WESTERN EUROPE, EASTERN EUROPE, AND WORLD DEVELOPMENT, 13TH–18TH CENTURIES

Studies in Critical Social Sciences Book Series

Haymarket Books is proud to be working with Brill Academic Publishers (http://www.brill.nl) to republish the Studies in Critical Social Sciences book series, edited by David Fasenfest, in paperback editions. Other titles in this series include:

WESTERN EUROPE, EASTERN EUROPE, AND WORLD DEVELOPMENT, 13TH–18TH CENTURIES

COLLECTION OF ESSAYS OF MARIAN MAŁOWIST

EDITED BY JEAN BATOU AND HENRYK SZLAJFER

Haymarket Books
Chicago, Illinois

First published in 2010 by Brill Academic Publishers, The Netherlands
© 2010 Koninklijke Brill NV, Leiden, The Netherlands

Published in paperback in 2012 by
Haymarket Books
P.O. Box 180165
Chicago, IL 60618
773-583-7884
www.haymarketbooks.org

ISBN: 978-1-60846-200-1

Trade distribution:
In the US, through Consortium Book Sales, www.cbsd.com
In the UK, Turnaround Publisher Services, www.turnaround-psl.com
In Australia, Palgrave Macmillan, www.palgravemacmillan.com.au
In all other countries, Publishers Group Worldwide, www.pgw.com

Cover design by Ragina Johnson.

This book was published with the generous support of Lannan Foundation and
the Wallace Global Fund.

Printed in the United States.

10 9 8 7 6 5 4 3 2 1

Library of Congress Cataloging-in-Publication Data is available.

CONTENTS

PREFACE
"MARIAN MAŁOWIST: AN APPRECIATION"

Immanuel Wallerstein

This collection is most welcome. The main articles of Marian Małowist are collected together (and in many cases translated into English) for the first time. Małowist, who is one of the major economic historians of the twentieth century, is also a much neglected one. Of the eighteen articles here, only five were published in English-language journals that are widely read by historians and social scientists, and even these journals are primarily read by economic historians. So most scholars have been missing out on one of the most fertile and cultivated minds who have written on the central issue of our times—the wide and widening gulf between the core and the periphery, the North and the South, western and eastern Europe.

Małowist was a polyglot and a person of wide geographic scope. He once complained to me in the 1970s about the decline of linguistic competence among his own students. He said that, when he began teaching, he used to require that students who wished to enter his seminars know at least four languages besides Polish. But, he sighed sadly, today I can only insist upon two.

The scope of his comparative research seems remarkable: between Poland and other "eastern European" countries (Hungary, Bohemia, Moldavia, etc.); between Poland and Russia; between eastern Europe and Scandinavia; between eastern Europe and western Europe; between eastern Europe and southwest Europe/Latin America; between Poland, Spain, and the Ottoman Empire as empires; between mediterranean Europe and the western Sudan.

What he had to say in making these comparisons is always interesting and is always based on such data as are available. But he never hesitated to infer possible explanations when definitive data is absent, saying things like "I cannot provide proof," or "a possible hypothesis is...." For he was always interested in the generalizations that can be made, while always being very prudent in suggesting them. He did theoretically-informed empirical research. He was to be sure a hesitant theoretician. He always sought to find the equilibrium point between the two tasks.

In addition to the wide comparisons, he always showed himself sensitive to the multiple cascade of boundaries, in terms both of causes and effects. He knew that what was an economic advantage from the point of view of the widest geographical unit could be a negative from the point of view of regions within it and perhaps once again a positive from the very local levels. He felt at ease moving between the different levels. Hence we always get a very textured picture of economic and social reality from his descriptions and analyses.

He always noticed the crucial role of debt mechanisms as a basic constraint on economic activity and a major means of transferring capital from the debtor to the creditor. Furthermore, he approached all these problems with the eyes of someone coming from a less-favored zone who was concerned to understand not only why the zone was less favored but what that zone might do about it. In his response to Anthony Hopkins's critique of his article on the western Sudan, he says:

> With regard to Dr. Hopkins's view that we must above all answer the question why only a few countries developed, while the majority of mankind remained in backwardness, I think that this is a question of our point of view. Dr. Hopkins lives in a highly developed country, while I in my country have experience of the difficult struggle with the remainders of backwardness. It is not surprising that I am intensely interested in understanding them. I think this is essential if we wish to overcome them. (Chapter 13, p. 286)

He has bequeathed some with some fascinating, insufficiently explored questions that are at the heart of these issues. For example, he points out that the sixteenth century saw a relative decline of three powerful states—Spain, Turkey (Ottoman Empire), and Poland. He offers a tentative and tantalizing explanation. "My view is that their territorial expansion in each case saddled them with onerous obligations which their still fragile economies were unable to cope with in the long term." (Chapter 5, p. 142) This is in a text that was published in 1973.

In an earlier text (published in 1965), he elaborates on what he calls the "self-evident" "negative results for the Spaniards and Portuguese of their great expansionist efforts." These countries lacked "a solid basis of national production," and hence "the very Empire itself was an important factor in the progressive exhaustion of economic life in Spain and the ossification of social structures too backward to ensure any dynamic development of the mother country." He sees this as parallel to what Poland did "within the far more modest framework of eastern Europe." (Chapter 11, pp. 256, 257).

Małowist says that those states who had "the nucleus of industrial organization and of capital accumulated in the course of trade"—that is, the Dutch, the British, and the French—then "insinuated themselves into the traffic between Spain, Portugal, and their colonies," and used their profits "to supply themselves with agricultural and forestry products from Eastern Europe," contributing thereby to the "consolidation and further spread of serfdom." (*Ibid.*, p. 257)

Here we have at least an explanation of how it is that the seemingly strong position of Spain and Portugal on the one hand and Poland on the other was turned on its head and led to their marginalization in the process of overall economic development in Europe. But it is also an argument why the nation-centered variety of economic history which had been (and still is) so preponderant in these analyses makes it difficult to understand what is really going on. This is why I consider Małowist a pioneer of world-systems analysis, even if he himself was reticent to assume this title. I could go on, but it is better that the reader delve himself into these rich texts and ponder the data, the inferences, and the theoretical paths upon which Małowist leads us. For we have far from exhausted the issue that Małowist himself insists drove his scholarship—understanding why the development of the modern world has been such an asymmetrical process, with big winners and even bigger losers, and then try to draw some conclusions on what can be done to rectify the grievous imbalances.

INTRODUCTION
"I CHASED AFTER POLISH GRAIN ALL OVER THE WORLD"

Jean Batou and Henryk Szlajfer

A two-volume translation of Josef Kulischer's fact-loaded book *Allgemeine Wirtschaftsgeschichte des Mittelalters und der Neuzeit* (an enlarged 1954 edition) appeared in Poland in 1961 on the initiative of Marian Małowist (1909–1988). Why did Małowist not choose the superb, problem-oriented short synthesis entitled *Economic and Social History of Medieval Europe* by Henri Pirenne, whom he valued highly? One of the reasons he gave was the inevitable obsolescence of great theoretical designs, "even those as excellent as Pirenne's work." As a result, he argued, these maintain their scientific value "only for a narrow circle of experts who are able to take a critical stand on the author's line of argument."[1] The other reason, however, was more weighty: it had to do with teaching Polish students. After years of being indoctrinated with Stalinist dogma, Kulischer's work offered "an enormous amount of information" and "a wealth of historiographic material." In the Polish edition, the bibliography in Kulischer's book was supplemented and updated by a disciple of Małowist's, young Dr. Bronisław Geremek.

Although he was skeptical about overambitious generalizations, Marian Małowist did not avoid asking key questions and putting forward—particularly in informal conversations—bold, even risky hypotheses. However, he was wary of constructing far-fetched theories. One of Małowist's most talented disciples, the late Professor Antoni Mączak, wrote that "Małowist did not like theories. His daring lay in suggesting hypotheses, not in proclaiming them." Mączak added that some of his interpretative ideas—as, for example, his idea of a negative impact of the serf-based economy in the Renaissance period (assessed as Poland's "golden age"), "obvious to his regular interlocutors"—had been published by other people.[2] The fact that he did not evade key

---

[1] Marian Małowist, "Wstęp" in J. Kuliszer, *Powszechna historia gospodarcza średnio-wiecza i czasów nowożytnych*, Vol. 1, Warszawa: Książka i Wiedza, 1961, p. V*f*.

[2] Antoni Mączak, "Wstęp" in H. Zaremska (ed.), *Marian Małowist: Europa i jej ekspansja XIV–XVII w.*, Warszawa: PWN, 1993, p. 9.

questions, however, is directly linked to the subjects he dealt with: Flanders, and the expansion of its trade in the late Middle Ages, the rise of Sweden and its activities in the Baltic Sea area in the 15th–16th centuries, and then Kaffa, on the Crimean coast, and the Genoese trade in the period preceding the great discoveries and conquests. The next step was the study of that part of west Africa which in early modern times came under Europe's expanding sphere of influence, particularly that of Portugal, and of the Dutch as well. But that was not all.

He never lost sight of central and eastern Europe, and of Poland in particular. As Immanuel Wallerstein accurately points out in the Preface to the present volume, that subject is not just an important part of Małowist's reflections, it was part of his biography. He grew up and worked in a backward region. Consequently he not only searched for the inner causes of central and eastern Europe's underdevelopment but also tried to precisely define its place in the general panorama of economic relations in Europe in the 13th–15th centuries. With the beginning of the Iberian countries' expansion overseas in the 15th and 16th centuries, Poland's and the region's economic situation changed in a far-reaching manner. The book *Wschód a Zachód Europy w XIII–XVI wieku. Konfrontacja struktur społeczno-gospodarczych* [*East and West Europe in the 13th–16th Centuries. Confrontation of Social and Economic Structures*], published in 1973, was the result of his pioneering reflections and research.

He did not refer to such theory-loaded concepts as centre—periphery or, in the 1970s, to Wallerstein's terminology, although one might infer such terminology from his studies. But, as already said, Marian Małowist avoided involvement in heated theoretical disputes. That is why we do not find in his works much of an echo of the famous "Dobb-Sweezy debate" of the 1950s or of the "Brenner debate" of the 1970s. Much earlier however, he had attempted an analysis of economic relations within the Baltic area presenting them as fitting in the category of "colonial" relations. Yet, owing to the historical inapplicability of the term "colonialism" to the region, he gave up such a radical perspective, even though in his handwritten changes to the final part of *Wschód a Zachód Europy*... he wrote about a *sui generis* economic colonization of Eastern Europe.[3] *Sui generis*, because in his reflections on the back-

---

[3] Henryk Szlajfer has the copy of *Wschód a Zachód Europy*... with these handwritten changes.

wardness of Poland and of the region, he attached great importance to "inner factors," i.e. those related to the economic motivations and behaviour of the upper class elites (the nobility-*szlachta*) which strength-ened the tendency leading to a crystallization of the serf-based system ("second serfdom"), the underdevelopment of towns, of crafts and of domestic trade.[4] In *Wschód a Zachód Europy*...he also turns down any geographic or geopolitical determinism as a possible explanation of backwardness. Still, Antoni Mączak devoted a book to the "colonial" hypothesis. He validated the centre/core—periphery concept (to use modern terminology), although not in the radical "colonial" variant.[5] Incidentally, another great Polish economic historian, Witold Kula, who was much more theoretically inclined,[6] did not hesitate to refer to east-European "grain plantations" as an equivalent to Latin American "sugar or cotton plantations," i.e., a "pre-colonial" situation.[7] And last but not least, Marian Małowist brought up what appears at first glance to be an exotic topic, that of Tamerlane and his powerful though short-lived empire, which had stretched from Samarkand to Delhi, the Persian Gulf, Aleppo and Ankara. The economy of that empire, based on trade and plunder, that "plundering empire," Małowist pointed out, had acted as a special connection between Europe and the Asiatic East (with its hub of commerce situated in Samarkand). Tamerlane, who fascinated both Christopher Marlowe and Edgar Allan Poe, had made an art of massacre, too.

To this list, one should add the monograph on the Portuguese con-quistadors (*Konkwistadorzy portugalscy*), which provides a very clearly-drawn panorama of Portuguese colonial expansion in Africa, Asia and

---

[4] Another outstanding Polish economic historian, Jerzy Topolski, fails to notice that in his book, *Przełom gospodarczy w Polsce XVI wieku i jego następstwa*, Poznań: Wydawnictwo Poznańskie, 2000, p. 40f. When Anna Sosnowska describes Małowist's views on the genesis of Poland's backwardness as a "putative model" of colonial development, her own position on this issue remains unclear. See A. Sosnowska, *Zrozumieć zacofanie. Spory historyków o Europę Wschodnią (1947–1994)*, Warszawa: Wydawnictwo TRIO, 2004, pp. 203–208. The co-founder of modern historical sociology Theda Skocpol, "Wallerstein's World Capitalist System: A Theoretical and Historical Critique," *The American Journal of Sociology*, Vol. 82, No. 5, 1977, p. 1081f, does not make such mistakes. She interprets M. Małowist's hypothesis correctly.

[5] Antoni Mączak, *Między Gdańskiem a Sundem. Studia nad handlem bałtyckim od połowy XVI do połowy XVII wieku*, Warszawa: PWN, 1972.

[6] Witold Kula, *An Economic Theory of the Feudal System*, London: NLB, 1976 (Polish edition 1962).

[7] Witold Kula, *Historia, zacofanie, rozwój*, Warszawa: PWN, 1983, p. 165.

Latin America. Małowist returned in that book to the question of the genesis of modern slavery.

Once again he emphasized the relationship between experiments on the island of São Tomé and the Brazilian plantation. "It is my impression," he wrote, "that historical science has underrated this aspect of [Brazil's] history." When analysing the slavery and plantation "experiment" which the Portuguese had carried out on that small island, he did not conceal an emotional touch: "In the 16th and 17th centuries, this really dreadful island played a considerable role in the emerging world economy."[8]

If we were to join all these "research points" with lines, the picture becomes clear. Małowist, in parallel with Fernand Braudel, was carrying out an ingenious project, a novel one in the world of historiography: an insight into the "moment" of the birth of the modern world economy, which Wallerstein calls "European world-economy". At the same time, he was looking for an answer to the question which had perplexed him all his life: how come, that the birth of modern world economy was accompanied by modern backwardness, particularly in central and eastern Europe—the other facet of western Europe's triumphant transition to developed capitalism. Speaking figuratively, he said that in his research he had "chased after Polish grain all over the world" in order to understand the connection between "second serfdom" and West European modernity. Also, it was obvious that this issue inevitably implied adopting a clearly defined methodological position: a preference for placing "national histories" in the context of general history and stressing the importance of comparative studies. Mączak wrote that he owed to Marian Małowist his "conviction that we do not understand our past unless we capture it in a comparative way."[9]

Fragments of an answer to the fundamental question concerning the complicated tangle of modernity and modern backwardness can be found in the works of his disciples. The subjects that were of particular interest to Malowist were: the fate of towns and crafts in Poland at a time when a dynamic economic centre emerged in western and northern Europe; the double-edged role that trade played simultaneously in strengthening the serf-based economy and in facilitating the

---

[8] Marian Małowist, *Konkwistadorzy portugalscy*, Warszawa: PIW, 1976, pp. 175, 169.
[9] Antoni Mączak, *Klientela. Nieformalne systemy władzy w Polsce i Europie XVI–XVIII w.*, Warszawa: Semper, 2000, p. 6.

emergence of the skewed, non-dynamic economic structures in eastern Europe; and the beginnings of the European expansion in Africa, Asia and later in Latin America.

The output of the "Małowist school" was impressive although in later years some of his disciples concentrated on other subjects as well, or abandoned economic history altogether. For example, the late Benedykt Zientara, whom Małowist called his "dearest" disciple, carried out studies, among other things, on metallurgy in Little Poland (Małopolska) in the 14th to 17th centuries and on spontaneous German settlements on Polish territories in the Middle Ages (important because of the transfer of skills and institutional patterns), and next, on the nation-forming processes in mediaeval western Europe.[10] Antoni Mączak, already mentioned, was the author not only of books on economic relations in the Baltic area and on what was, in fact, the export-oriented free peasants' farming system in northern Poland at the beginning of the 17th century,[11] but also of an analysis of the industrial revolution in England and of a collection of works by western historians, dealing with "the genesis of modern England."[12] Moreover, Mączak attempted a comparative analysis of the slave plantation in colonial Brazil with the grain-export economy of Poland in the period of the "second serfdom"; in addition, he emphasized the similarity of the roles those two export-oriented economies played in the emerging modern world economy.[13] Bronisław Geremek defended a Ph.D. thesis

---

[10] Benedykt Zientara, *Dzieje małopolskiego hutnictwa żelaznego XIV–XVII w.*, Warszawa: PWN, 1954; "Z zagadnień terminologii historycznej 'Drang nach Osten'" in S. Herbst (ed.), *Społeczeństwo, gospodarka, kultura. Studia ofiarowane Marianowi Małowistowi w czterdziestolecie pracy naukowej*, Warszawa: PWN, 1974; *Świt narodów europejskich. Powstawanie świadomości narodowej na obszarze Europy pokarolińskiej*, Warszawa: PWN, 1985.

[11] Antoni Mączak, *Między Gdańskiem a Sundem...*; *Gospodarstwo chłopskie na Żuławach Malborskich w początkach XVII wieku*, Warszawa: PWN, 1962.

[12] Antoni Mączak, *U źródeł nowożytnej gospodarki europejskiej*, Warszawa: Wiedza Powszechna, 1967; *Geneza nowożytnej Anglii*, Warszawa: PWN, 1968 (articles by F. J. Fisher, E. J. Hobsbawm, H. R. Trevor-Roper, J. Thirsk, J. U. Nef, D. C. Coleman, L. Stone, G. E. Aylmer, B. Manning and Ch. Hill). In the Poland of the time, where access to literature was very difficult, such selection led students in particular into the heart of great disputes that were going on among leading European historians.

[13] Antoni Mączak, *Le Modéle de l'économie bresilienne de Furtado et la production agricole pour l'exportation dans Pologne du XVIᵉ et du XVIIᵉ siècle*, paper presented at the international colloquium on "Recherché historique et recherché économique. Agriculture et développement du capitalisme" organized by the Gramsci Institute, Rome, 1968 (unpublished). Following Mączak but also Witold Kula's model of Polish serf-based export economy, Marcin Kula perceived strong functional similarity of

presenting certain aspects of the history of crafts in mediaeval Paris,[14] thus continuing one of the research subjects Małowist took up (with regard to Poland) at the beginning of the 1950s. Henryk Samsonowicz studied the history of Polish crafts and the economy of Polish towns in relation to the activity of the Hansa, and, together with Maria Bogucka, published an excellent history of Polish towns up to the mid-18th century.[15] Recently, referring to Małowist's *Wschód a Zachód Europy...*, he produced a brief review of "economic zones" that appeared in mediaeval and early modern Europe.[16]

The younger generation was represented by Michał Tymowski, who elaborated on Malowist's studies on Africa,[17] and by Jan Kieniewicz, who first published an analysis of the methods of early modern European expansion in Africa and Asia, and then authored a history of India, and an interesting attempt at a theory of colonialism.[18] Finally, to bring this list of Marian Małowist's younger generation of disciples to a close, Jan Szemiński, now Professor Yohanan Bar Yafe of the Hebrew University of Jerusalem, who, among other things, has devoted his studies since the end of the 1960s to the rebellions of Indians and peasants against Spanish rule.[19]

"the slave" and "the serf." See his *Początki czarnego niewolnictwa w Brazylii. Okres gospodarki cukrowej XVI–XVII w.*, Wrocław: Ossolineum, 1970, p. 138f.

[14] Bronisław Geremek, *Najemna siła robocza w rzemiośle Paryża XIII–XV w.*, Warszawa: PWN, 1962.

[15] Henryk Samsonowicz, *Rzemiosło wiejskie w Polsce XIV–XVI w.*, Warszawa: PWN, 1954; *Późne średniowiecze miast nadbałtyckich. Studia nad dziejami Hanzy nad Bałtykiem w XIV–XV w.*, Warszawa: PWN, 1968; Maria Bogucka, Henryk Samsonowicz, *Dzieje miast i mieszczaństwa w Polsce przedrozbiorowej*, Wrocław: Ossolineum, 1986.

[16] Henryk Samsonowicz, "Strefy gospodarcze Europy w średniowieczu i wczesnej epoce nowożytnej. Próba analizy porównawczej" in K. Baczkowski, J. Smolucha (eds.), *Europa środkowowschodnia od X do XVIII wieku: jedność czy różnorodność?*, Kraków: Societas Vistulana, 2005.

[17] Michał Tymowski, *Historia Mali*, Wrocław: Ossolineum, 1979. On the "Małowist school" of African studies see M. Tymowski, "Badania historii Afryki Czarnej w ośrodku warszawskim w latach 1960–2002: szkoła Mariana Małowista" in J. Łapott (ed.), *Afryka. 40 lat penetracji oraz poznawania ludów i ich kultur*, Szczecin: Muzeum Narodowe, 2004.

[18] Jan Kieniewicz, *Faktoria i forteca. Handel pieprzem i ekspansja portugalska na Oceanie Indyjskim w XVI wieku*, Warszawa: PWN, 1970; *Historia Indii*, Wrocław: Ossolineum, 1980 (3rd rev. ed. 2003); *Od ekspansji do dominacji. Próba teorii kolonializmu*, Warszawa: Czytelnik, 1986.

[19] Jan Szemiński, *La utopia tupamarista*, Lima: PUC, 1982; "In Search of an Inca" in S. J. Stein (ed.), *Resistance, Rebellion, and Consciousness in the Andean Peasant World, 18th to 20th Centuries*, Madison, Wis.: University of Wisconsin Press, 1987.

Nowadays, in discussions in Poland, Małowist's main work *Wschód a Zachód Europy*... (2nd edition, 2006) is referred to more and more often. This, however, does not quite apply to economic historians. Unfortunately, this field of science has been in crisis since the 1980s in Poland.[20] On the other hand, Małowist's "come-back" is noticeable primarily among young sociologists and political scientists. To some extent, this is a natural reaction to Poland's new situation after 1989 (and also to the publication of Polish translations of some of Wallerstein's works). The world economy, the history of its emergence, the place of Poland and east-central Europe in European and global economic structures, the problem of interplay—in the process of catching up—between externally induced changes and internal structures and vested interests, these and other topics gradually become elements not only of scientific thinking but of a *Weltanschauung* as well.

Marian Małowist was a teacher—a Master—in the noble, mediaeval, sense of the word: Antoni Mączak recalls that his first disciples had called him "Homeister," in analogy to *Hochmeister*—"great Master". His graduate seminar was an uncompromising school where it was difficult to get in. But it is thanks to Małowist, and also to Witold Kula, mentioned earlier, and to their disciples that Polish economic history, which had been developing in difficult (a euphemism!) political circumstances, opened itself to the world in the post-Stalinist period, particularly in the 1960s and 1970s, when Polish economic historians became not only "consumers," but also major "producers" of scientific knowledge.[21]

Małowist's works as well as an array of his disciples at the same time testify to the fortitude of the man who had seen a lot in his life, having been entangled in the infernal period of European interwar history and subsequently of the German occupation and the extermination of European Jews by the Nazis. He came from an assimilated, non-religious and not very wealthy family, his father was a Łódź doctor. As a child, he contracted polio. And to get somewhat ahead of the story, a few months after the Red Army had driven the Germans from the territories east of the Vistula River and Małowist came out of hiding, he met with a

---

[20] See Andrzej Wyczański, "Wstęp" in *Historia Polski w liczbach. Gospodarka*, Vol. II, Warszawa: GUS 2006, p. 8.

[21] On this see the balanced evaluation by Jacek Kochanowicz, "Economic Historiography in Communist Poland" in *Studia Historicae Economicae* (Poznań), Vol. 27, 1997.

serious accident, leading to severe disability and limited mobility. Yet, all his most important books and articles were still to come.

When at the end of the 1980s he agreed to a long conversation about his life and scientific development,[22] he remained quite detached when describing the beginnings of his scientific activity under the direction of two very different scholars, Marceli Handelsman ("he taught me the craft") and Stefan Czarnowski ("he cured me of dogmatism"). He had fond memories of both of them, although he did not conceal his criticism of the research horizons of Polish economic historiography of the time. About the interwar period, particularly about the 1930s, he spoke with reserve. When he, a Polish Jew, had finished his doctorate on Swedish expansion in the Baltic Sea region (distant relatives had financed his one-year visit to Stockholm, to the Uppsala archives), his road to a further academic career was blocked. The 1930s was a bad time for people like him. In the second part of the 1920s, his involvement in the then illegal Polish communist movement—which sent him for a short period to prison—turned into a serious disappointment to Malowist: "the period during which one could think freely had come to an end, and the still illegal bureaucracy was taking power".[23] He did not fit in with Stalinist communism, and broke off with it. A trip to the USSR—the Crimea and Leningrad—in the summer of 1939 reinforced his critical judgment. After the war, he did not join the communist party, although he remained, as he said, a Marxist. At the end of the 1930s, although those were though times, he had gathered notes and materials for a future work on the activity of the Genoese in the Black Sea area in the 15th century. Fortunately, despite the upheavals of the occupation, the materials survived. In 1947, the Warsaw University's Institute of History published his book entitled *Kaffa—kolonia genueńska na Krymie i problem wschodni w latach 1453–1475* [*Kaffa. The Genoese Colony in the Crimea and the Eastern Question, 1453–1475*].

To the assimilated Polish Jew, war meant confinement in the ghetto and the threat of extermination. In the Warsaw ghetto he taught; he loved that profession. At the same time, he worked with Dr. Emanuel Ringelblum, organizer of the unique, underground, Warsaw ghetto

---

[22] Those to participate in that conversation were Bronisław Geremek, Ryszard Stemplowski, Henryk Szlajfer and Michał Tymowski. Its extensive fragments were published as "Sobre la historia y los historiadores habla Marian Małowist" in *Estudios Latinoamericanos* (Warsaw), Vol. 12, 1989.

[23] *Ibidem*, p. 16.

archives.[24] On 13 August 1942, the tragic day of the destruction of most of the Warsaw ghetto, Marian Małowist's wife was sent to the Treblinka *Vernichtungslager* (extermination camp). He himself escaped from the ghetto. With the help of historians who had contacts with the underground Home Army (AK), primarily Stanisław Herbst, Witold Kula and Helena Brodowska, he found shelter in a village east of Warsaw. As "Józef Mil" he secretly taught peasant children. He also cooperated with the BCh Peasant Battalions, guerrilla troops created by underground peasant parties. The same peasant guerrillas defended him against the Germans, but also against rabid anti-Semites from guerrilla troops of the NSZ National Armed Forces (some of them already united with the Home Army), since the latter hunted down not only German invaders but also "Jews and communists" as well.

It was a traumatic experience for Małowist. In one small village and its surroundings, he met both heroism and heinousness. BCh troops defended their teacher effectively. In 1968, almost a quarter of a century later, when the communist authorities launched an anti-Semitic campaign in response to the student rebellion, Marian Małowist decided not to leave Poland. And in the 1970s, when Henryk Szlajfer asked him why, Małowist recalled the village which had given him a haven and saved him: "It wouldn't be right for me to emigrate."

The tragic experience of the ghetto and of the ravages wrought by the German invasion made him resistant to any kind of totalitarian temptations, but also to romantic concepts such as the "noble conqueror" (like Tamerlane) or the "noble slave." During the above-mentioned conversation he said, "I have come to believe that oppression, that suffering is not a school of heroism at all, it is a school of dehumanisation, that's what it is. This belief turns out to be useful now, in my studies on slavery."[25] But, also with reference to the much grater tragedy of the twentieth century, in his work on Tamerlane he emphasized that he was interested in whether, in the opinion of Central Asian people living in the 14th- and 15th-century, Tamerlane "was regarded as a criminal

---

[24] The archives kept documents and accounts (approx. 25,000 pages) describing the situation of Polish Jews under the German occupation until early 1943 and the first stages of the *Endlösung*.

[25] At this point Małowist refers to the book *Niewolnictwo*, Warszawa: Czytelnik, 1987, he wrote together with his second wife Iza Bieżuńska-Małowist, the late Professor of Hellenic and Roman history at Warsaw University.

or a hero. [...] [Because] we would make a fundamental mistake if we judged him according to our own ethical criteria."[26]

It was obvious that during the student rebellion in March 1968, he would sympathize with the young people. In the 1970s, he sided with the nascent democratic opposition, and was glad to help when his signature and name could be used to defend the persecuted. In 1978, he was among the co-founders of the underground "Flying University" (TKN), associated with the democratic opposition.[27] But let us make things clear: Marian Małowist was an authority, not a political activist.

Marian Małowist's first article to appear in the West was published in 1931 by the *Revue belge de philologie et d'histoire*, to which Henri Pirenne contributed regularly.[28] In 1935–37 he also published two articles on Baltic and Scandinavian countries. Almost a quarter of a century later, a second article in French by Małowist appeared in a volume published in Warsaw in 1955, entitled *La Pologne au Xe Congrès international des sciences historiques à Rome*. But it was only towards the end of the 1950s that he started contributing regularly to western publications, not only to books but also *Festschriften*—in honour of Armando Sapori in Italy (1957), Jaime Vicens Vives in Spain (1965), and Fernand Braudel in France (1973); to conference proceedings; and to prestigious journals in his discipline: *Past and Present, The Economic History Review, Journal of European Economic History, Annales E.S.C.*, etc.

Most of Marian Małowist's contributions in languages other than Polish were written in French. His early affinity to Henri Pirenne in Belgium and the Annales School in France probably explains this bias. In 1972, a collection of his essays was published in Paris under the title *Croissance et régression en Europe, XIVe–XVIIe siècles*, in the *Cahiers des Annales* (n° 33). Marian Małowist made indeed a significant impact on French historiography of the Middle Ages and the Renaissance.

---

[26] Marian Małowist, *Tamerlan i jego czasy*, Warszawa: PIW, 1985, p. 6.

[27] The aim of the TKN was, among other things, to arrange a series of special self-help lectures on forbidden historical subjects. Małowist together with Władysław Bartoszewski, Tadeusz Mazowiecki and others were involved in critical evaluation of the history textbooks used in schools. See Andrzej Friszke, *Opozycja polityczna w PRL 1945–1980*, Londyn: ANEKS, 1994. pp. 500–508, and Antoon De Baets, *Censorship of Historical Thought: A World Guide, 1945–2000*, Westport, Conn.: Greenwood Press, 2002, p. 394f.

[28] For his publications see the Selected Bibliography at the end of this volume.

However, one should not overlook his contributions to the *Storia d'Italia* in 1978 and to *The Cambridge Economic History of Europe* in 1987.

Subsequently, his influence was even more pronounced in writings dealing with the world-system theories in the 1970s. As Walter L. Goldfrank pointed out: in Wallerstein's Volume I of *The Modern World-System*, "in terms of individual citations, Braudel is by far the most-quoted (45), followed by Małowist (19) and Chaunu (19), with Bloch (15) and the Marxist economic historian Maurice Dobb (15) next."[29] Wallerstein always acknowledged his indebtedness: "Fortunately, I was reading both Braudel and Małowist. What I discovered in Braudel was two concepts that have been central to my work ever since: the concept of the world-economy and the concept of the *longue durée*. What I discovered in Małowist (and then in other Polish and Hungarian authors) was the role of Eastern Europe as an emergent periphery of the European world-economy in the sixteenth century."[30] On one occasion, he added that Małowist and his colleagues gave "sudden flesh to the concept of periphery, as has been initially adumbrated by the Latin American scholars grouped around Raúl Prebisch in the Economic Commission for Latin America (ECLA)."[31] This constitutes one more, very important reason to make this work, a large part of which has never been translated from Polish, available to a wide English-speaking audience.

---

[29] Walter L. Goldfrank, "Paradigm Regained? The Rules of Wallerstein's World-System Method", *Festschrift for Immanuel Wallerstein*, Part I. *Journal of World-system Research*, Special issue, Vol. 11, N° 2, Summer/Fall 2000, p. 163.

[30] Immanuel Wallerstein, "The Itinerary of World-Systems Analysis; or, How to Resist Becoming a Theory" in Jospeh Berger and Morris Zelditch (eds.), *New Directions in Contemporary Sociological Theory*, Lanham: Rowman and Littlefield, 2002, p. 361.

[31] *Ibidem*, p. 363.

ESSAYS OF MARIAN MAŁOWIST

CHAPTER ONE

COMMERCIAL CAPITALISM AND AGRICULTURE*

In this article, the problem of reciprocal influences between commercial capital and grain farming will be examined, based on available sources concerning medieval and early modern Italy. The debatable term "mercantile capitalism" will not be used, for in my view it is poorly defined, coined as it was in an attempt to outline an economic system where commercial capital determines both the overall economic development and the essential problems of its functioning. This kind of approach in fact raises many questions. Farming, and to some extent breeding, were predominant factors in the economy of all preindustrial ages, not only because the great majority of the population lived and worked on the land, or at least outside the main cities, but mainly because dependence on the supply of grain and other products from the rural economy was present in all spheres of social life.

At the very time when agriculture was least productive, its level and its potential for development were dependent upon possible population increases and decreases. These in turn determined the situation of the sectors in the economy not directly linked to rural activities. The essential task of urban policies during the Middle Ages lay in ensuring the delivery of food products to the inhabitants of the city. This was a constant concern for all the political and State bodies of the time. Indeed, this situation was not resolved until the agrarian revolution brought about an enormous increase in agricultural productivity, first in England and later in various western European countries. The recent work of British scholars clearly indicates that the industrial revolution was only made possible by the growth in productivity of British agriculture in the 17th and 18th centuries. Nor does this phenomenon apply to England alone. Commercial capital was only one of numerous elements that affected the agrarian revolution and one cannot credit it with a decisive role. A similar situation can be observed in central and

---

* Originally published as "Capitalismo commerciale e agricoltura", in *Storia d'Italia, Annali I: Dal feudalismo al capitalismo*, Torino: Einaudi, 1978, pp. 451–507. Translation from Italian by Serena Anderlini-D'Onofrio, revised by Robin Kimball.

eastern Europe between the 16th and 17th centuries, when the second serfdom began. We have known for some time that increased demand and higher prices paid for agricultural products from eastern Europe largely contributed to the massive exports of grain and other farming, breeding, and forestry products to western countries. Commercial capital had an important function in the organization of these exports, but it was certainly not the decisive cause of the generalized diffusion of serfdom in the rural areas of eastern Europe. What determined that phenomenon was the immensely superior military and political organization of the nobility with respect to the peasants, as well as the close collaboration between the nobility and the State, interested in seeing society develop in this direction rather than otherwise.

Commercial capital was thus one of numerous elements in the social development denoted by these two phenomena, but it did not necessarily determine its direction. In the first case, both the economy and the social structures were rendered so dynamic and so profoundly transformed as to revolutionize England and the whole of western Europe. In the second case, they became fossilized to the point of causing a veritable return to feudalism. This article attempts to demonstrate that the situation of grain farming, where Italian commercial capital was employed, was not dissimilar to the one described above. Given the current state of research, these observations are perforce only suggestions of a general nature, which will no doubt be considerably modified as later studies are published.

In the course of the last twenty or thirty years, research on Italian rural history has made great progress. This formerly neglected area has attracted the attention of eminent scholars, thanks to whom our knowledge of farming and breeding, as well as of the relationship between producers and landowners, has been greatly increased. The intervention of commercial capital, and of bourgeois capital in general, in Italian country life between the 16th and 18th centuries has been at the centre of numerous debates. On the other hand, the equally fascinating period of the Italian Middle Ages would seem to have elicited less interest, even though Imberciadori and Giorgetti have made essential contributions to the study of sharecropping (*mezzadria*). It is regrettable that the study of trade in agricultural products and its attendant problems has generally been neglected, since this impoverishes the framework from which we can analyse the problem as a whole. Research on the relationship between agriculture and the market is of great importance in clarifying the issue of rural economy, its mercantile character and productivity, beginning with issues related to the circulation of currency and its penetration into rural areas. It seems that, in this field, the results obtained by Italian scholars do not compare favourably with those of British and East-European historians. Certainly, in eastern Europe and in England the geographical, climatic, and soil conditions were completely different from those in Italy. Nonetheless, some of the phenomena observed there are of comparable importance in the understanding of issues related to Italian economic development.

One of these phenomena, typical of the distribution of agricultural products in long-distance trade, is the system of advances paid by merchants to producers who were committed to delivering their products by a fixed deadline. According to R. Carande, this system, which was largely applied by the Hanseatic merchants with respect to agriculture and forestry products from Poland, Lithuania, and Livonia, was likewise practised in Spain by both local and Italian merchants, and in particular by the Genoese, who were major buyers of wool.[1] The Dutch had adopted this procedure at least by the 15th century. In Norway it dominated the relationships between the Hanseatic people and local fishermen (a fact that has caused animated debates between German and Norwegian historians). It was a very important element in the connection between numerous sectors of the rural economy on the one hand and the market-place on the other, as well as in the development of monetary and commercial relationships. Indeed, the system of advances created fairly close relationships between producers (who were often far away) and the market-place, while it also expanded the role of intermediary merchants. In the industrial world, this phenomenon can be compared to the putting-out system known in towns. The similarity is even stronger if we consider that, ever since Doren, the attractiveness for the rural population of the putting-out system has been clearly established. In particular, Posthumus has convicingly demonstrated this attractiveness in reference to examples from the northern Netherlands,[2] while I have also devoted some attention to it. Indeed, especially in southern Italy (the *Mezzogiorno*), the system of advance

---

[1] R. Carande, *Carlos V y sus banqueros. 1516–1556*, Madrid 1943, I, pp. 57–59; M. Małowist, *A Certain Trade Techniques in the Baltic Countries in the XVth to the XVIIth Century*. Poland at the XIth International Congress of Historical Sciences, Warszawa 1960, pp. 103–116.

[2] N. W. Posthumus, *De Geschiedenis van de Leidsche Lakenindustrie*, 's Gravenhage 1908, vol. I, *passim*.

payments was so common as to be deplored, in the 18th century, by
Ferdinando Galiani, who considered it an abuse that damaged the
southern economy. More precisely, this system was based on "country
merchants" lending money to the peasants in so-called *contratti alla
voce* (oral contracts).[3] It would be useful to examine the interrelatedness
of commercial capital and rural economy on this basis by comparing
it with the situation obtaining in the Netherlands, England, Germany,
and other countries. Important as are the results provided by statistical
methods in the study of rural Italy, the comparative method usually
allows a broader view and a more thorough understanding of phenomena in both social and economic history. Thus, through a comparison
between what was happening in the various regions of Europe, rather
than just in the Mediterranean and western European area, it is possible
to understand why so many aspects of the agricultural economy were
related to social relationships typical of feudalism. Moreover, despite
the profound differences existing between the various countries, it is
important to consider the significance of the fact that almost everywhere
the producer was placed in a position of dependence with respect to
the landowner.

This article will examine the relationships between commercial
capital and agriculture—mainly as concerns grain farming—from the
time of the flowering of the Italian medieval economy (between the
12th and 13th centuries) up to the severe crisis that befell the country
in the 17th century. In particular, it will explore some of the regions
where the activity of commercial capital is most manifest. These are
primarily regions outside Italy proper, sometimes situated quite far
from the peninsula, but which were no less Italian territories from
which merchants exported a great deal of grain, while providing other
kinds of merchandise, and investing their own capital to promote and
transform agricultural development according to their own demands
and necessities. Unfortunately, owing to the lack of studies on Sicily,
it is not possible to make a pronouncement on this important region.
Instead, it is the regions between the Black Sea and the Balkans, the
islands subject to Venice (and in particular Crete), central and southern
Italy, and the Venetian region that will be mainly considered here. All of
these regions exported grain mainly to cities in Tuscany and northern
Italy. Other regions exported cereals as well, but to a lesser degree. In

---

[3] Cf. S. J. Woolf, *La storia politica e sociale*, in *Storia d'Italia*, vol. III: *Dal primo
Settecento all'Unità*, Torino 1973, pp. 34–37.

this way it is hoped to examine the problem of whether, and if so to what extent, Italian commercial capital affected the structural development of agriculture and hence its attendant social structures.

I. *The Eastern Area and Grain Supply*

Ever since antiquity, the fertility of the lands on the shores of the Black Sea constituted a strong pole of attraction towards those territories, as shown by the numerous colonies founded by the Greeks in those fecund regions. Mainly for the purpose of supplying its own capital city, the Eastern Roman Empire successfully maintained a monopoly over grain imports from those countries for a long period. Indeed, this monopoly was only broken by Italian merchants as late as sometime between the 12th and 13th centuries. After their conquest of Constantinople, the Turks eventually resumed the political strategy pursued by Byzantium, making in turn some concessions to Italian merchants.

The first Italian merchants to establish direct contacts with the shores of the Black Sea were the Venetians, starting from the 12th century. Thanks to the powerful influence of Venice in eastern Europe, these relationships developed freely with the foundation of the Eastern Roman Empire, but still remained fairly brisk even after the restoration of the Paleologus dynasty. From the travel journal of the brothers Niccolò and Matteo Polo, *Il Milione*, we learn that the Venetians were present in the Crimea after it was conquered by the Mongols; indeed, the city of Soldania (today's Sudak) became the point of departure for Venetian expeditions in Central Asia and China. It is likely that Venetian exports of grain from the Crimea started at that time, though we have no specific information about it. During the 13th and 14th centuries, surpluses of grain available for export came from Thrace, Mesia, and Macedonia, whose northern and southern parts belonged to the Bulgarians and to Byzantium respectively. Thus the harbours of these three regions assumed a special importance at this time. Among them were Rodosto, on the Sea of Marmora, Sozopolis, Anchialus, Mesembria, and Varna, on the west coast of the Black Sea, and finally Thessaloniki (Salonica), whence the Venetians penetrated into the fertile territory around Philippopolis (today's Plovdiv).[4]

---

[4] Cf. *Ikonomikata na Blgaria do socialisticeskata revolucia*, Sofija 1969, Vol. 1, pp. 96–99. 106–8, 113, and 143.

The treatise by Francesco di Balducci Pegolotti describes the types
of cereals grown in the coastal region of the Black Sea, and indicates
that in the 14th century other Italians besides the Venetians were interested in trade with these regions and were aware that it was possible
to buy various kinds of grain from the East. According to Pegolotti,
the best wheat was that produced in the Crimea, followed by the
wheat from Mesembria and Rodosto.[5] Even though the Genoese were
the number one in trade with the Black Sea in the 14th century, the
Venetians continued to maintain their commercial relationships with
the Bulgarians, via Salonica, and above all via Varna.[6] After the fall
of the Eastern Roman Empire, the relationships between the Genoese
and the Mongol khans of Crimea grew closer. Indeed, the Genoese
founded their own Crimean colony of Kaffa, where the ancient city
of Theodosia once stood. In the meantime, since the late 14th century
they had been gradually acquiring the right to trade in the Bulgarian
kingdom against payment of a customs toll.[7] In fact, the commercial
contacts between Genoa and the Bulgarians go back to the beginning of
the century. As early as 1332, the Genoese already had a centre of their
own in Licostomo (today's Kiliya), on the Danubian delta, and later
they also took possession of Belgorod (subsequently called Akkerman
by the Turks) on the Dnestr, from which they were expelled by the
Moldavians only in the 15th century. Thus, the entire coastal area of
the western Black Sea and the Crimea fell within the commercial orbit
of the two Italian cities of Genoa and, to a lesser extent, Venice. The
kingdom of Bulgaria, the principalities of Wallachia, and the Crimea
together constituted an important outlet for Italian products such as
luxury fabrics, weapons and other metal items, salt, oil, etc. But above
all they represented an essential source of agricultural produce.

Once having destroyed the competition of the Greeks residing in
Bulgarian ports and having assisted Constantinople during a serious
famine, the Italians took control of the grain exported to the Byzantine
capital from those countries. By 1308 they had succesfully placed the
Paleologus rulers under their growing influence. They exported wheat
and barley from Thrace and Macedonia via Salonica, and probably also

---

[5] F. Balducci Pegolotti, *La pratica della mercatura*, edited by A. Evans, Cambridge
(Mass.) 1936, p. 25.
[6] *Ikonomikata na Blgaria*, pp. 134–38 and 141ff.
[7] *Ibid.*, pp. 139 and 145–48.

from the harbours on the western shores of the Black Sea.[8] Quantitative data on these exports are not available. But the fact that the Byzantine capital depended completely on supplies of wheat from Bulgaria and the Crimea, and that cargoes of Bulgarian and Macedonian grain were shipped directly to Italy, suggests that considerable amounts of cereals were exported.

This state of affairs was one of the consequences of the general development of Bulgaria during the 12th and 13th centuries. Bulgarian scholars have pointed out the growth in the country's urban and rural population during this period, despite the fact that, until handicrafts and commerce assumed a certain importance around the 14th century, most Bulgarian towns retained a typically rural character. J. Sakazov, a pioneer in studies of Bulgarian economic history, and his followers have emphasized the importance of vast farmland estates, and above all of the great monasteries, which were foremost in producing grain for sale. Indeed, monks left this commercial activity to the care of their agents or to local merchants, who in turn had connections with merchants from Constantinople and Italy. The land that belonged to large ecclesiastical institutions and to the local aristocracy (*boyars*) was farmed by peasants who were subject to corvées. While the *paroikoi* inherited land, the *ostroiki* were probably ex-slaves. Together they began to form a fairly homogeneous mass of serfs.[9] In the course of the 13th century, the great monasteries and the local aristocracy gradually subjected the *paroikoi* to their domination, and imposed on them tributes in kind and corvées similar to those demanded of the *ostroiki*. The *paroikoi* also owed tributes to the State, which often granted immunities to monasteries and their property. In fact, the monasteries controlled a considerable portion of agricultural production, their abundant manpower being drawn from small landowners and poor peasants. Craftsmen residing on monastic properties were also subject to the monasteries, including even highly specialized craftsmen such as goldsmiths. In the 13th century, the monasteries even started organizing their own fairs, which competed with the increasingly numerous city fairs.[10] It is difficult to establish to what extent the growth in agricultural production both in Bulgaria and in the surrounding territories was caused by the

---

[8] *Ikonomikata na Blgaria,* and J. Sakazov, *Bulgarische Wirtschaftsgeschichte,* Berlin-Leipzig 1929, pp. 104–6, 134, 139–42, and 152–60.
[9] *Ikonomikata na Blgaria,* pp. 108–11.
[10] *Ibid.,* p. 127; Sakazov, *Bulgarische Wirtschaftsgeschichte,* pp. 105–111.

growing demand for grain from Italian merchants. This growth might well have been determined mainly by population increase, combined with the progress, which took place in spite of all, in the social division of labour between country and town. Nonetheless, it is undeniable that the 13th century witnessed major agricultural development in the inland of Varna and other ports on the Black Sea, which in turn supports the hypothesis that this development was considerably motivated by the demand from the Italian merchants.

This situation basically favoured the big landowners, both lay and ecclesiastical, who were able to impose bigger corvées, thus obtaining more products destined for export. It is probable that the peasants put up resistance, as shown by their seeking shelter within towns or on the estates of less demanding landowners, and as can be also inferred from the insistence with which, during the 13th and 14th centuries, both clergy and nobility sought to bind peasants to the land.[11] Unfortunately, analysing this process is not easy, since Bulgarian sources in medieval history contain many gaps. While its general development seems similar to the better-known phenomena observed in central and eastern Europe during the 16th and 17th centuries, in the current state of research this line of comparison is merely a working hypothesis for future studies. On the other hand, the development of serfdom was interrupted by the Turkish conquest and the formation of new social relationships within the rural culture of the Balkan regions, initially, as will be seen, involving some advantages for the peasants of those parts.

1. *The Genoese in the Crimea*

No less difficult is the study of the formation of Italian interests in Crimean grain production, given the absence of sources on the history of agriculture in that peninsula. The 1287–88 acts by Lamberto di Sambuceto, a notary in Kaffa, make practically no mention of any grain trade in the Crimea.[12] The presence of other notaries in Kaffa is not sufficient to infer a lack of interest in this commercial activity on the part of the Genoese, while the disappearance of their papers precludes the examination of any transactions they may have facilitated. On the other

---

[11] Sakazov, *Bulgarische Wirtschaftsgeschichte*, pp. 108–11.
[12] M. Balard, *Gênes et l'Outre-Mer*, vol. 1: *Les Actes de Caffa du notaire Lamberto di Sambuceto 1289–1290*, La Haye 1973.

hand, we know that in the 1280s Kaffa was already an important artisan and commercial centre and must have had secure sources of grain supply. The fact remains that, for the 14th century, extant documents about the grain situation in Kaffa are somewhat scarce, and it is only for the following century that more relevant sources are available.

The 1449 statutes of the Genoese colonies on the Black Sea mention a right of six *aspri* on food supplies that entered Kaffa via land, while other taxes were levied on the trade in foodstuffs.[13] From the same source, we learn that the Genoese either rented or bought fields, meadows, and pastures in the environs of the town.[14] There they bred cattle and horses and probably farmed as well. This situation is similar to that of other cities, such as Sudak, where Italians and Greeks cultivated vineyards, or Cembalo (now Balaklava), where in all likelihood grain came from neighbouring farms owned by town dwellers. The correspondence between the Kaffa authorities and the Banco di San Giorgio between 1453 and 1473, published by Vigna, clearly shows that this large city (with more than 77,000 inhabitants in 1475) mainly depended for its grain supplies upon what the Genoese called the *campania Cafae*—a reference to the fertile lands that surrounded the city of Kaffa, but which were nonetheless subject to the local Tatar chief. Any interruption in the traffic between the *campania* and Kaffa could cause serious famines,[15] even though we have no exact information on who the producers were. It is doubtful whether they were citizens of Kaffa, even though this possibility cannot be entirely ruled out, at least in some cases, for we know that the inhabitants of numerous medieval towns did not despise agricultural labour. Nonetheless, it seems more likely that in the Crimea, well known for the importance of its slave trade, the rich landowners had serf labour at their disposal.

Jan Długosz (Johannes Longinus), the Polish chronicler of the second half of the 15th century, who was generally well informed on the Crimea, states that Hadji-Ghirey, the founder of the Crimean khanate of the time, sought to induce his subjects to give up nomadism, albeit

---

[13] V. Jurgevic, *Ustav dlia genuezskikh kolonii v Cernom More izdannyi v Genue 1449*, in "Zapiski Odesskogo Obscestva Istorii i Drevnostiei," 1863, V, pp. 672 and 698.

[14] *Ibid.*, pp. 725 and 742.

[15] M. Małowist, *Kaffa, kolonia genueńska na Krymie i problem wschodni (1453–1475)*, Warszawa, 1947, p. 44.

without much success.[16] It is, however, possible that small groups of Tatars adopted a sedentary lifestyle and farmed land, encouraged by the earnings made possible by major outlets in the neighbouring cities. Already some decades earlier, the khans of the Golden Horde had made land-grant agreements (*iarlyk*), in which there is mention of the Crimean landed property owned by high Tatar dignitaries and worked by slaves.[17] The only available later source covering the last quarter of the 16th century is provided by Marcin Broniowski, a Pole who was quite familiar with the Crimea, but it is not much clearer than previous documents.[18] Nonetheless, it seems plausible to conclude that, between the 14th and 15th centuries, a certain number of inhabitants of the Genoese colonies in the Crimea and some Tatar dignitaries devoted themselves to agriculture and breeding, utilizing serf labour and making profits from supplying Kaffa and other towns in the peninsula. It should be added that the inhabitants of Kaffa organized acquisitions of grain from the mouths of the Dnestr and the Dnieper, and from other coastal areas of the Black Sea, for the similar purpose of exporting it partly to Constantinople and partly to Italy.[19] Here too, however, we lack the necessary data to document the production and export volumes of this trade, though we may infer that both local needs and exporting activities doubtless contributed in some measure to the development of agriculture in the Crimea, as well as along the northern shores of the Black Sea. After all, it was the Greeks and the Genoese who introduced vineyards into the Crimea. As regards the Black Sea, the importance of Constantinople cannot be overemphasized, for it was there that the Italians supplied themselves with Bulgarian and Crimean grain.

2. *Venice and Cretan Feudalism*

For cotton, silk, wines, and cereals, the island of Crete was one of the main sources of supply for Venice, especially after the Fourth Crusade, when it fell under the domination of the *Serenissima* republic. A large

---

[16] *Dlugossi Joannis seu Longini Historiae Polonicae libri XII*, Cracoviae 1874, vol. V, book XII, p. 471; Małowist, *Kaffa*, p. 50.

[17] B. D. Griekov and A. Iu. Iakubovski, *L'Orda d'Oro*, Roma 1957, pp. 78ff.

[18] Martini Broniovii De Biezdzfedea, *Tatariae descriptio*, Coloniae 1595, p. 17. Broniowski mentions the farmlands of the great Tatar lords in the Crimea which were cultivated by Hungarian, Russian, Wallachian, and other slaves, evidently captured in the course of Tatar raids in those countries.

[19] Małowist, *Kaffa*, pp. 48–61 and 81–86.

part of the land on the island was granted to the Venetian aristocracy as a fief, thus causing long and bitter conflicts with local feudatories from Greece. While we do not know exactly what consequences this had for the peasants turned serfs (the *paroikoi*), the sources mention escapes and scarcity of manpower on the island. However, some of this might have been caused by reasons other than the material conditions of existence: for instance, the Venetians favoured the Roman Catholic church against the Greek church, thus causing the resentment of both the Orthodox clergy and the local population, often hostile to Italian domination. The same religious sentiments may well explain the subsequent spread of a favourable attitude towards the religiously more tolerant Turks.

For the Venetian Republic, the colonization of the island of Crete by the Venetian gentry was of great importance. On the one hand, the settlement of some poor aristocratic families on the island freed Venice from concerns due to insidious social tensions at the heart of the state, while on the other it reinforced its hold on such an important supply centre. In general, there is no mention of separatist tendencies on the part of the local colonists, who needed the support of the metropolis against the Greeks.

The plains of the southern coastal area, celebrated for their fertility, were essential to supplying both Venice and the islands under its dominion with grain. The Venetians developed the irrigation system and, to remedy the scarcity of manpower, often imported slaves onto their property from the coastal areas of the Black Sea and Anatolia. They also encouraged the immigration of Armenians into the countryside, albeit with results of minor relevance.[20] In 1301, they also settled on their lands, as *paroikoi*, many of their prisoners captured during the war against Byzantium.[21]

As regards supplies, trade, and various sectors of economic life, Crete's interests were strictly subordinated to those of the metropolis, as were those of the other Venetian colonies. As a rule, all the goods exported from the island had to be sent to Venice, firstly in order to meet the city's needs and secondly to be redistributed according to the Venetians merchants' best interests. In principle, Venice also

---

[20] F. Thiriet, *La Romanie vénitienne au Moyen Âge*, Paris 1959, pp. 264, 265, and 410.
[21] Thiriet, *Délibérations des assemblées vénitiennes concernant la Romanie*, Paris 1966, Vol. I, Nos. 37 and 41.

acted as intermediary for all imports into Crete, according to the same system of centralization. In practice, however, these rules did not always prove applicable, and in fact Crete did trade directly with Cyprus, Constantinople, Syria, Anatolia, and Rhodes. For their part, the Venetian authorities exercised a rigid control over Cretan commerce, especially the grain trade.

The registers of various commissions of the Venetian senate charged with the affairs of the island—published by F. Thiriet—clearly bear out the republic's policy with respect to this dominion. Yet this French scholar considers that grain imports from Crete were not a major item in the sum total of the city's supplies. According to Thiriet, in 1342 the granaries of Venice stored about 365,559 *staia* of wheat (about 30,680 hectolitres), of which 97,320 *staia* (some 8,000 hectolitres) were of good quality. Given that Crete was expected to supply about 40,000 measures per year, Thiriet observes that its contribution to the Venetian supplies was not a high one.[22] This assertion arouses some perplexity. In fact, the document that reports the amount of grain preserved in Venetian silos also points out that the granaries were full to the brim, and recommends that the wheat be quickly distributed among the population, lest it spoil.[23] It seems evident that this was an exceptional situation, since in general the Venetian authorities were more concerned with having in store sufficient wheat to provide for the city, rather than worrying about a possible surplus. One is thus inclined to think that the usual amount of grain in storage did not exceed two-thirds of the amount indicated in this document, or roughly 220,000 *staia* (about 18,300 hectolitres).

Another document, dating from 1331, i.e. eleven years prior to the minutes of the meeting quoted above, reports that at the time the feudatories of one of the most fertile districts in the island, Canea (Khania), were expected to deliver 50,000 measures (8,500 hectolitres) of grain to the city per annum.[24] This provision was paid for by the Senate. Ten years later, this amount might conceivably have been reduced to 40,000 measures (6,800 hectolitres), without taking into account the amounts of grain available for free trade, notably between local feudatories and Venetian merchants. All in all, the volume of this mandatory amount

---

[22] Thiriet, *La Romanie*, p. 329.
[23] *Ibid.*, p. 327.
[24] Thiriet, *Délibérations*, I/2, No. 484.

shipped from Crete to Venice was by no means so negligible in relation to the mass of grain usually stored there.

The Venetian government also exerted strict control over transactions between private parties, often forcing merchants who were citizens of the republic to sell all their imported Cretan grain to the city authorities. In the 14th and 15th centuries, the price paid by the government varied between 10 and 18 *soldi* (a twentieth of a lira) per *sterion* (83 hectolitres),[25] an amount equivalent to, and sometimes rather higher than, the current established price. Importers were seldom authorized to sell grain freely at the market price, and generally speaking this happened only at times when the senate did not fear a famine. Speculation in grain was very common in Europe at the time, but there were few opportunities to practise it in Venice, thanks to the vigilance of the senate, which helped to prevent such common calamities of the Middle Ages as famine and penury of grain. This goal was also scrupulously pursued in the regulations concerning Cretan grain exports, where prescriptions were often repeated owing to frequent violations.

Among Italian feudatories in Crete, not a few had received, as a fief from the republic, small islands devoid of sufficient food resources. The Venetian authorities accordingly allowed them to supply such places as Cerigo, Carpathos, and other minor islands. However, the Venetian senate soon became aware of the need to establish rigorous control systems to prevent the gentry from taking advantage of the permission granted them to export grain, not just to their own possessions but also to other regions. Such procedures were rendered easier by the fact that these export licences often laid themselves open to a wider interpretation as referring to all countries allied with Venice. In this way, despite prohibitions, exports of this kind took place repeatedly during the 14th and 15th centuries.

As we have seen, the Cretan feudatories were active in trading cereals, both in the mandatory delivery of grain bought by the Venetian government and in free trade. But it appears that more than once the senate, or rather its commission on grains, put down advance payments to Cretan feudatories on future deliveries of grain. Cases are known in which these feudatories borrowed money immediately after a consignment, to cover the expense of buying and dispatching grain. To take just one example, on the occasion of the August fairs in Milopotamo,

---

[25] *Ibid.*, No. 464.

Retimo, and Apokorona, the well-known Cretan feudatory Alessio Kalergi took out a loan of 6,000 *iperperia*, and pledged to pay it back to the Venetian authorities in grain within four years. The price of 100 measures of grain had been fixed at 15 *iperperia*. The Venetian archives confirm that loans of this kind were frequent.[26] These advances paid to producers to secure grain supplies present a case somewhat similar to those mentioned in the introduction. In fact, in the countries of northern Europe, loans of this kind were arranged both with direct producers and with titled landowners. It is also known that in some cases the debtor was forced to meet his obligations by complementing his own resources with grain bought from a third party. This system was widely practised in both Poland and Livonia, countries that exported agricultural and forestry products, while in Prussia it was practised by the Teutonic Order, which often drew inspiration from Frederick II of Swabia for its trading methods. Later the merchants of Gdańsk (Danzig) extended this method to the whole of Polish territory.

Credits granted in advance of future grain deliveries implied a risk for both parties involved in the operation, mainly in view of the difficulty of predicting the exact size of forthcoming harvests and the consequent price of their produce. On the other hand it should be noted that in some ways this procedure constituted an element of stabilization in the price of grain, which is by nature exposed to all possible causes of variation, beginning with climatic and atmospheric disturbances. At the same time, producers managed to secure cash for themselves during the dead agricultural season, while lenders secured a regular supply. The analogy with work at home lies in the fact that in this way those who had commercial capital available were able to penetrate the sphere of grain distribution, thus stimulating production and subordinating it to their own interests. This did not always entail brutal exploitation of grain suppliers, even though creditors, having more capital available than producers, were placed at an obvious advantage. It is clear that, in this way, the production of grain came to be closely connected with the market, and this in turn came to constitute a factor in economic development. In the relationships between Venice and Crete, the state had the role of creditor, although, even without evidence, it is fair to surmise that there may also have been cases of loans from private parties.

---

[26] Thiriet, *Délibérations*, 1, Nos. 79–82, 153, 161, and 221; I/2, Nos. 7, 92, 102, 103, 115, 126, and 142ff.

Around 1345 the Cretan feudatories experienced a time of hardship. In the current state of research, it is not clear whether or not this phenomenon was similar to the agricultural crisis that took place about this time in the West: the date is in fact somewhat earlier. In 1345, the feudatories, in agreement with the Cretan authorities, decided to send a delegation to Venice, to request an increase in the price of grain mandatorily provided to the main city from 20 to 25 *iperperia* for 100 measures (about 17 hectolitres). In case of rejection, the delegates would expound the ruinous situation of the feudatories and declare that they could no longer carry out the demands of the *Signoria*. In this case it was a matter of participating in the expedition against the Turks organized by the League of Italian States under the leadership of Humbert II, the dauphin of Vienne. The outcome of the senate's deliberation is not known, but we do know that the Cretan feudatories paid 3,000 *iperperia* for the expedition.[27] The document containing this information also reports that an ordinance from the Cretan authorities forbade the sale of both wheat and rye at a price lower than that obtaining in 1345. It appears that, while the situation of the market was unfavourable to the feudatories, the senate put pressure on Cretan producers in an effort to obtain their grain at a lower price. It seems probable that, as a result of competition from sellers, buyers obtained more favourable conditions and that the ordinance of March 2, 1347 sought to put an end to this situation.

During the same years, the islands around Crete suffered incursions by Turkish pirates who had settled in the powerful emirate of Aïdin (Palatia, Ephesus). When the emir was found to be an accomplice and protector of the pirates, a direct conflict with him broke out.[28] Although this particular incident came to an end in 1358, the Turkish pirates continued their incursions for a long time to come[29] and for the Cretan feudatories such incidents were to prove especially vexatious. The feudatories were responsible for protecting certain islands round Crete, such as Karpathos and Cerigo (Cythera), which were subject to them. In addition, the Cretans were accustomed to importing slaves, horses, and grain from Aïdin, especially in years of poor harvest.[30] Such acquisitions allowed them both to complete grain deliveries owed

---

[27] *Ibid.*, I/2, No. 102.
[28] *Ibid.*, Nos. 516 and 534.
[29] *Ibid.*, Nos. 513, 538, and 576.
[30] *Ibid.*, No. 639.

to Venice and to supply the neighbouring small islands with food. However, the major calamity was the black plague, which struck the island disastrously in two bouts; 1347–48 and 1361–62. In November 1348, the Cretan authorities went as far as considering whether or not they should repopulate the island.[31] A year earlier they had already granted fiscal exemptions and various easy terms to those willing to settle in Crete. The feudatories suffered greatly from this situation: in February 1349 they complained of the insubordination of peasants who, on the pretext that they were short in number, refused to work the land,[32] probably objecting to both corvées and salaried work, which was paid quite poorly at the time. This phenomenon was typical of the years following the plague that spread to Italy and the rest of western Europe. On the other hand, it is known that in 1352 a maximum wage was fixed for the services of diggers, carpenters, and coalmen,[33] classes of workmen who had attempted to improve their living conditions by asking for rises made possible by the new situation.[34] Meanwhile, slaves assigned to agricultural jobs took advantage of the disarray caused by the epidemic, by marking an increase in the number of escapes.

The Cretan feudatories appealed to Venice to grant them special repressive powers with respect to both *paroikoi* and slaves, but apparently did not obtain satisfaction. In the years between 1363 and 1366, growing demands from Venice (who had in its turn suffered grievously from the plague) led to a general insurrection of the Cretan gentry, both of Greek and Italian origin—an insurrection which swept the peasants into a state of revolt and even succeeded in enlisting the support of Pera, the Genoese colony in Constantinople. Venice had great difficulty in suppressing the revolt, and on this occasion went as far as attempting to enlist the support of the peasants, promising freedom to those *paroikoi* who were subject to the insurgent lords or to the city "commons," i.e. the island authorities.[35]

Thiriet, a specialist on Cretan history, maintains that in the last quarter of the 14th and during the 15th century the economic situation of the island improved distinctly, like that of the rest of "Románia"

[31] *Ibid.*, No. 617; II, No. 729.
[32] *Ibid.*, I/2, Nos. 545, 546, 547, and 553.
[33] *Ibid.*, No. 560, par. 8.
[34] *Ibid.*, No. 591.
[35] *Ibid.*, Nos. 560 and 564.

[former Roman dominions, tr.n.], and that this was mainly due to the general development of agriculture, especially of cotton and sugar-cane plantations, whose products were in high demand on the European markets.[36] Yet one questions whether this French scholar may have not been over-optimistic, especially in assessing the economic situation of the Greek islands subject to Venice during the second half of the 15th century, at a time when the republic had suffered major losses. One was the Turkish occupation of Eubea (Negroponte), which deprived Venice not only of a powerful naval base but also of an essential centre for the distribution of grain produced both on the island of Crete and on the Greek mainland. The conquest of Constantinople by Mohammed II, and the occupation of Greece, Albania, and many Greek islands, were also major blows for Venice, especially when viewed in the wider perspective of the rapid development of the Ottoman Empire into a naval power, capable of challenging the Republic of Venice even by sea. Nor was this negative balance compensated for by the fact that, in 1489, Cyprus and other smaller islands ended up under the dominion of Venice. The city found itself subject to continual Turkish pressure, and this included the problem of grain supplies. Since all the productive territories of the former Byzantine "Románia" eventually fell under Ottoman dominion, Venice now found itself increasingly dependent on the Ottoman Empire in this respect also. Other possible sources of supply included the kingdom of Naples, Sicily, and Lombardy but, inasmuch as their rulers were inclined to take advantage of Venice's hardships, the latter's freedom of action was severely restricted as a result of the new situation.

As far as the relation between grain production and commercial capital is concerned, it is worth recalling that the system of mandatory paid deliveries to which the Cretan feudatories were subjected highlighted their dependence on the huge commercial capital that was the foundation of Venice's power. Here the issues that need further study will be outlined. We know that the Venetian authorities resorted to private parties for their acquisitions of grain from Crete. They encouraged merchants by promising them a pre-established price for grain imported into Venice, provided it was sold to the republic first; only

---

[36] *Ibid.*, Nos. 700–9; II, Nos. 749, 757, and 758; cf. Thiriet, *La Romanie*, pp. 336, 346, 394, and 410.

under certain conditions did they allow its introduction onto the free market also. Unfortunately, little is known of mercantile activity regarding the traffic of grain in Venice. However, it is fair to assume that the strict control exercised by the state and the impossibility of selling grain outside the city severely restricted the opportunity for speculation and illicit profits. Even though the members of the Venetian government were tied to the interests of big commercial capital, they nevertheless saw the necessity of meeting the essential needs of the population, and not only in the matter of grain supplies. Indeed, settling these problems was an essential condition for maintaining that social harmony which was a basic feature of the republic of Venice.

A problem that deserves further examination is the commercial circulation of grain within the area controlled by Venice. The role of the Cretan gentry in these activities has already been mentioned; by contrast, we have no exact information on the participation of merchants and peasants in the grain trade. We cannot exclude the possibility that the Cretan gentry sold not only grain produced under its own control or through the services of the *paroikoi* but also that acquired more or less forcibly from the peasants. In order to clarify the situation that still requires extensive research, we may examine, by way of comparison, what happened in the coastal states of the Baltic, the great exporters of wheat from the Middle Ages to the modern era.

Ever since the 14th and 15th centuries, in the ports of this area of Europe, merchants and foreign businessmen tried to establish relationships with producers of foodstuffs and timber, mostly via the population of the small inland towns. There, merchants, gentry, and peasants who grew grain were engaged in finding ways to create direct contacts with foreigners, thus eliminating intermediaries as far as possible. For their part, Flemish and British businessmen tried to bypass barriers raised by harbour cities and establish direct relations with producers, albeit with little success. At the same time, with the system of advances on future harvests, merchants in the Baltic ports assured the delivery of timber and grain, thus managing to establish close relations with the inland population.

Subsequently, mainly from the 16th until well into the 17th century, the lay gentry and the higher clergy managed to assert themselves as major suppliers of raw materials and food products. Thanks also to their political power, they successfully eliminated a series of intermediaries, mostly from the inland markets, whom they confined at best to the role of agents. The peasants were thus forced into bigger corvées and were obliged to sell their surplus produce to their lords, who in this way took control of the main resources and dispatched them to the ports destined for export trade.

The examples of Gdańsk, Revel (today's Tallinn), and Riga show how both peasants and inhabitants of small inland towns were gradually excluded from the grain trade, to the advantage of the gentry. In fact, similar developments were observable throughout the inland area of the Hanseatic cities, from Livonia to Mecklenburg. This factor blocked the development of most inland towns. Eventually it threw the peasant masses into abject poverty, thus causing the situation of artisans and small urban merchants to deteriorate as well. The economy that connected small towns and rural areas dwindled considerably, to the point that on both sides there was a marked return to a natural economy. The social structures became ossified, and regressed.

This process of comparison attempts to underline the possibility of drawing valid analogies, not only with Crete and other grain areas within "Románia," but also with Italy, especially the south. In the harbour towns of the coastal states of the Baltic, the activities of merchants and foreign businessmen did not in fact determine the development of social and economic relationships; the decisive factor there was the overwhelming domination of the landed gentry over other social strata. It would be beneficial to investigate these and other open questions, as regards both the territories subject to Venice and the Italian south or *Mezzogiorno*.

3. *Relations with the Turkish Empire*

Some elements of the "economic model of Central-Eastern Europe" would seem to apply also to the grain trade between Italy and the Ottoman Empire, even though the latter presents notable chronological and social differences. As already pointed out, with the beginning of the second half of the 15th century, almost all of the eastern region that supplied Venice found itself under the domination of the Sultan. But this also applied to many other Italian city-states, such as Genoa and Florence, and to other towns such as Ancona. The importance of this phenomenon should not be underestimated.

As we know from the works of F. Braudel, M. Aymard, and Ö. L. Barkan, the economic policy of the Turks did not favour the development of grain exports on a large scale. In particular, Barkan has shown how, in the 16th century, the Ottoman Empire was the theatre of an extraordinary demographic growth, both in the cities and in the country, estimating this increase in population at around 60 per cent. Istanbul at first reached about 400,000 inhabitants, then 600,000, which were enormous figures for the time, while the population of other towns subject to the Ottoman Empire within the European regions also grew considerably, even though practically none of them had more than 20–30,000 inhabitants.[37] As a result, supplying towns, and especially the capital, posed a serious problem for the Ottoman authorities, who extended the system of imposing mandatory deliveries to the producer countries (not only of grain but also of various other foodstuffs), even though in his own time Solyman the Magnificent made an effort to render things tolerable for the peasants from the European provinces. Naturally, the need to supply the army was also at the root of the frequent bans on exporting grain proclaimed by the Ottoman government, concerned *inter alia* with keeping the price low. Thus the transportation of grain from one province to another, as well as its export, was only authorized through paid licences granted by the central authorities. In reality this control proved not always inflexible, owing to the corruption rife among civil servants.[38]

Another factor also deserves mention. Before the Turkish conquest, the great monasteries and the local gentry (*boyars*) were the main, though probably not the only, producers of grain destined for export. While the Turks tolerated the Orthodox ecclesiastical institutions, the Bulgarian and Serbian gentry had been partly massacred and partly forced to embrace Islam and become subject to the Ottoman system of military feudalism. The population subject to the *sipahi* (military feudatories) rendered relatively moderate services both in kind and labour. In addition, the *raja* (local subjects of the Sultan) paid taxes to the state, which obviously had no interest in bringing ruin upon itself.

---

[37] Ö. L. Barkan, "Research on the Ottoman Fiscal Survey," in M. A. Cook, *Studies in the Economic History of the Middle East from the Rise of Islam to the Present Day*, London 1970, pp. 168–170. Cf. also Ö. L. Barkan, "Essai sur les données statistiques des registres de recensement dans l'Empire Ottoman aux XVᵉ et XVIᵉ siècles," in *Journal of the Economic and Social History of the Orient*, I/1, 1957, and *idem*, "Les déportations comme méthode de peuplement et de colonisation dans l'Empire Ottoman," in *Revue de la Faculté des Sciences Economiques de l'Université d'Istanbul*, II, 1953.

[38] H. Inalčik, "L'Empire Ottoman," in *Actes du Premier Congrès des Etudes Balkaniques et Sud-Est Européennes*, III, Sofija 1969, pp. 90 and 92; *idem*, "Quelques remarques sur la formation du capital dans l'Empire Ottoman," in *Mélanges en l'honneur de Fernand Braudel*, Toulouse 1973, I, pp. 235–237; *idem*, *The Ottoman Empire, A Classical Age*, London, 1973.

The *timar*, the *zeamet*, and the *khass* were fiefs invested with various tax duties, ascribed to the *sipahi* and others. For those who made any gains during the period of the great Turkish conquests, the major sources of revenue were the continuing wars of aggression. From the 14th to the 16th centuries, this would appear to be the key to the extraordinary dynamism of Ottoman expansion, which was also based on population growth. Towards the end of the 16th century, however, the situation changed; demographic growth tapered off until it came almost to a standstill, while tax duties became more and more oppressive, driving the peasants to flee *en masse* towards the towns, and especially to Istanbul. Hence, while the countryside became depopulated, the towns were filled with parasitic and downtrodden masses.[39] According to Barkan, dramatic changes in prices, the high cost of living, and inflation all contributed to the economic and political decline of the Ottoman Empire, which had to face ever-increasing military expenses, especially after the battle of Lepanto.[40] Even in the structures of the rural areas, important transformations took place. The *sipahi* and other military feudatories suffered from a decrease in their income, the more so since, from the start of the 17th century, the Ottoman Empire found itself at a disadvantage in the face of western Europe and was thus gradually forced to abandon its aggressive policies. While the number of the decreasingly necessary *sipahi* diminished, the Empire called in regiments of mercenary soldiers, and developed its artillery and naval forces with enormous deployment of resources, all of which called for higher taxation.[41] At the same time, the dramatic increase in food prices throughout Europe, which started during the second half of the 16th century and continued until the third decade of the 17th century, also affected the Ottoman Empire, thus driving the feudal lords to engage in the direct sale of agricultural products. The example was set by the highest dignitaries and even the Sultan himself, although such a policy was contrary to the traditional strategy of the Ottoman Empire.[42] On the other hand, the system of minor fiefs did not favour the development of vast farmland estates under direct control of the lords. The

---

[39] Inalčik, *L'Empire Ottoman*, pp. 92–97.
[40] Inalčik, *L'Empire Ottoman*, pp. 92–97, and Ö. L. Barkan, "The Price Revolution of the XVIth Century. A Turning Point in the Economic History of the Near East," in *International Journal of Middle Eastern Studies*, 1975, 6, pp. 3–28.
[41] Inalčik, *L'Empire Ottoman*, pp. 96–97.
[42] *Ibid.*, p. 98.

laws in force, founded on Koran law, did not allow the imposition of taxes higher than the norm established at the time. Thus the peasants could appeal to the Sultan, whose power was still unquestioned, or to his main representatives, who were little disposed to see the power of their vassals grow, especially when this carried the risk of potential revolts and social disorders.

In such a situation, the number of fiefs (*timar* and *zeamet*) held by *sipahi* in the European regions of the Ottoman Empire decreased during the second half of the 16th century. Meanwhile, the great dignitaries, eager to take advantage of the favourable trend in the grain trade, used all possible means, some more and some less legal, to gather as many fiefs as possible under their control. To secure large quantities of foodstuffs for sale on the market or for export, they imposed on the peasants bigger and bigger corvées and tributes in kind. In the course of the 16th century, the first *ciftlik* emerged—the new type of estate that was to become dominant in the following centuries. Under the pressure of growing expenses, the central authorities contracted or sold state land to entrepreneurs, usurers, and other individuals who often had nothing to do with the obligations of military service. They established big firms (*ciftlik*), where work was done by slaves, salaried workers, and serfs. The exact process is still not well known. Sakazov and other Yugoslav scholars point to the beginning of the 17th century in Bulgaria and Serbia as marking the formation of the *ciftlik*, while Turkish historians place its appearance somewhat later.[43] In any case, in the 17th century the *ciftlik* was not yet a predominant form of farmland management. The majority of agricultural firms were to be found in the fiefs concentrated in the hands of the *sipahi*, the great dignitaries, or the relatives of the Sultan. Nonetheless, in time these lands also ended up by becoming *ciftlik*, their owners growing more and more involved in the domestic and foreign trade in agricultural produce. Later, the phenomenon was to favour separatist tendencies, such as became manifest in late Turkish feudalism.

F. Braudel rightly observed that this process presents many analogies with the transformations that took place in the same period in central and eastern Europe, even though profound differences can also be observed, due mainly to the absence of military feudalism in

---

[43] Sakazov, *Bulgarische Wirtschaftsgeschichte*, p. 188; Inalčik, *L'Empire Ottoman*, p. 97.

those regions. Somewhat similar phenomena can also be observed in Russia, where the possessors of *pomiest* were warriors and farmers at one and the same time. For obvious reasons, these points will not be dwelt upon here.

As regards the Ottoman Empire, it should also be mentioned that the introduction of rice and, from the end of the 16th century, of maize, enabled the food needs of the population to be met, leaving larger quantities of grain available for export (wheat, rye, barley).

It will be useful to examine briefly the participation of Italian commercial capital in the Turkish grain trade, and the influence this may have had on the socio-economic development of the Ottoman Empire. We have already mentioned the activities of the Venetians and Genoese in the Black Sea area and in Constantinople before the fall of the Byzantine Empire and the final Turkish conquest, which ended with the capture of Kaffa in 1475 and of Akkerman and Licostomo in 1484. In contrast to what various scholars (including myself) used to believe, the newly conquered regions were not hermetically sealed off from the Italian merchants. H. Inalčik has pointed out how, in the course of four months in 1490, 75 ships put into Kaffa; of these, 7 were Italian, and of the 157 merchants who arrived there, 4 were Italians. Compared with the overwhelming majority of Islamic ships and businessmen concerned, these figures are insignificant. The Italian ships mentioned belonged either to Italians who continued to live in the Crimea, and hence had become subjects of the Sultan, or to Venetians who imported wine from Chios and Crete.[44] One is immediately struck by the absence of the Genoese, who had been so powerful a force in the Black Sea basin not long before. Clearly, this scant data cannot be of significance in determining whether or not they were present in those regions once under their influence. Nonetheless, the Genoese would appear to have supplied grain mainly to southern Italy, now dominated by Spain, with whom Genoa had close economic and political ties.

It is not known whether the Venetian ships that put into Kaffa with Greek wine then loaded up with grain destined for Istanbul or Italy, though this possibility cannot be ruled out. In his important work devoted to the Venetian grain trade, M. Aymard shows that as late as around 1550 the Grand Vizier Roustem Pasha was still asking the Sultan to deny foreigners all access to the Black Sea, which implies

---

[44] Inalčik, *L'Empire Ottoman*, pp. 129–130.

that they continued to trade there.[45] We know that, some fifteen years later, the Venetians planned to transport Ukrainian grain to the Black Sea via the Dnestr, evidently in order to supply Istanbul and Venice itself. The plan failed, partly owing to the hostility of Poland, but above all owing to the categorical opposition of the Sultan.[46] The Poles were afraid that in case of war the trade would facilitate the penetration of the Turkish army into Poland, while the Turks wanted to close the Black Sea to all foreigners, so that navigation would be confined to the merchant and war fleets of the Ottoman Empire (as in fact happened shortly after), thus eliminating any concern regarding defence or supplying the capital.[47]

In this connection, we know little concerning the situation of Florence, Ancona, and other Italian towns that imported grain from the East. In the second half of the 15th century, Florentines, Anconians, and Genoese all took advantage of the war between Venice and the Turks to try and establish good relations with the Ottoman Empire.[48] They probably purchased grain in Istanbul and other ports of the Empire. In the 16th and 17th centuries, things must have developed along similar lines in Florence and Ancona, but very little is known on this score. As with Venice, the grain from Albania and northern Greece must have entered Italy via Ancona. Aymard rightly notes that it was easier for the Venetians (and probably other Italian merchants) to purchase grain on the western borders of the Ottoman Empire and on the islands rather than in other territories, where the stringent regulations forbidding the export of grain were more strictly adhered to. In those provinces, it was often the same local Turkish dignitaries who were financially interested in such trade.

The Venetians often received grain thanks to smugglers who used small boats called *caramursali*.[49] The purchase of grain from the Turkish Empire was a frequent matter of concern for Venetian ambassadors to the Sublime Porte. Towards the middle of the 16th century, the *bailo* (Venetian "Resident") Bernardo Navagero wrote that the Turks were persuaded (and in our view they had good reason to be) that Venice

---

[45] M. Aymard, *Venise, Raguse et le commerce du blé pendant la seconde moitié du XVIe siècle*, Paris 1966, p. 47.

[46] E. Alberi, *Relazioni degli ambasciatori veneti al Senato*, Firenze 1844, series III, vol. II, pp. 20–21.

[47] Aymard, *Venise*, p. 45.

[48] Małowist, *Kaffa*, p. 190.

[49] Aymard, *Venise*, pp. 46–47; Alberi, *Relazioni*, I, p. 183.

had an absolute need of Ottoman grain and that Venetian merchants could not prosper without trading with the Turks. Some years later, the ambassador Trevisan expressed similar sentiments, observing that the Ottoman Empire enjoyed an abundance of grain, which, however, was due to the vastness of its territory and its relatively scarce population, rather than to a high productivity rate.[50] Aymard, who called attention to this phenomenon, considered that at times during the 16th century there was overproduction of grain,[51] so that both producers and merchants regarded grain export as essential. At the same time, the Venetian ambassadors insisted in the senate on the necessity of intensifying the cultivation of cereals in the Venetian colonies of Dalmatia and in the Levant, so as to be no longer dependent on the Sublime Porte and avoid contributing to its power with the large sums paid for the purchase of grain.[52]

There were also other views on the state of agriculture in the Ottoman Empire. Marcantonio Barbarigo was well acquainted with Turkish affairs, having been *bailo* in Istanbul from 1567 to 1573. In his report written in 1573, he observed that the agriculture of the Empire was in a state of slow decline, the peasants abandoning the (often fairly fertile) fields, so much so as to provoke a scarcity of foodstuffs and a high cost of living. He reports having explained to the Turkish dignitaries that in the republic of Venice, as a consequence of the prohibitions against exporting grain established in the past by the Ottoman Empire, grain crops were now being grown on former swampy soil which had subsequently been drained.[53] These are clues that at least partly explain the transformations undergone by north Italian agriculture, which will be dealt with later. According to Barbarigo, in 1564 the failure of the Venetians to send ships to load grain dealt such a blow to the Turks that the Sultan ordered the wheat to be exported before it spoiled.[54] Whether from fear of retortion, or in order to strike a blow at the attitude of superiority of the Turkish authorities towards Venice, Barbarigo advised against buying export licences in Istanbul, and recommended that caution be exercised when buying grain.[55] This

---

[50] Alberi, *Relazioni*, I, pp. 183–184.
[51] Aymard, *Venise*, p. 45.
[52] Alberi, *Relazioni*, II, p. 290.
[53] *Ibid.*, III, p. 313; see also the pessimistic report by Marcantonio Barbarigo on the state of Ottoman agriculture in 1573.
[54] *Ibid.*, II, p. 22, Relazione di Barbarigo.
[55] *Ibid.*, pp. 46–47.

would appear to have been a political strategy designed to encourage the illegal exportation of grain from the Turkish Empire, a policy liable to provoke strong reactions.

In the last decades of the 16th century, one can observe a general tendency on the part of Venetian ambassadors and *baili* in Istanbul to emphasize the economic difficulties of the Empire, the depopulation of the countryside, and the decadent state of agriculture. They ascribed this to the tributes exacted by agents who worked for the government as independent contractors in the tax administration.[56] But some saw things differently. For example, in 1592 Lorenzo Bernardo observed that Istanbul continued to be well supplied with grain from the coastal countries of the Black Sea, the Morea, the Greek islands, and Anatolia (Egypt could be added), and that an abundance of agricultural products was available to the Sultan for his own needs and those of others.[57] At that time the harvests in the Mediterranean basin had been poor for some years, and in Italy there was a serious famine. Venice accordingly sent her ships to Turkey to load grain.[58] Genoa and Tuscany likewise drew on the great granary of the Levant and Turkish products were unloaded in Leghorn.

During the last decade of the 16th century, the price of grain on the domestic markets of the Turkish Empire underwent a major increase. According to the Venetians, while the *sipahi* tried to protect their Christian subjects from the tax collectors, they also demanded more services and, as the ambassador Zane reported, profited from higher prices to sell their grain on the domestic market and abroad. The *sipahi*, who collected for the Sultan the taxes paid by the *raia*, took advantage of their position to demand more than the sums due.[59] It would seem that they were driven into this by the fact that, in order to obtain the *timar* and other privileges from the Sultan, they had to pay established fees, and many palms had to be greased with sizable tips. The Italians frequently stressed the corruption that reigned in all sectors of Turkish life at the end of the century.[60]

---

[56] *Ibid.*, III, p. 313, Relazione di Barbarigo.
[57] *Ibid.*, II, p. 349.
[58] *Ibid.*, III, p. 386.
[59] *Ibid.*, II, pp. 218, 226, and 272–273; Relazioni di Contarini, 1583; Morosini, 1585; pp. 386–388.
[60] *Ibid.*, II, pp. 134–135; Relazione di Tiepolo, 1576.

Even though Italian grain buyers did purchase export licences from the Sultan and from high dignitaries, we know that they often resorted also to exporting illegally without a licence. Inevitably, information on those who sold the agricultural products required by the Italian merchants is scarce, but it is known that, during the first half of the 16th century (and perhaps even before), these included not only Ottoman feudatories and merchants, but also peasants. However, the situation changed in the second half of the century, when the amount of land concentrated in the hands of the great feudatories secured them large amounts of cereals from tributes in kind owed by serf peasants.[61] The growth of the urban population, the repercussions of the general increase in agricultural prices in Europe, and the growing demand for foodstuffs drove the great feudatories to become directly involved in the grain trade. Thus in 1553, the well-informed Venetian *bailo*, Bernardo Navagero, noted that the income of the Turkish high dignitaries had increased remarkably, the revenue of the Grand Vizier and the commander-in-chief of the fleet, Roustem Pasha, apparently reaching as much as 60,000 ducats per annum. We know that Roustem Pasha sold the grain produced on his widespread fiefs in the coastal area, which was then destined for export.[62] Other dignitaries made equally large profits from the sale of their own grain, especially in times of famine; we have already seen how, in the second half of the century, the *sipahi* also enjoyed higher revenues, thanks to the greater exploitation of peasants forced to turn in their surplus harvest. Their situation is analogous to what we know of the gentry from the coastal countries of the Baltic during the same period. It is fair to assume that the Italian merchants, giving up trade with the peasants, adjusted to the transformations taking place in the structure of property and in the division of revenue within the Ottoman Empire. They thus approached the big feudatories and the owners of *ciftlik*, who were able to offer them considerable quantities of grain and, thanks to their influence, at the same time facilitate exports of its grain, despite the frequently repeated bans on sale abroad.

Again, the analogy between the situation outlined in the Ottoman Empire and that obtaining in Central-Eastern Europe is striking. In both regions, we find the same basic socio-economic principle of

---

[61] Aymard, *Venise*, p. 50.
[62] Alberi, *Relazioni*, I, pp. 83–84 and 88–89.

excluding the peasants from the commercial circuits established by merchants and foreign businessmen in the harbour cities. Naturally the juridical aspect of the issue will not be covered here, beyond the fact that, in the 16th and 17th centuries in the Baltic, the process of absorbing subordinate fiefs into gentry estates had already come to a close, while in the Ottoman Empire *timar* and *zeamet* were still being absorbed into larger fiefs. This difference can be explained if we bear in mind the omnipotence of the Sultan's authority and the resistance of the Turkish administration to such transformations in farmland property, transformations to which it yielded only under the pressure of growing military and economic hardships.

It is not known exactly when the Italian merchants who purchased grain in Turkey started to suffer from the competition of businessmen from the Ottoman Empire. J. Tadič, in his study of trade within the city of Ragusa (Dubrovnik), placed the appearance of this phenomenon as late as the last quarter of the 16th century.[63] The merchants from the Ottoman Empire were for the most part Jews, many of whom had fled from Spain and Portugal, but there were also Greeks, Armenians, and Bulgarians among them. All displayed increasing activity and developed an intensive trade with Italy, especially with Venice, via Dalmatia and the coastal areas, while avoiding Ragusa, which was hostile to them.[64] We do not know whether the position of the Italians in the Ottoman Empire grew weaker as a result of this, but it can be fairly assumed that it did. At all events, from the end of the 16th century, British and Dutch merchants started plying the eastern Mediterranean more frequently and regularly, selling their goods at better prices than the Italian merchants and acquiring various products, including grain; their competition thus became increasingly threatening to the Italians. It is uncertain whether, in the course of their trade, the merchants from the Ottoman Empire and those from northern Europe frequented social milieux different from those that supplied the Italians. Unlikely as this may seem, new research in this direction is called for.

Another point that remains obscure, for lack of quantitative global data, is the possible influence exerted by Italian commercial capital on the development of the socio-economic structures of the Ottoman

---

[63] J. Tadič, "L'unité économique des Balkans et de la région Méditerranéenne," *Actes du Premier Congrès des Etudes Balkaniques*, p. 638.

[64] *Ibid.*, pp. 639–640.

Empire between the 15th and 17th centuries. Undoubtedly, the exceptional demographic growth and other domestic causes had a major impact. Nonetheless, it should be noted that the Italian merchants played a part in linking up Turkish agriculture with foreign markets, and introduced certain elements from the European economy, accelerating in particular the phenomenon of general price rises. It can thus be seen that to some extent the activities of Italian commercial capital played a not inconsiderable role in the complex process of the transformation of Ottoman military feudalism, which in the course of the 16th and 17th centuries took on an increasingly "civilian" character.

4. *Contacts with the Baltic*

To conclude these considerations, let us briefly review the attempt by Venice and other Italian states to arrange for provisions of grain from the Baltic and the basin of the river Elbe in the years between 1590 and 1592, when the great famine caused a dramatic rise in prices.[65] The main sources of information in this field are the reports by Marco Ottoboni, a Venetian agent sent to Austria and Poland in 1590 to organize the acquisition of grain there, at a time when famine raged in the Mediterranean area and grain prices were extremely high. But the high cost of transporting grain from central Europe to Italy by land ultimately rendered this project unfeasible. Ottoboni then proceeded to Poland, only to find that all the grain had already been bought up by the Gdańsk merchants while it was still standing, as had also occurred in the Baltic area. In fact, this grain was destined for the Dutch, who played a dominant role in the maritime traffic of the Baltic and the North Sea. Most of Ottoboni's commercial activity was concentrated in Gdańsk, since he realized that this city practically enjoyed a monopoly over Polish grain exports, even as regards the remote provinces of Volhynia and Podolia, situated at the south-eastern border of the kingdom, which produced the types of grain most suitable for long-distance transport.

At that time there was even an agent of the Pope in Gdańsk. After extended negotiations, he came to an agreement with that city whereby, over a period of three years, Civitavecchia was to be provided with 1000 *laszty* (32,824 hectolitres) of rye and 500 *laszty* (16,412 hectolitres) of wheat, at 100 *scudi* the *laszt*. Rome made a commitment to

---

[65] *Lettere di Marco Ottoboni al Senato di Venezia*, in *Archivio di Stato di Venezia* (photocopy in the possession of the author).

accept the merchandise even if it spoiled during transportation, and to deposit 100,000 *scudi* with the Gdańsk Senate. At this time, agents of the Grand Duke of Tuscany and of Genoese merchants were still active in Gdańsk and Lübeck, where they bought grain destined for Leghorn and Naples.

Meanwhile, Ottoboni, acting under pressure from the Venetian authorities, whose insistent letters described the dramatic situation in Italy, strove to obtain conclusive results. In northern Europe, cereals sold at prices lower than those in the areas that usually supplied Venice, such as southern Italy, Sicily, and the countries of the Ottoman Empire. Estimating that it would be more advantageous to import grain from there, Venice envisaged the possibility of creating a storage space where a constant amount of grain could be preserved. Yet, despite his best efforts, in the course of eighteen months Ottoboni only managed to get five ships sent to Venice, of which only three arrived at their destination with a few hundred *laszty* of wheat and rye. In fact, Ottoboni's plan was thwarted less by the presence of other Italian emissaries than by the Dutch, who had been the main buyers of Polish grain for at least a century. Besides, during those years the Dutch had already been sending Baltic grain to Leghorn and Genoa, whose ports were better situated than Venice on the sea route to the Levant. Indeed, together with British merchants, it was the Dutch who established a dominant role in grain exports from northern Europe to Italy. For their part, merchants from Gdańsk were afraid to sail to these remote Italian harbours, mainly for fear of the Barbary pirates established on the North African coast, but also of the risk of being kidnapped when in Spanish and Portuguese harbours, or seeing the deterioration of their merchandise during the long sea voyage. On the other hand, at that time it was impossible to transport grain direct from Baltic ports to Italy; once in a while a stop-over was necessary in order to move the cargo around, allow it to dry, and prevent it from spoiling.

The failure of these Venetian plans to ensure supplies is also interesting from another viewpoint. Here we find two large and rich commercial cities, Venice and Gdańsk, incapable of organizing an operation which would have guaranteed secure profits, even though it involved some risk. Aside from the various reasons mentioned, it would seem that this whole affair also reflects a change in the attitude of the Gdańsk merchants, who on this occasion objected to getting involved in a dangerous undertaking, precisely because by that time they had grown accustomed to their simple role of intermediaries between the Baltic inland and the Dutch, who possessed a good merchant fleet and the necessary entrepreneurial spirit. After drying out for a year in the silos of the Gdańsk harbour, Polish, Lithuanian, and Ukrainian grain was ready to be shipped to western Europe, but Gdańsk no longer had a fleet large enough to meet the current need. Besides, the Gdańsk gentry invested large sums in the less risky purchase of farmland estates, which in the circumstances ensured good profits, given the high price of agricultural products. Among the Hanseatic cities, Hamburg, more closely connected with the Netherlands, was the only one that gave evidence of still possessing plenty of "capitalistic spirit," which was clearly reflected in the emergence of its favourable situation.

II. *Italian Grain Agriculture and Commercial Capital*

Notwithstanding several recent studies by Italian historians, devoted to problems of agriculture, some of which have given excellent results, scarce attention has been paid to the trade in agricultural produce. I would like to examine here the influence of the grain trade on Italian agriculture, and outline the framework of the investment of commercial capital in agriculture. This latter problem has been especially widely discussed, constituting as it does an essential element in the understanding of the path covered by Italy in past centuries. Inasmuch as it is closely related to the issue of the troubled passage from feudalism to capitalism, it is also at the origin of the stagnation and economic regression the country suffered during the 17th century. It is regrettable that the investments of commercial capital made in agriculture during the Italian Middle Ages have not been analysed. Though less developed than in the 16th and 17th centuries, the phenomenon was already manifest at that time, and a careful study would throw more light on what transpired on the threshold of the modern age.

Three issues have attracted my attention. The first is *mezzadria* (sharecropping), the typical relationship between peasants and landowners since the beginning of the 13th century, especially in Tuscany. The second is the influence of the grain trade on the socio-economic structures of the *Mezzogiorno* (South). The third concerns capital investments in Venetian agriculture during the 16th and 17th centuries. In the absence of a complete knowledge of the local situation and the full availability of the relevant sources, my contribution is perforce limited to indicating a few working hypotheses.

1. *Urban Capital and Mezzadria*

In Italy, the European economic development that began towards the end of the 10th century, and continued for some three centuries more, got off to a very early start. It is generally acknowledged that the long succession of wars and invasions in the peninsula was followed by a period of relative peace which favoured the growth of the population, which in turn formed the basis for subsequent economic progress. Despite their state of desolation and destruction, numerous Roman towns survived, and this undoubtedly favoured the process of urbanization during the 10th century, made possible by the growth in rural population and by agricultural productivity. Henceforth, these two economic factors continued to influence each other, thus giving rise to a characteristic trait, common to northern and central Italian towns, namely their ability to assert not only their economic but also their political will on their rural counterparts.

This development will only be mentioned here, rather than covered in depth. Like all towns, Italian cities needed to establish close relations with the surrounding rural areas in order to secure the necessary supplies of food, to sell at least part of their products, and to encourage the immigration of peasants. This latter factor was a vital one for medieval towns, which needed manpower to compensate for their own low birth-rate. The town was thus forced to subdue its rural area. Naturally, trading merely within that area did not meet the needs of major cities which, as we have seen, soon ventured far beyond the boundaries of their immediate surroundings, having first subdued the surrounding countryside. Italian towns had laws designed to concentrate the essential products of rural areas on the city market, so reducing to a minimum the possibility of the rural areas under submission to export agricultural produce, especially wheat, to other markets. These measures were rendered necessary by the low agricultural productivity of the time, and the towns tried to enforce them in all possible ways. For this reason, especially in the early stages of the phenomenon, the penetration of city capital into the countryside must not be considered only as related to the profitability of the undertaking but also as a response to the desire of the municipality and of individuals to secure the necessary foodstuffs.

In the 13th century, the Tuscan municipalities secured the emancipation of the peasants, an event on which scholars have recently modified their attitude. As we know, this was an episode in the struggle waged by large towns against feudal lords who refused to submit to municipal authority.[66] Moreover, the emancipation of peasants facilitated investments in the countryside by the townsfolk, especially by merchants who succeeded in getting hold of much farmland that formerly belonged to the gentry. This was by no means a purely Tuscan or Italian phenomenon: in northern European cities, the bourgeoisie was no less willing to invest part of its capital in the countryside, thus securing foodstuffs and income from the sale of agricultural produce obtained as a service from the farmers. Many examples could be given, but here it will suffice to mention the Hanseatic markets and the Amsterdam bourgeoisie in the 15th and 16th centuries. Another case to be considered in this context is the investment of urban capital in the Tuscan countryside during the Middle Ages. It has been noted for some time that in the 14th century the possession of real estate, both in the town and in the country, elevated the prestige of Tuscan bankers and rich patricians. Both persons who deposited their own money with them and other businessmen with whom they traded were more disposed to grant them their trust, since those estates constituted a collateral security in the event of difficulties.[67] Eventually, both acquiring country property and building villas became the expression of a desire to "live civilized life," which in practice meant assimilating the manners of the aristocrats. As Giovanni Villani observed, the rich landowners lived off the food products of the countryside, especially when they resided there.

Imberciadori and other scholars have rightly observed that *mezzadria* developed from a pre-existing form of participation called *colonia parziaria*.[68] This system, which had been in existence in Italy and elsewhere for a long time, secured a part of production for the owner, but not necessarily one half of it, while it spurred the peasants, who were often tied to the land, to increase the productivity of the soil with improvements of various kinds. Thus *mezzadria* guaranteed not only continuity in contractual relationships but also farmland improvements such as the cultivation of new lots, land reclamation, or, conversely, irrigation (which was however a more difficult task for peasants). In Lombardy, these goals had been attained already in the 10th and 11th centuries,

---

[66] For a general account, cf. G. Luzzatto, *Per una storia economica d'Italia*, Bari 1967, pp. 143ff.

[67] Cf. A. Sapori, *Studi di storia economica (secoli XIII–XV)*, Firenze 1955, pp. 191ff.

[68] I. Imberciadori, *Mezzadria classica toscana, con documentazione inedita dal IX al XIV secolo*, Firenze 1957, pp. 36–37 and 52.

and perhaps even earlier, at a time when *mezzadria* had not yet been introduced. On the other hand, in Tuscany they stimulated the rise of *mezzadria*, which subsequently spread to other regions of Italy.

In its classic form, *mezzadria* existed between the beginning of the 13th and the middle of the 14th centuries. It was founded on a freely negotiated agreement between the landowner (*locator*) and the peasant committed to farming the estate (*conductor* or *mezzadro*). The two parties to the contract were free men who in some form became associated for a period of between two and five years, which was subject to extension. To revoke a contract, each party was required to give notice several months ahead of time.[69] Yet, from a contract drawn up as early as the beginning of the 14th century, it is already clear that only the *locator* had the right to revoke the contract, while the *conductor* accepted this important clause.[70] On the other hand, if the *mezzadro* broke the contract without notice, he was liable to pay a pre-established sum in damages. The *mezzadro* was committed to delivering half of the harvest to the owner, providing transportation free of charge, working with his entire family, and using all or part of the seed grain and any equipment supplied. He also accepted that his labour and the harvests be supervised by the owner or his agent, and undertook to return the estate in good order at the end of the contract. For his part, the owner entrusted the land to the *mezzadro*, usually together with a home, which however was not always mentioned in the contract. Often, the owner also provided some of the seed, the ploughing tools, and sometimes the livestock.[71] Thus the landowner and the *mezzadro* shared in a way a relationship of solidarity, but this solidarity should not be overestimated, as Imberciadori did, for in a sense it represented no more than the meeting-point of two contrasting interests, the owner's and those of the *conductor*. Nevertheless, in his brilliant *History of the Italian Rural Landscape*, E. Sereni states that the overall results of *mezzadria* in the Middle Ages were positive, for it contributed to the extraordinary development of viticulture, to the cultivation of better-quality grain and the abandonment of mediocre species, and to improvements in agricultural techniques. In general,

---

[69] *Ibid.*, p. 63.
[70] *Ibid.*, pp. 67 and 118–120.
[71] *Ibid.*, pp. 41 and 46–51.

these results were attained in the plains and hilly regions near towns, which in turn offered an outlet for the produce.[72]

The contract of *mezzadria* was thus originally negotiated between free men, and initially did not imply any bond of feudal dependence between landowner and producer. Nonetheless, the undertakings given by the producer remind one of the services a serf owed to his landlord: the obligation to be always present on the land, payments in kind, free transportation of the produce to the owner's home, and the prescription for the entire family to work on the owner's land. In fact, in the 16th and 17th centuries, the reactionary policies of landowners in these areas eventually led to patterns of "feudalization" in the *mezzadria* system.[73]. By contrast, during the Middle Ages and up to the beginning of the 14th century, the possibility that the *mezzadro* would become a completely free farmer, and perhaps even an owner, was unquestionably open, for his labour secured him an income higher than what was necessary to maintain himself and his family. Urban expansion caused an increase in the price of grain and agricultural products. While the overall population increase produced a higher pool of manpower in the countryside also, the growth of towns absorbed a growing number of workers, especially in the manufacture of silk and wool, and farmers thus saw their position strengthened with respect to the landowners.

Naturally, sharecroppers could easily fall into debt as a result of adverse weather conditions, famine years and the calamities that ensued, or epidemics and other natural disasters. In such cases, the *mezzadro* would find his freedom restricted and ran the risk of falling into a state of economic and even juridical servitude with respect to the landowner. In fact, as is well known, ever since the Middle Ages and well into modern times, the indebtedness of farmers was in various European countries a major cause of the feudal enslavement endured by the peasants. In contrast to what is implied by some widespread theories, feudal dependence, in its various forms, was also the result of indebtedness, and not only of forces outside the realm of economics; thus, the Russian *kabal'nye kholopy*, for instance, were nothing less than farmers reduced to slavery because of their debts.

---

[72] E. Sereni, *Storia del paesaggio agrario italiano*, Bari, 1958, p. 108.
[73] G. Giorgetti, *Contadini e proprietari nell'Italia moderna. Rapporti di produzione e contratti agrari dal secolo XVI a oggi*, Torino, 1974, pp. 282ff.

Most *mezzadria* contracts were negotiated for a period of a few years. At the expiration of the contract, it was possible for either party to modify the conditions or to make arrangements with other parties. The element of uncertainty implied in this system undoubtedly placed the owner in an advantageous position, since the farmer was economically the weaker. In fact, the period between the 13th and early 14th centuries witnessed a large growth in population; there was thus plenty of manpower available, and the situation of the *mezzadri* to some extent deteriorated. An indication of this is a clause noted by Imberciadori in a contract of the early 14th century, already referred to, whereby the option to cancel the contract before its expiration was restricted to the landowner.[74]

Nonetheless, scholars agree on a positive evaluation of the early centuries during which *mezzadria* was practised in Tuscany. There is no doubt that the investment of urban capital in agriculture favoured the development of its techniques and means of production. In addition, it must have attracted the commercial and monetary economy within its orbit, thus contributing in turn to intensifying production by supplying the town markets. Naturally, this form of management did not extend to all farmland, where older forms of ownership and production still survived. According to Sereni, *mezzadria* was most beneficial in the hills round the towns, which were best suited to horticulture and vineyards,[75] while in the plains where grain crops were grown its benefits were less in evidence. We also know that in this sector Tuscan production was usually insufficient, and that Florence was accustomed to imports from the south.

The studies by Conti give some idea of the social backgrounds common among *locatores*, who included not only merchants but also jurists, doctors, notaries, and master craftsmen.[76] Yet, for reasons already explained, the great mercantile bankers must also have invested major capital in agriculture. It is difficult to evaluate the number of landowners' country houses that existed in the environs of Florence between the 13th and 14th centuries. The famous description of Florence that we owe to Giovanni Villani shows how rich town dwellers generally spent the summer months in their rural residences and enjoyed the agricul-

---

[74] Imberciadori, *Mezzadria*, pp. 67–68.
[75] Sereni, *Storia del paesaggio agrario*.
[76] E. Conti, *La formazione della struttura agraria moderna nel contado fiorentino*, vol. I, *Le campagne nell'età precomunale*, Roma, 1965.

tural produce from their estates. To take just one famous example, in Boccaccio's *Decameron* we find the countryside frequented by town dwellers and, during the plague of 1348, it is the countryside that provides shelter for the group of young people whose story originated Boccaccio's. While we do not know the number of rural residences belonging to town dwellers in the Venetian region and in Tuscany,[77] there are good reasons for thinking that the tendency to invest capital in country estates, which became safer than commercial and financial transactions, developed mainly from the 15th century onwards. The crisis that hit most of Europe during the second half of the 14th and the 15th century led to a decline in the income from agriculture. This trend was reversed only towards the end of the 15th century, while in the 16th century agriculture once more became relatively profitable. Undoubtedly it was the large lay and ecclesiastical landowners, gentry and bourgeoisie, who drew most benefit from the situation, rather than the peasants.

In many western countries, the first half of the 14th century was characterized by a major crisis in the feudal structures; we do not know when this crisis started in Italy. Yet in Italy the 1348 plague and subsequent epidemics must also have brought about a notable transformation in the social structure of rural areas. According to C. Klapisch-Zuber, in the period between 1400 and 1430 the Tuscan population fell to its lowest level, rising again thereafter only slowly and to a limited extent.[78] In many European countries, this decrease in population resulted in a scarcity of manpower which in turn gave rise to improvements in the condition of the peasants and their agricultural contracts. In Tuscany, the situation would seem to have developed somewhat differently. Though the matter cannot be examined in detail here, I wish nevertheless to take a position thereon.

As we know, by the end of the 14th century the Tuscan luxury textile industry had already been hit by the crisis, and its situation worsened in the following century. It is likely that for new immigrants the possibility of finding work in the towns was reduced to zero. Hence immigration from the countryside abated, and this, together with the fact that some poor town dwellers flocked to rural regions, must undoubtedly have

---

[77] P. Villani, *Feudalità, riforme, capitalismo agrario*, Bari, 1968, p. 115; Sereni, *Storia del paesaggio agrario*, pp. 145 and 199.

[78] C. Klapisch-Zuber, "Villaggi abbandonati ed emigrazioni interne," in *Storia d'Italia Einaudi*, vol. V: *I documenti*, Torino, 1973, pp. 336–337.

weakened the position of the peasants with respect to the landowners. From 1400 onwards, the fall in the price of grain in Tuscany rendered the situation even more dramatic, especially for those peasants from areas most closely connected with the urban markets. The lower prices hit grain producers most of all, but to a lesser extent they probably also affected vegetable, fruit, and vineyard farmers from the hilly rural areas round Florence and other cities. To adjust to these new unfavourable conditions, many landowners tried replacing agriculture with breeding. This phenomenon was especially noticeable in Romagna, subject to the Pope, in the south, and in other regions (besides Italy, it was also current in England, Spain, and elsewhere). Both livestock and wool in fact fetched prices relatively higher than grain, while breeding demanded less labour than farming. In Tuscany, such measures were adopted by Siena, which dominated the vast depopulated coastal expanses of the Maremma. There, big landowners introduced migrant herding (*transumanza*), hoping, as Klapisch-Zuber noted, that it would contribute to rendering those lands fertile.[79]

A major effect of the crisis of the 14th and 15th centuries was the concentration of vast country estates in the hands of the Church and the rich bourgeoisie, especially in the regions where epidemics and war raged most. At the same time, as a consequence of the abandonment of ancient villages and boroughs (hamlets, etc.) and the formation of sparse settlements within the large estates, a transformation of the peasant population took place. In the second half of the 14th and throughout the succeeding century, *mezzadria* expanded steadily in Tuscany, as a kind of contract especially favourable to both ecclesiastical and lay landowners, and sometimes even to rich farmers, all of whom leased out a part of their land for several years. After 1350, in the environs of Pistoia, *mezzadria* extended to 55% and after 1400 to two-thirds of the land under cultivation.[80]

The development of *mezzadria* in the 16th and 17th centuries still requires extensive research. Giorgetti has shown that during those centuries a certain economic stratification took place among sharecroppers. Those who farmed the most fertile lands near the towns were capable of making an income that could eventually lead them to economic

---

[79] *Ibid.*, pp. 325–326 and 346–347.
[80] D. Herlihy, *Medieval and Renaissance Pistoia. The Social History of an Italian Town, 1200–1430*, Yale, 1967, pp. 136–137.

independence. But the majority of sharecroppers barely managed to make enough to live on, and often became indebted to the landowners, who imposed on them such material hardships and personal obligations as restricted their freedom in a feudal sense.[81] The root cause of that situation was probably the abundance of manpower caused both by population growth and by the crisis of the town economy.

Urban capital, and especially commercial capital, thus played a very important role at every stage of the development of Tuscan *mezzadria*. Between the 13th and the first half of the 14th century, it contributed to the extension of farmed areas, to the development of specialized agricultural techniques, and probably also to some improvement in the living conditions of the peasants. Beginning with the 16th and throughout the 17th century, *mezzadria* was still widespread in Tuscany, but the landowners managed to secure contractual relationships more favourable to themselves and thus acquired more wide-ranging powers at the expense of peasants. Sereni points to the proliferation of sumptuous villas built by rich landowners as the symbol of a refeudalization of Tuscan society.[82] This sound observation is borne out by the corresponding process sustained by commercial capital in most of Europe: agrarian investments were an inevitable way out for big merchants, so much so that even the Fuggers transformed themselves into feudal landlords. Agricultural and industrial productivity were still relatively low, while the living standards of the masses were extremely low; the markets available for products were thus very limited, and the overall situation was anything but favourable to industrial development. In the course of the 16th century and even more so in the 17th century, the merchants of north-western Europe surpassed the Italians in trade volume; it is thus not surprising that the rich Tuscan merchants should have invested their capital in country estates. The peasants' unstable economic situation, their relatively low income, and their vulnerability in the face of wars and famines placed them all too easily in a state of personal and economic dependence on the owners of landed estates. These were essentially the elements which governed the refeudalization

---

[81] G. Giorgetti, "Contratti agrari e rapporti sociali nelle campagne," *in Storia d'Italia Einaudi*, vol. V, pp. 704–723 and 747ff.; *idem*, "Contadini e proprietari", *op. cit.* On the refeudalization of Tuscany from the middle of the 14th century, cf. Sereni, *Storia del paesaggio agrario*, pp. 196–199.

[82] Sereni, *Storia del paesaggio agrario*, pp. 145–146.

during that period of Tuscany and of numerous other regions in Italy and Europe as a whole.

It seems fair to state that, in southern Italy and Sicily, both grain agriculture and the productive forces and relationships associated with it determined at once the development of the country and its subsequent stagnation and regression during the 17th century.

2. *The Grain from the Mezzogiorno*

Even though the economic recovery in southern Italy also set in around the 10th century, the conquest of the country by foreign dynasties, either through military exploits or in relatively peaceful ways, created special conditions, in particular providing the *Mezzogiorno* with solid feudal institutions and favouring the formation of a powerful group of barons, who dominated the minor gentry. Thus, kings from the Norman, Swabian, and Angevin dynasties succeeded in strengthening the central power, thanks mainly to the country's wealth and the royal treasury.

The barons' fiefs extended over vast regions. While the kings secured the most fertile lands for themselves, with time the aristocracy also managed to assemble immense estates yielding high profits from their livestock and agricultural products.

In the 13th century, most peasants were free men, even though they did not posses the land they farmed. They administered it for the king, the barons, the gentry, and later even the burghers. Ever since the Roman times, in southern Italy *latifondi* (vast landed estates) had dominated the rural landscape. In subsequent ages, this feature was preserved, thus establishing a typical way of settling the land, with the rural population living in large settlements or villages, whence they left each day to go and work on the owners' land or on parcels granted to individual workers. This system originally developed from the inhabitants' need to protect themselves against strangers, but it also proved an effective means of controlling the peasants. Similar settlements were at one time also widespread in central Italy, but later disappeared as a consequence of the crisis in the 14th century, when the inhabitants of settlements and small towns became dispersed throughout the land.

In southern Italy, besides *masserie* (large estates) administered by *magistri massariae* (representatives of the king), and great *latifondi* owned by barons, the *colonia parziaria* was also widespread; there peasants had the right to take over the lands assigned to them, but in so doing they in fact became tied to the land. Eventually this state of affairs rendered the peasants subject to the barons, not just as producers, but also because both judiciary power and other feudal privileges held by the landowners restricted the individual freedom of peasants residing on the lords' land. As in Sicily, these regions were large reserves of farm and livestock produce, which supplied not only other Italian regions but other Mediterranean countries also. This phenomenon merits some emphasis, since the (extremely dry) conditions of soil and climate did not favour grain farming. From the agricultural aspect, Abruzzi, Apulia, and Campania, with its volcanic soil, were especially important for the production of grain destined for export. By contrast, Calabria's fields, situated on mountain slopes, were mostly given over to fruit trees and vineyards; even so, at least in the late Middle Ages and the 16th century, this region remained self-sufficient in grain production.[83] The abundance of grain in some regions and its scarcity in others stimulated the development of the grain trade in the southern part of the peninsula. Indeed, it is difficult to imagine the rise of large urban centres such as Venice, Florence, Genoa, or Pisa without a constant influx of southern wheat. This problem has already been studied by G. Yver and others, and only certain aspects of the question will be examined here.

The Norman dynasty and subsequently the Swabians strove to obtain maximum profits from agriculture and from both the domestic and the international grain trade. There are some who even thought that Frederick II sought to secure a monopoly on grain production and trade, but the available sources would not seem to confirm this supposition. Nonetheless, both the domestic trade and the export of grain were subject to strong taxation, and foreigners had to buy purchase and export licences at high prices.[84] As a custom duty, the Norman, Swabian, and Angevin kings collected a fifth of the grain sent abroad by merchants, but this taxation was not so heavy as to curb this commerce; indeed, from the end of the 12th century, first the Pisans and the Florentines and later also the Venetians were actively engaged in the export of grain from the ports of Trani, Manfredonia, Barletta, Brindisi, Bari, Gaeta, Salerno, and even Naples, latter not being an important

---

[83] G. Galasso, *Economia e società nella Calabria del Cinquecento*, Milano 1975, pp. 115–124.

[84] G. Yver, *Le commerce et les marchands dans l'Italie méridionale au XIIIe et XIVe siècle*, Paris, 1903, p. 107.

export centre *per se*.[85] The Genoese also took part in this trade, albeit
to a lesser extent at first, and Provençal merchants likewise. Merchants
from Ragusa, Cattaro, and the Dalmatian ports also arrived from the
Levant in order to purchase grain.[86]

Here, too, we lack precise data on the global volume of grain exports
from the *Mezzogiorno* during the Middle Ages, though some fragmentary details are available for most of the 14th century. Thus, around
1316–17, the Venetians obtained a licence to export 105,000 *salme* of
wheat (1 Apulian *salma* was the equivalent of 160 litres; 1 Neapolitan
salma 166 litres). In 1329, the great Florentine merchants, the Acciaiuoli,
were authorized to export 145,000 *salme* of grain from the kingdom,
of which 125,000 were from Apulia and the remaining 20,000 from
Abruzzi. In 1335 and the following years, 33,000 *salme* were exported
on the basis of a contract negotiated directly with the king. Likewise in
1335, the Florentine company of the Bards was expected to load 10,000
salme of wheat and other cereals in Barletta, destined for the Papal
States.[87] Even though these data could be multiplied, they still would
not provide a general picture of cereal exports from the *Mezzogiorno*.
We only know that, from the beginning of the 13th and especially in
the first half of the 14th century, the grain trade within the southern
kingdom was dominated by the Florentines, the lively activity of the
Venetians in Trani notwithstanding.[88] The Florentines managed to take
charge of this trade sector, thanks largely to the loans they extended
to the kings of Naples. The very sums made available to the monarchs
were often returned in the form of grain produced on their lands, and
in this way the great Florentine merchants and financiers were able to
control the exports of grain and of other agricultural products from the
Mezzogiorno, thereby also achieving a position of prominence in the
kingdom's domestic trade.[89] Merchants from the other northern cities
arrived only later, to find lesser opportunities.

With whom did these foreign merchants negotiate? The data gathered
by Yver indicate that the most important contracts were drawn up with
the Crown, which is understandable inasmuch as the monarchs had

---

[85] *Ibid.*, pp. 106 and 122–126.
[86] *Ibid.*, p. 125; J. Božič, *Ekonomski i drustveni razvitak Dubrovnika v XIV–XV veku*,
in "Istoricki Glasnik", I, 1949, pp. 45–47.
[87] Yver, *Le commerce*, pp. 107–8, 115, 118, and 124–25.
[88] *Ibid.*, p. 123.
[89] Yver, *Le commerce*, pp. 121ff.

the largest amounts of grain available, produced in their lands. But neither should the role of the barons or the town merchants be ignored. Unfortunately we have no specific information on the character of these transactions, nor do we know whether they were paid for in cash or by credit. This second possibility seems plausible, since the big Venetian and Florentine companies had agencies within the southern kingdom directed by consuls. This is a problem that merits further study. At the same time, it would be useful to arrive at an understanding of whether, and if so to what extent, the peasants who produced grain had an interest in exporting it.

Foreign merchants were the major distributors of the grain exported both to their own cities of origin and to other countries, depending naturally on the advantages offered by the venture. Even Venice, otherwise so insistent on enforcing the principle that imported grain be unloaded in its own harbour, sometimes allowed and sometimes even demanded that it be unloaded in other ports of its maritime empire, as when grain was in short supply and was required for the basic needs of the garrisons and the local population.[90] It was not unusual for Syria and northern Africa to receive wheat acquired by merchants operating in the kingdom of Naples.

While grain had an important place in the commercial transactions between the merchants of central and northern Italy and the Kingdom of Naples, it should be pointed out that it was not the only merchandise in which they traded. Other items such as alum from Ischia, oil and silk, and certain products from the Levant could all be bought in Naples. But above all the merchants sold large quantities of cloth of various quality, mainly from Florence and Lombardy. A textile industry and goldsmithery also existed in the kingdom, but their products could not compete with those from central and northern Italy.[91]

It may be wondered why the southern merchants did not take on the role of exporters directly. Certainly, they cannot have been completely excluded from the foreign, let alone domestic, trade. Yet there is no doubt that their position was far weaker than that of the rich foreigners, and their role in maritime traffic was a relatively modest one. Evidently they did not have sufficient means available to them, and their capital

---

[90] For example in 1282, 1290, etc. Cf. Thiriet, *Délibérations*, I/1, Nos. 55 and 144, etc.

[91] Yver, *Le commerce*, p. 117.

was considerably smaller than that of their northern competitors. Perhaps the taxes imposed by the royal administration slowed down the pace at which commercial capital could be accumulated, while the policy of the Crown favoured those merchants who were able to lend money and pay high customs duties. This was a crucial problem in the economic life of the kingdom, and it would appear that, once past the period of its highest prosperity, southern Italy displayed less economic drive than other regions of the peninsula both in trade and in agriculture. From the 12th to the middle of the 14th century, the development of agriculture would seem to have been more quantitative than qualitative. The growth in both domestic and foreign demand for grain led to an expansion of the lands sown with cereals and there is no doubt that both local and foreign commercial capital had a major impact in this area. On the other hand, few changes are noticeable in production techniques and relationships. Certainly, the development of agriculture essentially favoured the monarchy and the great barons and greatly strengthened their position. Local merchants probably drew profits from foreign trade, yet they never came near the possibilities available to foreign merchants. Similar considerations apply to the majority of artisan production from the south. From the 12th to the middle of the 14th century, southern Italian artisan production still remained a non-negligible economic force, yet it was hardly able to oppose foreign competition, especially in the textile sector. But this is another problem, which still awaits exhaustive research.

Even less is known about the conditions of the southern peasants in those centuries. We know neither to what extent the better-off among them participated in the trade of agricultural products, nor what relationship existed between their debts and the taxation imposed by the State, the Church, and the barons. One may surmise that price increases were in some measure advantageous for those peasants who produced grain and other foodstuffs destined for sale, and that the overall commercial and agricultural situation was favourable to them; but on these issues detailed information is still lacking.

To conclude this point, I would call attention once more to the penetration of commercial capital in large landed estates. It is known that this phenomenon concerned in particular the powerful Florentine merchants and financiers active in the Kingdom of Naples, who not only granted important credits to those in power, but also occupied high administrative offices. Yver provides numerous examples, emphasizing the importance of farmland transactions negotiated with the Florentines, and their acquisition of lands belonging to barons who were unable to fulfil their obligations. The Crown itself was involved in similar transactions. In this way, several members of companies such as the Bardi, the Peruzzi, the Aldobrandini, and the Acciaiuoli acquired possession of large estates, thus becoming feudatories of the Kingdom of Naples.[92] Exactly what consequences this had on southern agriculture is something that remains to be seen. There is no doubt that the crisis of feudalism also affected these regions. Just as in the 13th, 14th, and 15th centuries, the struggles between rival barons had consequences also to the Roman countryside bordering on the kingdom, which was devastated and depopulated. The wars between the Aragonese and the Angevins had dramatic repercussions on the population, leading to a remarkable decrease in the number of inhabitants and settlements in the countryside. Yet the major disaster remains the black death of 1347–48. C. Klapisch-Zuber has recorded that, between the 13th and 14th centuries, in the Apulian lowlands, about one half of all populated centres disappeared, and almost as many (45 per cent) in the dioceses of Molise, while it would seem that Abruzzi and Calabria were less affected. Generally speaking, it may be said that in southern Italy and in Sicily the depopulation process hit towns and villages in equal measure.[93]

The rural economy had to adjust to these new conditions. At the beginning of the 15th century, the price of grain decreased, while the prices of wool and meat remained more stable. This fact can be explained by the lower price of bread, which allowed survivors to spend more on this type of food and on clothing. Large landowners tended to develop the breeding of farm animals, especially sheep, a policy explained both by the higher profits attainable from animal breeding and by the labour shortages caused by epidemics. In fact, there had been attempts to extend this activity ever since the end of the 13th century, but the year 1443 marked a radical turning point when Alfonso the Magnanimous allotted the depopulated Apulian lowlands exclusively to breeding. At that point, a conflict arose between shepherds and peasants, caused by the shepherds' desire to extend the lands destined for pasture, a policy which caused severe damage to crops. From then on, the Apulian

---

[92] *Ibid.*, pp. 326–28.
[93] C. Klapisch-Zuber and John Day, "Villages désertés en Italie. Esquisse," in *Villages désertés et histoire économique XIᵉ–XVIIIᵉ siècles*, Paris, 1965, pp. 446–450; Klapisch-Zuber, *Villaggi abbandonati*, pp. 342–344.

lowlands, which had once been one of the granaries of the Mediterranean countries, lost much of their importance in this respect.

Sereni has pointed out other important details. The large landowners did not restrict themselves to occupying pastures and incorporating within their lands municipal properties previously used by peasants, but they also put up fences.[94] All that did great harm to both breeding and peasant farming, since those enclosures prevented proper manuring of the soil. That process continued in the 15th and 16th centuries, leading to the expulsion of many peasants from their lands and their emigration towards urban centres. In this period the dioceses adjacent to the Apulian lowlands underwent an increasingly serious process of depopulation, while centres like Foggia and Lucera were growing.[95] As was the case in Castile and Aragon, the royal authorities generally favoured livestock breeding because of the large sums they collected from leasing pastures.

Such developments call to mind what happened in Spain during the formation of the Mesta. There is no doubt that, in organizing Apulian breeding, Alfonso the Magnanimous kept in mind the experience gained in his country of origin. Castilian wool was of good quality, and had quickly assumed a major role in the country's economy. It was even used abroad by Dutch clothmakers, and in England it was mixed with locally produced wool. In contrast, the wool from the Italian *Mezzogiorno* did not prove of very good quality; yet, even though it was inferior to Spanish, and especially to English wool, it was used by clothmakers from the Kingdom of Naples and other Italian regions.

At this point it might be worth comparing and contrasting developments in the Kingdom of Naples and in England between the end of the 14th and the 15th centuries. The development of sheep breeding, the enclosure of pastures, and the beginning of the gradual expulsion of peasants from their lands are all analogous phenomena. However, the effects of the crisis were somewhat different in the two countries. In southern Italy, the *latifondi* did not disintegrate, and only the enclosure of pastures took place. In England, the farmlands were also enclosed. According to Sereni, in the Italian *Mezzogiorno* agricultural techniques regressed, while

---

[94] Sereni, *Storia del paesaggio agrario*, pp. 122–123.
[95] Klapisch-Zuber, *Villaggi abbandonati*, pp. 342–349.

in England some progress was made in this field.[96] Lastly, while Neapolitan textile production remained practically stagnant, that of England grew markedly from the end of the 14th century onwards. Those differences in the economies of the two countries were there when the economic and political crisis reached its peak in the course of the 15th century. The reasons are not easy to establish. Perhaps it should be noted that in England commercial capital had made an important contribution to the development of a rural textile industry, first in the western provinces and later in other parts of the country. Furthermore, English merchants had immediately become involved in supplying woollen cloth to the domestic market and in exporting them to other countries. Meanwhile, as the textile industry developed in the Kingdom of Castile, albeit at a slower pace than in England, both local and foreign merchants, especially the Genoese, boldly embarked on the international wool trade. Probably owing to its mediocre quality, the wool of the Italian *Mezzogiorno* did not arouse as much interest among merchants and so only contributed in much smaller measure to the expansion of the country's textile industry. While these questions lie outside the framework of this study, it should nonetheless be noted that in this respect commercial capital, both local and foreign, did not greatly influence the transformations that took place in rural areas.

For the Kingdom of Naples, the second half of the 15th and the first three decades of the 16th century were a very difficult period. First of all came the bloody battles between King Ferrante and the barons, followed by the French attempt to take over the kingdom, the Spanish intervention, and the war between the houses of Valois and Habsburg. Meanwhile, the conflict between the monarchy and the barons continued. In 1480 the Turks landed in Otranto, after which the Neapolitan and Sicilian coasts lived under the constant threat of the Ottoman fleet or the Barbary pirates. The Turkish peril and the Kingdom's coming under the influence of Spanish politics led to a growing increase in public expenditure and fiscal oppression, even though the darkest period for southern Italy only started at the end of the 16th century.[97] In fact, between 1505 and 1595 the population of the Kingdom of Naples grew from about one million to over two million, the growth rate being especially rapid during the first half of the century. Naples,

---

[96] Sereni, *Storia del paesaggio agrario*, pp. 189–191.
[97] Cf. Galasso, *Economia e società*.

which counted some 150,000 inhabitants at the beginning of the century, had more than 280,000 in 1606. Less important towns also experienced a period of prosperity.[98] For a certain time sericulture flourished in the Calabrian countryside, and the production of sugar cane developed.[99] In general, all sectors of the kingdom's agriculture participated in the economic boom which Europe enjoyed in those years. Economic differences among the peasants became more pronounced in direct connection with the growth in grain production and in the cereal trade. In fact, one observes the formation of a richer group, in league with the merchants for whom they acquired agricultural produce. Some were even able to avail themselves of capital advanced by the gentry. The Venetians became increasingly active in the Kingdom of Naples, and acquired large amounts of grain, legally or otherwise.[100] Sometimes they obtained goods direct from the producers and, in certain cases at least, settled accounts in gold. Nonetheless, in the 16th century the Genoese still remained the primary buyers, and established ever stronger economic links with the empire of the Spanish Habsburgs. They managed to establish direct and regular contacts with well-off peasants, to whom they paid advances on future deliveries of grain, thus transforming those peasants into minor entrepreneurs.[101]

In contrast, the situation evolved unfavourably during the last twenty years of the 16th century. In the first quarter of the 17th century, a succession of bad crops and an economic slump threw into disarray an agricultural system which was already suffering under the pressure of large-scale breeders. At the same time, the production of sugar, cotton, and to some extent silk did not match foreign competition and consequently declined. This situation was accompanied by an economic offensive from the aristocracy, which successfully sought to restore its ancient rights and privileges and reclaim feudal tributes that had fallen into disuse. At the same time, the aristocracy appropriated commons, depriving the peasants of pastures and stifling their ability to farming.

---

[98] A. Bellettini, "La popolazione italiana dall'era volgare ai giorni nostri. Valutazioni e tendenze," in *Storia d'Italia*, Vol. V: *I documenti*, Torino 1973, pp. 507ff.; R. Romano, "Napoli: dal Viceregno al Regno." *Storia economica*, Torino 1976, p. 10; Galasso, *Economia e società, op. cit.*, pp. 100ff.

[99] Galasso, *Economia e società, op. cit.*, pp. 143–52 and 175–81.

[100] Galasso, *Economia e società, op. cit.*, pp. 125–28 and 207–11; Aymard, *Venise, op. cit.*, pp. 42–45 and 94. For the "*massari*"; cf. R. Villari, *La rivolta antispagnola a Napoli*, Bari 1966, p. 61.

[101] Galasso, *Economia e società*.

Banditry became widespread and discontent spread throughout the rural areas,[102] while poverty caused massive migration towards the towns, especially Naples. Scarce opportunities to find work forced large numbers of these new town-dwellers to live by their wits on the margins of society, a situation which led to the revolt of Masaniello in 1648.

Meanwhile, the gentry reinforced its own position. Though subject to a Spanish viceroy, the gentry held on to its own economic power, and even strengthened it by assimilating rich families of ex-merchants and bankers such as the Spinola, the Grimaldi, the Doria, and the Imperiali. Urban stagnation drove many town-dwellers, merchants, jurists, etc. to buy land, but this was not enough to reinvigorate agriculture and the rural economy. Its only effects were to aggravate peasant oppression, owing to the deterioration of material conditions, and, following the failure of Masaniello's revolt, to plunge vast masses of the people into apathy and abject poverty.[103]

3. *Venetian Expansion and Agricultural Problems*

The problem of the investment of Venetian commercial capital in farming property and its influence on the republic's agriculture has long been the object of lively discussion. The first, somewhat optimistic, pronouncements by Beltrami, concerning the period between the 16th and 18th centuries, have been subsequently corrected, among the others by their very author.[104] The most pessimistic picture of the situation is perhaps that of R. Romano, who regards the agriculturization of Venetian commercial capital in the modern age as one of the manifestations of the refeudalization that came with the socio-economic regression that befell Italy in the 17th century.[105]

The problem is undoubtedly complex. It is undeniable that, even in the second half of the 16th century, investments of commercial capital in both the Venetian region and Lombardy were at the source of major

---

[102] *Ibid.*, pp. 376ff.; Villari, *La rivolta*, pp. 58ff. and 161–166.

[103] Sereni, *Storia del paesaggio agrario*, p. 195; Villari, *La rivolta*, pp. 172–184.

[104] Cf. D. Beltrami, *Storia della popolazione di Venezia dalla fine del secolo XVI alla caduta della Repubblica*, Padova, 1954; *idem, La penetrazione dei veneziani in Terraferma. Forze di lavoro e proprietà familiari nelle campagne venete dei secoli XVII e XVIII*, Venezia-Roma, 1961.

[105] R. Romano, "Agricoltura e contadini nell'Italia del XV e XVI secolo," in *Tra due crisi: l'Italia del Rinascimento*, Torino, 1971, pp. 57–68.

agricultural progress, especially as regards regulation of the waterway network, the draining of marshlands, and the introduction of new rice crops, and later of maize. Even though the nutritional value of the latter is inferior to that of wheat, it is higher than that of other grains usually eaten by peasants, and its high yield helped to reduce the recurrent threat of famine. On the other hand, it would be mistaken to narrow the problem of commercial capital investments in agriculture exclusively to modern times. In fact, Stuart J. Woolf has pointed out that the Venetians possessed lands in the Venetian countryside at least from the end of the 14th century, if not before; despite all existing restrictions, they took advantage of the confiscation of possessions owned by the Carraresi, acquiring vast estates in the adjacent mainland, the Terraferma conquered in the 15th century, especially in the areas surrounding Padua. It appears that around 1446 about one-third of the lands around Padua belonged to Venetians, and some years later they made important acquisitions in the areas around Verona and Vicenza.[106] According to Beltrami's estimate, through land taxation Venice collected an income that grew between 1510 and 1537 from 33,000 to 42,000 ducats, reaching 93,000 ducats in 1566, and 134,000 in 1582.[107] This spectacular increase in tax revenue gives some idea of the steady expansion of Venetian possessions on the mainland. It has been calculated that these amounted to 150–160,000 hectares, in the areas round Padua, Treviso, Vicenza, and Verona, and in general they were the best arable areas. These agrarian investments continued to grow between 1580 and 1630.[108]

The Venetians displayed a propensity for acquiring lands as early as the 14th and 15th centuries. How is this tendency to be explained? At the time, this phenomenon was in fact widespread throughout Europe. Everywhere rich merchants sought to invest part of their money in real estate and especially in land property, as a way of protecting their capital against the usual risks of commercial operations. Ups and downs in the economy contributed to this policy, since it was not always easy to find good ways of investing capital in commercial and financial transactions. Another factor to be borne in mind is the merchants' desire to

---

[106] S. J. Woolf, "Venice and the Terraferma. Problems of the Change from Commercial to Landed Activities," in B. Pullan, *Crisis and Change in the Venetian Economy in the Sixteenth and Seventeenth Centuries*, London, 1973.
[107] Beltrami, *La penetrazione*, pp. 48–51; Woolf, *Venice*, p. 182.
[108] Beltrami, *La penetrazione*, pp. 51–53; Woolf, *Venice*, p. 182.

ensure their own provision of foodstuffs in years beset by tragic famines and growing difficulties in importing grain. Finally, a motivation that should not be overlooked is the sense of social prestige that these country residences conferred on their new buyers. In the 15th century, the great Venetian expansion on the mainland favoured these tendencies. It is difficult to establish to what extent this activity expressed a specific interest in land ownership on the part of some groups within the Venetian aristocracy, or whether it was solely the consequence of the republic's territorial expansion on the Italian continent. It would also be pertinent to take into account the fact that some merchants felt driven to restrict their investments in trade because of the continuing conflicts between Venice and the Turkish principalities in Anatolia, and the subsequent reverses which Venice suffered in the fight against the Ottoman Empire. Such investments were at risk of rising losses and, while pouring money into real estate was probably less profitable, it was much less risky as well. This factor might also explain the increasingly aggressive policy of Venice in the peninsula.

While Venetian investments of commercial capital in farmland property in the late Middle Ages were not an isolated phenomenon, they would not appear to have caused any major changes in either the cultivation of the soil or in existing social relationships within the regions subject to the republic. At that time, new owners neither introduced new agricultural techniques nor did they extend farmed areas. On the other hand, no reasons existed for such initiatives at that time inasmuch as, up till the middle and even at the very end of the 15th century, agricultural prices remained relatively low. Furthermore, Venice was still in a position to purchase agricultural products from the Levant, and only later did the restrictions imposed by the Sublime Porte contribute to the increased cost of imported wheat. At any rate, the situation did not appear too serious to Venice, since powerful groups within Ottoman society had an interest in grain exports.

The researches of F. Braudel and other scholars from the Parisian École des Hautes Études have shown that Portuguese expansion into India disrupted Venetian trade with the Orient only for a short time. Indeed, in the second half of the 16th century the republic managed to re-establish her own position on the Eastern markets, albeit only for a few years. While Venetian trade remained powerful, investments in farmland on the nearby mainland continued to grow. In the first half of the 16th century, the rapid demographic growth in the capital and the consequent development of outlets for agricultural produce encouraged new investment in rural areas. From the end of the 15th century onwards, the rise in prices rendered the purchase of property advantageous while, in the Terraferma and in Lombardy, one could observe the development of industrial activity, and hence a rise in population, in the towns subject to the *Serenissima*.

For the Venetian authorities, agricultural use of the mainland was a matter of deep concern, as is manifested in their interest in the well-known memorandum by Alvise Cornaro who, towards the middle of the 16th century, called attention to the vast uncultivated areas in the region surrounding Venice, the Veneto, left uncultivated either for want of water or, conversely, for their swampy nature.[109] The government decided to undertake a vast operation of reclamation, to be funded by both state and private contributors but, when the time came to start work, only public funds were available. This nothwithstanding, remarkable results were achieved, and the extension of cereal growing and of pasture land enabled gradual progress from a system of rotation every three years to one of continuous exploitation of the soil.[110] This initiative can probably be seen as a reflection of changed conditions in the country; both the rise in population and the higher price of agricultural produce encouraged research into new means of providing these goods, even at the cost of sizable investments. As already mentioned, in the import sector the situation was deteriorating; the consequences of the restrictions imposed by the Turks and the difficulties encountered by agriculture in the Ottoman Empire were making themselves felt. At the same time, importing grain from southern Italy, Sicily, and Lombardy made Venice dependent on Spain, to whom these regions were now subjected. On the other hand, attempts to import grain from central and eastern Europe had failed, even at a time of dire need, while in the Mediterranean English and Dutch competition were frustrating the activities of Venetian merchants. All these reasons must have induced the government of Venice to develop mainland agriculture.

R. Romano rightly considers that the Venetian government, in financing on its own the reclamation of swamps and the subsequent extension of farmlands, was acting in the best interests of the great aristocratic families.[111] And if, between the mid-16th century and the 1580s and

---

[109] Woolf, "Venice," pp. 180–181.
[110] Romano, *Tra due crisi*, pp. 194–196; Villani, *Feudalità*, pp. 117–118.
[111] Romano, *Tra due crisi*, pp. 194–196.

1590s, the enthusiasm for these initiatives on the part of the Venetian gentry was at best moderate, this was due to the exceptional situation that favoured trade with the Levant. During this period, investing capital in commercial enterprises was probably more profitable than locking up large sums in improvements of farmland, especially as long as the state paid for them. P. Villani observes that the work of land reclamation, pursued vigorously throughout the second half of the 16th and the early 17th century, practically ceased with the first signs of the crisis of the 17th century. This was due to a fall in agricultural prices, especially of grain, in the first three decades of the 17th century. This fall was in turn due partly to the European depression and partly to the closure of many markets within Venice itself, which was severely hit by deadly epidemics. The new developmental phase did not take place until the 18th century, with a general recovery in agriculture and with population growth.[112]

Italian scholars agree in pointing to the disastrous effects which the reorganization of agriculture had on the rural population of Lombardy and Veneto. The formation of large estates led to communal property being absorbed within them, so depriving the poorer peasants of their right to use them. The expulsion of small farmers from their fields increased the supply of labour, which became available at extremely low cost. In general, this process may offer an analogy with the development of English agriculture in the 16th and 17th centuries, which formed an essential prelude to the future industrial revolution. Yet in point of fact the situation in Italy and Venice was diametrically opposite. Even when deprived of their fields, British peasants found work in the rural and urban industries, which grew steadily, despite crises, and adapted to the needs of both domestic and foreign markets. Thus we know that, in the Levant, English and Dutch textiles—cheaper than the Italian ones due to their lower production costs and inferior quality—eventually replaced Italian textiles, which were of a higher standard but too expensive. In England, industrial expansion, which was partly due also to progress in the mining and metallurgy sectors, absorbed most of the manpower driven from the countryside and stimulated the farm produce market.

---

[112] Villani, *Feudalità*, p. 116.

In contrast, 17th-century Italy was the theatre of a reverse process. Industrial production fell dramatically and gave way to produce from north-western Europe, while agricultural products, in particular raw materials, started to dominate the export trade. Compared with the situation in the Middle Ages, economic interrelations in Europe were now turned upside down to the detriment of the Italian states.[113] Poor peasants from the Venetian Republic and Lombardy were unable to find job openings in the towns. Free only in theory, many of them were forced to take on employment on large land estates, thus being reduced to a state of utter dependence on the landowners and their agents. For all the undeniable progress made by north Italian agriculture during the 16th and 17th centuries, that progress nonetheless became bogged down in the kind of vicious circle typical of the eastern European countries in the same period. The peasants became impoverished, but could not find jobs in a sorely depleted industrial world. Industry in turn could not develop owing to the limited purchasing power of the local population and the availability of foreign products at competitive prices. In this situation one should seek the reasons for the inability of Italian industry, at one stage so buoyant, to convert to mass production and produce cheap goods in the 16th and 17th centuries. The excessive conservatism of the guilds would not appear to have been the only reason for this "missed opportunity." Both peasant impoverishment and foreign competition led to a gradual shrinking of outlets, and this in turn perforce affected the situation of towns linked to local markets. Everything contributed to reducing the possibility of selling cheap goods, while in the small Italian states the governments in charge were not sufficiently concerned with protecting their own industries. Naturally, this picture represents no more than a framework for a working hypothesis; clearly, new research is indispensable in order to explain how it came about that Italy, once in the forefront of the European economy, became transformed into a backward and, in some respects, underdeveloped country.

---

[113] Cf. R. Romano, "La storia economica: Dal secolo XIV al Settecento," in *Storia d'Italia*, vol. II: *Dalla caduta dell'Impero romano al secolo XVIII*, Torino, 1974, pp. 1908ff.; C. M. Cipolla, "Il declino economico dell'Italia," in *idem, Storia dell' economia italiana*, Torino, 1959; Pullan, *Crisis and Change*, pp. 127–145.

4. Provisional Summary and Open Questions

If the relationships between commercial capital and agriculture are to be examined in their complexity, as they have been outlined here, despite the great gaps in sources and the lack of specific studies on essential points, one should begin by observing that they varied enormously from one region to another for somewhat diverse reasons. The situation presents sharply contrasting features, depending on whether the owners of commercial capital in a given region wanted, mainly or exclusively, to buy grain, or whether they tended to invest in land property. But it is not a question of drawing a sharp distinction between these two phenomena, since the regular provision of grain in one region often led directly to the investment of capital in the purchase of land. This was the case in almost all the Italian regions between the 14th and 15th centuries. An analogous situation perhaps obtained in the Crimea under Genoese influence, but there the issue is somewhat less clear. In any case, the phenomenon involving commercial capital was relatively widespread throughout Europe from the end of the Middle Ages to the beginning of the modern age.

In attempting to determine the influence that grain purchasers exerted on the development of productive forces in agriculture and on the system of social relationships linked to them, we come face to face with very complex questions. There is no doubt that owners of commercial capital who regularly bought major quantities of grain were an essential force in the economic system to the extent that they encouraged production growth. However, this did not necessarily entail technological progress, nor did it always improve the living standards of direct producers, those peasants who constituted the vast majority of the population even in the most advanced states of medieval Italy. Production growth could also be obtained by farming lands ill-suited to cultivation (as became apparent during the crisis of the 14th century). A similar effect could be achieved by exploiting peasant labour further, as landowners did in Bulgaria and its surrounding regions between the 13th and 14th centuries, when Italian merchants used to buy local agricultural products. It should be emphasized that in such cases the influence of merchants on the relationships of agricultural production was not a direct one, even though their activity did encourage the great monasteries, the boyars, and the state to deprive peasants of most of their surplus production, in order themselves to export it at a profit. An analogous situation subsequently developed in central and eastern Europe, affecting the economy of those countries for a long time to come. In the Balkans, however, this process of deterioration would appear to have been slowed down by the Turkish conquest and the establishment of Ottoman military feudalism. Nonetheless, in the second half of the 16th and in the 17th century, the process resumed, leading to the increasing impoverishment of the peasant masses and to the decline of the domestic market. This situation was a major hindrance to the development of urban crafts. It should be added that the grain buyers who represented commercial capital were nearly always providers of industrial products also, thus further aggravating the difficult situation of the non-agricultural sectors of the local economy. Study of the situation of the Italian *Mezzogiorno* and Sicily in greater depth would be well worth the effort, for feudalism was there profoundly embedded in the rural areas, and would seem to have remained there until quite recent times.

The question of *mezzadria*, especially in central Italy, and the influence exerted by commercial capital investment on the rural economy of the Venetian State are both issues that have aroused much discussion. There is no doubt that, between the 13th and the middle of the 15th century in central Italy, *mezzadria* played an eminently positive role in the development of grain farming and agriculture in general. In fact, capital input (not necessarily commercial) enabled peasants to extend the areas under cultivation and to diversify their crops in line with regional opportunities and market demands. However, with time this inflow of capital would seem to have diminished, as landowners burdened peasants with almost the entire costs of production, so causing both their impoverishment and a deterioration in the state of agriculture as a whole. While this issue still requires more research, it is fair to state that the demographic situation, the fluctuating labour market, and the commercial climate were all the determining forces in the development of *mezzadria*.

The investment of Venetian and Lombardian capital in agriculture yielded important results as regards raising its profitability, and hence created the necessary preconditions for radical transformation in other areas of the economy. However, the positive effects of these transformations were not immediately apparent in the profoundly unfavourable economic climate that reigned throughout the 17th century. At the same time, it is fair to assume that they did have major consequences to the subsequent development of the Lombardian and Venetian economies.

Ever since the Middle Ages, the princes and great barons of the Italian *Mezzogiorno* knew how to derive maximum advantage from massive grain exports, even if some profits also accrued to well-off peasants. Both the crisis of the 14th century and the Italian wars between the end of the 15th and the beginning of the 16th century inflicted hard blows upon both these social groups, even though agriculture continued to enjoy favourable conditions for quite some time during the economic boom of the mid-16th century. The old gentry and the new aristocracy of foreign merchants and financiers were the first to take advantage of the situation, thus establishing their economic predominance. The crises of the 17th century, together with the imposition of Spanish taxation and the process of refeudalization that took place at the end of the 16th century, produced a situation of poverty and economic backwardness which characterized the whole of social and productive relationships in the Italian *Mezzogiorno*.

CHAPTER TWO

MERCHANT CREDIT AND THE PUTTING-OUT SYSTEM: RURAL PRODUCTION DURING THE MIDDLE AGES*

There is a large literature on credit and the putting-out system in medieval production. By the turn of the nineteenth century, scholars such as Doren, Davidshon, Pirenne, Espinas, Nubling, and others had examined the history of the system of financing medieval industrial production in Florence, Flanders, and part of southern Germany. They concluded that many prosperous merchants made artisans dependent by supplying them with indispensable raw materials on credit or by advancing cash payments for their work. Such dependent artisans were limited to the production of finished or semifinished products at a pre-arranged price. Merchants concentrated larger amounts of commodities in their own hands and saw to their distribution, frequently in distant markets. The economic premises for this system, according to these historians, were as follows:

1. A demand existed, especially for commodities of higher quality, the production of which called for the purchase of expensive raw materials as well as costly transportation in order to sell them, frequently, in very distant markets.
2. Direct producers were, on the whole, too poor to meet these conditions.
3. The concentration of larger material means in the hands of merchant-entrepreneurs made it possible for them to conduct indispensable trade and organizational operations. This was frequently accompanied by a concentration of political power in the hands of these same merchant-entrepreneurs, thanks to which they considerably limited the freedom of economic action of dependent artisans, as, for example, in Florence or in thirteenth-century Flanders.

---

* Originally published in *Review*, IV, 4, Spring 1981, pp. 667–681.

The results of the early research conducted by Doren, Espinas, and Pirenne have already undergone certain modifications. It is now known that the entrepreneurs originated not only from among a section of merchants, but also from among the more prosperous artisans, and that the organizers of the putting-out system in the cloth industry did not have great capital resources. Nevertheless, the essential reasoning seems to have been correct. Research undertaken by Strieder and many central European historians has shown that the putting-out system was widely applied also in medieval mining and especially in the exploitation of silver and nonferrous metals.

The aim of this paper is to ask whether we can also talk about the existence of certain forms of the putting-out system in the rural economy and especially at its intersection with trade. I also wish to consider the problem of the possible preconditions for these social and economic phenomena in medieval Europe.

The putting-out system was a form of credit. One should not, I believe, separate these two phenomena from each other but only define their specific traits. The putting-out system produced very real profits for the investors since it transferred the risk which accompanied production, especially, for example, in mining, totally onto the shoulders of the producers. This also explains the fact that up to the Fugger era capitalists rarely exploited their superiority over the producers by concentrating them in larger groups under the capitalists' supervision and directing their work at the capitalists' own risk. Of course the situation in technology was an important factor hampering the entire process by being unfavorable to the emergence of centralized manufactures, but one cannot nonetheless neglect the purely economic elements.

Let us return to our main subject, the examination of whether the putting-out system existed in the Middle Ages only at the point of intersection between the rural and the market economy or whether it had other uses as well. One should begin with the well-known forms of investment in agriculture. First, it is widely recognized that when the gentry organized settlements and furnished peasants with new plots of land, it was also forced to give them material aid by supplying them with certain sums of money or cattle. Members of the gentry counted on the fact that in the future profitable farmsteads would bring them gains in the form of various payments in kind, monetary dues, and so on. Another form of credit given by the gentry and well-known in certain countries of eastern Europe, for example in Russia or Livonia, resulted from the fact that peasants were threatened by natural disasters and war alongside a very low productivity in agriculture and were forced to take loans from their masters, church institutions, or burghers. Loans made by the gentry led, at times, to a total economic and personal dependence of the peasants on the lords, bordering practically on slavery. Also, urban creditors in Livonia made the peasants dependent by giving them loans. The townspeople of Revel (Tallinn) and Riga took part of the surplus production from the peasants in this way, intending it for their own use or for sale and, at times, they seized a part of the livestock of the debtors together with their tools. One theory, now abandoned, claimed that, in Livonia in the fourteenth and fifteenth centuries, the indebtedness of the peasant population towards its lords contributed to a great extent to the development of a serf-labor economy and the personal subjection of the peasants who were unable to pay back their loans in cash or in kind and were forced to return it as serf-labor. I would not include these phenomena in the category of the putting-out system because the creditors, as a rule, did not intend to seize products intended for further distribution. They were mainly concerned with obtaining the highest profits possible from this source by exploiting the weak position of the peasants. This situation was not always so unfavorable to the peasants since it depended upon many factors.

It would be worthwhile to examine more closely the case of the well-known Italian institution of "mezzadria", which was quite profitable for both parties concerned in the thirteenth to fifteenth centuries and only later became decidedly detrimental to the peasants. Initially, under conditions of a compelling growth of demand for foodstuffs by the large towns of central Italy, their inhabitants were willing to enter into agreements with the peasants, assigning them land for a few years and covering the costs of its cultivation in return for a given portion of the produce (one half, hence "mezzadria", or some other part). Moreover, the peasants sold part of the surplus products on the urban market and even achieved a certain degree of prosperity. On the other hand, towns-people, not only the wealthy merchants but even artisans, guaranteed for themselves a supply of indispensable food products which, in the Middle Ages, with frequent famines and low agricultural productivity, was no trifling matter. Changes occurred as late as the sixteenth and seventeenth centuries when an increase in the size of the rural labor force enabled the burghers (and the nobility) to force upon the peas-ants increasingly severe economic conditions and even a limitation of their personal freedom. However, neither the phenomena mentioned above which took place in eastern Europe nor the "mezzadria" were aimed at concentrating larger amounts of agricultural products in the hands of the creditors in order to sell them in the market which, in my estimation, was a characteristic trait of the putting-out system.

The development of the situation in the Hanseatic region and later Dutch activity in central, eastern, and northern Europe presents itself differently. In German and Norwegian works a controversy, which has not been resolved entirely, was waged for a long time on the subject of the influence of the German merchants on the decline of Norwegian towns and burghers in the Middle Ages. From the thirteenth century on, the Hanseatic merchants had an important outpost in Bergen to which they sent grain and other food articles from Germany and the Baltic countries. A part of those products was given to fishermen and hunters who arrived in the town from northern Norway, in return for future deliveries of dried fish and furs at predetermined prices. Such credits in kind enabled a part of the northern population to survive through the difficult winters, while the Hanseatic merchants guaranteed for themselves regular supplies of Norwegian fish, very much in demand in the European markets. This system worked efficiently from the thirteenth to the sixteenth centuries which shows that for a long time it was a necessity for both sides. It should be stressed at this point that, as a rule, one does not come across complaints that the Hanseatic merchants did not meet their obligations. Obviously that would have been unprofitable for them. Hence, the system presented here resulted in the emergence of permanent and, as a rule, regular economic links between producers from the distant regions of northern Europe and its central parts. Of course, this gave rise to great discontent among the Norwegian townspeople who were totally eliminated from this exchange by the direct contact between the Hanseatic merchants and the suppliers from the distant North. Since this was a very important sphere in the medieval Norwegian economy, one can believe that the activity of the Hanseatic merchants actually did, for a long time, hamper the development of Norwegian trade and towns. The latter were too weak to counteract effectively the more prosperous Hanseatic merchants who for some time were able to intercept grain supplies to Norway, causing famine and an increase of prices. We know that the Hanseatic merchants used this method from the beginning of the thirteenth century. In this system of Hanseatic trade in Norway, I notice elements characteristic of putting-out despite the fact that the producers did not get raw materials necessary for their work from their creditors, although they sometimes got tools.

In the fourteenth, fifteenth, and sixteenth centuries, the giving of credits on account of future supplies of rural products can be detected in central-eastern Europe and, to a certain extent, in southern Italy. This system aimed at the regular provision of distant markets with sought-after agricultural products brought in by the local and, especially, by the foreign merchants.

Let us begin with Italy. It is well known that in the Middle Ages one of the main sources of grain supplies for Tuscany, Venice, and certain other nearby regions was the Kingdom of Naples and Sicily. Research conducted by Yver and later Italian historians shows that it was mainly the Florentines, as well as the Venetians and Pisans, and later also the Genoese, who dominated the export trade from the Kingdom of Naples, obtaining many privileges from the local rulers. The notorious financial difficulties of the kings of Naples were the reason for frequent loans received from the Florentines, in return for grain which came from the crown's vast estates and payments in kind made by their subjects. These trade operations resulted in foreign control of a significant part of the export trade in grain as well as of other agricultural products from the south. This problem also has many other aspects which call for elucidation. For example, even today the nature of the contacts between merchants from northern Italy and the Neapolitan and Sicilian feudal lords who, one might suppose, actively participated in the transport of agricultural products from their estates is not clear. We also have no concrete information about the economic relations of the foreign merchants with the peasant population of the Kingdom of Naples and Sicily. Thus one cannot say whether, and to what extent, these merchants used the system of advance payment for future supplies of products. It seems that as far as the late Middle Ages are concerned, the northern Italian financiers followed a rather different pattern of conduct. Taking advantage of the frequent insolvency of the Neapolitan Crown and the indebtedness of the local barons, great merchants such as the Bardis, Peruzzis, Aldobrandinis, Acciaiuolis, and others purchased large landed estates. In this way the wealthy Florentine citizens became great Neapolitan feudal lords, which furnished them with important prestige gains and at the same time, enabled them to participate in the profitable grain trade. One should also add that both Florentine and Venetian firms maintained permanent factories in the Kingdom, which participated in both domestic and foreign trade in agricultural products. Perhaps using their financial superiority the foreigners made payments in advance to both merchants and local producers in order to insure regular supplies. This is, however, a hypothesis which I am unable to justify on the basis of source materials.

In the fourteenth and fifteenth centuries Neapolitan agriculture experienced a sharp crisis which was partially overcome during the period of a general rise of grain prices in the sixteenth century. During this stage of new prosperity a considerable material differentiation among the peasants of the Kingdom of Naples occurred. A group of prosperous folk emerged, clearly connected with the merchants. These peasants received payments in advance from the merchants for supplies of silk and agricultural products. At the same time, they did not limit themselves to their own crops but also bought from other peasants, thus transforming themselves into small-scale entrepreneurs. The recipients of these commodities and simultaneously the suppliers of capital were primarily merchants from Genoa, very active in the Kingdom of Naples in the fourteenth century. In turn, they exported grain and other agricultural products to Liguria and other parts of Italy. The Venetians also continued to make grain purchases in this region, but we do not know in what form they did this. At any rate, one can suppose that credit transactions could have contributed to the growth of agriculture and the prosperity of a part of the Neapolitan peasantry.

Much better known is the system of purchases of agricultural and woodland products in the late Middle Ages in the Baltic region. Originally the Hanseatic merchants dominated this region. In the fifteenth and, above all, in the sixteenth and seventeenth centuries, they gave way to the Dutch who won enormous economic influence.

At this point one should draw attention to several other circumstances thanks to which the regions of northwestern and central Europe became economically complementary. Already at the end of the fourteenth century in Flanders and England and perhaps even earlier and during the next century in Holland and Portugal, an insufficient supply of timber appropriate for shipbuilding was acutely felt. This was a period of a considerable increase in the fleets of all those countries with the exception of Flanders, where, however, the township of Sluys, the outer harbor of Bruges, began to play a very significant role as a center for the distribution of timber on an international scale. From the fourteenth century on, the new Flemish, Brabant, and, especially, English and Dutch textile industry found extensive markets in the Baltic region which also imported cloth, Breton salt, Dutch herrings, and many other items from the west, even including a certain amount of Levantine goods. This was one consequence of a growing prosperity in the central-eastern European countries which were left unharmed by the economic and social crises of the fourteenth and fifteenth centuries and, on the contrary, were experiencing a stage of rapid expansion of agriculture and the urban economy, although they still remained at a lower economic level than that of western Europe. They did, however, possess resources that were very important at the time for their eventual trading partners. Hence, imports from the west could have been at least partially counterbalanced by exports of timber and its by-products and, in the fifteenth and sixteenth centuries, by the export of grain. Certain nonferrous metals as well as furs and hides of various kinds also entered into the picture. At the turn of the fourteenth and fifteenth centuries oak, pine, beech, etc. became extremely important articles of export from Poland and the Grand Duchy of Lithuania. The Carpathian region exported yews, which eventually became almost entirely extinct. Alongside building timber such byproducts as potash, tar, and pitch, used for caulking ships, also became saleable products. Gdańsk assumed the role of the main center for exporting these articles. Here, in early spring and autumn when the level of the Vistula River and its tributaries rose, innumerable rafts arrived from the Polish and Lithuanian hinterland carrying timber and other items. After their unloading the rafts were also dismantled and sold as timber. This was the situation in Gdańsk and initially, although on a smaller scale, in Riga and Königsberg, with the latter two towns receiving goods, above all, from the Lithuanian-Byelorussian hinterland.

The Hanseatic Baltic merchants tried to retain their role as intermediaries in trade between the west and countries of their own hinterland, and basically they succeeded. In relation to newcomers from the west, above all the English and Dutch, they used compulsion of various kinds to make it difficult to penetrate into Poland and Lithuania. As far as Poland was concerned, the problem was more complicated. The prosperous merchants from Cracow and certain neighboring towns and, in the fifteenth century, the merchants from Wilno in Lithuania won, for a period of time, the right to direct contact with Western trading partners which, however, they were unable to exploit fully. Journeys by Polish merchants from Gdańsk to the west were also rather rare. The Cracow and Wilno merchants conducted trade transactions in Gdańsk and other Baltic ports by using their own capital. Those from Cracow dealt in a more expensive category of goods, especially Hungarian copper, Western cloth, and so on, which already implied the possession of greater capital. Among them there were wealthy people whose heirs entered the ranks of the Polish gentry or even of the magnates.

The situation in central Poland, and expecially in Mazovia and nearby regions, was different. There were extensive woodlands and arable land but a lack of larger towns and wealthy merchants. The Vistula and its northern and central tributaries such as the Niemen and Dvina constituted an extremely convenient waterway well suited for transporting timber and subsequently also grain to the Baltic ports. This took place, as I have mentioned, primarily in the spring and autumn when heavy rainfall raised the water level in the rivers. In the winter the rivers froze and became unfit for sailing. Difficulties also occurred in the summer when the water level fell excessively.

Thanks to a considerable number of source materials it is possible to obtain information regarding the character of trade as it existed, at the latest, from the end of the fourteenth century. I have examined this problem elsewhere, and at present I should like to draw attention to the particularly characteristic traits of early trade in agricultural and sylvan products.

It seems that the initiative to exploit the forest resources of Poland can be ascribed to the Teutonic Order, which was not only a powerful political and military but also an economic institution. Extant records show that from the last quarter of the fourteenth century the so-called Schäffer of the Order made numerous agreements intended to safeguard a steady supply of timber, potash, tar, and pitch, above all, from eastern Mazovia. Their partners were the lesser Mazovian gentry, inhabitants of the numerous townships on the Bug and Narew rivers, tributaries of the Vistula, and even, so it seems, local peasants. It was the population of these areas at that time still densely wooded. The Order made payments in advance to its partners in winter obligating them to deliver given supplies of timber to Gdańsk at a predetermined price whenever sailing became feasible in spring. After their arrival at Gdańsk the remaining payment was made. In practice, such agreements were extended from one year to the next. Trading partners of the Order frequently included the same people for long periods of time. Payments in advance were made in the Order's own very highly valued money but also sometimes in cheap Western cloth.

What purpose did these payments serve? The suppliers of forest items did not in the least limit themselves to the export of their own products but also brought them in their own region and then sent them from river ports to Gdańsk. All this called for much expenditure for which there was a lack of local cash. At this point it was precisely the Order which joined in by making permanent contracts with the suppliers of timber pitch, potash, and other forest products. Representatives of the Order organized a steady network of supplies of these commodities to Gdańsk. They sold the timber to the English and Dutch merchants who came to the mouth of the Vistula or themselves transported it to these countries, and especially to Sluys in Flanders. They also used the timber for shipbuilding. The merchants from Gdańsk and Toruń followed in the footsteps of the Order. In the course of the fifteenth century the export of Polish timber to Portugal, with the mediation of the Hanseatic merchants, also increased. This had many consequences of an international importance. In the first place, a relatively strong economic tie between the Western markets and the heretofore backward regions of central-eastern Europe was formed. This resulted in growth in the forest economy, an influx of money, and the development of trade and towns. Already in the fifteenth century the significance of Warsaw and nearby towns grew, with the inhabitants organizing the transportation of forest products to Gdańsk either on the basis of credit in Gdańsk or at their own expense. In the fifteenth century Gdańsk became not only an exporter of timber but also the largest Baltic producer of ships sold to the Dutch and Portuguese. It would be worthwhile to recall that John II, King of Portugal, supported energetically in the last quarter of the fifteenth century the transportation of timber from Gdańsk, which was closely connected with Portuguese expansion into West Africa at that time. As far as the Dutch were concerned, originally they were dependent not only on timber supplies from Poland via Gdańsk but also purchased many ships. This changed as late as the turn of the fifteenth and sixteenth centuries when shipbuilding developed on a large scale in Holland itself, although based on raw materials supplied from the Vistula regions and Norway. In the course of the sixteenth century, Norway became the main source of timber for western Europe, because Poland's already much devastated woodlands were insufficient. A rather strong position was, however, retained by neighboring Lithuania and Byelorussia exporting mainly timber by-products to Gdańsk, Königsberg, and Riga, sent subsequently to the west. No concrete information is available about the methods used in the Königsberg trade. The Riga merchants, on the other hand, followed the same system of advance payments to the producers as was customary in Gdańsk.

Hence, even relatively cheap commodities became an element in the emergence of an international market. One should stress that the system of giving credit in advance for future supplies fulfilled an important task. It contributed to a considerable economic stimulation of areas previously practically isolated from the circulation of major commodities and accelerated the liquidation of the remnants of the natural economy which still prevailed there. This system had certain traits similar to those of the industrial putting-out system, but it brought more real profits to both of the directly interested parties.

The method of credit lending to the suppliers of commodities also played a large role in the period of extensive trade in agricultural products from central-eastern Europe and particularly from the Baltic region. In this instance, beginning with the fifteenth century, the Gdańsk merchants tried to attract to their town grain and, especially, rye, wheat, flax, and hemp from the hinterland. Their aim was not only the feeding of the local population but, above all, export, especially to Holland, Flanders, and, in exceptional situations, also to England. In the sixteenth and the first half of the seventeenth centuries, markets for new sales emerged in Portugal and in Italy. This problem has been frequently discussed in historical works because it is connected with the emergence of the so-called second serfdom in eastern Germany and Poland.

The export of grain from Poland began in the fifteenth century. Documents from the Gdańsk archives show that gradually it embraced practically the entire Vistula basin. Gdańsk merchants and their agents bought grain wholesale and their debtors obliged themselves to supply crops to Gdańsk at their own expense and at given prices, regardless of fluctuations caused by better or worse harvest periods.

In the fifteenth and at the beginning of the sixteenth century, the Gdańsk merchants not only bought Polish grain on credit but even delivered larger boats for its transportation. This brought protests from many Pomeranian towns incapable of competing with the prosperous Gdańsk burghers as well as energetic actions on the part of the Pomeranian gentry, directed already in the 1450s against the organization of grain imports by the Gdańsk traders since this supposedly resulted in a fall of prices for agricultural products in Pomerania itself.

Nevertheless, the Gdańsk burghers maintained their position in the Vistula grain trade and also became its chief supplier to the Western markets. With time, in the sixteenth and seventeenth centuries the transportation of grain from Gdańsk by sea to the west was taken over by the Dutch and became a very important element in their trade activity on the route Baltic-Holland-Portugal and even Italy. The Gdańsk merchants, on the other hand, retained their role as intermediaries in supplying harvests from the Vistula basin to their port, which furnished them with large profits. They never forsook the system of making payments in advance for supplies. It is known that, for example, in 1592 when the Venetian agent Ottoboni attempted to buy in Poland larger amounts of grain for Venice which, at the time, suffered famine and high prices, nothing could be obtained because all the grain was allotted for export and had been purchased earlier by the Gdańsk traders with further export in mind. It seems, however, that the dependency of the Polish grain exporters on the Gdańsk merchants was weaker than it was in the timber trade. Exporters of grain in time included the middle and prosperous gentry as well as magnates. These groups, in contrast to the more modest timber suppliers, had at their disposal a sufficient amount of cash and the unpaid labor of their serfs, and thus were not so dependent on advance payments. This development, which calls for further research, is best known from the example of Livonia in the fifteenth and sixteenth centuries. There the local merchants tried in various ways to guarantee a supply of grain, flax, and hemp from the agricultural hinterland. They sold salt and other indispensable commodities to the peasants for prices as high as possible thus bringing about their indebtedness and compelling them to return debts in the form of agricultural products, calculating the prices of the latter at a very low level. They used a different method in dealings with the more prosperous peasants. They entered into agreements with them which consisted of long-term loans in return for which their partners supplied them not only with a part of their own crops, but also those bought from other producers. Because in this case as well the merchants were concerned with agricultural products not so much intended for consumption in the country as for export to distant Western markets, merchant credit was here a factor in the creation of extensive trade connections on a European scale. This is even more important in the case of the Gdańsk burghers where certain proof exists that in their grain trade they operated with credit not only on the basis of their own capital, but also that in the sixteenth century they used sums borrowed from the Dutch in return for supplies of an appropriate amount of grain to Amsterdam. During certain periods in the sixteenth century even the wealthy grain merchants from Antwerp became involved in this procedure, giving loans to the Dutch who were, in turn, the creditors of the Gdańsk traders. The latter, by basing themselves on their own capital and sums borrowed as described above, already reached the rural producers directly, i.e., the Polish gentry. This is an interesting example of the influence of merchant capital on the rural economy and the linking of the latter in this way not only with Gdańsk, but also with extensive foreign markets. The profits which the gentry and merchants gained from this source, in turn, made possible the purchase of Western commodities. We are faced with an interesting premise for the formation of an all-European market and, in a certain sense, also of a world market since timber and grain from central-eastern Europe facilitated to a considerable degree the Portuguese and Dutch expansion which, in the sixteenth and seventeenth centuries, was of a markedly commerical nature.

It is precisely this element of linking rural production in the less-developed countries with the markets of the dynamic regions and the creation of a *sui generis* international division of labor which I consider to be the most important result of the influence of merchant capital on the rural economy. I should like to make clear that this was influenced also by many other factors and especially by social structures as well as the level of economic development of the regions involved.

It could be said that the initiative for these commercial influences on the rural economy was supplied obviously, as a rule, by the milieu and the countries that were economically stronger, who thus influenced not only the economic situation of their weaker rural partners but also their socio-economic structures. Hence, the enormous grain exports from the Baltic countries had a considerable impact on the shaping of the serf-labor economy in the whole of central-eastern Europe and this, with time, resulted in a long-lasting period of stagnation and even economic and social regression. Foreign capital was not always the decisive factor here. Indigenous merchant capital was also highly important. It accumulated within the same economic sphere and was active in its own more backward hinterland, although it was prepared to satisfy the needs of distant markets and drew profits from this procedure.

I see in these phenomena a *sui generis* analogy to the putting-out system in artisan production and mining. In all these cases merchant capital created stimuli for the intensification of the production which, to a certain extent, was conducive to the emergence of a great international market. In certain circumstances this process favored the increase of the producers' prosperity and in others, especially in the long run, caused their pauperization.

CHAPTER THREE

SOME REMARKS ON THE ROLE OF MERCHANT CAPITAL IN EASTERN EUROPE IN THE LATE MIDDLE AGES*

In this essay I wish to return to certain controversial questions which, although by no means new to historical science, are still a cause of many disputes and much confusion.

The first question concerns the function of merchant capital in the late medieval economy. In this respect, the problems of East-Central and Eastern Europe have long been the object of particular interest and discussion.

The second question, linked closely with the first, I would formulate in the following way: can research into merchant capital circulation in Eastern Europe make it easier for us to grasp the undeniable fact of the development of many East European countries in the 14th and 15th centuries, i.e. at a time when a large part of Western Europe was experiencing an acute socio-economic crisis? Perhaps an attempt to answer these two questions will throw some light on the origins of the division of Europe into separate economic regions in the 15th and 16th centuries.

The functions of merchant capital in the feudal economy were and are a subject of much debate. Many scholars still consider merchant capital to have been the main development factor in stimulating the economy, a sort of *deus ex machina* with an outside influence on the feudal economy, causing its transformation. To this common denominator belong the old theories of Pirenne, Klincevskii and Rörig, held dear by many historians and economists such as Sweezy and others.

There is another view, too, which rightly emphasizes the leading role of the rural economy in the life of medieval Europe, but which nonetheless reduces the effect of merchant capital to almost nil. This view, sometimes pushed to extremes, caused serious omissions in research

* Originally published as "Uwagi o roli kapitału kupieckiego w Europie wschodniej w późnym średniowieczu" in *Przegląd Historyczny*, Vol. 56, 1965, pp. 220–231. Translation from Polish by Maria Chmielewska-Szlajfer, revised by Robin Kimball.

into major areas of the economy of Eastern Europe's feudal countries, especially into the problems of commodity circulation, primary accumulation, etc.

At present, practically all scholars are agreed that the feudal economy was based on the rural economy, first and foremost on agriculture. This is an undeniable fact as regards not just medieval Europe, but also those countries which even today practise a feudal type of economy or are only now trying to abandon it. Medieval Europe was, above all, a vast agricultural region where rural economy predominated. The advancement of handicraft and industrial production, as also of trade was, as a rule, much greater in the West than in the East. Between the 13th and 15th centuries, the majority of East European countries were passing through a stage of rapid social development, making up largely for their lagging behind the West. The 14th and 15th centuries in Western Europe were marked by economic recession. Although it brought about important and inspiring economic and social transformations, it temporarily stopped the growth dynamics of many lines of production and exchange.

After all, in East-Central and Eastern Europe one can observe serious differences in the chronology and rate of development of particular countries and regions. Taking the 13th century as the point of departure for my considerations, I would roughly distinguish three geographical regions. Bohemia, Silesia, the Carpathian countries, Little Poland, and, in a broader context and somewhat later, also western and southeastern Russia (despite the Tatar invasions) were the areas of fastest growth. The Baltic countries as far as Novgorod made up the second region. The third region, spreading from central Poland far to the east and north-east, in the 13th and 14th centuries showed relatively lower growth dynamics. At this point, one should exclude those Russian territories whose development was checked by the Mongol invasion and long-lasting oppression.

Bohemia and the Polish territories and also, to a smaller degree, the Slovak territories had long been the main areas where agriculture and animal breeding had been developing. Moreover, in the light of archaeological research of the past few years, it is impossible to call in doubt the existence of Slavonic towns in the so-called pre-colonization period. Nevertheless, it was precisely in the 13th century that substantial qualitative changes occurred and the three above-mentioned regions of economic growth began to appear. It must be emphasized here that, for many reasons, the source of these changes cannot be confined to the pressure of German peasant and urban population. Only in certain Baltic countries and in the eastern Margravate did this population force its way into the new areas of expansion. In all other cases, the initiative and plan for colonization were provided by the local feudal lords. The initiative was a result of local needs, although with time it led to developments menacing Bohemia, Poland, and the Baltic peoples. It is worth remembering here that in Poland and Bohemia, so-called German law went far beyond the areas of dense German colonization, and played a cardinal role in the history of the Polish and Czech population between the 13th and 16th centuries. I cannot here go deeply into the history of the Polish and Czech countryside, but it must be emphasized that both the settlements requiring money rent as well as the fast spread of German law over the territories of the old rural settlements indicate that in the 13th and 14th centuries rural economy in Bohemia and Poland reached a relatively high level. This enabled a gradual introduction of money rent, thanks both to the productivity of local agriculture and to the existence of towns, the natural market for agricultural produce. Next, the application of German law and the improvement of agricultural techniques speeded up the process of economic development in general.

Returning to the three above-mentioned regions of socio-economic development, I would underline the obvious imbalance among them with regard to the development of towns, urban trade, and long-distance foreign trade in particular. There is no doubt that, in the 13th and 14th centuries, the southern and Baltic regions were far ahead of the immense central region, and that in point of fact it was only as late as the 15th century that the situation in Poland, Lithuania, and Russia began to change radically. In the light of the studies carried out so far, it is clear that, at both stages of the economy of Eastern Europe (Bohemia included), merchant capital played an important role, without necessarily exerting a good influence on development as a whole. How then to explain merchant capital's great interest in the Czech, Carpathian, and Baltic areas in the 13th and 14th centuries, and its subsequent growth, aided by the inflow of foreign capital in the 15th century? The mere fact that a large number of German, Italian, and other merchants arrived in the southern area in the 13th and 14th centuries does not clarify anything; it can only provide a point of departure for further considerations. We would do better trying to find out the reasons inducing them into visiting and often settling in those territories. They certainly hoped for some profit and, as a rule, their hopes came true. The question is

important, as the 13th and 14th centuries were marked by an influx of
merchants in Bohemia, Poland, and south-western Russia (with regard
to the latter, merchants arrived not from the West alone).

The problem was most glaring in Bohemia where, in the 12th and
especially the 13th century, local silver and gold mining, i.e. the mining
of metals particularly precious at a time of increased use of bullion in
the European economy, became especially dynamic. Silver, or rather the
silver coin, formed, according to Czech scholars, the basis of Bohemia's
late-medieval foreign trade.[1] Similar occurrences took place in the
Slovak and Transylvanian territories of Hungary, in Silesia, and in Little
Poland. In all these countries, deposits of copper (Silesia and Hungary)
and of lead and salt (Little Poland) were a major enticement to affluent
people, merchants among them. I think that, despite the many studies
on mining, not enough attention has yet been given to its effect as a
development incentive to other areas of the medieval economy, such as
trade, agriculture, animal husbandry, etc. After all, it was precisely the
metal resources of Bohemia, Hungary, Silesia, and Little Poland that
left their very strong mark on foreign trade[2] and affected other industries in those countries. This is why I propose treating these territories
as a relatively uniform economic zone, characterized, from the 13th
century, by both an inflow of foreign capital as well as the formation
of a local merchant class. It would be a mistake however to consider
mining as the only factor to have brought about economic growth. Of
utmost importance to the growth of merchant capital, and singularly
to the influx of foreign merchants, was the formation of the class of
rich feudal secular and ecclesiastical lords who were both consumers
and suppliers of many goods. This is the usual explanation given for
the immigration of many well-to-do foreigners to Prague, Cracow,

---

[1] F. Graus, "Die Handelsbeziehungen Böhmens zu Deutschland und Österreich
im 14. und zu Beginn des 15. Jahrhunderts," in *Historica*, No. 2, 1960, pp. 107–108.
Graus expressed similar views in *Cesky obchod se suknem ve 14. a pocatkem 15. stoleti*
(Praha, 1950). In my essay, I also rely on the studies of J. Koran concerning the history of Czech mining.

[2] Suffice to remember here the importance of the exports of silver and copper
from Hungarian Slovakia, and of gold from Transylvania. On the probable exports
of gold and silver from Silesia to Flanders in the 13th century, see M. Małowist, "Le
développement des rapports économiques entre la Flandre, la Pologne et les pays
limitrophes du XIIIe au XIVe siècle," in *Revue belge de philologie et d'histoire*, Vol. 10,
1931, pp. 1020–21. Problems of trade in Little Poland's lead were recently tackled in
D. Molenda, *Górnictwo kruszcowe na terenie złóż śląsko-krakowskich do połowy XVI
wieku* (Wrocław, 1963), p. 203.

Wrocław, and many other centres where various feudal courts were established. Still, not even in Bohemia can the increased wealth of the feudal lords be explained by the rise in their profits on mines alone. It was the rural economy that was these countries' main source of wealth. Precisely at the time when agriculture in Western Europe was facing a setback or even retrogressing, in the East it was developing dynamically. The development of agriculture and animal husbandry, accompanied by the concurrent development of silver, copper, and lead mining, was favourable to the growth of marketable products and especially to the monetization of the economy, offering, so to speak, increasingly more scope to the merchants and their operations.

I mean here both the petty urban traders and the so-called great merchants oriented towards satisfying the needs of the affluent parts of feudal society; the latter often invested large sums of money in mines. In the economic sphere we are discussing, all kinds of merchant activity were apparent, their intensity growing with time. Over the whole territory, the rising number of merchants, the size of property, and flourishing trade were reflected in the growing number of fairs and markets in Bohemia, Poland, and, in the 14th-century, south-western Russia. All this encouraged the formation and growth of local merchant capital and attracted foreign merchants: central and southern Germans in Bohemia, Poland, the Carpathian countries, and Russia, and Italians, particularly numerous in Little Poland and Russia starting from the 13th century, and in the 13th and 14th centuries penetrating even into the cities of the Golden Horde. At the same time numerous Armenians and Jews from East and West, and even Greeks, arrived in south-western and south-eastern Russia. These migrations of merchants were habitually attributed almost exclusively to the emergence in the 13th-century of new long-distance trade routes connecting the West, via Polish and Russian territories, with the East. There is much truth in this view but not, I believe, the whole of it.

There is no doubt that routes to Italian colonies on the Black and Azov Seas from the West and from Italy, crossing Poland and south-western Russia, and those connecting the Baltic, Black, and Azov Seas, contributed to intensified activity on the part of the merchants from Cracow, Wrocław, Volhynian Włodzimierz, and then from Lwów and from some minor centres of Silesia, Little Poland, and Russia. These routes attracted the attention of German and Italian merchants. From the 13th through to the 15th century, many of these foreigners did not confine themselves to sporadic trips through Poland and Russia, but

settled down in cities for a longer period of time or even for good. We
do not know enough about their activities, but arrivals from Germany
played a major role in Poland as the organizers of urban and rural
settlements which paid rent money. Many of them invested in salt and
lead mines. The purchase of real estate in town and even village became
a familiar occurrence. It was particularly common in 14th- and 15th-
century Little Poland, where these events are better known thanks to
earlier research by Ptaśnik. This scholar examined the immigration of
Italian and High German merchants to southern Poland and Russia. He
showed that many of these immigrants invested large sums of money in
salt and lead mining in Little Poland and Russia, acquired real estates
in towns and villages, and, with time, a number of these immigrant
families rose to the ranks of nobility. Next to them, an increasingly big
role was played by arrivals from Nuremberg, who formed the advance
guard of quite a strong wave of merchants emigrating from southern
Germany to East-Central Europe.[3] The problem has not been sufficiently
examined yet, but even the available data concerning transactions
entered into by Italians and natives of Nuremberg, merchants from the
banks of the Lake of Constance, etc., permit us to state certain facts.
These merchants did not treat Silesia, Poland, and Russia as merely a
transit area, as they supplied many goods for local consumption there.
It is worth emphasizing here that they imported not only German and
Netherlands merchandise but also eastern products they had acquired
in Venice, not in Tana or Kaffa. They showed keen interest in Polish,
Russian, and Lithuanian produce such as wax, kermes, wool, hides, furs,
and later also cattle.[4] They must also have been interested in woollen
cloth from Silesia and textiles from southern Great Poland, which could
be found in many places of southern, central, and eastern Europe.

Thus a massive inflow of foreign capital to these southern regions
took place in the 13th and 14th centuries, permitting trade to flourish, the more so since the trade routes ran in the proper direction.
To this latter factor I personally attach rather less significance than is
usually done. It should be stressed here that the marked formation in

---

[3] J. Ptaśnik, *Kultura włoska wieków średnich w Polsce* (Warszawa, 1959), p. 47ff.

[4] M. Scholz-Babisch, "Oberdeutscher Handel mit dem deutschen und polnischen
Osten nach Geschäftsbriefen von 1444," in *Zeitschrift des Vereins für Geschichte
Schlesiens*, Vol. 68, 1930, pp. 61–62, 66–67; J. Ptaśnik, *Italia Mercatoria apud Polonos
saeculo XV ineunte* (Romae, 1910), *passim*.

the 13th century of strong states in the southern region, i.e. the strong Kingdom of Bohemia, the Polish state, and, in a way, the Principality of Galicia, was not only related to the economic development of the southern region, but also fostered this development. These two factors also found reflection in the rapid cultural development of that part of the southern region discussed here, especially of the Czech and, slightly later, of the Polish territories.

It is worth turning our attention to the situation that emerged in the steppes of south-eastern Rus at the time when the Golden Horde was still thriving. This area saw the growth of great trade centres such as Saray, Astrakhan, and Kazan, and the concentration of Italian, Armenian, Greek, and Jewish merchants in Tana, Soldai, and later in Kaffa and other towns along the Black Sea coast.

No doubt major trade routes linking this area with the Middle and Far East played an important role in their growth. Nevertheless, it would be a grave error to underrate the role of local goods—including hides, wax, grain, salt, fish, and furs imported from the banks of the middle Volga, and also of slaves, originally primarily of Tatar or Caucasian extraction—in furthering the domestic and foreign trade of this area. It would seem that in the 15th century it was precisely the slave trade that attracted Italian merchant capital to Tana and Kaffa.[5] The destruction of the Golden Horde by Tamerlane, the decline of the steppe nomadic economy, and a very probable demographic decline in these territories in the 15th century made any revival of the trade centres on the lower Volga and the Don, and especially of Saray and Tana, impossible. It would seem that Kazan, a centre for trade with Rus, the Middle East, and western Siberia, profited from all this. As regards the Genoese colonies in the Crimea and on the borders of the Caucasus, the importance of the slave trade, carried on largely by Italian merchants, increased in the 15th century. On the other hand, the significance of sales of eastern products diminished, as this kind of trade had long been concentrated primarily in Alexandria and Syria. As regards contacts between the Italian colonies and the emerging towns

---

[5] B. Grekov, A. Jakoubovski, *La Horde d'Or* (Paris, 1939), pp. 135–62; M. Małowist, *Kaffa—kolonia genueńska na Krymie i problem wschodni w latach 1453–1475* (Warszawa, 1947), pp. 68–94; Ch. Verlinden, "La colonie vénitienne de Tana, centre de la traite des esclaves au XIVe et au debut du XVe siècle," in *Studi in onore di Gino Luzzatto*, Vol. II (Milano, 1950), pp. 1–25.

of north-eastern Rus, they would appear to have greatly influenced the economy of the upper Volga basin, but not to have seemed very attractive to the Genoese and Venetians. From time to time the latter returned to plans to develop trade with Tana, but these projects never reached fruition. Meanwhile, precisely in the 15th century, and long before it lost its colonies, Genoa began concentrating on the West. The trade of Kaffa and other towns of that region passed to the residing Armenians, Jews, Greeks, and, after 1475, to Turkish merchants as well. None of them however was able to invest as much capital as the Italians. At the same time, starting from the 14th century, some of them showed definite interest in the economy of awakening north-eastern Russia. We will deal with this issue somewhat later.

The latest statements by Johansen and von Brandt[6] as well as other studies indicate that, as regards the northern region, we often overrate the significance of the profitable transit trade for the growth of towns, particularly in the 13th and 14th centuries. While I have the impression that Johannsen exaggerates when he argues that medieval Rus could, in point of fact, have made do without western products, and the West without Rus furs and wax,[7] it is still hard to imagine how Hanseatic towns could have survived without adequate food and general agricultural support in the early stages of their development. Unfortunately, we still do not know much about economic ties between Hanseatic towns and the countryside, i.e. peasants and feudal groups, in the 13th and 14th centuries. While by no means denying the stimulating effect of merchant capital on the whole of the Baltic economy, I am opposed to overrating its influence, a tendency which started with Rörig.[8] Obviously

---

[6] P. Johansen, "Der hansische Russlandhandel, insbesondere nach Novgorod, in kritischer Betrachtung," in *Arbeitsgemeinschaft für Forschung des Landes Nordrhein-Westfalen. Wissenschaftliche Abhandlung*, Vol. XXVII, n.d., pp. 39–55; A. von Brandt, "Die Hanse," in *ibid., passim*.

[7] P. Johansen, *Der hansische Russlandhandel*, pp. 39–44. In my view, the author underestimates the significance of the imports of silver to medieval Rus. Until the 15th century, Hanseatic merchants had been the only silver suppliers; later they were joined by competitors from south Germany and the Netherlands. It seems to me that the relative inadequacy of bullion imports to the economic needs of 14th- and 15th-century Rus delayed the transition to money rent in the rural economy and the improvement of the monetary system there. After all, until the 16th century, all the silver at Rus' disposal had been coming from the West. Imports of salt and, more often than not, of grain were indispensable to north-western Rus between the 13th and 15th centuries.

[8] F. Rörig, *Hansische Beiträge zur Deutschen Wirtschaftsgeschichte* (Breslau, 1928) (eds. note).

the merchants, arriving in the East in great numbers, settled where they saw fit, and this depended on the prevailing standard of production in definite geographical areas. Even before the advent of Hanseatic merchants, Pomerania was an area of developed agriculture and, at a certain point, of important towns. The same can be said of Swedish mining, fishery in Skane, or the stock of furs and wax in Novgorod. All of them existed before Hanseatic merchants appeared there. It is evident that the flood of German merchants and rural population in Mecklenburg and Pomerania, like the flood of merchants and miners from Sweden, speeded up the economic development of those lands. Unfortunately, the poor condition of available sources hampers the study of the situation the settlers found on the spot. Nowhere did they find an economic desert, as suggested by earlier historiography concerning German settlements along the Baltic coast. It seems to me that the majority of Baltic-coast countries showed a lesser growth dynamics, particularly in the 13th century, than the above-mentioned southern region, but they were also much poorer in natural resources. Along the Baltic coast, communication routes, above all the Baltic itself and the inland roads, played an important role by enabling merchants to circulate a large number of wares even from a very deep hinterland, from southern Hungary, south-western and north-western Rus, etc. At work here was yet another important factor of a political nature, by which I mean the powerful orders of knighthood.

As is well known, they engaged in trade directly. In addition, thanks to their political and military power, they succeeded in obtaining, both for themselves and their subjects—merchants from Prussia and Livonia—many invaluable privileges in the entire Baltic hinterland. At this point one should mention the political and economic pressure of the Teutonic Order on Poland and Lithuania, particularly relentless in the 13th and 14th centuries, and of the Order's Livonian branch on north-western Rus, where they aroused the resistance of towns, at that time much more developed than, for example, in central Poland; also the Teutonic attempt to conquer Gotland, etc. One must not minimize the influence of the political power of the military orders on the attitude of Danes and Swedes to Hanseatic merchants. After all, in the 14th and even the 15th century, the Teutonic Order was usually seen as the Hanse's virtual protector. Given the state of economic, political, and geographical relations in the Baltic region, the situation in the 13th and 14th centuries was favourable to investment and to the growth of merchant capital. This is how we explain the powerful intervention of German merchants.

Of course, the situation in particular regions must have varied. It is worth noting here the relatively low rate of profit that Hanseatic merchants obtained in specific transactions with Novgorod, as emphasized by Lesnikov and Khoroskevic. The same however could not be said, according to Samsonowicz, of Danzig's trade with its agricultural and forest base.[9] One can put forward a hypothesis that, in the first case mentioned, Russian traders were strong enough, both economically and politically, to protect themselves against Hanseatic exploitation. The Hanseatic merchants, for their part, were nevertheless trying to pursue and develop trade in furs and wax, if only for the mass-production character of Russian exports. We already know that the furs exported by north-western Rus in the Middle Ages were mass-production rather than luxury goods. In their contacts with agricultural and forest producers in Prussia or Livonia, Hanseatic merchants were economically the overwhelmingly stronger partner; what is more, from the 13th through the 15th century, in the majority of countries they enjoyed clear political supremacy. In the 13th and 14th centuries, both their political and economic superiority and their favourable geographical position allowed the Teutonic Order and Prussian merchants access to the metal resources of the Carpathian region, and to trade with the Black Sea coast. It is worth remembering here the remarks by Lesnikov and Khoroskevic concerning the big role of the silver which the Order conveyed to Novgorod at the turn of the 14th century. The Teutonic Knights obtained that silver presumably from trade with Hungary and Little Poland.[10]

Summing up this part of my argumentation, I would say that, in the Baltic region in the 13th and 14th centuries, the situation was especially fortunate for representatives of merchant capital, and this not only because of the production level achieved by the local population. Of

---

[9] See M. P. Lesnikov, "Niderlandy i vostochnaya Baltika v nachale XV v.," in *Izvestiya Akademii Nauk SSSR. Seriya istorii i filologii*, Vol. VIII, 1951, p. 451; *idem*, "Die livländische Kaufmannschaft und ihre Handelsbeziehungen zu Flandern am Anfang des 15. Jhrh.," in *Zeitschrift für Geschichtswissenschaft*, Vol. 6, No. 2, 1958, p. 300, and other works by this scholar. A. L. Khoroskevic, in his excellent *Torgovlya Velikogo Novgoroda s Pribaltiyskoy i Zapadnoy Evropoy v XIV–XV vekakh* (Moskva, 1963), usually agrees, albeit more cautiously, with Lesnikov's hypothesis. However, H. Samsonowicz, *Badania nad kapitałem mieszczańskim Gdańska w drugiej połowie XV w.* (Warszawa, 1960), presents an opposite view on the situation in Gdańsk's trade.

[10] M. P. Lesnikov, "Torgovye snosheniya Velikogo Novgoroda s Tevtonskim Ordenom w kontse XIV i nachale XV v.," in *Istoricheskie Zapiski*, Vol. 39, p. 264; A. L. Khoroskevic, *Torgovlya*, p. 283.

great importance here were the political power of the military orders, the economic and political frailty of the majority of partners, and last but not least a favourable geographical situation. I would ascribe the strong influx of merchant capital from Germany to the Baltic countries to all these factors. The question of the rate of profit that Hanseatic merchants gained on their transactions requires much further research. Were the hypotheses of Lesnikov and Khoroskevic concerning the low rate of profit earned by Hanseatic merchants to prove fully justified, that would not only throw plenty of light on the accumulation of merchant capital but would perhaps make it easier to understand the undeniable fact of the backwardness of the organization of Hanseatic trade when compared with the Italian system. I mean here the relatively primitive forms of organization of merchant credit, the absence of a developed banking system, insurance, etc.

Formerly, the peak of the Hanse's development was often associated with the signing of the treaty of Stralsund. This was Rörig's view, though this outstanding scholar, more than his predecessor, examined not only the political but also the economic and systemic history of Hanseatic towns. Historians also pointed, correctly, to the increased activity of the English and Dutch, from the 14th century, as competitors of Hanseatic merchants. It seems to me, however, that they overlooked one other factor. I mean here the expansion of the towns of the deep interior, such as Nuremberg, Wrocław, Cracow, and many other centres of trade, towards the Baltic region.

Maybe, from this point of view, we should also examine the efforts of the emperor Charles IV to develop the trade of Prague. Meanwhile, Novgorod resumed its struggle for its right to lucrative trade in Livonia and for access to Baltic navigation. All these tendencies were clearly connected with the economic growth of the above-mentioned southern region, i.e. of mining, crafts, and trade in developing southern Germany, Bohemia, Little Poland, and the neighbouring countries, and in reviving Rus. These matters are too well known to need repeating here. When all is said and done, at the turn of the 14th century Bohemia suffered a protracted recession, which applied to foreign trade in particular.[11]

---

[11] F. Graus, "Die Handelsbeziehungen", and J. Janáček, "Der böhmische Aussenhandel in der Hälfte des 15. Jhrh.," in *Historica*, Vol. 4, pp. 39–51, emphasize that at the time of the Hussite revolution, trade relations with southern Germany, so important to Bohemia, were not broken off. Yet, from Janáček's argument, it irrefutably results that

With time, the Bohemian recession had its repercussions in Vratislav (Wrocław) and in many other towns of what was then Bohemian Silesia, which made them even more dependent on economic relations with Poland than before. The situation of Cracow and other towns of Little Poland in the 15th century was rather auspicious. The prices of goods offered in Cracow were showing an upward trend, whence from time to time we encounter the opinion that 15th-century Little Poland must have been beset with economic difficulties. This was, however, an erroneous view. While the slump in copper and silver mining in Slovakia and Nuremberg competition were unfavourable factors for the merchants of Cracow, trade with southern Hungary still continued. Otherwise, there were no symptoms of stagnation in Little Poland. Rural settlement and growth of towns continued, while salt and lead mining were developing. Foreigners from Italy and southern Germany kept flooding into Cracow and Lwów, and settled down and invested their capital there, which they would hardly have done, had there been a business slump there. Until mid-15th century, Cracow had been in the van of those Polish towns struggling for free access to the Baltic trade. Thanks to the favourable turn in Poland and Lithuania's fortunes *vis-à-vis* the Teutonic Knights, the situation was advantageous to the Polish towns. In the 15th century, I perceive some symptoms of a crisis in the feudal system, expressed in complaints of manpower shortage and high wages demanded by labourers, declining revenues from rental dues, etc. These factors never assumed the same proportions as in the West, and would seem to have been of only a transitory nature.

During the 15th century, in Poland, Lithuania, and Rus, the central area, previously underdeveloped, became economically the most dynamic. Great Poland and Mazovia from the 14th century, Lithuania and the Grand Principality of Muscovy from the 15th, were the territories where rural and urban settlements developed rapidly. The products of these countries, such as wood, grain, hides, wax, and others, soon assumed a relatively great importance in foreign trade. In all this region, one can observe a revival in domestic and foreign trade.

The local merchant class was developing. Foreign merchant capital surfaced, searching for new areas for profitable investment. We well

---

those relations were reduced to a minimum, and that this situation lasted well into the 15th century. Perhaps the long-drawn out difficulties of Bohemian mining, including a considerable fall in coal exports, contributed to those severed relations.

know the great significance of Nuremberg capital for the early development of Leipzig, strongly connected since the 15th century with eastern
Europe. The same could be said of Warsaw, Wilno, and Lublin. As
regards Mazovia, Kujavia, and other neighbouring Polish territories,
the insufficient accumulation of their own merchant capital offered
great possibilities to merchants from Prussia, from Danzig in particular.
Following the example of the Teutonic Order, the Prussians restored
the already widespread system of granting loans in advance of future
deliveries. Whether or not that system always led to the exploitation
of the supplier (which personally I doubt), it certainly speeded up the
process of forming the local merchant class in towns and villages in
Mazovia, Kujavia, etc., and linked up their production with the market.
I think that the phenomenon discussed here—so common in every place
where foreign merchants met partners economically much weaker than
themselves—could, in the situation of Poland and Lithuania at the time,
be regarded as an important form of inflow of merchant capital which
could only accelerate extensive economic development.

Leaving aside the underresearched problem of Lithuania, I would
like to make some remarks concerning the Russian question. While
everybody seems to know that, in the 15th century, trade in Novgorod,
Pskov, Polotsk, and Smolensk flourished, the matter has not so far
been satisfactorily explained. We do not know enough about the local
merchant class and its capital reserves, though the existence of rich
merchants in 14th- and 15th-century Novgorod is beyond all doubt if
we consider, for instance, the volume of transactions we can identify.
Thanks to studies by Danilova, Gorskii, Khoroskevic, and other scholars,
it is already evident that the increased activity of north-western Rus was
closely connected with the economic development of Lord Novgorod
the Great and its substantial hinterland.[12] Soviet scholars have proved
moreover that north-eastern Rus, and especially the area along the
upper Volga, experienced rapid population growth and the development of agriculture and towns. In the second half of the century, the
city of Moscow came decisively to the fore.[13] Trade, both domestic and
foreign, in this part of Rus flourished rapidly, the active engagement

---

[12] L. V. Danilova, *Ocherki po istorii zemlevladeniya i khozyaistva Novgoroda i
Novgorodskoy zemli v XIV i XV vv.* (Moskva, 1955); A. D. Gorskiy, *Ocherki ekonomi-
cheskogo polozheniya krestyan Severo-Vostochnoy Rusi XIV–XV vv.* (Moskva, 1960);
A. L. Khoroskevic, *Torgovlya.*

[13] M. N. Tikhomirov, *Srednevekovaya Moskva v XIV–XV vv.* (Moskva, 1957), *passim.*

of grand monastic orders—explained by the weakness of the urban merchant class—being its peculiarity. However, in the 15th and 16th centuries, the urban merchant class gained in importance, especially in Moscow, Tver, Nizhny Novgorod, and the emerging towns of the north. In the 15th century, and in point of fact even later, the external trade of north-eastern Rus was primarily south-east-oriented, although trade expansion towards the north, and from mid-15th century towards the Baltic, gradually gained in importance. Bright trade prospects also attracted foreign merchants to this part of Rus, some of whom settled or spent long periods investing their capital there. Thanks to research by Syroečkovskii, Tikhomirov, Sakharov, and other scholars, we know that the group of the most important merchants of Moscow and other cities, the so-called Surozhane merchants, included Greeks from Byzantium and also Italians.[14] The latter, presumably with their roots in Genoa, reached Rus from the Italian settlements on the Black and Azov Seas. Tikhomirov concentrated his attention on the Italian Andrei Friazin, whose rights to the property on the Pechora River were recognized at the turn of the 14th century by Grand Prince Dmitrii Donskoi. The same rights had previously been granted to his uncle Matvei.[15] This information probably concerns the Genoese from Kaffa or Tana, who wanted to participate in the export of furs to the south. After all, in medieval Europe Genoese enterprise was well known. There is more material regarding rich Greek and Italian merchants in south-western Rus. They penetrated into the Muscovite state and often settled there. However, I cannot enter into all these details here. As regards the Hanseatic merchants of the time, they established contacts with Moscow, but did not settle there. By contrast, the merchants of Tatar and Armenian nationality did. Taken all together, it would seem that the influx of affluent foreigners ready to settle in Rus was smaller than in Bohemia or Poland.

Admittedly, not only religious and political but also climatic differences played a part here. Such a situation gave more scope to increasingly active Russian merchants. Suffice to point to their successes in westward expansion, through Lithuania and Poland to Germany,

---

[14] I did not manage to obtain the work by V. E. Syroečkovskii, *Gosti-surozhane* (Moskva, 1935). I refer to it on the basis of the footnotes in the above-quoted work by Tikhomirov and in the dissertation by A. M. Sakharov, *Goroda Severo-Vostochnoy Rusi XIV i XV vv.* (Moskva, 1959).

[15] M. N. Tikhomirov, *op. cit.*, p. 130.

and—according to some sources—as far as Italy. On the other hand, the relatively small inflow of foreign merchant capital impeded the advancement of the Russian merchant class as a clearly defined social group. Russian merchants moreover had to withstand domestic competition from the powerful and commercially active clergy and the *boyars*.

I wish to draw several conclusions from the arguments propounded above. They indicate the undeniably important role of merchant capital in the economy, albeit with this reservation, that this capital cannot be regarded as a major factor of economic growth. Merchant capital grew where growth in production and the effect of other factors were conducive to profitable investment. Trade continued to flourish and merchant capital to flow into Eastern Europe (with the exception of Bohemia), and even intensified at the time of the intense economic crisis in the West. Thus there arises the question as to whether contemporarily worse investment prospects in the West did not to some extent effect an increase in the outflow of capital to the developing East. Last but not least, we must pay attention to the fact that, although German and Italian investments acted as incentives to the development of a variety of East European industries, those investments were accompanied by a massive inflow of handicrafts and exports of raw materials which, with time, became very dangerous to those crafts which formed the economic basis of many East European towns.

CHAPTER FOUR

KAFFA. THE GENOESE COLONY IN THE CRIMEA AND THE EASTERN QUESTION (1453–1475)*

Part One

The problem of the Genoese colonies has not received sufficient attention from historians, notwithstanding the important role that these colonies played in the economic life, not only of Genoa itself, but also of the countries of Eastern Europe.

The old study by Canale is long outdated, and in any case contains errors arising from the author's uncritical use of his sources. Heyd, in his excellent history of the Levantine trade, accords a considerable place to the Italian colonies in the Crimea, but a really exhaustive study of the subject perforce lay outside the bounds of his work.

In preparing the present investigation, I naturally had recourse to the diplomatic code of the colony published by A. Vigna. To complement this instructive source, I examined the archives of both Genoa and Venice: in Genoa, I consulted the reports listed under the titles "Diversorum" and "Litterarum"; in Venice, those entitled "Senato mar" and "Senato secreta". I then compared the results of my researches with various documents from the Crown Archives held in the Warsaw Central Archives. Finally, I made use, especially in relation to the Eastern Question, of a large number of published documents, amongst which I discovered valuable information in the correspondence of Aeneas Sylvius Piccolomini (Pius II).

The first reliable references to Kaffa date from 1289 and 1290. By this time the Genoese colony was already in existence, on the site of the former Theodosia of the Milesians; it was an urban community administered by a consul, himself assisted by a council. It therefore seems reasonable to accept the date proposed by Heyd, who estimates

---

* Originally published in French under the title "Caffa—Colonie génoise en Crimée et la Question d'Orient 1453–1475" as a summary of *Kaffa—kolonia genueńska na Krymie i problem wschodni w latach 1453–1475*, Warszawa, 1947, pp. I–XXXII. Translation from French by Robin Kimball.

that the Genoese first settled in the Crimea shortly after the capture of Constantinople by Michael Paleologus, namely soon after 1261. The fall of the Latin Empire of Constantinople forced the Venetians to withdraw for a time from Byzantium and the Black Sea territories. Since the Crimea was at that time subject to Tatar domination, it was to Mengu Khan that Genoa turned for permission to found a colony there. The good relations which the Genoese entertained with Michael Paleologus also facilitated their access to the shores of the Black Sea.

During the second half of the 13th century, Kaffa enjoyed a brilliant wave of expansion and new Genoese colonies appeared along the southern shores of the Crimean peninsula: Soldaia (Sudak), Calamita (Inkerman), Vosporo (Kerch,) etc. There was also a Genoese settlement in Tana, on the lower Don (not far from the site of present-day Azov). The Venetians, having already established themselves in Tana and in Soldaia, became engaged in fierce rivalry with them but, while maintaining their commercial supremacy in the Mediterranean, were forced to give way to them in the Black Sea region.

In 1343, a conflict broke out between the Italians in the Crimea and Khan Janibeg; it lasted four years, but it would seem to have spared Kaffa, and even indirectly assisted it by weakening the influence of Tana. During the second half of the 14th century, following the collapse of the Golden Horde, the Genoese continued to strengthen their position in the Crimea. In 1365 they even captured Soldaia.

Towards the end of the 14th and the early years of the 15th century, the colonies suffered another powerful shock when Tamerlane's troops appeared at the estuaries of the Volga and the Don. The destruction of Astrakhan' and Saray, added to the troubles in Turkestan, put an end to the thriving commerce uniting the lower Volga with the Far East. Henceforth, Tana moved inexorably towards its decline, while Kaffa, in contrast, remained as the one great commercial centre among the Black Sea countries. However, as we shall later see, the oriental market no longer remained the principal base of the economic life of the colonies; little by little, trade in slaves and in local produce (especially grain and fish) achieved a status at least as important. The Genoese aim of extending their possessions led to confrontation with Hadji-Ghirey, the new Khan of Tatar Crimea who in 1434 inflicted a heavy defeat on them at Solgate and exacted tribute. Subsequently, the situation became stabilized for a time on the basis of the status quo: alongside the Tatars and the Genoese, there still existed the tiny state of Theodoros-Mangup, inhabited by descendants of the Goths who had taken refuge in the Crimea at the time of the great invasions.

From 1449 onwards, Kaffa is clearly recognized as the capital of all the Genoese colonies in the Crimea, and the power of its consuls is extended to all the possessions of the Republic in this region. According to sources dating from the first half of the 15th century, the town of Kaffa covered between 5 and 8 Italian square miles. It would appear that the houses were tightly packed one against the other; a Turkish census drawn up in 1475 records the presence of 8,000 houses inhabited by some 70,000 persons. These figures seem exaggerated, but unfortunately we have no other sources to draw upon.

The ethnic make-up of the population was anything but homogeneous. At the time of its demise, Kaffa counted 400 Italian families, that is to say some 1,600 to 2,000 persons. We also know that in more stable times the number of Italians in Kaffa was somewhat higher, and it seems fair to assume that between 2,500 and 3,000 Italians—Genoese for the most part—were settled there permanently. The majority of the population were Armenians who, under the threat of Mongol invasions, would appear to have abandoned their homes in Asia Minor and settled in the Crimea. According to Armenian sources, they made up some two-thirds of the total population. In addition there were, firstly, many Greeks, together with Tatars, Karaites, Jews, a tiny number of Poles, and perhaps even some Ruthenians and Wallachians. The Greeks were undoubtedly the most numerous after the Armenians, though the lack of source material makes it impossible to give a detailed breakdown. Among both the Armenians and the Greeks, and perhaps also among the Jews, there would seem to have been numbers of very wealthy persons.

Kaffa was the seat of the Catholic diocese, which was administered by the Dominicans. Both Greeks and Armenians had their own bishops, the Jews also had their ministers, and the same was presumably true of the Tatars. The Genoese authorities were scrupulous in their observance of religious tolerance, which they regarded as offering the best guarantee of social harmony in the town. At the same time, they exercised considerable influence on the nomination of those appointed to high ecclesiastical positions, selecting those whom they considered to be the most cooperative. A particularly delicate situation was that of the Greek bishopric, placed under the authority of Rome since the Union of Florence, but also exposed to the influence of the Byzantine patriarchate. This problem became even more acute following the capture of Constantinople, when the Patriarch became subordinate to the power of the Sultan.

On the social plane, Kaffa was divided into two groups of very unequal proportions. First came the Genoese, known as *cives*, amongst whom primacy was accorded to the nobility (*nobili*); only after these came the *burgenses*, who were, of course, far more numerous. The various magistratures were allocated on the basis of equality between the two groups—a system which naturally assured the Genoese of a preponderant influence patently disproportionate to their numbers, the more so since the consul, his deputy, and their two chief advisers, known as *massarii* (treasurers), were elected by the Genoese alone. This was the normal procedure in a colony. The entire organization of Kaffa was a faithful blue-print of Genoa itself. The consul, elected for one year and seconded by a deputy (*vicarius*), directed the administration, decided on policy, commanded the armed forces, and acted as judge. Until 1453, he was subject to a body known as "Officium Gazariae" (Khazaria-Crimea), which sat in Genoa and decided upon his nomination.

The consul governed the town and the colonies with the aid of two consultative bodies: one was the "Concilium Octo Antianorum", a type of council of municipal magistrates; the other was a larger council, made up of members of certain colleges of officials in charge of various administrative services. During the period which concerns us, the functions of the municipal magistrates were somewhat limited, whereas the two colonial treasurers (*massarii*) were the most influential personalities after the consul. In fact, the latter could not undertake any important measure without their accord. Moreover, any significant expenditure had also to be approved by the colleges, such as the four-member "Officium Provisionis", the "Officium Monetae", etc. The object of this system was to guard against all abuse. So far from achieving this, the collegial system in the administration merely gave rise to continual quarrels and rivalries amongst the colonial magistrates. In consequence of this, important decisions tended to be put off interminably, while the magistrates, whose responsibilities were poorly defined, sometimes investigated parallel cases without knowing it.

The Genoese *cives* monopolized the tasks of the council of treasurers and the consular syndics. The remaining offices were attributed on a basis of parity. It is clear that such an organization caused irritation among the native population, who sometimes vented their anger in popular risings. To remedy this situation, the authorities created the "Officium Quattuor Burgensium", designed to exercise control together with the consular and general syndics. This innovation provoked even more violent protests, and it was only when the colonies were already reaching their decline that the central authorities decided to restrict the exercise of public office to persons already living in Kaffa for at least 12 years (an exception, of course, being made for consuls and treasurers, who were always nominated from Genoa). It is worth noting that, as the situation of the colonies progressively declined, candidates for high office became noticeably more scarce, and those who accepted the dignity of consul frequently did so with the sole aim of enriching themselves rapidly at the expense of their fellow-citizens. No system of checks and controls succeeded in putting an end to these practices. The rivalry between officials also exercised an adverse effect on the administration of Kaffa: their attempts to find protectors in various groups of the population only led to further confusion and discontent. It should be emphasized at this point that in all this Kaffa was in no way an exception. With its administrative system copied from that of Genoa, it suffered from the same defects as other medieval Italian towns. The long distance from the metropolis and the difficulty of communications between Kaffa and Genoa only served to encourage these abuses.

The same considerations applied to the lower officials of the administration, in particular to the members of the police, who often received no pay beyond the proceeds of fines. Export and import customs duties, together with indirect contributions, formed the financial basis of the Kaffa administration. Customs duties applied to all goods arriving by land or sea, and so included food products. To these should be added the taxes raised on beer, wine, and salt, the latter tax being especially onerous for the population. The government did not directly concern itself with the collection of taxes but, as was common in several other Italian towns, farmed them out every year to private capitalists, the attribution being made by auction. Our researches suggest that taxes in Kaffa were not excessively high. Generally speaking, the population did not complain on this score, and the central authorities exercised great moderation in the matter. In the course of time, the citizens of Kaffa had to provide a part of the tribute paid to the Sultan and the Khan. The cost of administering the colonies was considerable: to the sums needed to maintain them in a proper state of defence was added the tribute due to the Khan (and later the Sultan also), as well as numerous "gifts" destined for the Tatar dignitaries. If to this we add the chronic treasury deficit resulting from a neglected economy and the abuses already described, it is not surprising to find that Kaffa, following once more the example of the metropolis, had recourse to public loans. It is well known what importance 15th-century Genoa attached to the bank of St. George (Casa di S. Giorgio), whose shareholders exploited all the sources of revenue in the town. The bank was directed by seven protectores, who not only administered the institution but also exercised a decisive influence on the affairs of the Republic. Kaffa likewise contracted debts and issued shares (known as *loca* or *luogi*) which conferred on their owners the right to participate in the profits derived from the colonies. As in Genoa, the shareholders formed an organization known as "Comperae Caphae", also directed by protectores, but we have no details concerning the activities of these latter. At a later stage, they doubtless had to cover part of the costs of the tribute owed to Turkey. The big shareholders of the "Comperae Caphae" doubtless belonged to the financial circles represented in Kaffa by the wealthy patrician families from Genoa, such as the Fieschi, the Di-Negro, the Spinola, etc. In all probability certain rich Greeks and Armenians were also associated. The bankers of Kaffa were not exactly the soul of integrity, and frequent bankruptcies caused enormous losses to large numbers of people. By and large, one is left with the impression that an unhealthy atmosphere reigned in Kaffa, especially during the 15th century: people amassed money with feverish haste, but with complete disregard for the means used to acquire it; the permanent sense of danger demoralized the entire population and created just that sort of "outpost" atmosphere in which a few resourceful and unscrupulous individuals thrive and prosper.

The public debt failed to remedy a serious deficit. It would seem that, between 1453 and 1456, the Bank of St. George, which had extended its activities to the Genoese Black Sea colonies, was obliged to furnish around 30,000 Genoese lire every year from its own funds. However, later on, in the period of prosperity during the war between Venice and Turkey, the deficit was finally covered, and the colonial government was even able to contemplate buying up the shares of the "Comperae Caphae" and liquidating the public debt. As a result, the price of these shares underwent a sharp rise, but this increase was unfortunately not maintained. Their nominal value would seem to have been equal to the *loca* "Societatis Comperarum S. Georgii" in Genoa, viz. 100 Genoese lire.

We have already mentioned that Kaffa traded primarily with the East via a vast route running from Astrakhan' and Saray, through Turkestan, and ending up in China. This was the route by which silks, spices, and other oriental products flowed into Kaffa. Some of these goods could also be purchased in Trebizond and in Constantinople, for Asia Minor was also in touch with the Far East via Persia. Incidentally, it would appear that merchants from Kaffa themselves made the journey to Sultaniyah, Tabriz, and other Persian trade centres. The ravages perpetrated in 1395 by Tamerlane in the lands of the lower Volga and Near Asia dealt a severe blow to this trade. Sources dating from the second half of the 15th century confirm the fact, already known from elsewhere, that at this time the centre of Levantine commerce shifted to the south, to towns in Syria and even as far as Alexandria. This development exercised an appreciable effect on the pattern of Kaffa's trade structure. In the second half of the 15th century, Kaffa showed little interest in its relations with Trebizond or with the other towns of northern Asia Minor. Despite the fact that oriental produce could only be obtained by this route, the colonial authorities paid scant attention to these problems. In our view, this decline in interest is explained by the following circumstances. During the 15th century, the Genoese were able to acquire oriental produce from Egypt, Syria, and from their own thriving colony of Chios. Seen in this light, Kaffa was for them of only secondary importance. In so far as Genoese merchants displayed an interest in the Black Sea colonies, it was for other reasons. For them, Kaffa represented first and foremost a source of supply in slaves and in grain. It was precisely for these reasons that the colonial authorities took special care to preserve their zone of economic influence in the Caucasus, the Crimea, and Moldavia.

An examination of the few sources available gives the impression that in this respect Kaffa presented a type of division of labour, trade in slaves and in grain being mainly concentrated in Genoese hands, while the Greeks, Armenians, Jews, and probably Tatars also, specialized in the traffic in oriental goods. The natives exported silk wares, other oriental cloths, and spices to the neighbouring countries (Moldavia and Poland) and even to far-off Muscovy. The Armenians' activities were of particular importance, enabling them to establish and maintain economic ties with the towns in eastern Poland and Moldavia where large numbers of their compatriots resided. We are also in possession of sources testifying to the fact that the Armenians and the Greeks also dealt in the slave trade, though in this domain the Italians would seem to have enjoyed superiority. Having more ample capital at their disposal, they could afford to meet the high costs involved in transporting slaves from Kaffa to Genoa. In this connection we have both direct and indirect testimony to hand. Slaves were transported either by sea or by land route, through Moldavia, Poland, or Hungary, to Austria and Italy. According to Sieveking, the number of slaves in Genoa during the first half of the 15th century amounted to 3,000, later falling to 1,200. We do not know on what basis Sieveking arrived at these figures. Be that as it may, it is certain that the slave trade found lively expression in Genoese documents of the second half of the 15th century. We also have firm evidence that many of these slaves had been bought on the Kaffa market. Genoese sources attest to their Tatar, Circassian, or Georgian origin. Most of these slaves were probably put to work in Italy as servants. At the same time, apart from Italy, the Genoese also supplied part of this living merchandise to Egypt, though this traffic, confirmed in reports of earlier centuries, finds no mention in sources from the second half of the 15th century. On the other hand, we do know that at this period the Sultan of Egypt still displayed a lively interest in trade with Kaffa. While the sources in question make no explicit mention of the matter, it seems quite possible that Kaffa at this time continued to supply Egypt primarily with slaves.

For the merchants of Kaffa, the Caucasus was the main source of supply of slaves, and it was there that they bought up men and women of Circassian or Georgian origin. The frequent internecine wars between the Caucasian tribes provided the Genoese with an inexhaustible supply of slaves. Moreover, it is known that in the 16th century poor parents used to sell their children to these merchants, and this traffic was almost certainly practised in the preceding century also.

But the people of Kaffa also acquired other products from the Caucasus. From Lo Copa, for instance, situated on the Kuban river estuary, they imported large quantities of fish, and probably timber also. In this field, they encountered keen competition from the Venetian colony of Tana. From time to time, Hadji-Ghirey, the Khan of Crimea, likewise competed with them on the Caucasian market. He strove to organize a vast slave traffic in the ports of Kerch and Inkerman. Kaffa felt itself threatened, but the danger did not last. In fact, up till 1475, the people of Kaffa maintained their leading position in the Caucasus, their rare disputes with the tribes of that region being of little consequence. There was one decisive factor in all this: the Kaffa merchants were virtually the sole customers for slaves and for other Caucasian wares, and in return supplied these countries with the most essential provisions, including valuable Crimean salt.

Their position in the Caucasus was accordingly a very powerful one. They also devoted keen attention to their Crimean neighbours. We have already referred to the importance of grain in Kaffa's trade; in this connection, the lands covering the south-eastern part of the peninsula were of particular importance. Crimean grain formed the basis of Kaffa's supplies, and part of this grain was perhaps exported to Italy and Turkey. We do not know which section of Kaffa's population was at that time concerned with agriculture: was it the Italians, the Armenians, the Greeks, or even the Tatar natives? Długosz records that Khan Hadji-Ghirey tried to interest his subjects in agriculture. In our view, it was primarily the presence of the Italian colonies that spurred on the Crimean peoples to cultivate the soil, with a view to ensuring the sale of grain. A more direct consequence of the settlement of the Genoese in the Crimea was doubtless the introduction of viniculture. Meanwhile, grain was also an important item of import from Moldavia and Wallachia.

Slaves, grain, fish, and a few other products (e.g. the red dye known as kermes) were the main items exported by Kaffa to Italy, Turkey, and the Mediterranean countries.

Kaffa's contacts with her immediate neighbours were of a very different kind. Amongst these, its relations with the Black Sea ports of Akkerman and Kilia were of particular importance. While it is true that a certain number of slaves were transported thence to Western Europe, their main importance lay in the export of oriental produce destined for the Danubian countries and Poland. It was via Akkerman and Suceava that routes finally led on to Lwów (Leopol), the biggest centre of eastern trade in southern Ruthenia in the 15th century. Merchants from Kaffa either made the journey to Lwów themselves, or else maintained contact with this town through Akkerman. By contrast, the citizens of Lwów only visited Kaffa in exceptional circumstances: generally speaking, the mediation of Akkerman merchants and the periodical visits from those of Kaffa sufficed their requirements. This oriental trade brought huge profits to Lwów traders and the right to place goods in bond protected them against the competition of less important Polish towns. The same traders also exported various wares to Kaffa: during the 15th century, these included German, Silesian, and Polish cloths, probably various hides, metal objects, wax, etc. The trade balance in all these transactions was almost certainly in Kaffa's favour, thanks to its ample supplies of valuable oriental goods. Among other Polish towns, Cracow was the main one to entertain direct or indirect relations with Kaffa. On their journeys to and from Kaffa, the Genoese frequently passed through Poland, all of which helped to strengthen the economic ties between the latter and the Genoese colonies. This trade was of great importance for Poland.

The routes running through Moldavia, Poland, or Hungary were also of prime importance for Kaffa. Quite apart from opening up extensive markets for oriental produce, they also ensured relatively safe communication with the metropolis at a time when, following the capture of Constantinople by the Turks, the latter became masters of the sea route between the Crimea and Italy.

Kaffa merchants not only exported their oriental wares to Moldavia or Poland, but also established ties with Kiev (admittedly of scant importance in the 15th century) and with Moscow. Both Russian and Kaffa sources contain information concerning merchants who travelled from the Crimea to Moscow and vice versa. This trade was not without its dangers, caravans often falling victim to raids by brigands. From what we know, however, it would seem that transactions between Kaffa and Moscow in the 15th century were of little importance to the colony.

In conclusion, it is clear that Kaffa played a key role in the economic life of the Black Sea countries, acting as intermediary in the trade in oriental goods arriving from Trebizond and other towns in Asia Minor and perhaps also in Persia. These goods were in turn exported to Wallachia, Poland, and Muscovy, in exchange for various products from Northern Europe. In all this traffic, the favourable economic status of the Genoese colonies played a useful role. The influence of the grain trade, stimulating as it did the development of agriculture in the Crimea and Moldavia, was of a similar nature. Grain from these countries was exported to Italy, Constantinople, and Asia Minor. In addition, Kaffa was an important centre for the supply of slaves, most of them of Caucasian origin, who were passed on to Italy or to one of the Muslim countries. It would appear that, in the second half of the 15th century, the slave traffic assumed an added importance, especially from the point of view of the Genoese, whereas the native population concentrated rather on the supply of oriental wares to the markets in Moldavia, Poland, and Muscovy.

Part Two

I. *The Eastern Question from the Fall of Constantinople to the War between Venice and Turkey (1463)*

The fall of Constantinople in 1453 surprised Europe. While no one entertained any illusions concerning the ultimate fate of the Eastern Empire, the capture of this stronghold, which had repulsed so many barbarian attacks in the past, produced a lively impression in the West. On the other hand, all idea of collective action against the Turks was out of the question. Venice, locked in struggles with Francesco Sforza and the Florentines, was in no position to take on the Turks as well. Alfonso V, the Magnanimous, King of Aragon and Naples, was engaged in a bitter feud with the Genoese over Corsica, and had ambitions of establishing hegemony in the Mediterranean; in addition, he was worried by the claims on Naples raised by the house of Anjou.

France continued to be embroiled in bitter struggles between the King and the feudal lords. In Germany, the Emperor Frederick III had no effective power and his authority was no more than apparent. Poland, in the light of its last experience, had no desire to launch a new war against the Turks; in any case, it was at that stage planning to wrest access to the Baltic from the Teutonic Order, a far more essential problem and one which absorbed its entire attention. Even Hungary, directly threatened by the Turks, was occupied elsewhere, for its young king Ladislas V had to defend his throne against both the Emperor and the attacks of the powerful nobles.

Among the powers, it was Venice who ventured furthest down the road of compromise, signing a treaty with the Sultan (18 April 1454) which, in return for payment of customs dues, granted it freedom of trade and for the time being guaranteed the safety of its possessions in the Morea (the Peloponnese). A similar attitude inexorably imposed itself on Genoa, far weaker than Venice and drained of its forces as a result of the war against Alfonso and internecine feuds. In order to preserve its trade with the East and the safety of its Black Sea colonies, it was forced in its turn to make concessions to the all-powerful Turks.

In these circumstances, the appeal for an anti-Turkish crusade launched by Pope Nicholas V and his successor Callixtus III had not the remotest chance of being heard either in Italy or beyond the Alps.

All the efforts of Papal diplomacy deployed in Italy failed to produce results; the same fate befell the mission undertaken by Aeneas Sylvius Piccolomini in Germany in the years 1454 and 1455.

From this confused situation, Sultan Mohammed II was quick to draw the maximum advantage. Undismayed by the failure of the expedition against Belgrade in 1456, he began by fortifying his position in the Balkans. His plans were indeed far-reaching: having swallowed up Constantinople, he entertained the idea of conquering Rome, the capital of Western Christianity; at all events, such ambitions were attributed to him by certain of his contemporaries, and a number of facts prove that they were not mistaken. Henceforth, his strategy consisted first and foremost in securing bases to support his attack on Italy. The realization of this plan absorbed Mohammed II's attention during the latter part of his reign. The first step involved eliminating Turkey's two great adversaries—Venice and Hungary—and ensuring the safety of the frontiers already established. Thus, in the years 1458–1460, the Sultan occupied the despotic states still held by the house of Paleologus in the Morea. In 1459, he captured Semendria, an important fortress on the northern frontier. In 1461, he captured Trebizond, so destroying the coalition of minor emirs in Asia Minor grouped around Uzun-Hassan, the sovereign of Persia—an event which had the effect of reinforcing the eastern frontiers of the Ottoman state. The following year, Vlad, the hospodar of the Multanes, was driven out and his place taken by Radu, a creature of the Sultan's. During all this period, the latter was patently preparing for a war against Venice which, by virtue of its dominance of Greek waters, posed a serious threat to Turkish interests. Mohammed's preparations were demonstrated by the capture of Lesbos in 1462 and the occupation of Bosnia the following year. Mastery of the latter placed him in an ideal position from which to attack northern Italy, as well as possessions in the Empire and in Hungary. The continuous aggrandisement of Turkish power and the growing threat which this presented was a source of great preoccupation for Pope Pius II. An eminent humanist, engaged in action against Turkey since the pontificate of Nicholas V, he seemed predestined to direct the struggle against the Ottoman Empire, in which he saw not only a dangerous enemy of Christendom but also an adversary opposed to the renaissance of letters. In his efforts to defend values dear to humanists of the 15th century, Pius II was anxious to enlist the support of medieval piety. His correspondence prior to his accession to the throne of Peter shows that he perfectly understood the difficulties of the enterprise.

He realized that, from the political point of view, the moment was not favourable for his plans. At the time of his accession, Italy was in a particularly complex situation. Genoa, having surrendered to France, had become the base of Angevin operations in Italy. Taking advantage of this base, John, Duke of Calabria, the son of King René, launched a war for the Neapolitan throne against Ferrante, the son of Alfonso the Magnanimous. The pretender was supported by a large part of the Neapolitan nobility. The growth of French influence in Italy deeply disturbed Francesco Sforza, Duke of Milan, who thereupon decided to make approaches to the Pope, who had no intention of surrendering his Neapolitan realm to the Angevins. The anti-French policy of Pius II aroused the displeasure of both Charles VIII and, subsequently, of Louis XI. Besides this, the Pope enjoyed an extremely bad reputation in Eastern Europe, where Poland reproached him with his sympathies for the Teutonic Order. Meanwhile, both Bohemia and Hungary were beset by internal political crises.

Faced with this thorny situation, Pius II took the initiative in convoking a large congress with the aim of preparing a war against Islam. He solemnly declared that he would place himself at the head of the expedition, doubtless hoping by this means to enrol enthusiastic masses in his wake. In fact, however, the Congress of Mantua (1459/1460), and with it the proposed expedition, ended in total failure. Occupied with numerous other problems, Europe did not stir one inch. During the night of 13th/14th August 1464, the Pope died in Ancona, while waiting in vain for the arrival of the Venetian fleet. It was slow in making an appearance because the Republic of St. Mark, even after the start of the war against Turkey, continued to eye the Pope with mistrust, suspecting him of having secret designs on the Adriatic shorelands. Thus it was that Pius II, whose conduct and whose policies admittedly gave rise to justifiable suspicions, died in an atmosphere of rumour and hostility.

II. *The Genoese Colonies in the Crimea in the Years 1453–1463*

For the Genoese colonies in the Crimea, the fall of Constantinople came as a severe blow. The main sea-route to the West, passing through the Bosphorus, was henceforth under Turkish control. Pera, the large Genoese colony on the Straits, was forced to surrender to the Sultan and conserved no more than the trappings of its autonomy. As we have

already seen, Genoa was at this time incapable of bringing any aid to
its colonies. The Doge therefore sold the colonies to the Bank of St.
George for 11,000 Genoese lire, in the hope that this powerful institution
might be better able to assist Kaffa than a weak government. In fact, the
proceeds from the sale of the other colonies were immensely valuable
for the clique in power in Genoa, engaged as they were in struggles
against the King of Naples on the one hand and the oppositional forces
of the Adorno and Fieschi families on the other.

Towards the end of 1453 and in the early part of 1454, Kaffa had no
more than intermittent contact with Genoa. Panic reigned throughout
the colony. At that time, Kaffa possessed neither fortifications nor arms.
There was a mass evacuation from the town, and those that remained
lived in constant fear of Turkish invasion or armed intervention by the
Khan. Divergences of opinion between the privileged classes of Genoese
and the rest of the population became extremely acute. The natives
endeavoured to gain some influence on the destinies of the town. In July
1454, a small Turkish expedition landed in the Crimea. These troops
made contact with Hadji-Ghirey but, not being in sufficient strength to
attack Kaffa, contented themselves with pillaging part of the peninsula
and the shores of the Caucasus. The Sultan's aim had been simply to
terrorise the Genoese and thus secure a durable peace on that front. At
this stage Turkey had no interest in antagonizing the Genoese, for the
idea of a crusade was still in the air, and the danger of a war against
Venice could not be discounted. One must admit that in all this the
Sultan attained his objective admirably: so far from contemplating any
action against Turkey, the Genoese, stricken with fear, did all they could
to win his favour. In an effort to prolong their existence, the Crimean
colonies agreed in 1455 to pay an annual tribute of 3,000 ducats. Even
the Khan took advantage of this situation to impose on Kaffa an annual
tribute of 300 sonmi. But the colonies' misfortunes did not stop there.
During 1455 and 1456, the poor state of the harvests in the Black Sea
countries ravaged Kaffa with famine and plague.

In the face of this dire situation, the local authorities, in the person
of the administrators of the Bank of St. George, set about attacking
the colony's affairs with energy. They realized the nature of Turkish
policy and this enabled them to control the widespread panic. They
also dispatched military reinforcements and even some provisions to
Kaffa. In an effort to arrest the decline in the population, in 1454 they
proclaimed a sweeping amnesty for all those who, for whatever reasons,
had meanwhile left Kaffa. At the same time, the protectors agreed to

meet a part of the demands of the *burgenses* by allowing the election of four members of their class to a body known as the "Concilium Quattuor Burgensium". This new institution supervised the magistrature and communicated directly with the central authorities.

Anxious to obtain increased financial resources for Kaffa, the protectors succeeded in obtaining Papal bulls in favour of the Crimean colonies.

All these measures, added to a period of relative political calm in the Black Sea region, combined to exercise a favourable effect on Kaffa's fortunes. As early as 1456, a clear improvement was visible: inhabitants returned to their homes and trade picked up once more. Despite this, however, the colony's budget continued to show a deficit, and the existence of social and religious conflicts aroused anxiety in Genoa. The temporary exile of Hadji-Ghirey in 1457 also proved a boon to the Genoese, inasmuch as his successor maintained friendly relations with the colonies. Neither the loss to the Moldavians of the fortress of Lerici (Oleshki) at the mouth of the Dnieper, nor local feuds with the duke of Gothia and certain Caucasian chieftains led to any grave consequences. In its relations with its neighbours, Kaffa displayed a spirit of conciliation, and strove to form alliances with Moldavia, Gothia, and with the Khan, in the hope of demonstrating to the Sultan the difficulties involved in any attack on the colonies, who asked for nothing more than peace, in return for loyally paying their tribute, supplying merchandise, and conducting themselves as impeccable neighbours. However, the occupation of Samastri in 1459 and the continued advance of the Turks along the northern shores of Asia Minor persuaded the authorities in Kaffa of the need to find a powerful protector. In view of the town's extremely unfavourable strategic position, however, this power must be one whose protection would not displease the Sultan. In the end, it was decided to appeal to Poland. Casimir IV of the Jagellons had steered clear of the anti-Turkish coalition; moreover, he exerted considerable influence on the policy of Hadji-Ghirey who, having recovered his throne, was now sovereign of the Crimea. A Polish "protectorate" would thus be in a position to improve Kaffa's position in the face of the Khan, the hospodar of Moldavia, and Turkey, without in any way compromising it in the eyes of Mohammed II. Such were the origins of the recognition of Polish suzerainty by Kaffa in 1462. It should be added that an additional motive behind this political manoeuvre was to facilitate the use of the Polish routes that were so important for Kaffa's economy. There was the further advantage that Kaffa could count on the King of

Poland's permission to enrol mercenaries for service in the colony. From
the Polish point of view, suzerainty over Kaffa represented a triumph
which strengthened the position of the Jagellons in the Black Sea region,
and this—which was extremely important—at no cost whatever. At the
same time, it should be stressed that Polish influence in the Crimea was
not strong: Casimir IV, distracted first by Prussia and subsequently by
Bohemia and Hungary, lacked the necessary forces to defend his position on the south-eastern frontier. The King was well aware of this,
and confined himself to the role of mediator in the political problems
of the Black Sea region.

III. *The Eastern Question during the War between* *Venice and Turkey (1463–1475)*

The temporary calm that ensued in the Black Sea basin is explained
by a shift in the centre of gravity of Turkish policy towards the West.
Having conquered part of the Morea, Bosnia, and several islands, the
Sultan was now in a favourable position from which to launch an
attack on Venice. Reckoning that he was by now strong enough to
deal with this ancient enemy of Turkey, he opened hostilities in 1463
in the Peloponnese. At this, the Republic of St. Mark effected a radical
change in its Eastern policy. Its revised aim was the formation of an
anti-Turkish league, or at least the receipt of aid from other countries
and from the Papacy. We have already mentioned the entente of 1464
between Pius II and the Venetians. However, lack of confidence in the
good will of the Pope and his enterprise persuaded Doge Moro to tem-
porize. The Venetian fleet finally reached Ancona—the starting point
of the crusade—after the death of Pius II, and thereupon immediately
returned to Venice. On the other hand, it would seem that the alliance
which Venice concluded in 1463 with Matthias Corvinus constituted a
great success for the Republic.

Hungary, alarmed by the Turkish invasion of Bosnia, was anxious
to drive out the Moslems with the aid of the subsidies provided by
Venice and by the Pope. In fact King Matthias did embark on a war
and occupied part of Bosnia, including the fortress of Jajce, but there
he stopped, having other political problems on his mind. In reality,
his main ambition was to conquer Austria, but he could not risk an
open break with Venice, whose subventions, together with those of the
Papacy, were of vital necessity to him.

Venice found itself in a grave situation. In practice, Hungarian aid proved insignificant. In the Morea, the troops of the Republic suffered a reverse and the Turks occupied the peninsula. In Rome, Pius II was succeeded by Paul II, who viewed Venice with hostility. Besides this, the Venetians became more and more dismayed at the activities deployed by Genoa, Florence, and Ancona in Turkey, all of whom took advantage of the absence of Venice to place their own commercial agents in the Levantine trade there. The situation of the Republic was critical on all sides. To compound the defeats encountered on the battlefield, Milan and Naples were drawing closer together, hoping by joint means to reduce Venetian influence generally. The Pope raised claims on Rimini, which belonged to the Malatesta, who were protégés of Venice. Moreover, Hungary, having recovered part of Bosnia, now began bringing pressure to bear on Dalmatia. In addition to the Turkish menace, Venice thus felt itself threatened in Italy and in the Adriatic. In 1466, supporters of a peace treaty with Turkey obtained a majority in the Senate, but their efforts failed in the face of the exorbitant terms put forward by the Sultan, his demands for Albania, the islands, and the Morea being quite unacceptable for Venice. Even so, discussions with the Turks continued in an effort to preserve the peace. This became especially desirable following the death of Francesco Sforza in 1466, at a time when his successor, Galeazzo Maria, was still a minor. This factor appreciably diminished the influence of the Milanese state, and the prospect of a renewed expansion on the Terraferma opened up before Venetian eyes. It was essential to take advantage of the situation in the Tuscan sector. The weak Piero de'Medici was not a dangerous adversary. Unwilling to engage themselves directly, the Venetians encouraged their old condottiere Colleoni to occupy Bologna, whence it would be possible to attack both Florence and the Papacy. All these partisan intrigues behind Venetian expansionist plans in Italy produced a new wave of anarchy throughout the Peninsula. The coalition formed against Colleoni, and hence against Venice, comprised Naples, Milan, and Florence. In the event, Colleoni, and Venice with him, were forced to abandon the fight. Apart from this, the Turkish victories undoubtedly contributed to a weakening of the expansionist aims harboured by the Republic of St. Mark. In 1468 Turkish troops occupied almost the whole of Albania, and the death of Skanderberg, its defender, severely aggravated the situation in this region. In 1468 and 1469, the Turks, operating from bases in Bosnia, pillaged Dalmatia and Istria and advanced as far as Italy's northern frontier. Not surprisingly, these events induced the quarrelling parties throughout Italy to reconsider the situation, at least for a time. In 1468, Paul II finally succeeded in forming a pan-Italian league, but neither the Pope nor the other signatories took their engagements seriously. A quarrel broke out between the Pope and the King of Naples, who supported the Orsini, the powerful Roman nobles, in their feud with the Papacy. In 1469, the Pope, anxious to enlist the aid of Venice against his enemies, concluded a 25-year alliance with the Republic of St. Mark.

During all this time, the Turkish menace grew from day to day. As we already know, the Turks were already present on the north-eastern frontiers of Italy. In addition, the Sultan was already in possession of a powerful fleet, and rumour had it that he had a number of aggressive plans for the future. Venice found itself in an extremely dangerous situation. All hope of outside aid had vanished. Hungary, in its striving to dominate Dalmatia, had thereby become an enemy of the Republic. In any case, ever since 1469, Matthias Corvinus had been completely engrossed in his battle for Bohemia. Poland was likewise engaged in this struggle. Countless interventions by Venetian diplomats at the Hungarian court, in an attempt to persuade Matthias to change his policy, failed to produce results. At this stage, the Turkish Aegean fleet took to sea and on 12 July 1470 captured Negropont (Euboea), so depriving Venice of one of its main naval bases. A wave of terror swept through Italy, where there were fears that the occupation of Euboea was merely the prelude to operations directed against Italy proper. Venice and Naples felt themselves particularly threatened. By contrast, Milan and Florence adopted a much more reserved attitude, and failed to join the new Italian league. Not even the Pope, with his eyes still fixed on Rimini, came to the aid of Venice. True, the latter managed, in April 1471, to conclude an alliance with the King of Naples, himself alarmed by the Turkish successes, but in the event this pact was to prove illusory.

Once King Ferrante realized that he was in no immediate danger, he resumed his anti-Venetian policy. This policy was dictated on the one hand by his fear of increasing Venetian influence throughout the Peninsula and on the other by his desire to increase his own influence along the eastern shores of the Adriatic—a policy already inaugurated by his father. Nor did Venice succeed in persuading the Emperor Frederick III to join the alliance, notwithstanding the fact that in 1471 the Turks had pillaged Gorizia and Carinthia. In these circumstances, it is hardly surprising that Venice continued to try and keep the peace

with the Sultan. All its efforts to form an anti-Turkish league must be
seen as nothing more than an attempt to place itself in a more favourable position in the event of negotiations with the Turks. The situation
of the Republic was going from bad to worse. On the battlefield, the
Turks held the upper hand, while in the background there loomed the
spectre of a dangerous anti-Venetian coalition formed by the rulers
of Naples, Milan, and Hungary. The Venetians were on the point of
agreeing to major concessions when, in totally unexpected fashion,
they discovered an ally in the person of Uzun-Hassan, the Turkmen
ruler of Persia. Defeated by Mohammed II in 1461, he was anxious to
profit from any war between Venice and Turkey in order to regain his
influence in the eastern part of Asia Minor. Aiming to drive the Turks
from Karamania, he decided to enter into negotiations with Venice in
the hope of obtaining financial aid and munitions. His embassy arrived
in Venice in 1471, and the following year Catarino Zeno visited Persia,
whereupon Uzun-Hassan decided on armed intervention. At first all
went well. The Turkmens occupied Tokat and in the autumn of 1472
Uzun-Hassan in person entered Karamania, where he was acclaimed
by the population. At the same time the Venetian fleet undertook a
series of successful operations along the shores of Asia Minor. The
Venetians took fresh courage. They began to contemplate victory over
the Sultan, or at least hoped that their successes would induce the Sultan
to conclude a peace treaty favourable to the Republic of St. Mark. Once
again, however, Venetian hopes proved vain. In early 1473, the Turks
laid waste Istria and Friuli and defeated the Venetians at Isonzo. But
of all these reverses, the most devastating was the crushing defeat of
Uzun-Hassan in the battle of Erzincan in August 1473. Thanks to this
victory over the Turkmens, the Sultan once again had his hands free in
the West. He next decided on clearing out the last Venetian redoubts
in Albania. In the middle of 1474, his troops laid siege to Scutari. It
is alleged that the Turkish infantry went into the attack to the cry:
"to Scutari! to Rome!" These were more than mere empty words: the
occupation of Albania would have provided the Turks with a relatively
easy means of transporting their troops to the Italian mainland. The
Turkish landing in Otranto, in 1480, clearly showed the direction in
which the Sultan's thoughts were moving. But in 1474 there was as
yet no sign among the Italians of any sense of the impending danger.
The interstate feuds continued as before. At this stage, Pope Sixtus IV
prepared to occupy the Tuscan locality of Città di Castello, a plan which
understandably spread alarm in Florence. Once again, the Italian league

was called into being, once again nominally for 25 years, but with few illusions anywhere as to its likely duration. The Venetians, who still held Scutari, endeavoured to alter the course of events by a series of diplomatic interventions in Hungary and Poland, but these two countries were so taken up with their mutual feud that Badoer, the Venetian envoy, failed to persuade either of them to join in the war against the Turks. During all that time, Venice succeeded in maintaining relations with influential persons in the Sultan's inner circle. Finally, following a lengthy period of futile interventions at the Turkish court, a 6-month armistice was unexpectedly signed in April or May 1475. This came as a boon to the Venetians, affording them a breathing space and the chance to fortify their positions. What lay behind this gesture on the part of the Sultan? In my view, the explanation is to be found in the Black Sea basin, where the position of the Turks was at that time an unfavourable one. Stephen the Great, the hospodar of Moldavia, had meanwhile become a veritable threat to the Ottoman Empire. True, in 1464 he had agreed to pay tribute to the Sultan, but it was clear that he was endeavouring to concentrate a force that would enable him to confront Turkey. He took advantage of aid from Poland, even though the Jagellon Casimir IV mistrusted his turbulent vassal. Stephen profited from the weakness of the Multanes (southern Wallachia), governed by the feeble Radu. In 1465, the Moldavians occupied Kilia, and henceforth Stephen kept up relentless pressure on his principal neighbour, whose territory he evidently hoped to acquire for himself. He even succeeded in repelling an attack launched by the forces of Matthias Corvinus, who was becoming alarmed by Stephen's growing strength and by the simultaneous increase of Polish influence along Hungary's eastern borders. In 1469, Stephen in his turn launched an attack on Transylvania—a move which was this time in Poland's interest. In 1473, he once more attacked the Multanes, apparently confident that the Sultan, absorbed in the wars against Venice and Persia, would not come to the aid of Radu. At this, Casimir IV became alarmed. Such excessive increase in Moldavian power was undesirable from Poland's point of view, and besides, Stephen's aggressive policy threatened sooner or later to involve war with Turkey. In 1474, the Polish King tried to mediate between the hospodars, but without success. Stephen considered himself to be in a very powerful position. Perhaps he even harboured a dream of creating a Black Sea power; at all events, he established family ties with the Duchy of Gothia in the Crimea, and strove to win the favours of the Genoese colonies.

The establishment of a powerful new Christian state on the lower Danube was something totally unacceptable for Turkey, who was determined to prevent any such undertaking. The Sultan dispatched troops into Moldavia, but on 17 January 1475 they suffered a crushing defeat at Birlad. Mohammed at once realized that the struggle against Stephen would require the deployment of immense forces. Besides, there now loomed before him the possibility of conquering the whole of the Crimea. It was in these circumstances that the Sultan agreed to an armistice with Venice, putting off the war against the Italians for another day.

IV. *The Genoese Colonies in the Crimea from the Beginning of the Turko-Venetian War until 1471*

The outbreak of war between Venice and Turkey in 1463 came as a very welcome development for the Genoese colonies in the Crimea. The situation forced Mohammed II to adopt a more friendly attitude towards the Genoese and the other Italians, all of whom furnished him with vital supplies. Contemporary documents certify that merchants from Genoa, Ancona, and Florence visited Turkey and that some of them even supplied the country with arms. In all this trade, the island of Chios, administered by a Genoese society, "La Maona", of the Giustimani, was an important transit centre. Kaffa likewise took full advantage of the situation: local merchants shipped grain to Constantinople, and the Sultan, loath to indispose the Genoese, allowed them free passage through the Straits. With this, sea communication between Kaffa and Genoa was greatly facilitated, and we know that even the transport of arms for Kaffa was effected by this route. The Turks turned a blind eye. Both the colonial authorities and the protectors of the Bank of St. George testified to a great improvement in the economic situation at this time.

The improvement in the colony's finances encouraged the Bank to invest new capital. Even the native population regarded the future with increased confidence. The combined effect of these two factors enabled Kaffa to undertake the construction of a second line of defences between 1465 and 1470. On the advice of the central authorities, wells were sunk and windmills constructed, to provide the town with improved means of water and food supplies in the event of possible complications on the political front. It should be emphasized that a number of wealthy

Greeks and Armenians voluntarily offered considerable sums to meet the cost of these operations—a proof of the good relations they entertained with the colonial authorities.

Notwithstanding these favourable aspects, the authorities in charge of the Bank of St. George were confronted with numerous problems in the life of the colonies. The native burghers strove constantly to increase their own rights at the expense of those of the consul and his aides. In an effort to curb these tendencies, the protectors recommended admitting Genoese members to the "Officium Quattuor Burgensium". The persistent feuds between the consul and his Council were even more disastrous, leading to disturbances in the town, as rival dignitaries sought the aid of supporters among the population at large. The attitude of the Catholic bishop of Kaffa, the Dominican Girolamo Panissari, provoked wide discontent amongst the Greeks and Armenians, questioning as he did their right to take part in the traffic of Catholic slaves. The Armenians and the Greeks both sent indignant protests to Genoa, accusing the Catholic bishop of himself practising that which he sought to deny to others. Apart from this, the bishop frequently interfered in the matter of mixed marriages, which caused much ill-feeling among the population as a whole. The protectors viewed this situation with disfavour and tried to persuade the bishop to adopt a more tolerant stance.

Nevertheless, none of these conflicts could be said to have adversely affected the life of the colony. True, the widespread corruption that reigned amongst the colonial bureaucrats aroused great dissatisfaction but, in the face of the favourable political and economic climate prevailing, it did not constitute a dangerous evil.

One of the principal preconditions for the successful development of the colony was the maintenance of friendly relations with the Khan of Crimea. During the closing years of his reign, Hadji-Ghirey adopted a very benevolent attitude towards Kaffa. In this respect, the beneficent influence of the King of Poland undoubtedly played an appreciable part. At the time in question, the Khan recognized Polish suzerainty and did all he could to maintain this alliance in order to ensure himself protection against the Golden Horde, which claimed sovereignty over the Crimea. From 1462 onwards, Kaffa likewise recognized the suzerainty of Poland, which had an interest in promoting amicable relations between its Crimean satellites. Kaffa also gained the favours of Mamay, the powerful leader of the Chyrynes, and hence master of the Crimean countryside that was of such importance for the colony. At that time Mamay represented a force equal to that of the Khan himself.

Hadji-Ghirey died in 1466. The chronicle of Długosz shows that in Poland he left behind him the best of memories. Once again Kaffa looked to the future with anxiety. Between Nur-Devlet, Ghirey's eldest son, and his brother Mengli-Ghirey, a struggle for the succession of the Khan's throne now set in. Initially, the former won a number of victories, but the fight continued. Ensuing events are recorded in two valuable sources, namely: the correspondence of the authorities of the Bank of St. George with the consul and Council of Kaffa; and the accounts of the government of the colony, entitled "Massaria Caphae", of 1468. It appears that Mengli-Ghirey managed to win over Kaffa to his cause by promising to reduce the level of tribute. In return, the inhabitants of the colony offered him financial, and probably diplomatic, aid during his struggle for the throne. Hostilities continued in the Crimea until January 1469, at which stage Mengli-Ghirey established himself firmly on the throne. Nur-Devlet was taken prisoner and, probably in accordance with a prearranged treaty, handed over to Kaffa. For the colony, this represented a great success, inasmuch as Mengli-Ghirey thereby became virtually a vassal of the colonial authorities, who, besides his rival Nur-Devlet, also held several other brothers of the late Khan in their hands. In these conditions, the Genoese were at last able to realize their long-cherished aim of forming an alliance of small Crimean states. This alliance was concluded sometime during the second half of 1469, Kaffa, the Khan, and the Duke of Gothia all participating. The Khan was very well disposed towards the colonists. When, in 1471, they came into conflict with Stephen of Moldavia, they urged Mengli-Ghirey to invade the territory of the hospodar, in order to force the latter to make good the losses which merchants from Kaffa had suffered at Akkerman. Even in this period of prosperity, however, the Genoese experienced a difficult moment. In 1470, the Sultan decided once more to strike terror into the hearts of the people of Kaffa, who in his eyes were increasingly allowing themselves excessive liberties in their relations with the Turks. On the pretext of a futile quarrel between Genoese and Turkish merchants, he raised the rate of tribute to 8,000 ducats and ordered the colony to hand over those allegedly guilty of provoking the feud. Panic seized the town, but in the end the Sultan relented, consenting to raise the tribute by a mere 1,000 ducats, making 4,000 ducats in all. The Genoese authorities were so terrified of the Sultan that the protectors

of the Bank of St. George ordered the consul of Kaffa to hand over
to the Turks immediately in future any citizens becoming involved in
disputes with the latter.

V. *Kaffa's Last Years as a Genoese Colony (1471–1475)*

The fall of Negropont, which created such a powerful impression in
Italy, also had profound repercussions on the shores of the Black Sea,
and created an oppressive atmosphere in Kaffa in particular. While the
colony was opposed to the Venetians, it could not fail to realize that
the Turks were gaining the ascendancy over the Christians, even on the
high seas. For the time being at least, however, the changed situation
did not influence the political attitude of the Black Sea colonies. The
war continued to rage, and for Kaffa this was the most important consideration. In fact, each time that there was talk of an imminent peace,
the colonies began to show signs of alarm concerning the future. In
1471, there was nothing to suggest that the situation might deteriorate.
The Sultan was absorbed by the war in the West, and besides this had
to prepare himself for the eventuality of a war against Uzun-Hassan.
For the moment, therefore, Kaffa had nothing to fear from the Turkish
side. In addition, the conviction reigned in the colony that the Khan
would not trouble the peace, given that the mere threat of liberating
Nur-Devlet, and possibly lending him support, was enough to fend off
any hostile designs that Mengli-Ghirey might be hatching. In a word,
peace reigned supreme in the region of Kaffa. Beside this factor, the
frequent feuds with the Caucasian princes and even the quarrel with
Moscow concerning compensation for the goods stolen during the travels of Kaffa merchants were of only minor importance. Even Stephen
the Great, hitherto harsh in his dealings with Kaffa, now sought to
draw closer. In the face of this changed attitude, both the consul and
his Council reacted with extreme reserve, for fear that excessively close
ties with Stephen might displease their fearful enemy, the Sultan. Apart
from this, the Crimean policy of the Moldavian voievode, who had
married Maria, princess of Gothia, and strove to extend his influence
over Theodoros, aroused considerable anxiety in Kaffa.

The international situation was favourable and continued to exercise
a beneficial effect on the economic life of the colony. The fiscal receipts
increased to such an extent that the colonial authorities decided to
set about writing off the public debt by the purchase of shares ("loca

comperarum Caphae"). The protectors of the Bank of St. George were satisfied with the situation in general, albeit disgusted with the widespread embezzlement rife among the higher dignitaries. The evil proved ineradicable, even at the top level of the Kaffa administration. Indeed, the corruptibility of the magistrates and the venality of officials, along with other abuses committed even by the consuls and their advisers, constituted a veritable scourge on the life of the colony. Meanwhile, the quarrels between the Catholic bishop and the non-Catholics continued. In an attempt to lessen the antagonism between the native population and the privileged citizens, the central authorities promulgated a decree stipulating that only citizens living in Kaffa for at least 12 years were eligible for public office. Not only did this measure fail to appease the natives, but new dangers loomed on the horizon. I have already emphasized the complex nature of the religious problem in Kaffa. In Genoa, the central authorities tried to manoeuvre in such a way as to avoid antagonizing the non-Catholics, while simultaneously influencing the choice of candidates to the main ecclesiastical offices of all the religions represented in the colonies. We have already seen how the conduct of the Catholic bishops aroused at once the hostility of the town-dwellers and the displeasure of the authorities. In an effort to counterbalance the influence of the Dominicans, who were dominant in the local diocese, the protectors of the Bank of St. George invited members of the Franciscan fraternity to settle in the colonies, the latter enjoying the reputation of being less fanatical and more open towards other religions. We have no sources indicating whether or not this measure met with any success. In 1471, the death of a Greek bishop gave rise to grave difficulties. Fearing the intervention of the Patriarch of Constantinople, now under Turkish influence, the protectors were anxious to see the vacant seat filled as rapidly as possible. For the Genoese, the maintenance of the Union of Florence was of immense political import. It would appear that the authorities managed to overcome all obstacles and to execute their plan. This measure became all the more urgent, given the fact that at the same period the Armenian community was experiencing a similar crisis in which the succession of their late bishop also played a part. The vote ended in a dual election, the poorer population supporting a certain Pangiager, while the wealthy members of the community gave their vote to Der Carabet. The intrigues of various Armenian cliques also played a part in all this, the more so since one of the candidates had influential cousins in the town. The affair was at first submitted to the Armenian patriarch, then to the authorities in Kaffa. All the evidence proves that the consul Antonio Cabella allowed himself to be bribed, and his aides doubtless behaved little better. All this provoked a mood of excitation and confusion in the town and led to a number of uprisings. The consul and his councillors accused each other of corruption, while the protectors, despite their best efforts, proved powerless to find a solution. This feud lasted until the occupation of Kaffa by the Turks, and had the effect of rousing the Armenian population against the Genoese. At the same time fresh troubles broke out as a result of the alleged attempt to assassinate Nur-Devlet and other Tatar prisoners. As a result, the latter were removed from Kaffa to Soldaia. There was a plan to kill off a large number of the prisoners, in the belief that the retention in captivity of one single hostage would suffice to ensure the loyalty of the Khan towards the colonies. Kaffa was in a state of effervescence. The situation did not constitute a danger so long as the favourable political position held good. But in 1472 a number of far-reaching changes took place. This date marked the death of a man whose power equalled that of the Khan, namely Mamay Murza, head of the Chyrynes and master of the Crimean countryside. The citizens of Kaffa had managed to remain on good terms with him, doubtless because they regularly offered him "gifts". It was in all probability the people of Kaffa who had won over Mamay to the cause of Mengli-Ghirey during the latter's struggle for the Khan's throne. Mamay's death now raised the question of his succession. In theory, Mamay's will should have settled the matter on its own, but in practice the situation also required the consent of the suzerain Khan on the one hand and that of the authorities in Kaffa on the other. The latter made contact with Mengli-Ghirey, who paid a visit to Kaffa especially to this end. It would seem that the candidature of Eminek, the brother of Mamay, was adopted by Kaffa against the wishes of the Khan. Eminek had an exceedingly tumultuous past behind him, but he declared that he asked nothing better than to pass the rest of his life peaceably in his abode. The people of Kaffa evidently had their reasons for believing him. Was it considerations of money that had "convinced" them? This was certainly the view of those who witnessed these events. In point of fact, Eminek had not the slightest intention of contenting himself with his new title, which he regarded as a mere stepping-stone to higher honours: his real ambition was doubtless the Khan's throne. He presented Mengli-Ghirey with a provocative demand that the latter accord him the hand of his mother in marriage. The Khan, infuriated by the pretensions of his vassal, refused even to countenance such a demand. Thereupon Eminek decided to force his hand through the mediation of Kaffa, calculating that Mengli-Ghirey would have no choice but to submit to the will of the colony. When the people of Kaffa refused, Eminek broke off relations with Kaffa in June 1474 and banned all sale of grain to the colony, hoping by this means to wring concessions out of them. The blow was a hard one, and a rise in the cost of living was soon felt in the town. The situation was further complicated by other adverse developments. The long-standing Polono-Crimean alliance came to an end, Casimir IV now making overtures to the Golden Horde, which was a natural ally of the Polono-Lithuanian state in its struggle against the rising power of Muscovy. On the other hand, the Horde was a mortal enemy of the Ghireys, and laid claim to power in the Crimea. Mengli-Ghirey, while trying to persuade Poland not to change its policy, was unable to resist the demands of the group of murzas, with Eminek at their head, who called for the invasion of Polish Ruthenia.

This invasion, directed by the powerful murza Aïdar, was launched in July 1474. At about the same time, the Muscovite envoy Beklemišev paid a visit to the court of the Khan and endeavoured, on the instruc-tions of Ivan III, to bring the Crimea into the alliance against Casimir. We know that Eminek was in favour of this plan.

The inhabitants of Kaffa were in a state of alarm. They made every effort to preserve the traditional alliance with the Khan, counting on Polish support and trying to deter Mengli-Ghirey from launching the invasion. In the event of such invasion, they demanded, to make plain their attitude, that no Polish prisoners be sold before the receipt of the corresponding ransom. The colonial authorities doubtless feared that the Polish government suspected them of participating in the traffic of slaves from Poland. As we know, good relations with Poland were of primordial importance for Kaffa, both politically and in the field of communications. This explains why the politicians in Kaffa continued to assure the Polish envoys of their good intentions, even though they were aware that the Tatars had already sold Polish slaves to the Turks.

The success of the invasion strengthened the authority of those in favour of a warlike policy, and notably that of Eminek. He kept up the food blockade of Kaffa, which lived in a virtual state of siege. In addi-tion, rumour had it that the head of the Chyrynes was acting in concert with the Turks. This was the moment when Mohammed II, following his successes in the war with Venice and his victory over Uzun-Hassan, was preparing for war in the region of Moldavia, and hence not far from Kaffa. The question of suppressing Eminek now became a matter of urgency for Kaffa. At this point, the widow of Mamay tried to obtain the protection of the colonial authorities for her son Saïdak. The latter, in the hope of succeeding to the throne of his father, had sought the protection of the Horde, a step which brought the Crimea face to face with the danger of an invasion by the Tatars from beyond the Volga, who were only too eager to intervene in Crimean affairs. For Kaffa, the prospect of a war in the Crimea was a disastrous one. It was perhaps for this reason that the colony decided to support Saïdak and began to put pressure on the Khan. Mengli-Ghirey, anxious to be rid of Eminek, agreed to collaborate with Kaffa on this occasion. The Khan succeeded in winning over to his cause two high dignitaries: Aïdar and Kara-Mirza. Eminek was exiled, and a successor had to be found for him. Kaffa gave zealous support to Saïdak, confident that the new master of the Crimean countryside would be under their influence. They continued to back him, even when things became dangerous. Contemporaries again accused the consul and his advisers of being in the pay of the mother of Saïdak, which is not at all improbable.

Kara-Mirza and Aïdar helped to overthrow Eminek, but protested against the candidature of Saïdak. In his will, Mamay had named Aïdar as his successor. When the authorities in Kaffa persisted, forcing the Khan to back their decision, a revolt broke out in the Crimea. In February 1475, the whole of Tatar Crimea rallied to the malcontents. In all probability, the insurgents acted in concert with the Turkish legate who was in the Peninsula at the time. Eminek returned. The Khan and his followers took refuge in Kaffa. Mengli-Ghirey offered to mediate, but his efforts reportedly broke down in the face of the stubborn opposition of Kaffa, unwilling as it was to abandon Saïdak. During March, rumours had it that a Turkish invasion was imminent, and that the Turks had reached an understanding with the Tatar insurgents. These rumours turned out to be well founded. The Sultan was preparing for a decisive struggle against Moldavia. It was because he realized that this campaign would require an immense effort that he had concluded the armistice with Venice. The disorders in the Crimea admirably suited his plans to subdue the entire Peninsula. In the Sultan's strategy, the Crimean Tatars were called upon to play a vital role, both in the struggle against Moldavia and in the event of a possible conflict with Poland. His concerted action with the Tatars was of great assistance to him in his reduction of Kaffa—a town of immense importance for the Turkish ruler, constituting as it did an ideal point of departure for an assault on Moldavia and an invaluable strong-point reinforcing the whole position of the Empire in the Black Sea region. The arrival of a Moldavian garrison in Theodoros alarmed the Sultan. After his successes against Venice and Persia, he no longer needed to take account of the Genoese. Nor did he stand in fear of Poland, which was fully taken up with its feud against Hungary, and lacked sufficient forces to defend its Crimean satellites, as had already become evident during the struggles with Moldavia. In this situation, he entrusted the grand vizier Kedük-Ahmed Pasha with the task of capturing the Crimea. On 31 May, Turkish troops landed at Posidonia, not far from Kaffa. Their force was made up of 1,000 janissaries, 10,000 soldiers from Anatolia known as "Azapes", and 1,000 horsemen. The rebellious Tatars joined forces with the invaders. The siege of Kaffa began on June 1st. The Turks made use of their artillery. Panic ensued throughout the city and disorders quickly spread. The Greeks and Armenians called for the capitulation of the town, threatening to massacre the Italians if the authorities refused. They saw no hope of victory, feared the impending carnage and acts of plunder, and hoped that, once they had surrendered, the Turks would allow them to resume their normal life. Kaffa capitulated on 6 June. The population were assured that they need have no fear for their lives or their possessions; foreigners were given the option of leaving the town, or remaining. But Kedük-Ahmed did not keep his word—the prize which fell into his hands was too tempting to resist. In so acting, the Turkish commander was in fact only following the example of his sovereign, who never kept the engagements he concluded with weaker adversaries. Witnesses of these events have left us a detailed description. On 7 June, the population were disarmed. On the 8th and 9th, the invaders imprisoned large numbers of Poles, Wallachians, Georgians, and other foreigners, some of whom were massacred. The 9th and 10th witnessed a census of the people and their possessions. All this was carried out by members of the Kaffa parliament who, having once signed the capitulation, henceforth acted on behalf of the invading forces. On 12 and 13 June, the Turks took away as prisoners numbers of children from Catholic families, boys and girls aged between 7 and 20, an act which spread terror and despair throughout the town. According to eye-witnesses, the number of boys involved lay between 1,500 and 5,000, the number of girls around 450. Following this, the Turks took charge of some 3,000 slaves belonging to the Kaffa population.

On 17 June, the inhabitants were ordered to resume their normal occupations. While the Armenians and the Greeks were left in peace, the Italians were told to surrender half of their possessions, with the stipulation that this contribution must be in cash. This measure spread fearful confusion and set off a sudden disastrous fall in prices. In order to acquire the sums demanded, the Italians were obliged to sell their goods for practically nothing; it appears that even precious metals lost two-thirds of their value. Finally, on 3 September, the Italians were embarked on board ship and taken to Constantinople.[1] By this time, the Turks had occupied the whole of the Crimea and Tana. Mengli-Ghirey was also dispatched to Constantinople. Aïdar took over the Khan's throne, but a few years later Mengli-Ghirey returned as a vassal of the Sultan and resumed power. Kaffa would remain Turkish for three centuries, and acquired sordid fame as the most terrible of slave markets, the victims being mainly men captured by the Tatars in the Polish and Muscovite territories, whom they sold in turn to the Turks.

The fall of Kaffa had tremendous political and economic implications. Henceforth, the lands of the Black Sea basin lay under Turkish domination. The loss of Kaffa as an important centre of Levantine trade represented a cruel blow to both Moldavia and Poland. Trade in the Black Sea area, once so lively and so prosperous, was dealt its final death blow with the occupation of Kilia and Akkerman by the Turks in 1484. Levantine commerce had to explore new avenues. Who can say whether the loss of the Crimean colonies was not a factor in spurring Genoa on to find a sea passage to India and China via the Atlantic? If this were the case, it would seem fair to admit that the great discoveries of the Genoese Columbus were not altogether unconnected with the painful losses suffered earlier by his homeland on the shores of the Black Sea.

Bibliography

Antonovič V., *Kiev, ego sud'ba i značenie s 14 po 16 stoletie (1352–1569)*.
Bachmann O., *Geschichte Böhmens*, vol. 2, Gotha, 1905.
Banescu N., "Contributions à l'histoire de la seigneurie de Théodoro-Mangoup en Crimée", in *Byzantinische Zeitschrift*, 35, 1935.
Battistella A., *La Repubblica di Venezia ne suoi undici secoli di storia*, Venezia, 1921.
Berchet G., *La Repubblica di Venezia e Inei Persia*, Torino, 1865.

---

[1] Before the Second World War, this description struck me as of doubtful credibility. Following my recent experiences during the German occupation of Poland, I have revised my opinion. (*Author's note*).

Bratianu G. I., *Recherches sur le commerce génois dans la Mer Noire au XIIIe siècle*, Paris, 1929.

——, *Recherches sur Vicina et Cetatea Alba*, Bucuresti, 1935.

——, "La Question de l'approvisionnement de Constantinople", in *Byzantion*, 5, 1929.

Brosset M., *Additions et éclaircissements à l'histoire de la Géorgie depuis l'antiquité jusqu'en 1469 de J. C.*, St. Pétersbourg, 1851.

——, *Histoire de la Géorgie depuis l'antiquité jusqu'au XIXe siècle*, vol. 1, 2, St. Pétersbourg, 1851–1859.

Bruun F., "Bereg Černago Moria meždu Dnieprom i Dniestrom, po morskim kartam XIV-go i XV-go stoletii", in *Černomore*, č. 1, Odessa, 1879.

——, "Materialy dlia istoni Sugdiei", *ibid.*, č. 2, Odessa, 1880.

——, "O poseleniakh italianskikh y Gazarii. Topografičeskiia i istoričeskiia zametki", *ibid.*, č. 1.

Byrne E. H., *Genoese Shipping in the Twelfth and Thirteenth Centuries*, The Mediaeval Academy of America, Cambridge, Mass., 1930.

Caggese R., *Firenze dalla decadenza di Roma al risorgimento d'Italia*, vol. 2, Firenze, 1913.

Canale M. G., *Della Crimea, del suo commercio e dei suoi dominatori*, vol. 1, 2, Genova, 1855.

——, *Nuova istoria della repubblica di Genova*, vol. 1, 2, Genova, 1858–1860.

——, *Storia del commercio, dei viaggi, delle scoperte e carte nautiche degl' Italiani*, Genova, 1866.

Chapman C., *Michel Paléologue, restaurateur de l'empire byzantin (1261–1282)*, Paris, 1926.

Charewiczowa L., *Handel średniowiecznego Lwowa. Studia nad historią kultury w Polsce*, 1, Lwów, 1925.

Dublecki M., "Kaffa, osada genueńska i jej stosunek do Polski w XV w.," in *Przegląd Pow.*, 12, 1886.

Enzyklopaedie des Islams, Leiden, 1913.

Eysser R., "Papst Pius II und der Kreuzzug gegen die Türken," in *Mélanges d'histoire générale*, Bucuresti, 1938.

Fraknól W., *Matthias Corvinus, Konig von Ungarn*, Freiburg i. Br., 1891.

Friedberg J., "Zatarg Polski z Rzymem w czasie wojny trzynastoletniej," in *Kwart. Hist.*, 24, Lwów, 1910.

Gołębiowski K., *Dzieje Polski za panowania Kazimierza, Jana Olbrachta i Aleksandra*, vol. 3, Warszawa, 1848.

Górka O., "Białogrod i Kilia a wyprawa r. 1497", in *Sprawozdania z posiedzeń Tow. Nauk, Warsz.*, t. 25, z. 1–6, Warszawa, 1932.

Hammer J., *Histoire de l'Empire Ottoman depuis son origine jusqu'à nos jours*, vol. 3, Paris, 1836.

——, *Geschichte der Goldenen Horde im Kiptschak*, Pesth, 1840.

Heyd W., *Geschichte des Levantenhandels im Mittelalter*, vol. 1, 2, Stuttgart, 1879.

Hruszevski M., *Istoria Ukraini-Rusi*, vol. 4, 6, Kijów, Lwów, 1907.

Jorga N., *Geschichte des rumänischen Volkes*, vol. 1, Gotha, 1905.

——, *Geschichte des osmanischen Reiches*, vol. 2, Gotha, 1909.

——, *Studii Istorice asupra Chiliei si Cetatii Albe*, Bucuresti, 1900.

Karamzin N. M., *Historya państwa rossyiskiego*, vol. 6, Warszawa, 1826.

Kolankowski L., *Dzieje Wielkiego Księstwa Litewskiego za Jagiellonów*, Warszawa, 1936.

Kretschmayer H., *Geschichte von Venedig*, vol. 2, Gotha, 1920.

Linovskij V., "Podole, Wołyń i Ukraina. Obrazy miejsc czasów przez A. Przezdzieckiego", Wilno, 1841, Zap. Odessk. Obšč., 1, 1844.

Manfroni C., *Storia della marina italiana dal trattato di Ninfeo alla caduta di Costantinopoli, 1261–1453*, Livorno, 1902.

Manfroni C., *Storia della marina italiana dalla caduta di Costantinopoli alla battaglia di Lepanto*, Roma, 1891.

Marinescu C., "Pape Calixte III (1456–1458), Alfonse V d'Aragon Roi de Naples et l'offensive contre les Turcs", in *Bull. de la Section Hist. Académie Roumaine*, vol. 19, Bucarest, 1935.

Marini C. A., *Storia civile e politica del commercio dei Veneziani*, vol. 5, Vinegia, 1800.

Miller W., *The Latins in the Levant. A History of Frankish Greece (1204–1566)*, London, 1908.

Neri A., "Di Gottardo Stella e specialmente della sua legazione al Concilio di Mantova nel 1458", in *Giornale Ligustico*, 1876.

Nistor J., *Die auswärtigen Handelsbeziehungen der Moldau im XIV, XV, und XVI Jahrhundert*, Gotha, 1911.

Pastor W., *Geschichte der Päpste seit dem Ausgang des Mittelalters*, vol. 1, 2, Freiburg i. Br., 1901.

Pierling, *La Russie et le Saint-Siège*, vol. 1, Paris, 1896.

Pułaski K., *Stosunki Polski z Tatarszczyzną od połowy XV vieku*, vol. 1, Kraków, Warszawa, 1881.

Reumont L., *Lorenzo de' Medici il Magnifico*, vol. 1, Leipzig, 1874.

Rodocanacchi E., "Les esclaves en Italie du XIIIᶜ au XVIᶜ s.," in *Revue des questions hist.*, 79 (1906).

Sieveking K., *Genueser Finanzwesen vom 12 bis zum 14 Jahrhundert*, Freiburg i. Br., 1898.

——, "Die Genueser Seidenindustrie im XV u. XVI Jahrhundert", in *Schmollers Jahrbuch*, 21.

Smirnov, *Krymskoe khanstvo pod verkhovenstvom Ottomanskoi Porty do načala XVIII veka*, St. Petersburg, 1887.

Stachón B., *Polityka Polski wobec Turcji i akcji antytureckiej w wieku XV do utraty Kilii i Białogrodu (1484)*, Lwów, 1930.

Syroečkovskii V. E., "Puti i usloviia snošenii Moskvy s Krymom na rubeže XVI veka", in *Izv. Ak. Nauk SSSR*, Nr. 3,1932.

Thallóczy L., *Studien zur Geschichte Bosniens und Serbiens im Mittelalter*, München u. Leipzig, 1914.

Vasiliev A. A., *Histoire de l'Empire Byzantin*, vol,. 1, 2, Paris, 1932.

Voigt G., *Enea Silvio de' Piccolomini als Papst Pius der Zweite und sein Zeitalter*, T. 3, B. 1, Berlin, 1856–1863.

Volkov, "Četyre goda goroda Kaffy (1453–1456)", in *Zap. Odessk. Obšč.*, 8, 1872.

Wright, John Kirtland, *The Leardo Map of the World 1452 or 1453*, New York, 1928.

Zinkeisen, *Geschichte des Osmanischen Reiches in Europa*, vol. 2, Gotha, 1854.

CHAPTER FIVE

LEVANTINE TRADE WITH EASTERN EUROPE IN THE 16TH CENTURY. SOME PROBLEMS*

Following the studies undertaken by Fernand Braudel and his school, it is now accepted as an established fact that the discovery of the sea route to the East Indies did not, after all, ruin the commercial exchanges of the Mediterranean countries with the Levant. In fact, despite Portuguese domination of the sea passages round the Cape of Good Hope, this trade resumed after only a brief interval.

Previously, it was long considered that the changes in the major trading routes effected at that time also exercised an adverse influence on the economic relations between the Levant and East Europe, but today this view likewise requires re-examination. Thanks to recent studies by historians from various countries, we are today fairly well informed concerning the movement of precious metals during the Middle Ages. During the 13th and 14th centuries, Czech and Hungarian silver, as well as gold, mainly from the lands subject to the Crown of Saint Stephen, fuelled the exchange of goods between these regions, the West, and Italy, passing mainly *via* Venice. The vacuum caused by the crisis in the mining industry in the areas of production was filled, in the 14th and especially in the first half of the 15th century, by the massive importation of silver from Bosnia and Serbia into Venice and other Italian commercial centres.[1] Nor should one underestimate the importance of the gold from the Sudan which found its way to the

---

* Originally published in French as "Le commerce du Levant avec l'Europe de l'Est au XVIᵉ siècle. Quelques problèmes", in *Histoire économique du monde méditerranéen 1450–1650. Mélanges en l'honneur de Fernand Braudel,* Toulouse, 1973, pp. 349–359. Translation from French by Robin Kimball.

[1] B. Krekič, *Dubrovnik (Raguse) et le Levant au Moyen Age*, Paris-La Haye 1961, p. 29; M. J. Dinic, *History of the Mining Industry in Serbia and Bosnia in the Middle Ages* (in Serbo-Croat), 2 vols., Beograd, 1925, 1962, *passim*; D. Kovačević, *Bosnian Commerce in the Middle Ages* (in Serbo-Croat), Sarajevo, 1961, pp. 18ff., 52ff., etc. By the same author: "Le rôle de l'industrie minière dans le développement des centres économiques en Serbie et en Bosnie pendant la première moitié du XVᵉ siècle", in *Studia Balcanica*, 3, 1970; J. Božič, "The Economic and Social Development of Ragusa in the 14th and 15th Centuries" (in Serbo-Croat), *Istoricki Glasnik*, 1, 1949, pp. 46; 49ff.

shores of the Mediterranean in the course of the 14th and 15th centuries. The work by John Day contains a series of figures demonstrating that, in the second half of the 14th century, Sudanese gold appeared in considerable quantities both in Spain and in Genoa, and that it was used by the latter in its trade with the Levant.[2] It was towards the middle of the 15th century that Venice established closer relations with the Barbary coasts, mainly, it would seem, with a view to procuring Sudanese gold at a time when sources of supply of this metal in Transylvania and Central Europe were becoming exhausted, and when Turkish conquests in the Balkan peninsula had momentarily disrupted Ragusa's trade with its hinterland, and consequently with the flow of silver from these regions towards Italy. By contrast, Sudanese gold continued to pour into the sea-ports of the Maghreb, and thence towards Italy and Egypt. It also found its way to Cairo via trans-Saharian routes. Notwithstanding all that has been written on this subject, we still lack decisive proof that Portuguese expansion in West Africa put an end, in the 15th century, to the export of Sudanese gold towards the North and towards Egypt—which latter constituted an important staging post for black Moslem pilgrims on their way to the Holy Places of Islam. The traffic in gold closely associated with these pilgrimages continued throughout the 15th and 16th centuries.[3]

What was the situation in the countries of Central and Eastern Europe as regards trade with the Levant? I have pointed out on another occasion that oriental merchandise, spices in particular, reached these regions by diverse routes. Polish historians formerly insisted primarily on the importance of the continental routes which linked southern Poland to the Italian colonies on the shores of the Black Sea. Today it is recognized that, in the course of the 15th century, there was an increase in the import of oriental produce into Poland by way of Venice and Nuremberg.[4] As for Prussia and northern Poland, they received spices and drugs, not only via Lwów, but also through the intermediary of Hanseatic merchants who brought them, first from Brugge and later from Antwerp. It is thus clear that in the course of the 15th century the

---

[2] J. Day, *Les Douanes de Gênes, 1376–1377*. I, II, Paris, 1963, *passim*.

[3] M. Małowist, *The Large States of the Sudan in the Late Middle Ages* (in Polish), Warszawa, 1964, pp. 301–305.

[4] M. Małowist, "Les routes du commerce et les marchandises du Levant dans la vie de la Pologne au bas Moyen Age et au début de l'époque moderne", in *Atti del VI Colloquio Internazionale di Storia Marittima*, Firenze, 1972, pp. 164, 165; J. Ptaśnik, *Italia mercatoria apud Polonos saeculo XV ineunte*, Roma, 1910, pp. 1, 2, 6, 19, etc.

maritime routes gained considerably in importance. Muscovite Russia conducted its Levantine trade, at first *via* Tana and Soudak (Soldaia, in the Crimea) and subsequently, in the 15th century, through Kaffa (for which there is relatively clear documentary evidence of its Muscovite connections towards the end of the century).[5] As for Novgorod the Great, it drew on its supplies of Levantine produce, in part at least, by the routes that linked it with Brugge, thanks to the presence of the Hanseatic trade centre there.

We have few details concerning the trade balance between the countries of Eastern Europe and the towns on the Black Sea during the Middle Ages. Following the upheavals caused by Tamerlane's invasion and the ensuing collapse of his empire, the transcontinental routes linking the Black Sea with China all but disappeared. At the same time, Kaffa continued to maintain its connections with Constantinople, Trebizond, and other ports in Asia Minor, situated at the western end of the routes used by the silk industry in Iran and the Persian Gulf. Kaffa thus possessed stocks of silk, processed by professionals on the spot, together with a considerable quantity of spices. Both Armenian merchants, particularly numerous in the Crimea and in Belgorod (Akkerman), and Genoese exported these products to Poland and Russia, either by direct route or through the intermediary of Lwów and of Moscow.[6] On the other hand, textiles and other wares from Poland and the West, dispatched in the opposite direction, were probably not sufficient to square the trade balance between Poland and the Black Sea region. In this respect, the situation of north-eastern Russia *vis-à-vis* the Levant was perhaps more favourable for, ever since the 14th and especially during the 15th century, the city of Moscow had become an important centre for the trade in high-quality furs from the far North. It also exported wax, large quantities of hides, falcons, and a small amount of Western textiles obtained *via* Novgorod or through Lithuanian merchants. In addition, 15th-century Russia had already established trading connections, not only with the Crimea, but also with the ports of Asia Minor. In spite of this, it seems likely that commercial exchanges between Russia and the Near East forced Moscow

[5] V. E. Syroečkovskii, *Gosti-Surožanie*, Moskva-Leningrad, 1935, pp. 17ff., 23, 26, 27, 46.

[6] M. Małowist, *Kaffa, the Genoese Colony in the Crimea, and the Eastern Question, 1453–1475* (in Polish), Warszawa, 1947.

to export southwards some part of the precious metals in kind earned in her trade with the West.[7]

The Turkish conquest of Kaffa in 1475, and of other European Black Sea ports a few years later, was long regarded by historians as having dealt a serious blow at Poland and neighbouring countries. Recent research, however, has shown that the opposite was the case. True, commercial transactions between Lwów and the Levant were adversely affected, but only for a very limited period. Inalčik, who examined the Turkish customs registers for Kaffa and the European ports on the Black Sea, established that there was no diminution in receipts at the end of the 15th century, a fact corroborated by the satisfactory state of the region's commercial exchanges with Poland and Russia.[8] As for the Polish conflicts with Moldavia, a subject state of the Ottoman Empire, and with that Empire itself in the early 15th century, these were finally resolved around 1530. Poland's trade relations with the countries conquered by the Turks had already been established prior to this, and the situation had become a favourable one for the respective merchants involved. In Poland, the towns of Lwów and Lublin became centres of trade with the East, thanks mainly to the activities of the Armenian merchants settled in Poland and in the countries occupied or annexed by the Turks. Somewhat later, Jews from the Ottoman Empire also played an important part in this trade. In 16th century Poland, Turkish merchants were also tolerated. Those of them who bought and sold directly on the Sultan's account were given privileged status and, if their conduct was not always in line with established rules concerning foreign merchants in Poland, the authorities tended to look the other way. In the 16th century, Polish merchants were also active in the Ottoman countries, following the routes which led *via* the Rumanian principalities to Constantinople and Bursa. Sometimes they boarded ships at Belgorod or Chilia sailing for the Turkish capital and the ports of Asia Minor, but their preference was for the overland routes, where they would travel in caravans, conditions of security in

---

[7] M. V. Fehner, *Torgovlia Russkogo Gosudarstva so stranami Vostoka v XVI*, Moskva, 1956, *passim*.

[8] L. Charewiczowa, *The Commerce of the Town of Lwów in the Middle Ages* (in Polish), Lwów, 1925, pp. 77, 78; H. Inalčik, "L'Empire Ottoman", in *Actes du 1er Congrès International des Etudes Balkaniques et Sud-Est Européennes*, III, Sofia, 1969, pp. 87, 163.

the Ukraine being at that time far from satisfactory.[9] A glance at the types of merchandise in circulation reveals that they became widely diversified and also increased in volume by comparison with former times. In the light of findings by Rybarski and contemporary historians, it is clear that, in the second decade of the 16th century, spices and oriental silk wares passed from Turkey into Poland, and even further westwards. In 1530–1531, the Lublin fairs, in full expansion at the time, attracted numerous merchants, in particular Armenians from Kamieniec in Podolia, who brought from Turkey saffron, ginger, rice, cloves, etc. In 1548 the town of Lublin received permission from the king to install a wax foundry, which also made it possible to check the *res aromaticae* imported from Greece and Turkey. In this privilege, Rybarski rightly detected proof of the regular import of these products. Such imports from the East, via the Rumanian principalities, included grapes, sugar, cloves, saffron, etc. In this connection, pepper is seldom mentioned,[10] the main reason being that it reached Poland chiefly by sea, either from Antwerp, and thence through Gdańsk, or by the continental routes which linked the Netherlands metropolis to Leipzig and to Greater Poland. The agents of King Emanuel in Antwerp counted the Poles amongst their customers for the pepper which the Portuguese imported into Europe.[11] This, however, should not be taken as implying that pepper did not also arrive directly from the East. As we have already seen, the basis of Poland's commerce with the Levant became considerably wider in the course of the 16th century, due to a number of significant factors which should be enumerated here. From the turn of the 15th century at the latest, the amount of silver finding its way into Poland increased, thanks to the expansion of its maritime trade based on the export of cereals. This trend grew considerably more marked in the course of the 16th century, especially during the second half, when the price of agricultural products on Western markets underwent a particularly sharp rise. There was likewise a sharp rise in the population of the country,[12] as well as in the living standards of

---

[9] A. Dziubiński, "The Trading Routes between Poland and Turkey in the 16th Century" (in Polish), in *Przegląd Historyczny*, 1965, pp. 232–257.

[10] R. Rybarski, *Polish Trade and Trading Policy in the 16th Century* (in Polish), 2nd edition, vol. 1, Warszawa, 1958, p. 153.

[11] A. Braamcamp Freire, "A feitoria de Flandres", in *Archivo Historico Portuguez* VI, 1908, pp. 413–415; *idem*, Documentos, Nos. 43, 50.

[12] I. Gieysztorowa, "Research into the Demographic History of Poland", in *Acta Poloniae Historica*, 18, 1968, pp. 8–11.

the nobility and an important section of the bourgeoisie. These latter factors were also evident in the Ottoman Empire of the 16th century, but on a far vaster scale.[13] In the towns of Anatolia and the Balkans, industry and commerce were booming. The long period of peace between Poland and Turkey encouraged the movement of merchants between the two partners. Nor was it only a case of merchants from the Empire visiting Poland. Towards the close of the 16th century, Polish merchants established direct contacts extending as far as Persia; however, it was mainly in Turkey that they purchased Indian wares, saffron and alum from Asia Minor, rice from the Balkans, and indigo. They acquired mohair (textiles derived from goat's hair), camlet and silks from Bursa, sheepskins, articles of clothing, and pottery. Greek wines, especially Malmsey wine, were imported into Poland in considerable quantities.[14] Some of the luxury articles imported from the Ottoman Empire were subsequently reexported to Russia, the Baltic countries, and Germany. At this point one should mention another trade item of prime importance: the import of calves from Moldavia—a vassal state of the Sultan's—assumed such proportions in the 16th century that the Ottoman sovereigns were forced to put an end to this trade, which was endangering the supply of meat to the Turkish capital.[15] At the end of the 16th century, the number of calves reexported from Poland to Germany and Bohemia exceeded 40,000 per annum and was still increasing. A large proportion of these cattle, probably more than half, came from Moldavia. This traffic aided the development of those industries in Poland which treated the hides.[16]

According to sources that are unfortunately somewhat imprecise, Poland exported to the countries of the Ottoman Empire articles from the cloth industries of the Netherlands, England, and especially Germany and Silesia. In the course of the 16th and the first half of the 17th century, there was also a rise in the export of Polish cloth of superior quality, mainly from the towns of Brzeziny and Biecz. Other exports included metals, notably lead, tin, copper, or articles made from these metals or

[13] Ö. L. Barkan, "Essai sur les données statistiques des registres de recensement dans l'Empire ottoman aux XVᵉ et XVIᵉ siècles", in *Journal of the Economic and Social History of the Orient*, I, 1958, pp. 19–29.
[14] R. Rybarski, *op. cit.*, p. 121; A. Dziubiński, *op. cit.*, pp. 245, 246.
[15] M. Alexandrescu-Dersa, "Quelques données sur le ravitaillement de Constantinople au XVIᵉ siècle", in *Actes du Iᵉʳ Congrès International des Etudes Balkaniques*, p. 670. "Les édits du sultan Selim II en 1566–1568".
[16] Rybarski, *op. cit.*, pp. 68–71.

from iron, in particular agricultural implements.[17] Some of these articles were of military significance—in Poland a great craze had developed for the types of damaskeened sword (known as *damascènes*) imported from the South-East. In return, furs from Russia and Poland-Lithuania were supplied to Turkey. The subjects of the Sultan, in particular the merchants operating on his behalf, did not bring money into Poland, bartering their goods instead against those they wished to purchase. By contrast, Polish merchants visiting Turkey were obliged to take with them cash in kind to cover part of the purchasing costs. We have no figures concerning the exchange of merchandise between Poland and the Turkish Levant, but the factor just mentioned, together with the protests from the Polish Diets against the flight of money towards the South-East, suggest that the overall trade balance was unfavourable to Poland. Venetian agents in Constantinople around 1544 expressed themselves in this sense, and in my view this situation is characteristic of the whole period in question.[18] In the absence of adequate documentary evidence, however, it is impossible to say anything more detailed in this respect; it seems possible that researches in the Turkish archives might throw more light on this problem. It should be noted that the reexport to the West of Turkish and Rumanian merchandise helped to strengthen Poland's trade balance. Studies by Pelc have shown that the prices of eastern produce in Cracow followed the same curve as those of other articles.[19] This affords further proof that trade with the Levant did not suffer any excessive disruption as a result of the Great Discoveries. Cracow supplied itself with eastern produce by the routes leading from Turkey and from Venice. In conclusion, it is clear that the exchange of goods between Poland and the Turkish and Persian Levant increased considerably in the course of the 16th century, and that the *pax turcica* in South-Eastern Europe and Anatolia probably made an important contribution to the establishment of closer ties between this area and the countries situated further to the North.

A similar picture can be observed in connection with the commercial exchanges between the Levant and Muscovite Russia. In the middle of the 16th century, the Russians conquered the Tatar khanates of Kazan and Astrakhan. The first of these acquisitions provided Russia

---

[17] *Ibid.*, pp. 156, 157; Małowist, "Les routes du commerce...", pp. 170, 171.

[18] E. Alberi, *Relazioni degli ambasciatori veneti*, Series III, vol. I, p. 160.

[19] J. Pelc, *Prices in Cracow from 1369 to 1600* (in Polish), Lwów, 1935, pp. 42, 66, 67, etc.

with access to the supply of high-quality furs from beyond the Urals: Kazan had, from time immemorial, enjoyed economic links with the Siberian tribes, as had formerly been the case with the Great Bulgars, on the banks of the Kama river.[20] It should likewise be mentioned that, in the early Middle Ages, the trade fairs of Nizhni Novgorod, on the Volga, were attended by merchants from the Tatar countries and from Turkestan. Meanwhile, the occupation of Astrakhan opened up vistas of maritime access to Persia, a factor which the Muscovy Company, established in northern Russia in the mid-16th century, endeavoured to turn to its own advantage, albeit with little success.[21] The work by Mrs Fehner informs us that, from the middle of the 16th century onwards, the Russians exported to Iran and Central Asia their furs, their industrial products, and their firearms, manufactured mainly in Moscow; in return, from the South, they acquired for themselves silks, cotton textiles, pearls, and spices.[22]

The researches of Syroečkovskii and Fehner have demonstrated that trade with the Turkish Levant was of extreme importance to the Russians. Even before the demise of Genoese colonies in the Crimea, Russian merchants travelled in caravans as far as Kaffa, while the Genoese, the Armenians, and the Greeks from Kaffa made the journey to Moscow.[23] This trade increased considerably once the Turks had established themselves in the Crimea and the steppes of the lower Don, and had pacified those regions which had hitherto been insecure for travellers. In the course of the 16th century, the Turkish town of Azov, near the site of the ancient Tana, became an important centre of trade with Russia. The local Turkish authorities regarded the presence of Russian merchants there as the basis of their prosperity and the source of the income derived by the Sultan's treasury from the town of Azov. Meanwhile, Russians continued to frequent the Crimea, Constantinople, and the ports of Asia Minor. A part of the routes linking Moscow with Turkey traversed Polish territories, a fact which presented certain dangers for the Russians, frequently at war with Poland as they were. As a result, Russian merchants did their best to avoid these heavily populated

[20] S. V. Bakhrušin, *Očerki po istorii kolonizacii Sibira v XVI i XVII vv.*, Moskva, 1927, pp. 88ff.

[21] T. S. Willan, *The Early History of the Russia Company 1553–1603*, Manchester U.P., 1956, pp. 57–62, 121, 122, 145–154.

[22] Fehner, *op. cit.*, pp. 51–66.

[23] Syroečkovskii, *op. cit.*, pp. 27, 40–43.

regions, preferring to cross the steppes of the Caspian and the Black Sea region. Russia and Turkey attempted to set up a relay system to provide shelter for the diplomatic agents and the merchants of their respective countries. Notwithstanding the dangers presented by the Tatar nomads in the 16th century, these commercial exchanges continued to flourish and subsequently played a part of considerable importance. This traffic was facilitated by Russian agricultural and military colonization in the steppes of the higher Don and the Volga. Thanks to the access gained to Turkey and Persia, 16th-century Russia participated in the Levantine trade in these countries, acquiring spices, silks, pearls, precious stones, quality arms, and oriental textiles, in return for high-quality furs and hides, falcons, and a certain (probably very limited) quantity of western textiles which had reached Russia via the Baltic and West-East continental routes. It is impossible to make a detailed study of the trade balance between Russia, the Turkish Levant, and Persia, but it is generally considered to have been favourable to the more easterly countries. In the 16th century, the influence of Eastern civilization was far more marked in Russia than in Poland. As yet, Russia did not exploit her own supplies of precious metals, but her trading connections with the West, in full development at that time, brought in a considerable amount of money. This explains why the Hanseatic merchants tried, albeit in vain, to establish trade with the Russians on a barter basis. Money had already been flowing into Russian coffers since the 14th and 15th centuries. Russia's economic ties with Lithuania and Poland had the same consequences. Attman, the Swedish expert, analysed the trade balance in Narva on the basis of the customs registers for the period 1583–1617. According to his findings, the value of the merchandise exported by Russia during this period considerably exceeded that of the goods imported. The trade balance was restored by means of payments in kind or in precious metals, representing some 928,362 *dalers*.[24] This applies exclusively to the town of Narva after 1581 (the date of Swedish occupation), that is to say after the most prosperous period (1558–1581), during which it belonged to Russia and profited in no small measure from the favouritism of Ivan the Terrible. Willan, the historian of the Muscovy Company, was not prepared to express an opinion on the question of the trade balance between England and

---

[24] A. Attman, *Den ryska marknaden i 1500—talets baltiskapolitik 1558–1595*, Lund, 1944, pp. 53–57, 88–93.

Russia for lack of reliable documentation on this score. We thus have no information concerning the situation at Port Saint Nicholas, Archangel, and other Anglo-Russian trade centres. On the other hand, the same author estimates that the export of English cloth, copper, and tin to north-eastern Russia was modest in volume, whereas the purchase of Russian goods—linen, hemp, wax, furs, etc.—took place on a large scale and was of considerable importance to England.[25] Foreigners visiting Russia in the 16th century were struck by the abundance of gold and silver in the treasury of the tsar and among the high Russian nobility. It should be emphasized that the Russian sovereigns of the 16th and 17th centuries were the most powerful traders in the land, and that the aristocracy, both lay and ecclesiastical, were not averse to sharing in the profits emanating from this type of activity. As a result, Russia disposed of the financial means to balance its trade with the East.

The facts enumerated above enable us to draw a certain number of conclusions. They demonstrate in convincing fashion that, even following the discovery of the Cape route, Levantine commerce with the countries of East Europe continued to thrive. While the first wave of Turkish conquests in Southern Europe had been accompanied by ravages and destruction, the *pax turcica* of the late 15th and the 16th century favoured the economic development of the European and Anatolian provinces of the Empire. This explains the solid basis on which Turkey's relations with its northern neighbours were established. It is clear that Ottoman trade with Poland and Russia contributed in marked fashion to the flow of money and precious metals to the Near and Middle East. While historians see evidence of a weakening in the economy and power of the Ottoman Empire at the turn of the 16th century, they attribute this to factors that have nothing to do with the Levantine trade. It would perhaps be useful to undertake comparative researches on the beginnings of the decline of various powers at this stage, notably Spain, Turkey, and Poland. My view is that their territorial expansion in each case saddled them with onerous obligations which their still fragile economies were unable to cope with in the long term.

---

[25] Willan, *op. cit.*, pp. 187, 279–281.

CHAPTER SIX

POLAND, RUSSIA AND WESTERN TRADE
IN THE 15TH AND 16TH CENTURIES*

What part trade played in the economic evolution of sixteenth century Europe has been much debated, and in recent years our information on the subject has grown considerably. Nevertheless, a great deal remains to be discovered and clarified. Western scholars have until recently, with few exceptions, shown too little interest in the problems of trade with the east-European countries. Moreover, they have tended to treat Eastern Europe as a single area without distinguishing sufficiently between the historically very different regions within it. On the other hand several historians in Eastern Europe, who hold the fundamentally just view that production, and especially agriculture, is fundamental to economic evolution in precapitalist epochs, have in recent years often tended to underestimate the importance of trade, notably of international trade. But while it is true that trade depends on the general state of the productive forces and class relationships, nevertheless it may also affect the shape of these quite significantly. In this article I propose to touch on some problems of Polish and Russian history in the fifteenth and sixteenth centuries, the period when overseas trade became important for both countries, while their trading relations with the west to some extent determined the shape of west-European economic development. What I want to consider is, how, given a certain pre-existing social structure, this trade affected production, the markets and the distribution of social income in the areas with which we are concerned, and notably the interesting divergences between Polish and Russian developments. In the present state of research these questions cannot be conclusively answered. It is therefore likely that we shall, for a long time to come, have to revise our views in the light of new discoveries.

In the fifteenth century Baltic trade began to change its character. The export of bulk goods from the East to the West became increasingly important—i.e. cereals, timber and its by-products, industrial crops like

---

* Originally published in *Past and Present*, 13, 1958, pp. 26–41.

flax and hemp, and later on even wool, etc.—though the former articles
of export continued to remain important—i.e. furs and pelts, wax, etc.
Conversely the imports now included not only the luxury textiles of
the Flemish *grande draperie*, which was already in decline, but also
cloth of middling quality from Flanders, Holland and England, and
Breton, later also Portuguese salt which was of enormous importance
for the coastal regions of the Baltic. At the end of the fifteenth and in
the early sixteenth centuries colonial goods made their appearance.
Western and southern wines, silks and other luxury goods continued
to be imported in the same ways as before. By the end of the fifteenth
century at the latest Holland had come to depend, for part of its food
supplies, on the deliveries of Baltic grain,[1] while the development of
Dutch and English shipping was unthinkable without a regular supply
of East European timber, hemp, pitch and grease. Potash, wood ash,
animal fats and other products of Eastern Europe were already essential
for the growing industries of Holland and England. However, grain was
undoubtedly by far the most important eastern export, whose markets
expanded beyond the countries of North-Western Europe to reach the
Iberian Peninsula in the sixteenth century, and by the end of that century even Italy. Hence the old view that Baltic trade lost its importance
in the age of the great discoveries has long become untenable. On the
contrary, we now know that the Baltic countries became both the source
of western raw materials and a market for their exports, thus facilitating their relatively rapid industrialisation as well as the development
of their shipping, which in turn was essential for their conquest and
exploitation of their overseas colonies.

This picture of a harmoniously developing international division
of labour looks somewhat less idyllic when seen from the perspective
of East European social and economic development, though we shall
observe very considerable differences in the evolution of the various
eastern countries.

Our statistical sources are limited. Nevertheless, the figures of customs
tolls in the Sound and some other data allow us to make a number of
quantitative statements. We know that at the end of the fifteenth cen-

---

[1] As shown frequently in the Dutch sources, e.g. Amsterdam Gemeente Archief,
Privilegieboek, II, bl. 20; Ijzeren, Kapell 12 *Handvesten ofte Privilegien...der Stad
Amsterdam*, I (Amsterdam 1748), p. 69. All these are from the first two decades of
the sixteenth century. Cf. W. S. Unger, *De levensmiddelvervorziening der hollandsche
steden in de middeleeuwen* (Amsterdam 1916).

tury the grain exports from Gdańsk to the West amounted to about 10,000 Lasts per annum, which may be regarded as a minimum figure.[2] Other sources suggest that this was a period of rapid increase in the demand for Baltic grain, which, incidentally, led the aristocracies of all Baltic countries (with the exception of Sweden) to show a vastly increased interest in the grain trade.[3] We may recall that in the West this period already showed a rising trend in the price of agricultural products. Unfortunately the Sound Toll figures for Baltic grain are not recorded before 1562. Earlier material regarding Poland is found only in the published customs calculations for Włocławek on the Vistula (1537–1576), which throw a good deal of light on the export of the areas in the Vistula basin south of that town.[4] Naturally these cover only a part of Polish exports. Thus exports from Eastern Great Poland and part of Kujavia, an extremely fertile and well-cultivated area, went through Bydgoszcz, while Toruń was a great export centre for Mazovian and Kujavian grain, and Polish Prussia, an important producing area, exported direct to Gdańsk. For the first half of the century only figures for 1537, 1544 and 1546 are preserved in Włocławek, which exported by water, respectively, 6,739, 2,562 and 6,483 Lasts, mainly of rye.[5] One is inclined to agree with Rybarski, that the total Polish grain exports at this time probably did not greatly exceed the quantities attained at the end of the fifteenth century.[6] By 1555 a startling increase had taken place: 19,000 Lasts were exported through Włoclawek, after which the figures fluctuate between 6,416 Lasts (1558) and 24,826 Lasts (1562). The average annual export for the period 1555–76 was about 14,719 Lasts; there are no figures for 1562–7 and I have neglected the negligible quantity of 426 Lasts exported in 1572, doubtless the result of harvest failure. If we leave out 1558, the minimum annual export (1560) was 10,595 Lasts.[7] As for the exports to Gdańsk in the last quarter of the sixteenth century, we must rely on the figures of the customs office of

---

[2] V. Lauffer, *Danzig's Schiff-u. Warenverkehr am Ende d. 15. Jh.* (Ztschr. d west-preussischen Geschichtsvereins, XXIII (1894), *passim*).

[3] M. Małowist, "Über den Handel des Adels in den Ostseelaendern im 15. u. 16. Jh" (*Hansische Geschichtsblaetter*, LXXV (1957)).

[4] St. Kutrzeba and Fr. Duda, *Regesta thelonei aquatici Wladislaviensis saeculi XVI* (Cracow 1915).

[5] *Ibid.*, pp. 14, 22, 36.

[6] R. Rybarski, *Handel i polityka handlowa Polski w XVI w.* (Polish Trade and Trade Policy in the Sixteenth Century) (Poznań, 1928), p. 29.

[7] *Regestra thelonei, passim*.

Weissenberg for 1579 and 1588, which point to grain exports of about 18,259 and 46,363 respectively.[8] This probably gives us something more like an order of magnitude for all Polish grain-export than Włocławek data. The enormous difference presumably reflects variations in the harvest yield in these two years.

After 1562 we have the figures for the Gdańsk grain exports to the West via the Sound. These also fluctuate sharply, but show a tendency to rise, especially in 1562–65, after which peak the exports nevertheless normally remain twice or three times as high as at the end of the fifteenth century. After 1591 we once again observe a rapid increase. However, the record figures of 1608: 66,397 Lasts, 1614: 52,716 Lasts—and above all of the peak year 1618: 84,493 Lasts—are somewhat exceptional. In other years it is the exception for exports to be higher than 43,000 Lasts, and indeed they are normally somewhat lower.[9] Of course it is commonly realised that the Sound Toll figures give us something near the minimum limits of grain exports to the West. Grain was smuggled through the Great Belt, in order to avoid paying customs at Oeresund, and it is likely that some grain was exported from Gdańsk on ships which made intermediate stops in the ports of Western Pomerania and Mecklenburg, and were listed accordingly, for it was the practice of masters to give the customs authorities at Helsingoer simply the name of the last Baltic port from which they sailed westward. Moreover, some Polish grain was transported by river to Stettin, where it was taken over chiefly by Dutch merchants for further delivery to the West. Grain exports by sea, and notably those of rye from Poland, were therefore almost certainly larger than the quoted figures indicate.

As for other products, Rybarski has drawn attention to the decline in Polish timber and allied exports, which may be explained by the expansion of the area under tillage at the expense of the forests. These underwent drastic contraction at this period, e.g. in East Mazovia, which had been formerly densely wooded. Lithuania and chiefly White Russia now became the chief suppliers of timber to the West, via the ports

---

[8] Rybarski, *op. cit.*, II, pp. 27, 38; D. Krannhals, *Danzig und der Weichselhandel in seiner Bluetezeit vom 16. bis zum 17. Jh.* (Leipzig 1942), p. 9.

[9] N. E. Bang and K. Korst, *Tabeller over Skibsfart og Varetransport gennem Oresund 1497–1660*, II, p. 98ff.

of Königsberg and Riga,[10] which also exported growing quantities of hemp and flax westwards.

Maritime imports to Poland and Lithuania in the sixteenth century included English and a certain quantity of Dutch cloth, salt, which was particularly important for the Riga trade with Lithuania and White Russia, herrings, wines, spices, silks, etc. It is extremely difficult to strike the balance of this maritime trade for Poland. Posthumus, who investigated the relations between Gdańsk and Amsterdam in the second half of the fifteenth century, suggested that Gdańsk had an export surplus. My own researches have led me to the same view. A. Christensen, who discusses the matter in the light of the papers of the firm of Adrichem in Delft for the end of the sixteenth century, comes to the same condusion.[11] I therefore believe that this hypothesis is correct, and applies to the whole of the sixteenth century. Admittedly, Heckscher long since pointed out that maritime commerce did not determine the total balance of trade of the East European countries. We know that Poland had overland trading relations with the West through Poznań and Silesia. Large herds of cattle were driven into Germany, very considerable quantities of skins and furs were exported and research is in progress to show that a good deal of grain also went that way; as did many goods of Russian origin—furs, pelts, wax, etc. Conversely Silesian, Lusatian and Czech cloth of middling quality, quite important quantities of English and Dutch cloth, a number of iron and steel products—notably agricultural implements—and similar goods were imported into Poland.[12] However, when we consider the high proportion of raw materials among the Polish exports, and the favourable terms of trade which these enjoyed in the sixteenth century, we may reasonably assume that Poland's balance of trade was active in this commerce also.

---

[10] Rybarski, *op. cit.*, I, p. 50.

[11] N. W. Posthumus, *De Oosterse Handel te Amsterdam* (Leiden 1953), p. 23ff.; M. Małowist, *Studia z dziejów rzemiosla w okresie kryzysu feudalizmu w Zach. Europie w XIV i XV w.* (Studies in the History of the Handicrafts in Western Europe during the Crisis of Feudalism in the Fourteenth and Fifteenth Centuries) (Warsaw 1954), p. 430; A. Christensen, *Dutch trade in the Baltic about 1600* (Copenhagen 1941), p. 390ff. Dutch and Danzig sources of the period agree that Dutch merchants exported coins, silver and gold eastwards, while Dutch ships often made the journey to Gdańsk in ballast.

[12] Rybarski, *op. cit.*, I, p. 160ff.; A. Mączak, *Sukiennictwo wielkopolskie XIV–XVII w.* (The Cloth Industry in Great Poland from the Fourteenth to Seventeenth Century) (Warsaw 1955), p. 228.

Trade with the West may well have enabled Poland and Lithuania to cover possible deficits in their trade with Russia and Turkey, which was lively in the sixteenth century. The country imported not only the valuable products of the North-East, but also (from Turkey) cotton and silk fabrics, spices, for which there was then a great demand in Poland, to some extent cattle and other goods. On the other hand it re-exported a significant quantity of Western imports to Russia, Turkey and Hungary, not to mention the export of the products of Polish mining and handicrafts. It is therefore unlikely that much of the stream of money which was presumably entering Poland from the West in consequence of its permanent export surplus, flowed out of the country to the East or South-East. The nobility and the wealthier burghers, especially in the great centres of sixteenth-century Polish trade, raised their standard of living rapidly. Even wealthy peasants sometimes still appear to have disposed of sizeable quantities of cash. This points to a country which was far from suffering a currency shortage.

That bullion was accumulated is clear. A more important question is, in whose hands it accumulated and for what purposes it was used. Here we must first draw attention to the remarkably privileged position which a few ports, chiefly Gdańsk and Riga, built up within the area of Polish maritime commerce. The flourishing state of Gdańsk in the sixteenth and the first half of the seventeenth centuries can be explained only on the assumption that the city was not merely the chief entrepôt for the growing grain exports to the West, but also the chief market at which the Polish grain suppliers who came there bought Western imported goods. Gdańsk must have earned considerable profits from this trade, some of which served to establish a growing domination over the producers for, as is well-known, the Danzigers granted them short-term credits which, in the course of time, became long-term credits. It is also well known that they attempted to influence the policy of the kings and of leading magnates through loans and "gifts." Though the occasions for these were often ostensibly political, they had economic objects, for any collapse of the political autonomy of Gdańsk would have undermined the city's privileged position as a trading monopolist, which was under frequent attack from the nobility.

This brings us to the second aspect of our problem, the enormous increase in the nobility's share in the trade with Gdańsk, and to a probably smaller extent, with Silesia and Germany, in the course of the sixteenth century. In the course of this century the nobles decisively outdistanced the urban merchants, who, in any case, often operated merely as agents of the aristocracy, particularly towards the end of our period.[13] This was of capital importance. For it is clear that under the circumstances a large proportion of the profits whose source we have just discussed fell into the hands of the nobles, especially those wealthier ones who were in a position to deal directly with Gdańsk. Another factor must also be considered. As in the West, the sixteenth century—and especially its second half—saw a marked price rise in Poland, the prices of agricultural products rising faster than those of other commodities. Since the foreign demand for Polish corn was increasing, the incentive to expand Polish agriculture was consider-able. The problem of technical progress in Polish farming during our period has not been adequately investigated, but we may assume that there were no particularly sensational innovations, for the agricultural handbooks compiled for the Polish nobility at this time do not record notable progress. Moreover, transport costs remained very high, even by water. In view of all this agricultural expansion led to a growth of an economy based on peasant labour services, as may already be observed by the end of the fifteenth century. This did not lead to particularly sharp opposition from the peasantry, for the brisk demand for farm produce softened their discontent. Part of the wealthier peasantry remained relatively prosperous in the sixteenth and even at the begin-ning of the seventeenth century, though the large number of landless men, the migrations of peasants and other symptoms of flight from the land suggest that many of the poorer peasantry were rapidly being ruined in the course of the sixteenth century. All things considered, we may assume that the undoubted increase in Polish grain production (and, notably in the eastern provinces, of animal production also) was initially achieved chiefly by increasing the cultivated area, i.e. by cul-tivating hitherto thinly populated or unpopulated lands. It seems also reasonable to seek a connexion between this increase in the demand for Polish farm produce and the increasingly obvious annexationist tendencies of Polish magnates in the Ukraine in the second half of the sixteenth and at the beginning of the seventeenth century, as well as with their politically dangerous adventures in Turkish Moldavia, where cattle breeding was highly developed. It might also be desirable to think of it in connexion with the settlement of numerous Polish nobles in Livonia, after that country came under Polish rule, and especially after

---

[13] This is almost typical of the entire Baltic area, except Sweden.

1581. (This colonisation led to an intensified exploitation of the local peasants, whose subsequent discontents were to be successfully utilised by the Swedes.)

Though the Polish price structure was in principle similar to that in the West, the local situation had certain peculiarities. The new prices arose at a time when the export of food and raw materials and the import of foreign industrial and luxury goods increased constantly, a process naturally enjoying the fullest support of the nobility which, as we have seen, greatly benefited from it. The Polish nobility was exceedingly powerful, thanks to its extraordinary numerical strength, its organisation and its military power. I have elsewhere described its policy as the very opposite of that of Western mercantilism:[14] they were for free trade. Under Polish (as under Pomeranian and Mecklenburg) conditions this economic policy could prevail. For the reasons already mentioned, it met with no great resistance from part of the peasantry. The merchants of the larger towns hastened to take part in the trade from which they derived considerable profit. But these developments tended not only to disadvantage the poorer, and numerically preponderant part of the peasantry, but also undermined the foundation of the handicrafts which produced for a mass market. Many branches of Polish industry collapsed towards the end of the sixteenth century, for obvious reasons: raw materials were expensive, and in short supply, living costs high, foreign competition acute, and a large part of the peasantry were on the road to pauperisation. We may thus observe that mercantile capital tended to withdraw from production, rather than to invest in it, a tendency which may be clearly observed even a century earlier. It is characteristic that the nobility, which controlled the ironworks in the second half of the sixteenth century, transformed most of them into corn mills.[15] Foreign trade, and especially Baltic trade, helped by the existing class structure of the country, favoured the conversion of the country into a purely agrarian economy, hindered the development of handicrafts and its transformation into industrial production. The classes interested in craft and industry were still too weak, and incapable of energetic resistance.

For all these reasons Poland gradually acquired an economy which, at bottom, is close to the classic colonial pattern. Nor was this without

---

[14] M. Małowist, *Über den Handel... op. cit.*

[15] M. Małowist, *Evolution industrielle en Pologne du XIVe au XVIIe siècle*, in *Scritti in onore di Armando Sapori*, I (Milan 1957), and the literature cited there.

influence on the country's culture, or even on its national character. Land became the only important source of wealth. The wealthy noble-man, exploiting his serfs, and thus able to acquire a standard of living suitable to his social station, became the only man worthy of respect. Large merchants, and many men from the circles of the more pros-perous industrial entrepreneurs were to ape the nobility. What were the ideals propagated by the two great Polish poets of the sixteenth century, Rey and Kochanowski, two men who, though they differed both in education and talent, nevertheless championed, in a manner very characteristic of the time, certain patterns of life which were to remain influential among many subsequent generations? The style of life of which they dreamed was that of retirement to the countryside, far from the storms of the world. The social groups in western countries, whose members blazed the trail of rapid economic development, had far different objects and ideals in life.

Such was the situation in Poland, or for that matter in the similar areas of North-Eastern Germany and Western Pomerania. In Russia, however, it was rather different. There the period since the sixteenth century saw, as we all know, a considerable growth of the productive forces and an increasingly close integration of the constantly expanding territory. There, moreover, the governments were proverbially anxious to secure their own "window on the world", though in our period they did not succeed in this object except along part of the White Sea. However, I should like to draw attention to some other factors which throw light on the importance of overseas trade in Russian economic life.

As we have seen, West European corn deficits were filled by imports from Eastern Germany, Poland and Livonia, countries which also exported a number of other agricultural and animal products. However, the corn trade was of no importance for Russian dealings with the West. Foreigners sought there mainly commodities like flax, hemp, and skins. In earlier periods they bought mainly, luxury goods such as furs and specialities such as wax, which played no fundamental part in the production or home market of the country. We know, thanks to the researches by Schroeder, Hollihn, Niitemaa and others,[16] that Russian trade through Livonia expanded so sharply at the end of the fifteenth

---

[16] E.g. V. Niitemaa, *Der Binnenhandel in der Politik der livlaendischen Städte im Mittelalter* (Helsinki 1952). G. Hollihn, *Die Stapel u. Gaestepolitik Rigas* (*Hansische Geschichts*, bl. 60 (1935)).

and in the first half of the sixteenth century, that both the eastern and western Hanseatic towns made efforts to repress it, or at least to confine it to the major Livonian trading centres. Owing to the rivalries among the local burghers, nobles and the Livonian Order those efforts failed. In spite of the hostility of the Hanseatic towns, the international commercial importance of the non-Hanseatic Narva, Ivangrod and the Swedish Viborg grew. At least the Russo-Livonian war of 1557 led to a temporary concentration of Russian trade with the West in Viborg, while the trade of Narva expanded rapidly during its Russian period (1558–1581). Attman's work has shown that Russia's main exports in this trade consisted of flax, hemp, grease, furs and wax,[17] i.e. in the main products of the North Baltic hinterlands of Pskov and Novgorod. Furs occupied only the second place in this list. Narva's chief imports from the West were English, and probably also Dutch cloth and salt, silks and other luxury articles, metal goods, including probably arms and ammunition. In spite of the obstacles put in the way of Narva by Poland and Sweden, its trade became rather important for England, Holland, the Southern Netherlands, the western Hanse towns, and even for France. The same period saw, from 1553–4, a rapid development of Anglo-Russian trade at the mouth of the eastern Dvina (Archangel), whence furs and pelts were primarily exported, but also other goods of the kinds already described. In the last quarter of the century the Dutch entered this trade, and almost excluded the English, French and other foreigners from it.[18] The English attached extraordinary importance to this White Sea trade, which appeared to open large markets for their textiles, but it was not without importance for the Dutch either.[19]

---

[17] A. Attman, *Den ryska marknaden i 1500—talets baltiska politik 1558–1598* (Lund 1944), p. 153ff.

[18] I. Lubimenko, *Les relations commerciales et politiques de l'Angleterre avec la Russie avant Pierre le Grand* (Paris 1933), p. 188ff.; J. E. Elias, *Het voorspeel van den eersten Engelschen Oorlog*, I (Hague 1920), p. 27; E. C. G. Brunner, *De ontwikkeling van het handelsverkeer van Holland met Oosteuropa tot einde der 16. eeuw* (*Tijdschrift voor Geschiedenis*, XLI (1926)).

[19] Lubimenko, *op. cit.*, p. 95ff.; T. S. Willan, *The Muscovy Merchants of 1555* (Manchester 1953), p. 24. For the importance of the Baltic and Russian markets for the Dutch textile industry, cf. the practice of the journeymen and servant "Lakenbereiders" in Amsterdam in the first half of the seventeenth century. They would draw up their wage demands in the period preceding the departure of the ships for the Baltic and Northeast. Cf. J. G. Van Dillen, *Bronnen tot de geschiedenis van het bedrijfleven en het gildewezen van Amsterdam* (Hague 1933), II, No. 1165.

What of Russia's balance of trade? Christensen and Attman consider that the country had a large export surplus in the sixteenth and seventeenth centuries.[20] Heckscher, and more recently Jeannin, have expressed reservations about this, arguing that the overland trade between Russia and Poland-Germany might well have had a different pattern, and that no balance of Russian trade can be struck without considering it.[21] Unfortunately Wawrzynczyk's study of trade between Poland-Lithuania and Russia in the sixteenth century, and Koczy's research into the trade of Poznań—an important centre on the relevant trade routes—do not clarify the matter.[22] However, the information collected in these studies does not suggest a Russian deficit. Łowmiański, who has worked on the history of Mohylów, whose importance in Lithuanian-Russian trade was considerable in the second half of the sixteenth century, inclines to the view that Lithuania was obliged to export coin to Russia in order to pay for imports from that country.[23] It is, of course, possible that a large part of the Western bullion which thus flowed into Russia as payment for goods bought there, continued its way into Turkey and Persia. Fehner's monograph on the subject of Russia's eastern trade unfortunately does not discuss the problem. However, she has conclusively shown that Russia sent large exports to the southern Orient, consisting not only of re-exported Western goods, but also of her own products, both of the kind which were exported to the West, and native handicrafts.[24] This must obviously have helped to redress the trade balance on Russia's side, though it is still likely that the country was in deficit with the East, in view of the expensive luxury goods imported from there. A certain flow of bullion eastwards out of Russia therefore seems quite probable.

---

[20] Attman, *op. cit.*, p. 87ff.; A. E. Christensen, *Sundzollregister und Ostseehandel* (*Pirma Baltijas Vesturniku Konference*) (Riga 1938), p. 398ff.

[21] E. F. Heckscher, *Oeresundstullräkenskaperna och deras behandling* (*Historisk Tidskrift*, II (1942); P. Jeannin, *L'économie française au milieu du 16e s. et le marché russe* (*Annales* 1954, I.).

[22] A Wawrzyńczyk, *Studia z dziejów handlu Polski z Wielkim Księstwem Litewskim i Rosją w XVI w.* (Studies in the Trade of Poland with Lithuania and Russia in the Sixteenth Century) (Warsaw 1956); L. Koczy, *Handel Poznania do połowy XVI w.* (Poznań's Trade until the Middle of the Sixteenth Century) (Poznań 1930).

[23] H. Łowmiański, *Struktura gospodarcza Mohylowa w czasach pomiary włocznej* (The Economic Structure of Mogilev during the Lithuanian Agrarian Reform in the Sixteenth Century), in *Roczniki dziejów społecznych i gospodarczych*, VIII (1939), I, pp. 64–5.

[24] M. V. Fehner, *Torgovla russkogo gosudarstva so stranami Vostoka v XVI vyeke* (Moscow 1956), p. 51ff.

It is natural to ask: what happened to the bullion which accumulated in Russia by this means? It has frequently been observed that the tsars disposed of considerable quantities of valuable goods, the yield of payments in kind: furs, pelts, wax and the like. The advance of the Russian frontiers in the North, in the South-East up to the Urals, and later the gradual conquest of Siberia, increased its potential supplies of these articles further. Thus the tsar's treasury acquired a mass of commodities, especially furs, admirably suited for export, all the more so as their very high price probably limited their sale in the home market.[25] Now the best expert on the history of Siberia in the sixteenth and seventeenth century, Bakhrushin, has shown how the export trade via the White Sea brought wealth to numerous native Russian merchants, and even facilitated the rise of peasants, who drew profits from it, to merchant status. The capital accumulated by these means, he argued, contributed to the rapid increase in mercantile wealth.[26] The Stroganov family, whose legendary wealth came from the Urals and the Siberian trade, was by no means the only case of its kind. (It is tempting, incidentally, to draw a parallel between the growth of the Stroganov fortunes and that of the contemporary dynasty of the Fuggers in the West). Bakhrushin held that the accumulation of capital through the White Sea trade, accelerated the colonisation of the thinly populated eastern regions, and the exploitation of their natural wealth, notably the development of the salt and iron industries.[27] I find myself in general agreement with this view, though this must not be thought to exclude the view that peasant migrations were of major importance in the economic development of eastern Russia and Siberia.

On the other hand, though the powerful Russian monasteries doubtless participated in foreign trade, Russian researches seem to show that their chief role, and an extremely important one, was in internal commerce. They appear to have traded with the mass of payments in kind (chiefly in grain) which they acquired from the peasants, and also to have provided a commercial link between Central Russia and the North

[25] A. G. Mankov, *Tseny i yikh dvizhenie v russkom gosudarstve XVI vyeka* (Prices and their Movements in the Russian State in the Sixteenth Century) (Moscow-Leningrad 1951), p. 61ff., has drawn attention to the modest part of furs in Russian internal trade, without explaining it.
[26] S. V. Bakhrushin, "Torgovye krestianie v XVII v." (Peasant Trade in the Seventeenth Century), in *Nauchnye Trudy*, II, p. 121.
[27] S. V. Bakhrushin, "Promyshlennye predpriatia russkych torgovych lyudei v XVII v." (Industrial Activities of Russian Traders in the Seventeenth Century), in *op. cit.*, p. 224ff.

and North-East.[28] Nor does it seem that the nobility, whether the old *boiars* or the new *pomieshchiki*, played a large part in Russian foreign trade in the sixteenth century, though this trade naturally affected their economy, if to a far smaller extent than in Poland. This brings us to a further problem. Grekov and other Russian historians have argued very strongly that the rise of serfdom, which began in Russia in the second half of the sixteenth century, was determined not by the demand of foreign markets, but by that of the home markets.[29] This is no doubt true for Russia, but the statement should also interest us from a slightly different point of view. How, we might ask, was Russian grain production linked with the internal grain deficit areas, which were often far distant? Russian students have long drawn attention to the importance of the grain exports from Central Russia to the North, the North-East, and in the early stages even to Siberia.[30] This greatly assisted the settlement of these territories, whose natural wealth was so vast, and eventually strengthened their political bonds with the centre of the Russian state.

Some general remarks may conclude this brief discussion of East European trade. It is clear that the international commerce of the Baltic and later of the White Sea cannot be regarded as something which unilaterally affected the economies of the East European peoples from outside. On the contrary, the economic expansion of Poland and Russia in the fifteenth and sixteenth centuries caused both the Polish-Lithuanian state, the Russian city-states of Novgorod and Pskov, and later the Muscovite state, to strive stubbornly for a direct trading link with the West, whither they wanted to send the excess products of their agriculture and cattle-raising, and whence they wanted to import craft products, luxury articles, salt, etc. As late as the fifteenth century Polish merchants still appeared on several occasions in the Netherlands, while the Russians pushed their independent trade in the north-eastern ports of the Baltic. Those developments coincided with the creation of

---

[28] Mankov, *op. cit.*, p. 26ff.

[29] B. D. Grekov, *Krestianie na Russi s drevneishikh vremen do XVII v.* (Russian Peasants from the Earliest Times to the Seventeenth Century) (Moscow-Leningrad 1946); *Ocherki Istorii SSSR, Konets XV v.— nachalo XVIII v.* (Moscow 1952); a German edition of this last work, under the title: *Geschichte der USSR*, Bd. III: *Ende des 15. bis Anfang des 17.Jh.*, Berlin, is in preparation.

[30] Kostomarov, *Ocherk torgovli Moskovskogo gosudarstva v XVI i XVII stoletiakh* (Sketch of the Trade of the Muscovite State in the Sixteenth and Seventeenth Centuries) (St. Petersburg 1862), pp. 98ff., 113.

national-territorial markets in Poland in the fifteenth century, in Russia
in the sixteenth century. Several obstacles had to be overcome in those
struggles for direct access to the Baltic, above all the resistance of the
two states of the Teutonic Knights (the Prussian and the Livonian)
which lay between Poland and Russia, and the sea. In this the eastern
states were only partially successful, Poland gaining access to the mouth
of the Vistula, Lithuania and Russia weakening the Livonian Order,
thanks to their own political and economic consolidation, and extorting
important trade concessions from it. The second important problem was
the Russo-Polish struggle for the weakening of the Hanseatic monopoly
over trade in the Baltic and its hinterland. Here again success was only
partial. For though Gdańsk, Riga and Revel (Tallinn) eventually lost the
support of their inland establishments in Kaunas, Polotsk, Novgorod,
etc., their great accumulation of capital enabled them to continue to
exploit the wealth of the hinterlands, and to maintain their position as
intermediaries between Eastern and Western Europe. In the course of
the fifteenth and sixteenth centuries the Polish, Lithuanian and Russian
movement to win access to maritime commerce was reinforced by an
analogous English and Dutch movement to conquer the markets of
Eastern Europe for their own manufactures, and to control the vital
import of foodstuffs, agricultural raw materials, timber, certain metals, etc., through the Baltic, as well as by other routes. In the fifteenth
and sixteenth centuries this led to several conflicts between England
and Holland on one side, the Hanseatic cities on the other. As a result
the former predominance of Lübeck in the Baltic trade was severely
weakened, though even in the sixteenth century the English and Dutch
had not wholly succeeded in destroying it, while on the other hand
the Hanseatic cities in the Baltic increasingly confined themselves to the
functions of passive intermediaries between their hinterlands and the
West, from which they continued to derive great profits.

It seems probable that this East-West trade gave the East a permanently active trading balance. Nevertheless the English and Dutch
gained enormous advantages from it. Not only did they gain considerable markets for their products, and a regular supply of basic raw
materials, essential for their subsistence and for the development of
their industry and high seas shipping. They also gained a number of
goods suitable for re-export to other Western countries, especially to
the Iberian Peninsula. This greatly favoured the expansion of Dutch,
but also English, trade and capital accumulation in both countries, a
matter of essential importance not only for the trade, but also for the

industry of England and Holland. France and the Southern Netherlands seem to have played a rather secondary part in all this. It is difficult to envisage rapid economic development in Holland, and partly also in England, in the sixteenth and seventeenth centuries, without the constant deliveries of East European grain, hemp, flax, timber, etc., and without the markets for Western and Colonial products which the East provided. When the Dutch States General called the Baltic trade the "mother trade" they were being no more than realistic.[31] Would the colonial, industrial and trading expansion of Holland and England have been possible at all without a prior strengthening of their contacts with Eastern Europe? It seems improbable.

Something like an economic division of Europe therefore appears in the fifteenth and sixteenth centuries. How are we to judge it, not in the Western perspective, but in that of Polish and Russian interests? The bitter struggles which both countries waged for access to the Baltic demonstrates the importance they attached to their participation in this international trade. So does the long-lasting Russian policy which aimed at the encouragement of English and Dutch trade on the White Sea coast. The sea trade gave to Russia and Poland a secure market for their products, facilitated the import of articles in short supply—i.e. not produced locally in sufficient quantities—and probably provided a considerable inflow of bullion, which in turn improved their trading possibilities with the countries further to the South and East. However, the trade developed in a form determined by locally prevelent social and economic circumstances, and affected those in turn. Here the histories of Russia and Poland diverge. Though both countries failed to make themselves independent of the expensive mediation exercised by the Baltic coastal towns, Russia, thanks to the opening of the White Sea route in the mid-sixteenth century, was more favourably placed than Poland. In Poland the trade favoured above all the interests of Gdańsk and of the nobility, partly also of the large merchants. The interests of the peasants (whose resistance to the growing enserfment was for a time weakened by the general boom in the demand for grain), and of the mass of townsmen—craftsmen, small traders, etc.—were sacrificed. The country was constantly drained of large quantities of foodstuffs and raw materials, and simultaneously flooded by quantities of industrial and

---

[31] W. S. Unger, "De hollandsche graanhandel en graanhandelspolitik in de middeleeuwen", in *De Economist* (1916), p. 264. The Dutch term was *moedernegotie*.

luxury goods, thus weakening small and middling crafts and traders, who had neither the skill nor the capacity to resist, and changing the social structure in the aristocracy's favour. Thus we observe a growing tendency towards a uniquely agrarian development which helped to turn the country into an agrarian and raw-material producing colony of the West. It is tempting to see certain similarities—perhaps rather remote ones—with the development of systems of monoculture in the colonial countries of the nineteenth and twentieth centuries.

In spite of superficial appearances, the situation in Russia developed very differently. As we have observed, grain played no part in Russian export trade of the fifteenth and sixteenth centuries, but a very considerable part in the internal colonisation of the country and its expansion towards Siberia. This internal grain trade facilitated the exploitation of other sources of wealth, brought the scattered areas of the country into closer contact with one another, and formed an important factor in the genesis of an all-Russian market. Moreover, Russian maritime trade operated in a different social situation from the Polish one. It provided the tsar with considerable assets, not only in customs revenues, but in the huge proceeds from the sale of the valuable products delivered to him in kind: furs, etc. The trade added considerably to the strength of the Russian merchant class, though its members frequently complained of the excessive privileges which the government granted to foreigners. It is thus clear that maritime trade not only favoured capital accumulation in Russia, but strengthened those forces whose interest lay in the unity of the country and the might of its state, a fact of considerable historical importance for Russia in the sixteenth and seventeenth centuries. Admittedly Russia's central power expressed above all the interests of the nobility (the *pomieshchiki*). Nevertheless, it made full use of the support and the financial help of the increasingly numerous and wealthy merchants, a class interested both in free trade within the country and political and commercial expansion abroad; for such expansion would enable it to make contact with the West via Lithuania and the Baltic, and would throw open the wealth of Siberia, and perhaps of the Middle and Far East. The conditions for capital accumulation in the hands of a native class of merchants were therefore much more favourable in Russia than in Poland, an advantage which was even greater, because the Russian nobility, which underwent very serious crises in the sixteenth and early seventeenth centuries, took no great part in large-scale trade.

Again, it seems that the capital accumulated locally was used for productive purposes to a much greater extent than in Poland. Its investment
accelerated the tempo of colonisation in the economically backward
regions of Russia and along its northern and south-eastern frontier. It
certainly helped to increase the quantity of products essential both for
the country's internal needs and its foreign trade. Merchants, moreover,
invested heavily in certain industries, such as salt-mining and the iron
industry of the Urals, which was to prove of considerable importance
for the equipment of the Russian armies. The quantity of commodities
essential to the country's population as a whole therefore grew; even
large numbers of peasants were drawn into the web of the commodity
economy. This is not to claim that Russian economic progress continued
unhindered. The intensified exploitation of the peasants by the state,
the nobility and the merchants, which is so characteristic of the East
European serf economies, began, from the end of the sixteenth and
during the seventeenth centuries, to limit the expansion of the internal
market, tending, in some ways, to preserve the elements of natural
economy, which still remained very large. However, the subsequent
evolution of the Russian economy no longer falls into the subject of
this article. The differences between Russian and Polish development
remain clear and significant.

CHAPTER SEVEN

THE PROBLEM OF THE INEQUALITY OF ECONOMIC DEVELOPMENT IN EUROPE IN THE LATER MIDDLE AGES*

We have all been accustomed for a long time to the existence of differences between the stages of development of various peoples, both in the modern and contemporary worlds and in antiquity. Although this seems to me to be a problem of great importance, historians of the Middle Ages have, however, rather neglected it. Comparing the phases of development of western and eastern Europe in the Middle Ages one can easily observe important differences. Rapid development in the economies of most of the eastern countries began late in the twelfth and thirteenth centuries, when the west had already reached the height of its medieval economic development. In the fourteenth and fifteenth centuries the situation changed markedly. Now it is the west which enters a period of long and grievous crisis, while most of the eastern countries take a considerable step forward. In the sixteenth century there is once again a new situation. Several of the western countries, and particularly the north western, enter into an economic expansion which, in spite of the crises of the seventeenth century, will lead them into a privileged position especially in economic matters. The economic advance of several of the eastern countries dies out at the turn of the sixteenth and seventeenth centuries and is followed by a regression of nearly two centuries. One should add that there were also considerable differences in stages of development and its dynamism between the different regions of the east and that the frontiers between the zones of economic development are not necessarily the same as the political frontiers.

I would like to begin by indicating briefly the predominant situation in the east for most of the period from the tenth to the twelfth and thirteenth centuries. The characteristic of this period is rather slow economic development. The territories of modern Bohemia and south-west Russia achieved the best economic results at this time, while the

* Lecture given at All Souls College, Oxford, on 8 May 1965, originally published in *Economic History Review*, 19 (1), 1966, pp. 15–28.

economy of Poland was still at a rather low level, but all these areas had some features in common. Thanks to recent investigations one can say that in the east, just as much as in the west, agriculture formed the basis of existence, but it was an agriculture of an extensive and primitive kind. Triennial rotation was little known and the iron plough was still something of a rarity. In spite of the natural wealth available, mining was little developed.[1] Commerce was dominated by luxury products destined for small groups within the population. Thanks to archaeological researches of recent years one can say that the east had towns in the economic sense,[2] but the vast majority of them were small agglomerations near the castles of princes and their officials, inhabited by populations of craftsmen and traders who were chiefly concerned to satisfy the needs of the restricted groups of the ruling class. There were contacts between the towns and the countryside, but the peasants living at the stage of subsistence economy did not yet provide a market as consumers on a large scale of the products of the towns. There was one institution among the Slavs of great interest which seems to me to prove that my supposition about the low level of productivity is correct. The embryonic states in Poland and Bohemia organized villages of service in which the population was compelled to do special and definite services.[3] The inhabitants were obliged to supply the prince and his followers with the products of agriculture and domestic industry. Probably it was difficult to buy these products because they were scarce and the ruling classes wished to guarantee themselves the minimum supply. The names of these service villages have sometimes survived to the present day and place-name investigations have been our greatest help in disentangling the social organization of the Slav peoples in the early Middle Ages.

A natural economy was, therefore, widespread in the Slav world during the tenth, eleventh and even the twelfth centuries, especially in the peasant sector. The same conclusions are indicated by the systems of taxation used by the princes. Everywhere in the east tributes in kind and labour services predominated. The circulation of money was very

---

[1] H. Dąbrowski, "Rozwój gospodarki rolnej w Polsce od XII do połowy XIV wieku" (Development of agricultural economy in Poland from the 12th to the middle of the 14th century), *Studia z dziejów gospodartswa wiejskiego*, V, 1 (Warsaw, 1962).

[2] *Les origines des villes polonaises* (Paris-La Haye, 1960). "L'artisanat et la vie urbaine en Pologne médiévale", *Ergon*, vol. III (Warsaw, 1962).

[3] K. Modzelewski, "La division autarchique du travail a l'échelle d'un Etat: L'organisation 'ministérielle' en Pologne médiévale", *Annales E.S.C.* XIX (1964), no. 6.

limited. Ibrahim-ibn-Jakub, the Judeo-Arab traveller of the second half of the tenth century, described the little pieces of cloth which were used as units of exchange by the western Slav. In Russia in the Kiev period, which was at this time more developed and in continuous commercial relations with Byzantium and the Arabs, the importation of moneys from these countries and their circulation were more important.[4] The same phenomenon is to a lesser extent to be seen in the countries bordering on the Baltic. In the tenth and eleventh centuries there developed Slav towns in western Pomerania and also Scandinavian centres of commerce. In the second half of the eleventh century there seems to have been a certain amount of economic progress also in central and southern Poland. It is shown, amongst other things, by the appearance of regular issues of local coins which fairly rapidly supplanted the foreign currencies in internal circulation.

Wars and invasions provided princes and lords with a source of revenue which one should not neglect. Poland and Kievan Russia disputed the fertile regions situated at the sources of the River Bug. For a certain period at the beginning of the eleventh century the Poles occupied the Moravian Plain and enjoyed the excellent agricultural land there. But one has the impression that these states were not only fighting for the possession of land. Each invasion brought the victors a certain number of captives. During the eleventh century and certainly in the preceding century, these prisoners were installed as serfs on the domains of the conquerors. Place-name evidence is a great help to us here. But one may also wonder whether in the tenth and even in the eleventh century some Slav princes did not engage in the slave trade. We know from Arab and even Italian sources that slaves of Slav origin were exported from the eighth and the ninth centuries into Spain, Arabia and towards Baghdad. The town of Prague was at that time an important market for slaves destined for export.

The export of slaves from Slav regions is fairly well known thanks to the Arab writers from the tenth century.[5] Very probably it was older than

---

[4] R. Kiesnowski, "Coin Finds and the Problem of Money in Early Mediaeval Poland", *Polish Numismatic News* (suppl. fasc. of vol. V (1961) of the *Wiadomości Numizmatyczne*); S. Tabaczyński, "Les fonctions pécuniaires des trésors", *Annales E.S.C.* XVII (1962), fasc, 2; J. Sztetyllo, "Czeki i morawski pieniądz pozakruszcowy wczesnego średniowiecza" (rés. fr. La monnaie non-métallique tchèque du haut moyen âge), *Kwartalnik Historii Kultury Materialnej*, XI (1963), fasc. 3–4.

[5] T. Lewicki, "Osadnictwo słowiańskie i niewolnicy słowiańscy w krajach muzułmańskich według średniowiecznych pisarzy arabskich" (rés. fr. La colonisation

this. Various things suggest that the incomes of the Slav princes and of the seigneurial class in formation were, at least up to the twelfth century, rather meagre, especially the revenues derived from economic activity. The lords could not yet exact considerable dues from the mass of the native population because the majority of the peasants were probably free men. It seems that this situation changed slowly in Poland during the eleventh and the twelfth centuries. At the beginning of that period there was in Poland a great insurrection directed against the unitary state in which the serfs seem to have participated, but our information about this revolt is too sparse for us to draw more detailed conclusions. It seems also that at this period Bohemia and Kievan Russia were more advanced on the road of development and feudalization of the economy than Poland and the other countries of the western Slavs.[6]

How then should one explain the great change in the economic situation in Poland, Bohemia and in Hungary which appears so clearly in the thirteenth century, but which had also begun in the preceding century?

One cannot explain it by any remarkable increase in the population because one knows that the lords of these countries encouraged at this time the introduction of German colonists, sometimes on a large scale. German historians and even those of the eastern countries previously supposed that this German colonization was the decisive factor in determining progress. This was attributed to the superior cultural level of the colonists, to their possession of more developed agricultural techniques than those of the native peoples, and also to more important material means. One cannot absolutely deny these factors, but there are strong arguments weakening this over-simple hypothesis. Researches of recent decades show that in most of the eastern countries German emigration was in fairly small numbers. Now the economic development which is so noticeable in the thirteenth and fourteenth centuries in eastern Europe, except for Russia, extended far beyond the areas reached by the German colonists. Other factors encouraging

slave et les esclaves slaves dans les pays musulmans d'après les écrivains arabes du Moyen-Age), *Przegląd Historyczny*, XLIII (1952), fasc. 3/4, pp. 473–91. Cf. Ch. Verlinden, *L'esclavage dans l'Europe médiévale*, Tome I (Péninsule ibérique—France) (Brugge, 1955), pp. 211–25.

[6] M. N. Tikhomirov, *Drevnerusskie goroda* (*Old Russian Towns*) (Moscow, 1956); B. A. Rybakov, *Remeslo drevnei Rusi* (*Old Russian Industry*) (Moscow, 1948). F. Graus, *Dejiny venkovskeho lidu v Czecach v dobe predhusitske* (*History of the Peasants in Bohemia before the Hussite Revolution*), Vol. I (Prague, 1953).

advance must therefore be sought. Richard Koebner believed that the socio-economic structures of the Slavs in the early Middle Ages were so sterile that they did not lend themselves to this evolution.[7] It was possible to accept this hypothesis at the time when it was still believed that the Slavs knew very little about agriculture, that they lived primarily by fishing and hunting and that they did not have towns. But historical and archaeological researches of more recent years have shown that the economic level of the Slav peoples before the German coloniza-tion had been seriously underestimated. I would like to suggest here a quite different hypothesis. Clearly the development of the peoples of eastern Europe was slower than that of the westerners during the period between the tenth and thirteenth centuries. But in spite of that they did achieve considerable results at this time. I think that from the twelfth century in particular the situation began to change to their disadvantage. The circulation of Arab money came to an end and the import of German money was relatively restricted. At this period there was a balance of power established between the Poles, the Czechs, the Hungarians and the Russians which meant that their wars and inva-sions of each other's territories became much less profitable. They had to defend themselves against the attacks of the Germans and those of the Lithuanians and Prussians, who were organizing their own states. Kievan Russia was already weakened by intestine wars and the inva-sions of the nomads from the southern steppes. Towards the middle of the thirteenth century it fell prey to the Mongols. Its fate was sealed for more than a century. The Mongol invasion also touched the other countries of eastern Europe, but its ravages were not followed by a prolonged yoke as in Russia. It was just in the thirteenth century that there began the great economic rise of Bohemia, Hungary and Poland. I have indicated earlier the general economic situation of these areas. Henceforward the aristocracy of these countries had to take particu-lar care of its property. Now the exploitation of these properties was still primitive. Certainly in the course of the twelfth century the state and the aristocracy had succeeded in driving the great majority of the peasants in these countries into serfdom, but the revenues drawn from their dues were small while the needs of the seigneurial group

---

[7] R. Koebner, "The Settlement and Colonisation of Europe", in *Cambridge Economic History of Europe* (Cambridge, 1942), p. 59. See also H. Aubin, "The Lands East of the Elbe and German Colonisation Eastwards", *ibid.*, pp. 396 sq.

were growing. Internal and external circumstances and the rising cultural level required increases in the revenues of the aristocracy. They
had to extract more work from the serfs. Further pressure was almost
excluded in the existing circumstances. With the population still very
fluid in some places peasants could avoid constraints by fleeing from
the lands of lords who were too demanding, especially as competition
for manpower was acute amongst the nobility. We know first of all that
the *hospites*, people recently installed on the properties of various lords,
were numerous in the course of the twelfth and the thirteenth centuries. There was no longer the possibility of introducing prisoners from
neighbouring countries, as had been done previously. It was necessary,
therefore, to interest the native people and also foreign colonists in the
reorganization of the economy and particularly in the intensification
of agriculture.[8] To attain this end it was necessary to introduce strong
economic incentives which would not only attract foreign immigrants,
but also encourage the natives to end the old routine of work and apply
more productive methods. In the thirteenth century we find in the east
the same profound changes which had taken place in the west in the
tenth and eleventh centuries. Bohemia, Poland and Hungary saw at that
time the introduction of the norms of seigneurial law which had long
existed in the west. This law, imitated in Poland and Bohemia from
the norms used in Germany, was here described as the privileges of
German law.[9] At the same time one sees everywhere the reorganization
of peasant dues to the lords and the reduction of their obligations to
the state. In Bohemia and a little later in Poland it was already possible
to introduce commutation of rents into money. This was an enormous
step forward because it gave the peasants more liberty and encouraged them to more intensive work. If the peasants could accept the
obligation to pay their dues in money, it must have been the case that
they already had a surplus of products which they sold in the towns
and in the rural markets. At the same time, also, the number of towns
and markets increased in Bohemia, in Poland and in Hungary. It is
therefore difficult to accept the hypothesis of the Czech scholar Professor
Graus that the great reform of the economy weakened the position of

---

[8] K. Tymieniecki, *Historia chłopów polskich* (*History of the Polish Peasants*), Vol. I
(Warszawa 1965); F. Graus, *op. cit.* vol. II.
[9] S. Trawkowski, "Zur Erforschung der deutschen Kolonisation auf polnischen Boden
im 13. Jahrhundert", *Acta Poloniae Historica*, vol. VII (1962).

the peasants.[10] German law also affected the whole structures of states. In order to give the privileges of the new law to the peasants and to the inhabitants of the towns the lords had to have rights of immunity from the princes. Otherwise they could not have reduced the dues that their subjects previously paid to the state. This considerably modified relations between the princes and the lay and ecclesiastical aristocracy. They were strong enough to compel the rulers to renounce certain rights. The latter had at first taken part in this movement and drawn great benefits from it. The areas of cultivation were rapidly increasing and towns and markets were growing in number and wealth. The revenues of the state and of the aristocracy were expanding considerably, but it is important to notice that this general progress did not take place on an equal scale on all the territories in question. There were great differences which did not correspond to the frontiers of states, frontiers which were at first very fluid. I would suggest that there were in eastern Europe three zones of differing development. The first zone, the most dynamic during the thirteenth and fourteenth centuries, was the area of which the Czech mountains and the Carpathians were the principal axis. It extended from the Czech plateau in the west as far as Transylvania and included in the north Silesia and Little Poland and in the south the areas of the Slovaks in Upper Hungary.

The second zone of dynamic development from the thirteenth century included the countries situated on the shores of the Baltic. Everything between these two regions was the third zone, the middle zone, in which economic progress was much less marked. This consisted of central Poland, Lithuania and a great part of the lands of Russia. Not until the fifteenth century was there a profound reversal of this situation. Then the middle zone produced a remarkable dynamism and tended to subordinate to its own interest the other two zones, whose evolution then became slower.

The characteristic feature of the southern zone from the thirteenth century was not only the progress of agriculture and of sheep farming in the mountains and cattle farming in Hungary, Ruthenia and Moldavia. Another very important factor of development was mineral wealth, the exploitation of which on a great scale had begun in the thirteenth

---

[10] F. Graus, *op. cit.* II, 159 sq.

century.[11] The German immigrants and the miners' law of this country played a considerable role in the mines of eastern Europe, as later on in the rest of Europe. Bohemia was particularly rich in mineral resources. There was a wealth of silver at Jihlava and above all at Kutna Hora. There were mines of gold and copper in the same country. This wealth attracted German merchants and entrepreneurs especially to the mining areas in the west of the country and to the capital. This mineral wealth, together with the fertility of its soil, explains the economic and political leadership of Bohemia in east-central Europe in the thirteenth and fourteenth centuries. The coincidence of these favourable circumstances certainly accelerated the expansion of a commercial economy in the economic life of Bohemia. Thanks to this coincidence dues of peasants paid to their lords in silver already predominated in the thirteenth century. The wealth of precious metals permitted the kings of Bohemia to create a sound currency. The position of the country in relation to the great routes of international commerce was not particularly favourable. But thanks to its mineral wealth, Prague became the great centre of commerce in precious metals. F. Graus has shown that during the thirteenth and fourteenth centuries the import of cloth from the west and of various other luxury goods was paid for above all by the export of Czech currency.[12]

Czech historians believe that the first two kings of the Luxemburg dynasty in the fourteenth century exported precious metals from the country to such an extent that they seriously disturbed its economic situation. Thanks to these favourable circumstances Prague with more than 30,000 inhabitants became one of the biggest towns of Europe north of the Alps. The other much smaller towns were also fairly well populated and numerous in comparison with the other countries of eastern Europe.[13]

The abundance of grain and mineral wealth increased the power of the great lay and ecclesiastical lords and of the rich merchants of the towns, who were mostly of German origin. It attracted into the coun-

---

[11] J. Koran, *Prehledne dejiny ceskoslovenskeho hornictvi* (*Outline History of Czechoslovak Mining*) Vol. I (Prague, 1955): D. Molenda, *Górnictwo kruszowe na terenie złóż śląsko-krakowskich do połowy XVI wieku* (*Lead and Silver Mining in the Silesia-Cracow Region to the mid-16th Century*) (Wrocław, 1963).

[12] F. Graus, *Cesky obchod se suknem ve 14. a pocatkem 15. stoleti* (*Czech Cloth Trade in the 14th and the Beginning of the 15th Century*) (Prague, 1950).

[13] F. Graus, "Die Handelsbeziehungen Böhmens zu Deutschland und Österreich im 14. und zu Beginn des 15. Jahrhunderts", *Historica*, Vol. II (1960).

try merchants of south Germany and especially the Nuremburgers, who inundated Bohemia with their manufactured products, especially objects of iron and copper. Urban industry in Bohemia itself could not develop to any great extent in these circumstances and remained for a long time rather weak. In the second half of the fourteenth century technical difficulties in the mines became for a time insurmountable. Discontent grew amongst the middle and smaller nobility, the Czech artisans and some of the peasants because of the predominance of the great lay and ecclesiastical lords and the merchants of German origin. Pressure from that side and the exorbitant fiscal exactions of the kings of a foreign dynasty led to the Hussite revolution. It is necessary to emphasize that the expulsion of the Germans from Prague and from mining towns certainly weakened the economic situation, especially in the mining areas. But it changed radically the distribution of wealth. It was the middle Czech nobility, the craftsmen and the better-off peasants, who enriched themselves most during the Hussite period. The internal market for native industry was enlarged and from the fifteenth century it made considerable progress inside the country and also beyond its frontiers. Agriculture, which suffered some setbacks during the struggles against internal enemies and against the Crusades, nevertheless developed and Bohemia at the end of the fifteenth century was in a position to pay for the import of necessary products such as salt, lead, etc. by increasing the export of cereals and of the products of fisheries, which were considerably modernized at this period especially in the southern part of the country. The new rise of the mining industries from the beginning of the sixteenth century helped to make the period from then until the Thirty Years' War a relatively prosperous one for Bohemia.[14] This country is the extreme case, even in the southern zone of which I have spoken. But features similar to this development are to be seen in Silesia and Upper Hungary and in southern Poland. The riches of the earth in these regions were less than in Bohemia, but they were considerable. There it was gold, silver and lead and iron in Silesia; salt, lead and also iron and a little copper in Little Poland. Upper Hungary had rich deposits of copper, iron and silver and also a little gold. In the mountains of Transylvania, gold mines were exploited. The

---

[14] J. Janaček, *Diejiny obchodu v predbelohorske Praze* (*Trade History in Prague before the Thirty Years' War*) (Prague, 1955); J. Janaček, *Remeslna vyroba v ceskych mestech v 16. stoleti* (*Industry in the Czech Towns in the 16th Century*) (Prague, 1961).

relation of these areas to the routes of international commerce was
more favourable than that of Bohemia. But I would like to dispute here
an ancient historical conception about the role of these commercial
routes, which seems to me to be in part mistaken. We have long
acknowledged that the rise of the towns of Silesia and Little Poland
from the thirteenth century owed much to the routes of communication which linked the west with the Italian colonies of the Black Sea
and the Baltic to Bohemia, Hungary and Mediterranean countries.[15]
These routes crossed in Silesia and Little Poland, and according to some
historians they provoked the development of the economy, especially
the economy of the towns, from the thirteenth to the end of the fifteenth
centuries. This theory seems oversimplifed to me. The routes of international commerce certainly attracted the attention of merchants
towards the lands of southern Poland and south-west Ruthenia, but it
was not only the advantages of transit trade which attracted merchants
and foreign capital into this zone. Nor did native merchants concern
themselves exclusively with trade in the products of the Orient and of
the west areas as was previously believed. Contracts of sale and purchase
between foreigners and natives in the fifteenth century (older ones are
not preserved) show clearly that local products, especially metals, salt,
cattle, wax, hides, furs and crimson (the red dye which was so much
sought after before the coming of American cochineal), the cheap cloths
of Silesia and Little and Great Poland, played a considerable role in the
international commerce of the southern zone. It was supposed previously that the commerce was based on the transportation of oriental
products from the Italian colonies of the Black Sea towards the west,
while the cloths of the Low Countries and of England went towards
the east and to Hungary. The first part of this picture is only partially
true. Commercial contracts from fifteenth-century Poland prove that
the Italians, the south Germans and also native merchants often
imported foreign products from Venice in the fifteenth century, and
sometimes even from Brugge. The Nuremburgers, who were very
numerous in Poland and in Hungary from the fourteenth century,

---

[15] S. Kutrzeba, *Handel Krakowa w wiekach średnich* (*The Trade of Cracow in the
Middle Ages*) (Cracow, 1903); S. Kutrzeba, "Handel Polski ze Wschodem w wiekach
średnich" (*Poland's Trade with the Orient in the Middle Ages*), in *Przegląd Polski
148–150* (Cracow, 1903): L. Charewiczowa, *Handel średniowiecznego Lwowa* (*The
Trade of Medieval Lwów*) (Lwów, 1925); H. Wendt, *Schlesien und der Orient* (Breslau,
1916); M. Małowist, *Kaffa, kolonia genueńska na Krymie i problem wschodni* (rés. fr.
Caffa—colonie génoise en Crimée et la question d'Orient) (Warsaw, 1947).

imported a great quantity of their cheap manufactured products, especially objects of copper and iron. Here it must be underlined that Italians and south Germans frequently invested capital on a relatively large scale in the salt industry of Little Poland.[16] Several of them bought real property in the towns of Little Poland and Silesia and cases of the acquisition of landed property in the Polish countryside were not rare. During the fourteenth and fifteenth centuries several rich strangers established themselves in Little Poland and took part in the fiscal administration of the kingdom. Certain families joined the nobility, even the upper nobility. From all this I draw the following conclusion. It is true that the existence of great international routes attracted the attention of foreign merchants towards Poland. But one cannot consider commercial transit as the principal factor in the great development of economic life, especially urban life, in central eastern Europe in the late Middle Ages. The development of agriculture and of mineral industries which was so important in Bohemia, in Silesia, in Little Poland, in Upper Hungary, is the real basis of the economic rise of these countries from the thirteenth century. A favourable relationship to the commercial routes contributed greatly to progress, especially in Silesia, in southern Poland, in Ruthenia, in Upper Hungary. The period in question coincided with the restriction of the opportunities of merchants in the west. They sought out new perspectives in the countries of the east which were in full prosperity. They invested their capital there and often settled there. In this way they contributed to the economic rise of eastern Europe. It must be added that it was not only westerners who interested themselves in the economic life of eastern Europe. There was also an immigration into that area of Armenian, Jewish and even Greek merchants, who settled especially in the towns of south-west Ruthenia and especially in Lwów. The general crisis of industry and of mining at the end of the fifteenth century introduced various economic difficulties in the southern zone. This crisis was overcome thanks to the investment of capital by foreign and native merchants which permitted the introduction of new methods to exploit the mineral wealth

---

[16] H. Amman, "Wirtschaftsbeziehungen zwischen Oberdeutschland und Polen", *Ergon*, Vol. III (1962); M. Małowist, "Le développement des rapports économiques entre la Flandre, la Pologne et les pays limitrophes du XIIIe au XVe siècle", *Revue belge de philologie et d'histoire*; X (1931); A. Mączak, *Sukiennictwo wielkopolskie XIV–XVII wieku* (*The Cloth Industry of Great Poland from the 14th to the 17th Century*) (Warsaw, 1955); F. Graus, "Die Handelsbeziehungen...".

situated not only at the surface but also at a certain depth. In the course
of the sixteenth century and especially in its first half, the mines of this
area contributed considerably to the further development of all these
countries.[17] In spite of all these favourable circumstances, the towns of
these countries, except for Bohemia after the Hussite revolution, did
not succeed in establishing urban industry on the scale of the west.
Craftsmen could scarcely defend themselves against the competition
of manufactured products imported in quantity by foreigners. The
merchants who governed the towns had no interest in the defence of
native trades. They quickly adjusted themselves to taking part in the
import trade in foreign goods and the export of the products of mines
and of agriculture. The urban industry of Poland and Hungary remained
relatively primitive and its leaders were poor and technologically backward. They could continue to exist as long as the internal markets were
growing, but the weakness of urban industry condemned the towns to
a precarious situation, especially as they had relatively small populations
and their influence on the politics of their countries was slight. It must
be added that really rich merchants tended during the sixteenth century
to join the nobility.

    I now pass to the Baltic zone which I regard as the second zone of
rapid development from the thirteenth century onwards. Hanseatic
commerce in general is too well known to require detailed treatment
here and I would like only to draw attention to a few problems which
are at present being debated by specialists. It was for a long time almost
a dogma amongst historians of the Baltic that the immigration of
German merchants in the twelfth and thirteenth centuries was the cause
of the development of large-scale maritime commerce on the Brugge-
Novgorod line and that this trade became the basis of the prosperity
of the Hanseatic towns of the Baltic region. More recently historians
of the Baltic have at last perceived close economic links between these
towns and their immediate agricultural and forest hinterlands.[18] Various
investigators have shown that Hamburg, Lübeck, Szczecin, Gdańsk,
Riga and Revel, not to speak of Stockholm, were in the thirteenth

---

[17] J. Koran, op. cit.; D. Molenda, op. cit.
[18] B. Zientara, "Einige Bemerkungen über die Bedeutung des pommerschen Exports
im Rahmen des Ostsee-Getreidehandels im 13.–14. Jahrhundert", in Hansische
Studien (Berlin, 1961); E. Engel, "Bürgerliche Lehnbesitz, bäuerliche Produktrente
und altmärkisch-hamburgische Handelsbeziehungen im 14. Jahrhundert", Hansische
Geschichtsblätter 82 (1964); V. Niitema, Der Binnenhandel in der Politik der livländischen
Städte im Mittelalter (Helsinki, 1952).

century in close relationship with their hinterlands from which they drew not only food supplies, but also various goods destined for distant markets. Study of this problem has only just begun. Certain scholars, such as the late P. Johansen, have even advanced the hypothesis that large-scale maritime commerce was not a necessity for the peoples of the Baltic zone.[19] This is an extreme position and, I believe, an exaggerated one. Certain types of merchandise were absolutely necessary for the Baltic countries. In most of these countries salt was lacking. North-west Russia had neither salt nor metals and could acquire these only by the sale of furs and wax to the Hanseatics. Sweden, which was still undeveloped in the fourteenth and fifteenth centuries, had no salt. These examples could be extended. The Baltic had a wide range of forest products and cereals which it exchanged against western merchandise. I think, therefore, that the maritime commerce of the Baltic was of great importance for the inhabitants of the countries bordering on this sea. But there is another observation to be made. It is often said that the Baltic was the Mediterranean of the north-east. This is true, but it must be added that it was a poor man's Mediterranean. An analysis of the structure of the Baltic commerce shows clearly that luxury goods played a minute role there. Thanks to the researches of Russian historians, and especially those of Lesnikov, Danilova, Khoroshkievich and others, it is now known that the famous furs of Novgorod were derived above all from the hunting of squirrels in the immense hinterland of that town.[20] Luxury furs appeared on the Novgorod market in a restricted quantity. I believe that it was the relatively low price of these furs which enabled them to be exported in large quantities to the west. The other goods exported from the Baltic countries were for the most part relatively cheap forest and agricultural products. The same is true of Swedish copper and especially iron in the Middle Ages. If one analyses the goods imported into the Baltic from the west, one notices immediately the importance of salt. But even amongst the more valuable

---

[19] P. Johansen, *Der hansische Russlandhandel, insbesondere nach Novgorod, in kritischer Betrachtung* (Köln/Opladen, 1962).

[20] M. P. Lesnikov, "Der hansische Pelzhandel zu Beginn des 14. Jahrhunderts", *Hansische Studien* (Berlin, 1961); L. V. Danilova, *Ocherski po istorii zemlevladeniia i khoziatsva Novgoroda i Novgorodski zemli v XIV i XV vv.* (*Studies on the History of Agriculture and Economy of Novgorod and its Country in the 14th and 15th Centuries*) (Moscow, 1955); A. L. Khoroshkievich, *Torgovlia Velikogo Novgoroda s Pribaltikoi i Zapadnoi Evropoi v XIV–XV vv.* (*The Trade of Great Novgorod with the Baltic Countries and Western Europe in the 14th and 15th Centuries*) (Moscow, 1963).

products, for example western cloths, it appears that it was only those of medium or low price which found really numerous consumers in the Baltic and its hinterland. All this reflects the material level of the population of the Baltic countries at the period of the commercial domination of the German Hanse. Similar conclusions are to be drawn from an analysis of the transactions between the traders of the Baltic zone. Most of the contracts of purchase and sale concerned relatively small quantities of merchandise and if these transactions involved a large number of different products, they were also in general of low price. The number and financial potential of the great merchants even of Lübeck and Gdańsk are not to be compared with similar classes in Italy or Catalonia. It has always been a matter of surprise to historians of this area that the forms and techniques of commerce remained so primitive into the sixteenth century. Lesnikov has proved that at least in the important commerce between Novgorod and Flanders the profits of merchants of the Hanse remained modest in the fourteenth and fifteenth centuries.[21] We still do not know whether this is also true of other sectors of commerce. But if the conclusions of these scholars prove to be valid also for other aspects of Baltic commerce, it will be easy to understand why the Hanseatics did not need a more advanced commercial technique. I believe that the accumulation of mercantile capital was still so limited amongst the Hanseatics that it did not require the application of credit and insurance methods of a more developed kind. It has recently been shown that some of the Hanseatic towns, and especially the richer ones, had close links not only with maritime commerce but also with continental commerce. W. Koppe has shown that relations with the Frankfurt fairs were of enormous importance for Lübeck in the fourteenth and fifteenth centuries.[22] It has long been known that the merchants of Teutonic Prussia were deeply engaged in the fourteenth century and later in commerce with Hungary and Ruthenia, from which they drew copper and silver and oriental products, the latter ultimately from the Black Sea. At the turn of the fourteenth century the Teutonic Order and its subjects exported large quantities

---

[21] M. P. Lesnikov, "Die Livländische Kaufmannschaft und ihre Handelsbeziehungen zu Flandern am Anfang des 15. Jahrhunderts", *Zeitschrift für Geschichtswissenschaft* (1958), fasc. 2.

[22] W. Koppe, "Die Hansen und Frankfurt am Main im 14. Jahrhundert", *Hansische Geschichtsblätter* 71 (1952).

of Hungarian silver to Novgorod in return for furs. It appears that the Hanse was neither so powerful nor so rich as was long thought and that its trade was affected by various continental influences which were outside its control. It should also be mentioned that until the beginning of the fifteenth century the Teutonic Order, at that time an organization of nobles, was the largest commercial power in the Baltic zone and that it was far more powerful than the merchant towns, with the possible exception of Lübeck. The Teutonic Knights protected the Hanseatics in Poland and even in Russia. The Order defended their interests in Flanders and England. In return it profited from the privileges of the Hanseatic organization. The collapse of the political, financial and military power of the Teutonic Order considerably weakened the position of the whole Hanse. From the thirteenth century onwards the merchants of the Hanse contributed greatly to the economic development of the Baltic zone by organizing commercial links between the peoples of that area amongst themselves and with the west. But in this way they contributed also to the awakening of forces which were to be directed against themselves. From the end of the fourteenth century it is no longer possible to speak of the existence of a Hanseatic League. Each sector of this organization acted politically in defence of its own interests. The Swedish, Danish, Polish and Russian merchants, like the English and the Dutch in the west, tended to free themselves from the commercial domination of the Hanse. A long struggle began which was resolved in a different fashion in the course of the sixteenth and even the seventeenth centuries.

The other important factor was the character of exchanges between the Baltic zone and the west. Exports from the east were above all primary products and the products of forest and agriculture. Imports from the west included, apart from salt, important quantities of industrial products which limited in a sense the development of the urban trades in all the Baltic countries. One might say that even at the time of the prosperity of the Hanse and in part in consequence of the activity of the Hanseatics themselves, the character of economic relations between west and north-east Europe became unfavourable to the full development of that zone and of eastern Europe in general.

I now pass to the third zone of economic development of eastern Europe in the later Middle Ages. This is central Poland, Lithuania and Russia, later to become Muscovy. In the first of these countries one observes important but not spectacular progress in the course of the thirteenth and fourteenth centuries. Agriculture developed there both quantitatively and qualitatively, but the industrial and commercial development of the towns was relatively feeble. Natural wealth and commercial stimulus were lacking. But population grew and new lands were put into cultivation. In the course of the fourteenth century not only Great Poland, but even the most distant Polish provinces such as Mazovia show an increase both in the cultivated area and in the number of little towns and markets. Peasants and lesser nobles settled in the towns and engaged there in commerce and industry. In the course of the fifteenth century one sees the first signs of a favourable set of circumstances for the forest, agricultural and pastoral economy of these countries. The growth of towns encouraged the peasants to increase their productivity. Western countries, especially the Netherlands and England and later Portugal and Spain showed a lively interest in the timber and other forest products as well as the cereals of the Baltic region. I have shown elsewhere how the merchants of Prussia, following the example of the Teutonic Order, succeeded in directing towards Gdańsk and other Baltic ports a substantial stream of forest and agricultural products from the fifteenth century. They achieved this by giving the producers and local intermediaries credits which their partners had to repay in kind. This method already produced excellent results in the fifteenth century and it was also used in the course of the two following centuries.[23] Apart from this, many merchants and nobles of central Poland organized on their own account exports which, in the course of the second half of the fifteenth century but even more in the sixteenth century, came to involve an increasing proportion of the cereal production of Poland and Lithuania. But the possibilities of selling these products internally and externally presented great difficulties to the noble producers. They wished to profit from such a favourable set of circumstances, but they lacked the means to do it. A depreciation of the currency and of their revenues in money deprived them of the possibility of organizing their economy by using the wage labour which was first lacking. One has the impression that towards the turn of the fifteenth century the economy of the Polish nobility was passing through a crisis. It was at that time that there began the introduction of the system of labour services which

---

[23] M. Małowist, "A Certain Trade Techniques in the Baltic Countries in the 15th–17th Centuries", in *Poland at the 11th International Congress of Historical Studies in Stockholm* (Warsaw, 1960).

is called the second serfdom.[24] This painful process lasted more than a century, but in the long run it ruined the majority of the peasants. It also had other very serious consequences. The ruin of the peasantry which was already marked towards the end of the sixteenth century, had a disastrous influence on the economic life of the towns, and in particular of those little towns which were tied to local markets. Industry and small-scale commerce disappeared. The rise in the price of cereals, especially in the second half of the sixteenth century, strengthened the greater and middle nobility as well as the rich merchants of Gdańsk, the intermediary between Poland and the western markets. But this enrichment encouraged further increases in the import of luxury products and the products of western industry which further weakened the position of this branch of the economy of Poland itself. The nobility even succeeded in limiting the activities of native merchants, except for those of Gdańsk, in the sphere of commerce with foreigners. Growing serfdom absorbed all the strength of the peasantry and paralysed the inhabitants of the towns, who were obliged to struggle against foreign competition supported by the nobility. At the beginning of the seventeenth century the Polish economy showed several features characteristic of colonial countries.

A new economic system was not limited to the middle zone which is here being discussed. The second serfdom tended to extend itself in all directions.

The growth of the demand for cereals which was reflected in the rise of prices, especially in the second half of the sixteenth century, and the difficulties caused by the expensiveness of labour had in nearly all the countries of eastern Europe the same influence on the system of agricultural production and through that on the economy as a whole. There were naturally variations in the time-scale between different regions. The great seigneurial demesnes were established at first mainly on the banks of navigable rivers which facilitated transport towards the Baltic ports. But later the same system spread out towards less well-situated areas. The Polish nobility pushed towards the east and the north-east in search of new territories suitable for agriculture. This happened in the Ukraine and partially in Lithuania and Livonia. Economic development in Russia shows similarities with what happened in Poland, but

---

[24] M. Małowist, "Über die Frage der Handelspolitik des Adels in den Ostseeländern im 15. und 16. Jahrhundert", *Hansische Geschichtsblätter* 75 (1957).

there were also differences. In the second half of the fourteenth century and in the course of the fifteenth century the disastrous economic and demographic consequences of the Mongol invasions were overcome. At this period remarkable progress is to be seen in the sphere of agriculture in the region of the upper Volga and Oka and a great movement of colonization in the north-east of Russia.[25] The powerful Russian abbeys played an important role in these movements of expansion. There was also a considerable development of towns and markets which often became fixed centres. In the course of the fifteenth century, at first in the territory of Novgorod and later in more central regions, the peasants were already in a position to pay part of their dues in money, which flowed into this country chiefly because of Baltic commerce. But this system had not the time to develop in Russia as far as amongst the western Slavs. As I have said, it is also the period of the growth of towns of which Moscow became particularly important. It profited greatly from the export of agricultural and pastoral products towards the north and especially of high-quality furs derived from the region of the Volga and of the north-east, and exported to the west. It attracted the immigration of rich Armenian, Tatar, Greek and even Italian merchants. The development of agriculture in the lands in the basin of the upper Volga and Oka enormously facilitated the Russian colonization of the immense regions of the north-east, which in exchange supplied furs, salt and later metals. The growing demand for agricultural products presented the Russian nobility with similar problems to those of which we have spoken in Poland. In the second half of the sixteenth century and especially towards the end of this period, one sees the second serfdom with all its consequences developing in Muscovite Russia.

I would now like to draw some conclusions from my survey.

From the thirteenth century there is to be observed in eastern Europe a dynamic development, but one which is not equal in all regions. This process was particularly clear in the domains of agriculture, pastoral farming and mining industries. It did not lead to the development of a really important urban industry. The weakness of the towns was an important factor. From the fifteenth century, and particularly later, circumstances which were so favourable for eastern European agriculture

---

[25] L. V. Cherepnin, *Obrazovaniie russkogo tsentralizovannogo gosudarstva v XIV–XV vekakh* (*The Organisation of the Centralized Russian State in the 14th and 15th Centuries*) (Moscow, 1960), chs. 2–3.

led to the introduction of labour services and the second serfdom. This phenomenon enriched and strengthened the nobility and, in Russia and for a certain period in Poland, merchants linked with agricultural interests. Urban industry, which was undeveloped, struggled against the competititon of foreign products and the difficulties caused by the smallness of interior markets and either remained insignificant or, as in Poland, was destined to disappear. Eastern Europe became for a long time a region complementary to the expanding west.

CHAPTER EIGHT

PROBLEMS OF THE GROWTH OF THE NATIONAL ECONOMY OF CENTRAL-EASTERN EUROPE IN THE LATE MIDDLE AGES*

This study covers the regions stretching from the Baltic to the Adriatic Sea in one direction and from Saxony to the Grand Duchy of Lithuania in the other. In choosing this area I was influenced by the following considerations:

1. Between the XIIth and XIIIth centuries and the beginning of the XVIIth century these countries experienced very similar phases of development. Although valuable, many previous studies however have been carried out in isolation to some extent, as analysis of individual countries did not allow for a fuller understanding of the general principles of economic growth and development which affected the whole area under discussion.

2. Because national markets had not yet come into existence, political boundaries played a limited role in economic life. For this reason the object of study during the later period should not be individual countries but rather the smaller regions where tangible economic links emerged. Alternatively, groupings of such regions, which I would describe conventionally as economic zones, should be studied within this general framework, economic interdependence being of great importance for the area as a whole. The territories mentioned in this case did no not always coincide with political boundaries but could considerably exceed them.

It would appear in the light of present-day research that in the territories of Central-Eastern and Eastern Europe during the early Middle Ages conditions for economic development were less favourable than those of Western Europe. As a result rural economy and urbanization progressed less in the territories over a long period. Thus, until the XIIth and XIIIth centuries the two-field system was dominant in agriculture, as was probably the burning of forest land, and the three-field was not generally in use.[1] Wooden implements

---

* Originally published in the *Journal of European Economic History*, III, 1974, pp. 319–357.
[1] H. Łowmiański, *Początki Polski*, t. III, Warszawa, 1967, pp. 235–244.

were unsatisfactory for cultivation of the heavy soil which was the most fertile, and H. Łowmiański considered this to be a factor in the very low agricultural yield, when assessing an average ratio of sowing to harvest at to 2 or at most 3. He claims that the yield often fell below 1:2. It was this which precluded the possibility of any larger natural growth of the population.[2]

Wheat, which became so important from the beginning of the XIIth and XIIIth centuries, was not well distributed and left many areas quite untouched. Few now deny that many settlements in the Slav countries and in Hungary had economic characteristics of early towns, but they were on the whole considerably smaller communities than those in the West, in Italy and in Kievan Russia, and they had much less scope for manufacture and trade. Of course there were exceptions, such as Western Pomerania.

How can this situation be explained? It is very difficult to throw light upon the problem but I believe that the main factor which slowed down the rate of development was the density of population which was appreciably lower than in the territories of the former Roman Empire in particular. This is shown by demographic evidence for the first half of the XIVth century and thus for a period before the outbreak of the Great Plague.

In this period the density of population per square km in the West and in Italy was approximately as follows:[3]

France	35
Italy	27 to 30
England	10
Germany	10 to 11 (somewhat hypothetical figures)
Netherlands	data are lacking but the southern part was very heavily populated

In the same period, the density of population in Central-Eastern Europe was:

Poland	6 to 7
Bohemia	8 to 10 (some estimates are as high as 15)
Hungary	somewhere between these two countries.

---

[2] *Ibid.*, pp. 296, 307.
[3] I. Gieysztorowa, *Research into the Demographic History of Poland*, "Acta Poloniae

Data referring to the so-called average density of population does not preclude large variations for individual regions, but the figures available do indicate conditions which were markedly unfavourable to the development of the Eastern part of the area under discussion. Attempts to estimate the population in AD 1000 indicate that, although the figures were different, there was nevertheless a similar disequilibrium.[4] This is of considerable significance since under the conditions prevailing at that time man was an essential agent of production, and so the density of population and the dynamics of its increase acted as a very important stimulant to economic growth. In this case, however, it is clear that weak economic growth itself affected the population increase.

The less favourable conditions for economic growth were due to invasions and the subjection of Central-Eastern Europe to nomads such as Avars, Hungarians, Protobulgarians, etc., and later in the XIIIth century the Mongols which lasted longer than in the west. Although most of them eventually settled down and some were assimilated by native communities, there was considerable destruction, although it was not as serious as in Russia in the XIIIth century. Also the legacy of the civilization of the Roman Empire which was more lasting and accessible in France, the Rhineland, and even in parts of England than in the territories of Eastern Europe should not be underestimated. In Panonia and particularly in the Balkans it was more difficult to take advantage of this legacy because of the invasions and the later struggles for power over the richer territories (e.g. Southern Macedonia). The XIIth century and particularly the XIIIth century brought radical changes in the situation in Central-Eastern Europe which then entered the stage of faster economic growth. This is what F. Braudel would have called a long phase of the trade cycle with a marked upward trend which lasted until the end of the XVIth century. There were, however, occasional major disturbances during this period, e.g. in the Balkans during the Turkish conquest from the mid-XIVth century to the late XVth century and during the Hussite revolution in Bohemia, as well as to some extent in Silesia.

Historica", t. XVIII, 1968, pp. 9–10, J. C. Russell, *Late Ancient and Medieval Population*, "Transactions of the American Philosophical Society", New Series Vol. III, 1958, pp. 100–112; E. Fuegedi, *Pour une analyse démographique de la Hongrie médiévale*, "Annales E. S. C.", 1969, No. 6, pp. 1300–1306.
   [4]. I. Gieysztorowa, *op. cit.*

German, as previously Polish and Bohemian studies, attempted to explain the changes in the XIIth and XIIIth centuries by attributing them exclusively to the immigration of the German settlers who represented a higher economic potential and a more advanced level of civilization than the native population. After lengthy debates Polish and Bohemian historians managed to emphasize, correctly, the importance of Teutonic Law or, as K. Tymieniecki wrote, of Western Law. The latter covered a much wider area than the territories colonized by the Germans, and was adopted by the local populations. Here, however, some reservations must be made. Tymieniecki and his followers tried to prove that the institutions of so-called Polish Law, which were formulated in Poland before the introduction of Germanic Law, had in fact evolved by themselves in such a way that there were no great differences between the two systems. In Tymieniecki's work there are references to the supposed decline of the peasants' legal rights, and to their cultivation of land as a result of the introduction of the new system. In his study of Bohemian villages F. Graus tried to prove that the introduction of Germanic Law increased the charges levied on peasants. However, it is evident from the same work that not only did the area under cultivation increase appreciably but also the productivity of the rural economy and its links with markets during the XIIIth and XIVth centuries.[5] Furthermore, there is no evidence of particularly acute poverty among the Bohemian peasants during the period under discussion, which would have been unavoidable if, as a result of the increased taxes, they had had to deprive themselves of their crops at the expense of their own already meagre consumption. This cannot be shown to have happened in any of the countries with which we are concerned where foreign settlers or new systems of village organization were introduced or, as most commonly happened, both appeared jointly. It would seem, however, that the growth in the output of urban and rural craftsmen supplying local and regional markets largely to meet the needs of the peasant population is a proof of the increase in purchasing power. I would also explain the development of iron foundries and, linked to that, the production of agricultural implements in (Małopolska) Galicia, by the XIVth century at the latest, in the same way.[6] Besides, would there have been any for-

---

[5] F. Graus, *Dejiny venkovskeho lidu w Cechach v dobe predhusitske*, t. II, Praha 1957, pp. 30–78.

[6] B. Zientara, *Dzieje małopolskiego hutnictwa żelaznego XIV–XVII w.*, Warszawa 1954, pp. 85–92.

eigners or immigrant colonists, some of whom originally came from very distant places, if they had not expected to improve their position under the new conditions? There is no evidence to suggest that they were disappointed. I have paused here, at some length, to explain the problems of the new settlements and of the new law because, in the discussion of this subject, too much space has been devoted to the controversy concerning legal, institutional and ethnic factors and too often the economic problems have been overshadowed by them. I believe, as historians have known for a long time, that the attempts which were still made in the XIIth century in Silesia and (Małopolska) Galicia to reorganise the economy on the basis of Polish law as well as to introduce Germanic Law in Poland, Bohemia and in some of the provinces of what was then Hungary, represented an important watershed in the history of these countries. The large estates which had already been formed did not have sufficient manpower, which was essential for the cultivation of the land. The period of aggressive wars came to an end. It was these wars which in the past had provided the rulers and the gentry of Poland, Bohemia and Hungary with slaves to be used as a labour force on their estates or as "goods" for trade. Instead there now arose the need for defence from external attacks, particularly from the Germans.

The cultural needs of the aristocracy were intensified through contact with the countries which had already attained a higher level of civilization. But the aristocracy lacked the necessary means for the proper exploitation of their estates. It would have been unrealistic to increase the pressure on the serfs as there were ample opportunities to escape as well as strong competition among the feudal lords for labour. Neither they themselves nor the state authorities had any adequate administration which could prevent the escapes or even catch the runaways.

This applied to Poland in particular during the disintegration of the kingdom, whereas the stronger government in Hungary even succeeded in carrying out compulsory resettlement of the peasants from the northern province to the Panonian plain.[7] Nevertheless, as Hungarian scholars have stated, foreign settlements based on better rights conferred on the colonists, played a very important part in the creation and the development of towns in the centre of the country, and especially in

---

[7] B. Hóman, *Geschichte des ungarischen Mittelalters*, Vol. II, p. 161.

the rural and urban settlements of Slovakia and Transylvania.[8] It was essential to confer Germanic Law on the immigrants in the two border provinces, even though great natural wealth had been discovered there—itself a great attraction. It is worth mentioning that a similar phenomenon probably occurred in central Sweden in the XIIth century and certainly in the XIIIth century. The influx into Sweden of miners of German origin and the introduction of a law which was territorially binding at an earlier date in the German mining territories, led to a rapid increase in the production of iron ore and later of copper in these provinces, particularly in Dalarna which was sparsely populated as yet at the turn of the XIIth and XIIIth centuries.[9]

Thus the increase in population and new legal codes were of great importance to the economy of Central-Eastern and Northern Europe. The second factor was undoubtedly more important. This is shown by the fact that foreign rural settlements retained their German ethnic character only in the territories of Eastern Germany, Silesia, North Western Bohemia, Western Pomerania and partly in Eastern Pomerania. In other areas these settlements were relatively quickly absorbed and assimilated by the local population. The survival of strong German communities in Slovakia and Southern Transylvania can be explained both by the large scale of the immigration and by the small size of the native population. The German element survived longer in the towns but there too, from the XIVth century and the XVth century, it was on the whole assimilated as a result of native immigration. Germanic Law in various forms also applied to areas where foreign immigration was very restricted or did not occur, e.g. in Mazovia (Mazowsze), leading on the whole to very positive economic results in the form of increased production and turnover of goods etc. This happened because with the new law peasants' dues and the taxes on burghers were regularized, and were undoubtedly reduced by restricting or by abolishing the rights of princes to levy taxes, by defining the quota of the Church tithe, by the introduction of a system of personal freedom, and for varying periods by the exemption from payment of feudal dues, thus enabling the set-

---

[8] G. von Probszt, *Die niederungarischen Bergstädte*, München, 1966, pp. 23–29; S. Pascu, *Die mittelalterliche Dorfsiedlung in Siebenburgen*, "Nouvelles Etudes d'Histoire", II, Bucarest, 1966, pp. 135–139, 142, 144–145.

[9] T. Soederberg, *Stora Kopparberget under medeltiden och Gustav Vasa*, Stockholm, 1932, pp. 59, 67; L. Kumlien, *Sverige och Hanseaterna*, Stockholm, 1953, pp. 57, 61–64.

tlers to establish themselves on a solid basis. Under these conditions they had an interest in achieving bigger increases in production. It was a system of long-term economic incentives which encouraged serfs to work more intensively, to expand the area under cultivation and to increase manufacture and trade. This was reflected in the development of the three-field system which automatically required the manufacture and introduction of heavier ploughs to enable cultivation of the richer soil. The brake on the growth of population and division of labour was released. It has been understood for a long time that an action of this sort could only be taken, particularly at the beginning, by the wealthy feudal lords who were able for a time to forego a large share of their current income from levies in the hope of increasing it later. Intermediary forms developed which were easier for the feudal lords to exploit. The connection between the German conquests, in the territories with which we are concerned, and the flow of urban and rural settlers of German origin is well known and obvious. In this case colonization served both a political and a military end. However, both the Teutonic Knights in Prussia and their Livonian branch in particular, had, in this respect, limited scope and perhaps limited needs. Many came from Germany to the Order's towns in Prussia but in Livonia they were not a majority, with the exception perhaps of Riga and Dorpat. In the remaining centres in Livonia, natives and Swedish immigrants outnumbered people of German origin and later there was also Russian immigration.[10]

The Germans, however, acquired control of trade and were dominant in the craft industries, but German colonization of the countryside in Livonia was never achieved. It is not known whether this was because there was a sufficiently numerous native population after the conquest, or whether the deciding factor was the shortage of people willing to settle in those distant territories which were constantly threatened by Lithuania and the neighbouring Russian States. A possible factor might have been the relatively weak economic potential of the branch of Teutonic Order in Livonia as compared with that of the Order in Prussia, which had links with the rich Hanseatic burghers and, thus, greater material resources which made the organization of colonization easier. Nonetheless, the speed with which the Prussian Order succeeded

[10] V. Nitemaa, *Der Binnenhandel in der Politik der holländischen Städte im Mittelalter*, Helsinki, 1952, pp. 56, 121–124, 324–326, 341; *idem, Die undeutsche Frage in der Politik der livländischen Städte im Mittelalter*, Helsinki, 1949, *passim*.

in becoming an economic power in the Baltic area deserves greater attention than has been given to it hitherto. But this problem has still not been properly explained. The system of monopolies copied from Sicily under the reign of Frederic II certainly had same limited importance, serving as a model for concentrating in the hands of the Order the sale of amber, which was so highly valued at the time, but this does not explain much. It is known that the Teutonic Knights encouraged colonization by German knights, peasants and burghers, but after 1350, when immigration from Germany ceased, they made wide use of Polish colonists from the region of Chełmno, Dobrzyń and also of Eastern Mazovia. The major group they oppressed was the poorer peasants subject to Prussian Law, but even in this case the Teutonic Knights did not go so far as to persecute them for the survival of pagan beliefs among them, the existence of which was fairly generally known.

The subject of migration in the Middle Ages has been studied in many countries for some time now. With the low rate of natural population growth migration was an especially important factor in the colonization of sparsely populated territories and towns. This applied both to the native and to the foreign population. So far as the latter was concerned there was, for example, an influx on several occasions from the highly populated France to Spain. In Central-Eastern Europe migration of both foreign and native population occurred. After the first, not very large, wave of Walloons and Flemings into Silesia, Poland and Bohemia, and of a few Frenchmen, particularly in Hungary,[11] Germans appeared everywhere and in much greater numbers. Later in the XIVth century came Jews, and Armenians also arrived in Poland and Russia. In Poland foreign colonization was strongest in the towns, whereas in the countryside the decisive role was played by the native population. The policy of toleration and encouragement to settlers of all kinds to establish themselves, which was pursued by the authorities and by private feudal lords, in an epoch when hostility to and mistrust of everything foreign was very strong, indicates how great were the economic difficulties created by population shortages at that time.

The beneficial effects of this action on the feudal lords influenced them to impose Germanic Law on the native people, in both rural

---

[11] B Hóman, *op. cit.*, pp. 157–162; E. Fügedi, *Formation des villes hongroises*, pp. 976–980.

areas and in the towns, at an early stage, from the middle of the XIIIth century. The benefits also influenced the Teutonic Knights and later the authorities of the Grand Duchy of Lithuania to encourage the flow of settlers from the Polish territories as well, and at the same time to confer advantageous rights on them. This policy was essential for success in sparsely populated and backward areas and also stimulated those who had settled previously to work more intensively. I have paused to discuss these well known facts but not with the intention of presenting them as "discoveries". But it is important that the problems of colonization and the acceptance of the new legal codes should be treated in a scholarly and not an emotional fashion. Some German scholars have, for instance, been guilty of attributing the role of the all-powerful "Kulturträger" on Slav soil to the colonists who were their fellow countrymen. Naturally Czech and Polish scholars reacted sharply and not infrequently overemphasized the problems of nationality, whereas the crux of the matter lay, in fact, in the demographic and economic difficulties which the feudal lords in Central Europe tried to deal with in various ways. This also happened in Scandinavia, Spain and France. As I stated twenty years ago, the XIIIth century changes were extremely beneficial both to the ruling classes and to the peasants and burghers. The benefits were obtained at the cost of concessions to the last two groups. It was these changes that initiated the long-lasting period of economic, political and later also cultural development referred to at the beginning of this article.

Demographic and economic growth in the XIIth, XIIIth and XIVth centuries in Central-Eastern Europe contributed to a large extent to the formation of several zones of economic development of varying dynamism. The areas of relatively early and rapid development were firstly the Baltic region and secondly the area comprising the Bohemian basin, Silesia, Galicia (Małopolska), and northern region of what was then Hungary and Transylvania. In the XIVth–XVth centuries there was a very noticeable economic revival in Serbia, Bosnia and also partly in Bulgaria which had been disturbed for a long time during the Turkish conquest.

The territories between the zones mentioned, or in their neighbourhood, showed a slower rate of economic growth in the Middle Ages but accelerated considerably during the XVth century. This was particularly true of Wielkopolska (Greater Poland) and Mazovia, of the Hungarian basin and, to some extent, of Moldavia. Here I shall confine myself to a brief description of the zones mentioned as I have discussed them

elsewhere in greater detail.[12] In all the zones agriculture and livestock
rearing were of basic importance, but in the area of the most dynamic
growth there were other favourable factors and circumstances as well. In
the Baltic, for example, trade played the most prominent role. The aim
of the Hanse and its success from the XIIIth to the XIVth centuries lay
not only in organizing trade among the Baltic states but also in establishing links between them and the countries of North-Western Europe,
and still more distant territories. Even in the second half of the XIIIth
century, furs (mainly squirrel pelts), wax from Novgorod and Pskov,
rye from Mecklenburg, Brandenburg and Western Pomerania, copper,
lead, metals from Poland, Silesia and Hungary, tin from Bohemia, and
iron from Sweden played an important part in the imports of Brugge.[13]
English scholars have recently agreed that the importing and distribution of furs and Baltic wheat was not only a very important factor in
the growth of London in the XIIIth century, but also greatly strengthened the position of the groups of wealthy merchants who dealt in furs
(skinners) and in foodstuffs from the Baltic area (victuallers).[14] It has
been known for some time that the Hanse made Norway economically
dependent on them during this period, as corn was essential for her
economy and they were the only suppliers importing it from the Baltic
area.[15] Supplies of timber and its by-products as well as corn from the
Baltic area were already of great importance for the Netherlands in the
XIIIth and XIVth centuries. All this favoured the Hanse gaining control
over the active trade between North-Western and Central and Eastern
Europe. Consequently, they established a monopoly for a long period
over the import of cloth from the Netherlands, and at first also from
England, as well as over the imports of manufactured and luxury goods
into the Baltic territories and their widespread hinterland, reaching as far
as Bohemia and Hungary. All this would have been unthinkable without
an increase in purchasing power which reflected the development of
the countryside and the towns, and without an increase in production
in the whole area under discussion in this article and in particular in

---

[12] A work on this subject is in the press.
[13] R. Häpke, *Brügges Entwicklung zum mittelalterlichen Weltmarkt*, Berlin, 1908,
pp. 90–120.
[14] G. A. Williams, *Medieval London. From Commune to Capital*, London, 1970, pp.
13, 63–66, 106, 158–165; E. M. Veale, *The English Fur Trade in the Later Middle Ages*,
Oxford, 1966, pp. 39, 67–70.
[15] O. A. Johnsen, *Norwegische Wirtschaftsgeschichte*, Jena, 1939, pp. 101, 105,
113–126.

the areas near to the Baltic Sea. The relative wealth of the Hanse, their initial solidarity and co-operation with the Teutonic Knights of Prussia and Livonia, as well as the economic and political weakness of their trading partners in the Baltic zone, enabled them to achieve rapid and considerable success not only in these territories but also, indirectly, in England and Flanders. But taking all this into account it must be understood that an enormous difference existed between the economic potential of the Hanseatic and Italian cities. A comparison shows the former to have been at a disadvantage, for the Hanse trade, on the whole, was in much cheaper goods (including furs) than the Italians and dealt with less affluent customers, not only in the Baltic region but also in Scandinavia and England. As a result the accumulation of merchant capital in the Baltic area was much smaller and slower than in the Mediterranean. Besides, in the 1370s, prices of corn, furs and other goods of Baltic area origin dropped more sharply than prices of manufactured articles. This must have weakened the position of the Hanse, at the same time strengthening that of its English competitors, and later also of the Dutch and those in the Baltic regions, as they were based on their own developing cloth manufactures, the foremost branch of production outside agriculture.

During the XVth century a noticeable disintegration of the Hanse as a league of towns began even though, individually, the towns continued to develop. They began to integrate more with their hinterland and in the second half of the century there was a marked tendency on the part of the countries of the hinterland to subordinate the towns to their own interests. Because of the economic superiority of the Hanse, however, this did not produce any great results. The change in the balance of power between the English and the Dutch damaged the Hanse, in spite of transitory successes in the struggles with their increasingly more important partners who were now also dangerous rivals.

On another occasion I have discussed the very dynamic Sudeten/Carpathian area, and the important Western Balkan region, and I drew attention to the enormous importance of the mining of metals, iron ore and salt for the economic growth of these countries between the XIIIth and the XVth centuries.[16] It is sufficient here to mention only the

---

[16] M. Małowist, *Górnictwo w średniowiecznej Europie Środkowej i Wschodniej jako element struktur społeczno-gospodarczych w XII–XV w.*, "Przegląd Historyczny", LXIII, 1972, 4, pp. 589–603. This article contains a list of the most important bibliography.

most important factors. The supply of lead from Galicia (Małopolska) and Silesia was essential for the exploitation of iron and silver ores in Slovakia and also in Bohemia,[17] while Galician (Małopolska) and later Russian salt constantly reached Bohemia and the border territories of Hungary, and similarly Russian and Transylvanian salt was brought to Poland before the extraction of rock salt began in Wieliczka and Bochnia.[18] Silesia and Galicia (Małopolska) supplied Hungary and Bohemia in the XIIIth, XIVth and XVth centuries with considerable quantities of cloth and linen of their own manufacture as well as those imported from Wielkopolska (Greater Poland), Southern Germany, the Netherlands and later from England and Holland. They supplied fish, particularly herrings, and other goods and in turn imported copper, tin, gold and silver which were essential for trade, mints and manufacture from their Southern neighbours. Later, wine was also imported. The interdependence between Galicia (Małopolska) and Silesia was very strong. Due to the wealth of the region of Olkusz and Slawkowo, the former was the main producer of lead in this part of Europe. From the middle of the XIIIth century rock salt from the region of Cracow, wool, skins and furs of Polish, Lithuanian and Russian origin, also some corn and iron, and later cattle were sent to Silesia. Among the goods imported were textiles from Silesia and Lusatia and Western metal products, etc. All these territories became involved in distant trade due to the convenient network of roads running from Germany and Italy to Tana and Caffa in the Black Sea basin, and from the Baltic to Hungary, Bohemia, Austria and further South. The wealth of the mines in Hungary, Bohemia and, to some extent, in Silesia as well, must have influenced the formation of these great routes. The mountain ranges in this area were not an obstacle to communications because of numerous valleys, and the whole of the area mentioned lay as it were on the point of contact of the Hanseatic, Italian and Upper German systems of trade. This increased the variety of the goods traded, particularly of manufactured and luxury goods, and widened the circle of foreign suppliers and local buyers, so quickening the accumulation of capital in all the countries of the region. This was also of considerable cultural significance. The end of the Middle Ages and the beginning of the Renaissance at

---

[17] D. Molenda, *Górnictwo kruszcowe na terenie złóż śląskokrakowskich do połowy XVI w.*, Wrocław, 1963, pp. 82–84.

[18] J. Wyrozumki, *Państwowa gospodarka solna w Polsce do schyłku XIV w.*, Kraków, 1968, p. 35 n.

the close of the XVth century were of much greater interest in the field of science and art in this region than in the Baltic area itself, without mentioning the other areas of Central-Eastern Europe.

In an article referred to earlier, I also touched on the problems of the development of Serbia, Bosnia and part of Bulgaria in the XIIIth and XIVth centuries and in the first half of the XVth century in connection with the expansion of the mining of silver ores and lead. I also mentioned the great importance of Dubrovnik and Venice, and of the relatively less significant ports of Dalmatia, as the intermediaries in the export of silver and lead to Italy and other countries of Mediterranean Europe and the Middle East. I also referred to these towns as the intermediaries in the import of textiles and other goods from Italy and Dubrovnik into the interior of the Balkan Peninsula.[19] The local need for metals, and even more the demand for gold and silver as well as for tin and copper, which became apparent in Western Europe, in Italy and to some extent also in the Baltic trade, strongly affected the development of both the mining areas mentioned. From the XIIth century searches were made for metal ores in Silesia, Bohemia and Galicia (Małopolska) while in Hungarian Slovakia mining had been undertaken for a very long time, but only of surface ores.[20] In these countries, as in the western part of the Balkan Peninsula, between the XIIIth century and particularly the XIVth century, the pioneers in mining were Germans. They were the leading specialists in this field in medieval and early Renaissance Europe and to some extent later in Central and South America. As we have seen the Baltic region, already from the beginning of the XIIth century, became an important source for supplying furs, hides, food, iron and timber products to markets in the Netherlands (particularly in Brugge), in England, and to some extent in other countries of Western Europe. At the same time, the Bohemian basin, the Carpathian central ridge, and later the Balkans, supplied the West and Italy with silver and gold. From 1325, Bohemia and Hungary also supplied them with very considerable quantities of silver and gold coins. Bohemia was the main source of silver and tin, Hungary of gold and copper, although she, too, exported a lot of silver.[21] This was of enormous importance for Italy, particularly for Venice

---

[19] M. Małowist, *op. cit.*

[20] Von Probszt, *op. cit.*, p. 23; J. Vlachovic, *Slovenska med v 16 a 17 storoci*, Bratislava, 1964, p. 22ff.

[21] M. Małowist, *op. cit.*, and the literature mentioned there.

and Florence, after the introduction of ducats, florins and silver coins of high value. Bohemian silver coins reached not only Italy, Upper Germany and the Rhineland, but also the Netherlands and, from there, undoubtedly England as well. Hungary's export of gold and silver, first in its natural state and from 1325 in the form of coins, was huge, as we shall see. In the XIVth century and the first half of the XVth, a similar function was performed, though undoubtedly on a smaller scale, by Serbia and Bosnia, and by numerous other places which were not as big but where silver and lead were mined. Dubrovnik's heyday in that period, as well as its extensive trade in the XVIth century, the intensity of which was disproportionate to the size of the town and the number of its inhabitants (about 3,000–5,000), would be inconceivable without the considerable accumulation of mercantile capital obtained from the trade in Balkan metals. From the XIIIth and XIVth centuries Dubrovnik, and to a lesser extent Split, Trogir and Sibenik, came to occupy a position in the Adriatic region similar to that of the Hanse in the Baltic, Great Novgorod in North-Western Russia and Vienna in relation to Hungary.[22] In the absence of a strong merchant class in their Balkan hinterland the towns on the Eastern coast of the Adriatic drew considerable income from acting as intermediaries between the Peninsula and more distant trading partners. Due to their location in Central-Eastern Europe, the Hanse and Dubrovnik, and to some extent Nuremberg, managed to achieve and maintain for a very long time a strong position in both the inland and coastal areas also in the West and to become indispensable to their trading partners.

In the XIVth century Central-Eastern Europe proper and the Balkans did not experience either the severe economic and social crisis characteristic of the Western countries, or the accompanying economic depression arising from the readjustments of the means of production to changing social conditions. This was undoubtedly a consequence of the delay in their economic development. In these territories (with the exception of Russia) the Black Death and the recurring epidemics in the second half of the XIVth century and during the XVth century caused less damage in the interior than in the West and in Italy, perhaps because of the slighter degree of urbanization. In contrast, in

---

[22] J. Božič, *Ekonomski i drustveni razvitak Dubrovnika v XIV–XV veku*, "Istoricki Glasnik" 1949, No. 1, pp. 21–23; M. Mirkovic, *Ekonomska Historija Jugoslavije*, Zagreb, 1958, p. 55.

Poland, Bohemia, Hungary and in the Balkans (until the time of the Turkish conquests), there was a relatively fast expansion of land under cultivation, investments in breeding and of towns. However, mining in Bohemia felt the effects of the crisis from mid XIVth century, most likely due to technical difficulties. In some areas of Northern Hungary (and perhaps earlier in Transylvania) this happened in the mid XVth century, but on the whole the area with which we are concerned developed without major interruptions.[23] In Bohemia and indirectly in Silesia only the Hussite revolution created a major interruption which resulted in the end in strengthening local manufactures and the economic contacts between town and countryside.[24]

During this period of crisis and depression in the West, the developing countries of Central-Eastern Europe acquired special importance for Western merchants who were restricted in their fields of activity. In Eastern Europe increasing opportunities were developing for the sale of goods and the profitable investment of capital. This would account for the English and the Dutch selling cloth in the Baltic region and explain the growing interest in Hungary, Bohemia and Poland shown by merchants from Nuremberg and other towns in Upper Germany and also by Venetians, Florentines and the Genoese. This would also explain the activity of the Italians in the Balkans and in the Northern part of the Black Sea which, until recently, had been poorly developed partly because of the threat from the Tatars from the XIIIth century and before then from other nomads.[25]

The interest of the Italians goes back even further however. In the first half of the XIVth century, two Italians, undoubtedly Genoese from a colony in the Crimea, were receiving grants from the grand Muscovite princes in the area of the Peczora river, most certainly in connection with the proposed supply of valuable furs from the distant North to the Crimea. Besides, in the XIVth and XVth centuries, economic contacts between the distant Moscow and Soldaia (Sudak) and later Caffa were

---

[23] J Koran, *K periodisaci dejin ceskeho hornictvi*, "Sbornik pro hospodarske a socialni dejiny", Vol. I, 1946, Nos. 1–2, 1946, *passim*.

[24] This emerges from the work of J. Janaček, *Remeslna vyroba v ceskych mestech v 16 stoleti*, Praha, 1961, pp. 29–60.

[25] I. Sakazov, *Bulgarische Wirtschaftsgeschichte*, Berlin/Leipzig, 1929, pp. 104, 123–134, 139, tables; Fr. Balducci Pegolotti, *La pratica della mercatura*, ed. A. Evans, Cambridge (Mass.), 1936, p. 38: data refer to export of corn from Varna and other ports and the Black Sea in the first half of the XIVth century.

fairly close.[26] It has been known for some time that merchants from the Rhineland (particularly from Cologne) showed a great interest in the purchase of silver and gold in Bohemia and Hungary from the XIIth and XIIIth centuries. By the XIVth century the dominant position in this trade was achieved by rich merchants from Nuremberg, Regensburg and other towns in Upper Germany, who came to Hungary through Moravia. In the course of time they also came through Vienna.[27]

Up to the outbreak of the Hussite revolution merchants from Regensburg and Nuremberg dominated foreign trade in Bohemia. By the second half of the XIVth century, at the latest, newcomers from Nuremberg were very active in Poland, at first particularly in Cracow, and then they reportedly reached the Black Sea and Constantinople through the South-Western part of Russia which had been absorbed into Poland.[28] Already by the end of the century their activity had affected Hanseatic craftsmen and merchants in Prussia and Livonia and they established contacts with Great Novgorod. They occupied particularly strong positions in copper and silver mining, and directed exports of metals to Venice. At the turn of the XIVth–XVth centuries, they attempted, somewhat unsuccessfully in this case because of the opposition of the Hanse, to participate in the coastal trade between the Baltic ports and Brugge. Besides the large firms and big merchants from Nuremberg, merchants from other mining centres were also active. They found ready markets in the Polish territories, in Prussia and in Livonia for the metal products in which Nuremberg specialized, and even for small articles such as needles. There were ready markets also for other articles of daily use—German and Italian fustians, linens of high quality, fabrics from the Netherlands and Italy, and also silk. The situation was similar in Hungary and also in Bohemia before the outbreak of the Hussite revolution. Energetic expansion by merchants from Upper Germany, who reached not only the urban but also the village markets,

---

[26] V. E. Syroečkovskii, *Gosti-Surožanie*, Moskwa-Leningrad, 1935, pp. 15–17, 23–27ff.; M. Małowist, *Kaffa—kolonia genueńska na Krymie i problem wschodni 1453–1475*, Warszawa, 1947, pp. 75–79.

[27] Th. Mayer, *Der auswärtige Handel des Herzogtums Oesterreich im Mitteltalter*, Innsbruck, 1909, pp. 5, 11, 46f., 74ff.; F. Bastian, *Das Runtingerbuch 1383–1407 und verwandtes Material zum Regensburger-Südostdeutschen Handel und Münzwesen*, Vol. I, Regensburgrg, 1944, pp. 86, 179, 430, 632–640; Vol. II, pp. 61f., 71ff.; W. Von Stromer, *Oberdeutsche Hochfinanz 1350–1450*, Vol. I, Wiesbaden, 1970, pp. 19f., 25, 55, 58–60, 69, 91–99.

[28] H. Amman, *Wirtschaftsbeziehungen zwischen Oberdeutschland und Polen im Mittelalte*, "Ergon", Vol. III, 1962, p. 339.

aroused strong, though rarely successful, opposition from the Polish and Prussian burghers who were exposed to dangerous competition from this quarter.[29] Prussian sources appear to indicate that both knights and peasants welcomed the newcomers as suppliers and buyers of goods because of the effect of this trade on village prices which tended to be unfavourable when compared with prices of town products, particularly of manufactures. Rich merchants from Upper Germany—for example Boner, Ber and other families—settled in Cracow, invested money in property and bought estates. They held high administrative posts in the Polish and Hungarian treasuries, and invested capital in lead and salt mining in Galicia (Małopolska) as citizens of the capital city of Cracow. It should be emphasized that this type of immigration intensified in the XIVth century and particularly in the XVth century, in spite of the fact that the flow of settlers from Germany to the East completely ceased after the Black Death. Merchants from Upper Germany in Bohemia and in Hungary bought mainly silver and gold but also iron, copper and tin which were used for manufactures in their own country. In Poland they bought furs, hides of Polish, Lithuanian and Russian origin, wood, cinnabar (red pigment) and certainly cattle. They were very active in Cracow and Lwów in the XVth century and also from the middle of the century in Poznań and Warsaw, whose fairs they valued highly as sources of furs. In the territory of Silesia, which belonged at that time almost entirely to the Bohemian Crown, in Galicia (Małopolska) and Wielkopolska (Greater Poland), agents of the Diesbach-Watt Company operated as well as those of other merchant houses such as Stromer, Cress, etc.[30]

The case of merchants from Venice, Florence, Genoa and Bologna in the XIVth and XVth centuries, was similar, as was that of the clothiers from Florence who settled in Cracow.[31] At first the Italians acted here

---

[29] C. Nordmann, *Nürnberger Grosshändler im spätmittelalterlichen Lübeck*, Nürnberg, 1933, pp. 7–16, 35, 67, 71, 109ff., 115, 119, 122, 138, 143, 144; G. Hollihn, *Die Stapel- und Gästepolitik Rigas in der Ordenszeit (1201–1562)*, "Hansische Geschichtsblatter", Vol. 60, 1935; p. 148f.; J. Ptaśnik, *Akta Norymberskie do dziejów handlu z Polską w w. XV*, "Archiwum Komisji Historycznej", Vol. X, 1909–1913, Nos. 6, 9–11, 13, 15, 32.

[30] H. Amman, *Die Diesbach-Watt-Gesellschaft. Ein Beitrag zur Handelsgeschichte des 15 Jahrhunderts*, Sankt Gallen, 1928, pp. 108, Nos. 17, 27, 60, 77, 84, 86, 88, 129–131, 134, 143, 161, 169, 171, etc.; Von Stromer, *op. cit.*, pp. 55f. 94, 109, 113, 121, 125ff., 146–153.

[31] In addition to sources published long ago by J. Ptaśnik, cfr. J. Wyrozumski, *Drapery in Małopolska in Late Middle Ages*, Kraków, 1972, p. 40. This work shows that weaving in Biecz, Felow and in many other towns had been relatively highly developed.

as collectors of Papal tributes but undoubtedly they had also been attracted to Silesia, Galicia (Małopolska) and Lwów by the prospects of trade with the east on the routes to the Black Sea. Nevertheless, in the XIVth, and particularly in the XVth centuries, they often settled in Wrocław and Cracow and established their agencies there. Their offices in Wrocław acquired the function of transferring to the Papal Treasury levies coming from Poland and Prussia. This job had previously been performed by the agents of Italian firms in Brugge. It seems that a member of the Medici firm operated in Cracow, but this is not clear. Contact with the royal court and with the magnates of Galicia (Małopolska), to whom they supplied luxurious Italian fabrics, helped the Italians in their moves to lease salt mines in Galicia and Ruthenia. In this field newcomers from Florence and Genoa played an important role in the XVth century in spite of competition from local merchants. There is information on the urban property and on the country estates acquired by those Italians who either settled or stayed in Poland for a long time.[32] Italian influence was strong particularly in Cracow even as late as the XVIIth century.

I believe that these developments together with the beginning of Jewish and Armenian settlements in towns, which were established in the Eastern provinces of Poland, were linked with the rapid economic growth of the country, particularly in the XIVth and XVth centuries. At the same time, this meant that there was now a flow of capital, which previously had been scarce in Central-Eastern Europe, and that new methods in trade and finance wore introduced. Venetians became important suppliers of both Italian and Levantine commodities when the trading centres with the East in the region of the Black Sea became weaker during the XVth century. In the more northern provinces of Poland there was also an economic revival in the XIVth and XVth centuries. In North Western Europe, from the second half of the XIVth century at the latest, and in Portugal from the XVth century, demand for Polish and Prussian timber for building purposes and for other timber products began to grow. In the Netherlands and temporarily in England, demand grew for corn, mainly rye, but also to some extent for wheat which was exported from Gdańsk (Danzig) but which in fact came from the Teutonic Knights' Prussian territories and from bordering areas of the Polish state. This became of greater importance

---

[32] J. Ptaśnik, *Kultura włoska wieków średnich w Polsce*, Warszawa, 1959, *passim.*

during the XVth century. It was a major economic problem for Prussia at that time, involving the sharply conflicting interests of the Order, the knights and the merchants from the towns.[33] The Order and the Prussian merchants, particularly from Gdańsk (Danzig), developed a system which depended on making payments in advance to the suppliers and producers for future supplies of timber, ash, pitch and corn, especially from Kujawy and Mazovia. From there, it was easy to float these products down the Wisła (Vistula) and her tributaries to Gdańsk (Danzig), particularly in the spring and autumn when the water level was high. On the Polish side many small merchants from a number of towns, as well as the gentry and even the peasants participated in the trade. It is difficult to say to what extent the Polish suppliers were exploited by their creditors as there is little information on the conflicts. But this whole phenomenon was important. It led to an increased flow of Prussian money into the interior of Poland and quickened its circulation. In Mazovia in particular local coinage was of low value and appeared in limited quantities.[34]

The most important factor, however, was the stimulating effect of the credit given both by merchants from Gdańsk (Danzig) and Toruń and from the towns in the old provinces of Central Poland and Mazovia, for forestry and agriculture in this less developed region. This opened new markets for these products at home and abroad and accelerated the development of Warsaw which until then was of little significance. However, there arose other opportunities for Warsaw, Poznań, Lublin and other smaller and medium-sized towns in Central Poland. The union of Poland and Lithuania at the end of the XIVth century made access to the interior of the Grand Duchy of Lithuania which had a small population and a low level of economic development but possessed plentiful supplies of skins, furs and timber easier for merchants from central Poland. Furthermore, it dominated the routes leading not only to Pskov and Novgorod but also to Moscow. The Grand Duchy of Moscow, which was in the process of consolidation, and in particular its capital, became an important trading centre not only in cheap squirrel skins but also in valuable furs coming from the far Northern

---

[33] M. Małowist, *Studia z dziejów rzemiosła w okresie kryzysu feudalizmu w Zachodniej Europie w XIV i XV w.*, Warszawa, 1954, p. 419ff.

[34] M. Małowist, *Podstawy gospodarcze przywrócenia jedności państwowej Pomorza Gdańskiego z Polską w XV w.*, "Przegląd Hist.," XLV, 1954, pp. 2–3, *passim*. M. Biskup, *Zjednoczenie Pomorza Wschodniego z Polską w połowie XV w.*, Warszawa, 1959, pp. 47–133.

Russian territories and also from Western Siberia. Simultaneously the even faster economic growth of North-Eastern Russia in the XIVth century increased the demand there for metal products, Polish and German textiles, for other goods and, particularly important, for money. The area's own currency system began to develop anew. This offered important opportunities for merchants from Poland and Lithuania who, as Contarini ascertained, had already visited Moscow by the 1470s.[35] The supply of skins and furs from Lithuania and Russia contributed to the fast growth of tanning and furriery in Poland and in Lithuania, where they came to occupy an important place among local crafts. Simultaneously, towns in central Poland and in Lithuania drew income from brokerage in the export of furs, skins and wax from their own territories and Russia to Wrocław and Leipzig who shared in this trade. This was a threat to the interests of the Hanseatic towns and they were aware of the fact.[36] Gdańsk (Danzig) took part in the overland trade.

Due to all this Poznań grew rapidly and activity of the Gniezno markets intensified.[37] Warsaw, Lublin, even Cracow and other smaller towns benefited. The traffic attracted the merchants from Upper Germany, who have already been mentioned, to Central Poland and Lithuania and also at times Italian merchants, although in small numbers.[38] During the XVth century the rate of economic growth in the central territories of Poland was probably faster than in Galicia but the level of economic development which had been achieved there earlier was still appreciably higher. In terms of land cultivation and livestock breeding the development of the two main provinces of Central Poland, Wielkopolska and Mazovia, is clearly noticeable. Admittedly there were many deserted fields in the former, but these were due to the migration of the peasants and the lesser gentry to the towns where they engaged in crafts and trade. Later sources indicate that many of

[35] *Il viaggio del Magnifico M. Ambrogio Contarini Ambasciadore della Illustrissima Signoria di Venetia*, Biblioteka Inostrannych Pisatielei o Rossii, t. I, Sankt Peterburg, 1836, p. 179. The author who stayed in Moscow in the second half of the XV century reported on numerous merchants from Germany and Poland who spent the winter in Moscow with the object of buying furs: sables, ermine, etc. These furs were brought to Moscow from very distant places. Contarini emphasized plentiful supplies of all types of food in the town. There was a sizeable colony established by the Italians. He also mentioned a goldsmith from Kotor.

[36] M. Małowist, *Studia*, p. 440f.

[37] L. Koczy, *Handel Poznania do połowy XVI w.*, Poznań, 1930, p. 92ff.; *Dzieje Gniezna*, ed. J. Topolski, Warszawa, 1965, p. 292f.

[38] Cf. note 30.

the fields which had apparently been abandoned were, in fact, cultivated on a permanent or temporary basis by neighbouring peasants who paid a fairly low rent to the owners. Nevertheless, the landowners found this worthwhile in view of the lack of possible tenants willing to take over the whole estates. In both these provinces colonization continued but the rate was faster in Mazovia.[39] By this time territorial expansion was achieved entirely through the indigenous population. In Wielkopolska sheep rearing became of considerable importance, supplying raw material for cloth manufacture which developed not only in the south-western but also in the eastern regions of this province.[40] Although data on cattle breeding in Mazovia are scanty, they allow us to conclude that the output met not only local needs but also those of neighbouring Prussia.[41] Cloth manufacture also developed in Mazovia but as in Wielkopolska (Greater Poland) the product was generally of cheap and medium quality for consumption by the poorer section of the population of the home country and for export to Prussia. Despite earlier doubts it is now certain that an important feature appeared in Poland in the XVth century, namely the strengthening of the economic links between the country's provinces, so establishing the beginning of a national market. In this Prussia (which had been included in Poland after the war with the Teutonic Knights 1454–1466) played a very important part. Although the division between the less and more developed zones persisted then, the economic gap between central, northern and southern provinces diminished.

A new feature characteristic of the XVIth century, particularly in the area along the Wisła (Vistula) and in Mazovia, was the beginning of the change in the organization of agriculture. The increased demand for corn in the Polish towns, specially in Galicia (Małopolska), and the increasing absorption of exports from the northern and central provinces by Gdańsk (Danzig), as well as the depreciation of rents paid in cash, all encouraged the gentry to enlarge their estates. An increase in weekly corvées began. L. Zytkowicz assumes, probably correctly, that the low productivity of agriculture (yields of 3 to 4:1) and the resulting low income for the gentry, combined with the low prices of

---

[39] I. Gieysztorowa, *op. cit.*, p. 10 draws attention to the faster rate of urbanization.
[40] A. Mączak, *Sukiennictwo wielkopolskie XIV–XVII w.*, Warszawa, 1955, pp. 26–41, 244–245. There are many indications that the Sieradz-Łęczyca region already existed in the XVth century.
[41] M. Małowist, *Podstawy gospodarcze*, p. 159.

agricultural products until the last quarter of the XVth century, made it impossible for farm administrators to rely fully on hired labour and led them to impose compulsory services and serfdom on the peasants.[42] It is known from other sources that in the XVth century, in Prussia as well as in Galicia (Małopolska), the gentry protested strongly against both the seasonal and permanent migration of peasants to the towns and complained about the high price of labour. All this, however, was but a small indication of the later radical changes in the rural economy. In the second half of the century the pace of change accelerated.

Bohemia and Hungary experienced great difficulties in the XVth century. In this area a decline in silver mining from the mid XIVth century resulted from the exhaustion of seams near the surface and mine owners lacked material resources and knowledge of methods of dealing with underground water. This made it impossible to reach seams which were at a greater depth, and neither were the problems of ventilating the deeper mines easy to solve. Nevertheless, during the period under discussion Kutna Hora in Bohemia in particular became almost a model for the mining area of this part of Europe. But the Hussite revolution caused the flight of the rich mining entrepreneurs and of a large proportion of merchants from the towns. Bohemia was boycotted and at war with hostile Catholic Germany and as a result of the attacks, which she fought off successfully on the whole, and as a consequence of the internal disorders, she experienced serious upheavals for nearly thirty years. However, it would appear that there were also developments which later had very positive effects on the future of the country. It would be very interesting to study to what extent the expropriation of the great estates belonging to the Church improved the economic position not only of the lay magnates but also of the minor nobility and the peasants. Bohemian scholars drew attention to the fact that craft guilds during the Hussite period managed to strengthen their position in relation to the merchants and patricians who up till then had been the ruling class in towns. This had positive effects on the development of the crafts in the country. Output of tin and iron products and also of textiles went up, and after the revolution they were to be found on Polish markets and were also exported

---

[42] L. Zytkowicz, *The peasant's farm and the landlord's farm in Poland from the 16th to the middle of the 18th century*, "The Journal of European Economic History", 1972, No. 1, p. 141.

to Russia, Hungary and the Balkans.[43] Although Schenek claims that
in the second half of the XVth century merchants from Nuremberg
regained their former strong position in Prague as suppliers of luxury
goods and manufacturers, Bohemian crafts succeeded in consolidating
their position both in the country and to some extent in the territories
further to the east. This was an important factor in the growth of the
towns. Czech scholars are of the opinion that in the second half of the
XVth century and in the XVIth century, it was the towns which had
the private backing of the great lords that grew, whereas in the royal
towns conditions were not so easy. It should be noted however that the
growth of towns, irrespective of type, led to an increased demand for
rural products. This was particularly beneficial for the peasants under
the prevailing system of taxes in Bohemian villages and in view of the
relatively high level of agricultural development. As for the gentry, it
would appear that their income was sufficient for their needs. They
attempted their own administration in fact only in Southern Bohemia,
where they began to organize the exploitation of numerous lakes with
the aim of exporting fish abroad. At the beginning of the XVIth century Bohemian mining entered a period which, although lasting only
half a century, saw it established on a worldwide basis, and there were
profitable investment outlets in this field for the material resources of
the rich gentry.[44] The corvée system and intensified serfdom began to
develop seriously only at the start of the XVIth and XVIIth centuries,
mainly after the Habsburg victory at Bila Hora (White Mountain) in
1621 and the ravages suffered by Bohemia during the Thirty Year War.
These events played an important role. It is much more difficult however
to grasp the situation in Hungary in the XIVth and XVth centuries.
There is no doubt, in the light of recent research, that during the period
referred to here Hungary had been a major European power in the field
of gold mining (about 4/5ths of European production) and of copper
mining. As regards silver it was inferior to Bohemia, producing 10,000
monetary units annually.[45]

E. Kovacs, and more recently O. Paulinyi, re-examined Hóman's
views in this field. Paulinyi came to the conclusion that the production

[43] Cf. note 24.
[44] J. Majer, *Tezba stribrnych rud v Jáchymove w 16 stoleti*, "Sbornik Narodniho
Technickeho Muzea", Vol. V, 1968, p. 137f., *idem, Tezba cinu ve Slavkovskem Lese v
16 stoleti*, Praha, 1960, pp. 5–6.
[45] B. Hóman, *op. cit.*, p. 353.

of gold calculated by Hóman (on average 1,000 kg. annually) remained at this level only in the early period, roughly from the beginning of the XIIIth century to 1325. Paulinyi accepted for the subsequent 60 years a figure of 3,000 to 4,000 kg. of gold as the average output, which also included Slovakia and the main mines of Transylvania. Afterwards output dropped to half that amount, while during the second half of the XVth century an acute crisis was experienced, brought about by technical difficulties but mainly by the lack of substantial amounts of capital required for constructing galleries and installations designed to protect the mines from flooding.[46] So far as the extraction of silver and copper is concerned, output increased towards the end of the XIVth century, partly due to Florentine investments. The first signs of crisis at the beginning of the XVth century were not as yet dangerous, but in the second half of the century they were acutely felt in central Slovakia, particularly in the copper ore mining industry. Even in such important centres as Kremnica and Banská Štiavnica the supply of large amounts of capital and the application of new methods of mine drainage became essential.[47]

Metals and ores had enormous importance for Hungary, both politically and economically. As a result of the reforms introduced by King Charles Robert (1325–1327) which encouraged an increase in the supply of miners and the creation of mining towns, the income of the Hungarian crown greatly increased. Besides the levy (*urbura*) amounting to 1/8th of the mined silver and 0.1 of gold, the crown derived very substantial profits from the compulsory purchases of the remaining crude ore for coinage, which was then valued in the neighbouring countries also. This system was modelled on the one introduced in Bohemia by the last of the Premyslids. The export of copper to Poland, the Baltic regions, Russia, Flanders, England and Upper Germany also brought in a large income from customs' duties. The rapid rise to power of Hungary under the Anjou dynasty would be incomprehensible had they not had such sources of wealth at their disposal. O. Paulinyi rightly draws attention to the disproportionately strong development of mining compared with the relatively low levels in other fields of economic life in

---

[46] O. Paulinyi, *Der erste Bau eines Stausees in Ungarn zur Bekämpfung der Wassernot der Zechen. Die Versuche Johann Thurzo's van Bethlenfalva für die Relonstruktion der Goldbergwerke in Nagybanya*, pp. 1–4. Photocopy of the article was kindly sent to me by the author.
[47] B. Hóman, *op. cit.*, p. 355f.

medieval Hungary.[48] One must also mention the fragility of its political power. In fact, as Z. Pach rightly insisted, the large-scale change from payments in kind by the peasants to money rents in the XVth century[49] is proof of the retarded development of Hungary in comparison with Bohemia and Poland, although in Hungary there is some evidence of payments of money rent from the XIIIth century onwards. It is worth mentioning that urbanization in central Hungary was in fact rather weak and, consequently, the demand for rural products was somewhat limited. The capital city of Buda had, at the beginning of the XVIth century, only about 8,000 inhabitants. The king's own court, together with those of the numerous magnates, often exceeded the burghers in number. A similar, or slightly higher, proportion of burghers was to be found only in the three main towns of Transylvania.[50] Hungarian scholars have drawn attention to the weakness of the craft industries of the country. Even copper was exported mainly as an ore in the XIVth century. In the XVth century in the numerous "*oppida*" (counterpart of the German *Marktflecken*) several hundred inhabitants were engaged primarily in agriculture, livestock breeding and in working vineyards, but craftsmen were not numerous.[51] It would appear then that the Hungarian economy was unfavourably affected by both the possession of natural wealth and its exportation.

Foreign merchants were interested in Hungary from the XIth century on account of its gold resources, and from the XIIIth and XIVth centuries also because of its silver and copper. This led foreigners to bring in large quantities of goods for which there was a demand in Hungary. Records of the customs office in Passau, which was on the route from Bavaria to Vienna, show that even in 1402 very large supplies of cloth from the Netherlands and Germany, metal products, etc. were being imported. According to Th. Mayer the bulk of these goods was assigned for Hungary whose main trading partner at that time was Vienna.[52]

---

[48] O. Paulinyi, *op. cit.*, p. 20.

[49] Z. P. Pach, *Das Entwicklungsniveau der feudalen Verhältnisse in Ungarn in der zweiten Hälfte des 15. Jahrhunderts*, "Studia Historica", 1960, p. 12, 15, 18; *idem, Abliegung der ungarischen Agrarentwicklung von der Westeuropäischen*, "Agrartörteneti Szemle", 1961, No. 1, p. 8f.

[50] E. Fügedi, *Pour une analyse*, p. 1306. Population of Buda later fell. *Din Istoria Transilvaniei*, Vol. I, Bucuresti, 1961, p. 133; J. Perenyi, *Villes hongroises sous la domination ottomane au XVIe et XVIIe siècles*, "Studia Balcanica", Vol. III, Sofia, 1970, p. 26.

[51] E. Fügedi, *op. cit.*, p. 1306.

[52] Th. Mayer, *op. cit.*, p. 39f.

The records of the customs office in Bratislava for 1457–58, which Ember analysed and later substantially adjusted, are very informative. Approximately 15,000 pieces of fustian and linen were sent to Hungary at that time. The value of the imported textiles reached 130,000 ducats and amounted to 79% of the value of the total imports. Goods of all qualities were included, same being 8 to 10 times as expensive as others. Besides expensive woven fabrics from Italy, the Netherlands, the Rhineland and Upper Germany, there were medium-priced products from Bohemia, Moravia, Silesia and Poland, and the cheaper Flemish and English kersey of medium quality, etc. An important place was held by metal products, which accounted for about 12% of the total imports. Oxen were the main item in Hungarian exports via Bratislava and in that year reached the as yet relatively small number of 1,466 head. Other exports included some horses, hides, wax, small quantities of copper etc. So Hungary's balance of trade in this field (as in others) was very much in debit. Ember estimated that the amount of money necessary to balance the account was 400,000 ducats[53] but as a result of more recent studies this figure has been reduced to 100,000–150,000 ducats. Nevertheless, Hungarian scholars estimate Hungary's total foreign trade deficit in the XVth century at between approximately 300,000 and 400,000 ducats per year. Of this, about 146,000 ducats went for trade with the West, 100,000 ducats for trade with Italy through Dalmatia and 50,000 ducats for trade with the North-Western area, i.e. Silesia and North-Western Europe.[54] According to Paulinyi the sum total was equal to two-thirds of the annual production of gold, which at that time in Hungary was approximately 6,000 marks (1,500 kg.).[55] This subject is very interesting for a number of reasons. Allowance has to be made for the fact that part of the imports from the West and from Italy was in theory intended for sale in the two Duchies on the Danube and in the Balkan countries, but this was made much more difficult by the war with Turkey. Ember did not take this into account.

---

[53] I quote from an accurate summary in Z. P. Pach, *Osteuropa und die Anfangsperiode der Entstehung des modernen internationalen Handels im 15. Jahrhundert*, "V Internationaler Kongress der Ökonomischen Geschichte", Moskva, 1970, pp. 1–3.

[54] E. Fuegedi, *Der Aussenhandel Ungarns am Anfang des 16 Jahrhunderts, Der Aussenhandel Mitteleuropas 1450–1650*, ed. I. Bog, Köln-Wien, 1971, pp. 56, 63–85.

[55] O. Paulinyi, *La formation générale de richesse de métal précieux et l'économie nationale de la Hongrie dans la période du féodalisme épanouissant et développé (1000–1526)*. Summary of the work published in Hungarian in "Szazadok", 1971, No. 108, pp. 561–602.

Nevertheless, in relation to the size of the population, imports into Hungary, both of luxury goods and necessities, were on a huge scale. This must have badly hampered the development of the country's weak craft industries and thereby reduced the rate of growth of the urban population and also the division of labour. From this point of view, exploitation of its natural wealth and its exportation from a country which was relatively poorly developed proved harmful to Hungary. In the XVth century, a large proportion of the income from the mines went to foreign merchants on whom the rulers conferred considerable privileges as buyers of metals, since there were no burghers of sufficient wealth in the country. As a severe mining crisis was on the way, the Hungarian crown found itself in difficult financial circumstances at a time of increasing pressure from the Turks. King Matthew Corvinus tried to save the situation by fighting the powerful magnates who were hostile to him and through an aggressive policy of conquest aimed at Bohemia, Austria and Poland. Although revenue from mining was still an important item in his budget, he tried to conquer North-Eastern Bosnia where there were, at that time, important centres of silver mining, particularly in Srbrnica. By 1475 the king conferred on John Thurzon and his partners, who were rich merchants from Cracow, privileges in connection with the drainage of mines in central Slovakia in return for 1/6th of the mined silver, as both capital and specialists were lacking in the country.[56] Matthew's successor, Ladislaus Jagiellonicus, had to extend these privileges considerably and, after 1494–1496, accepted the takeover of the most important Slovakian mines in Banská Bistrica and its neighbourhood by the partnership of John Thurzon and James Fugger, thus foregoing sales and part of the customs duties on the export of silver, gold and copper. This move, particularly during the first 25 years of the Fugger lease of the mines (Thurzon withdrew as time went on and joined the ranks of the aristocracy) led to an enormous increase in the production of copper and iron ores due to the use of water treadmills and the construction of deep galleries.[57] Under the prevailing conditions, demand for both metals was very large because of the use of copper and brass in the making of armour, especially in the Rhineland and on the Meuse. These metals were also in demand because of the large-scale exports of brass and copper articles

---

[56] I. Vlachovic, *op. cit.*, pp. 25–29.
[57] *Ibid.*, pp. 30–39.

from Antwerp, Lisbon and Seville to the Portuguese and Spanish colonies, and from Venice to the Middle and Far East. The Hungarian
crown was thus guaranteed an income from the leases and from some
other payments. Nevertheless, control over mining, which had once
given the Anjou dynasty and to a lesser extent Matthew Corvinus a
strong financial position, slipped from the hands of the Hungarian
Jagellons. But the enormous income of the Fuggers and their partners
annoyed the Hungarian gentry, and they met with strong opposition
from the mining towns of Slovakia because local entrepreneurs felt
themselves forced out by the powerful leaseholders. Disturbances broke
out in 1525 in which miners took part mainly because of the fall in the
value of money and an increase in prices. Nevertheless, the Fuggers
held out in Slovakia until 1546 and extended their influence to mines
in Transylvania although apparently with less success. The backing
given to the Fuggers by King Ladislaus and King Louis is explained by
their efforts to save their wealth in face of increasing danger from
Turkey. After the disaster at Mohács (1526) and later during the disintegration of the Hungarian Kingdom (1541), the Hasburgs continued
this policy partly because the Slovak mines were important for arming
their troops which were defending the rest of the Kingdom from the
Ottoman advance. However, it was this threat as well as the drop in
the production of silver and metals in Slovakia which influenced the
Fuggers to withdraw from this territory in 1546, but for a long time
they retained a monopoly position as buyers of these metals.[58] Hungarian
Slovakia still maintained an important place in iron ore mining. It is
worth recalling that industries producing iron goods in Nowy Sącz in
the XVIth century and at the beginning of the XVIIth century relied
on supplies of raw materials from the Carpathians.[59] Little is known
about the situation of the mines in Transylvania in the XVth and XVIth
centuries, and more recent Rumanian studies provide little in the way
of new information. It would appear that in Transylvania the production of iron, gold, silver and lead was particularly strong during the
reign of the Anjou dynasty and there were important exports of salt to
the interior of Hungary, to the Balkans (through the merchants of
Dubrovnik), to the Duchies along the Danube and also to the ports of

[58] G. Von Probszt, *op. cit.*, pp. 65, 70–72; F. Von Pölnitz, *Anton Fugger*, Tübingen,
Vol. II, p. 154f.
[59] A. Żaboklicka, *Kapitał mieszczański Nowego Sącza na przełomie XVI–XVII w.*,
Warszawa, 1967, pp. 43–46, 108–112.

Belgorod and Kilia. Lead was also extracted in Transylvania and in the Duchies. This caused some anxiety in Poland because of the competition. From a report of 1552 it seems that the production of gold dropped very noticeably. In the XVth century an important centre, Baia Mare (Hungarian Nagybánya) gave the crown large revenues in gold and silver, but later there was a drop in production, as also happened in many other regions in the country. Iron ore production was maintained, however, particularly in the region of Hunedoara, and during the XVIth century extraction of mercury increased.[60]

The situation of the Balkan territories, which in the 1460s came under Turkish rule for the next 300 years, is a debatable issue. In the early stages of the conquest the devastation was massive. The military tactics of the Ottoman commanders were based on terrorist raids preceding, as a rule, the main attack. This also gave the Turks considerable economic benefits in the form of prisoners who became slaves, in addition to other kinds of plunder which the Sultan shared with his army commanders and soldiers. A colony of merchants from Dubrovnik still operated in Turkish Belgrade in the XVIth century, systematically buying war loot from the Turkish soldiers returning from the conquests.[61] After the conquest of the Balkans however, the Turkish administration proved to be efficient and was probably no more oppressive for the population than the authorities of Christian states operating under similar conditions in conquered territories. A very favourable event was the shift in the military theatre to the territories further North. From the end of the XIVth century, waves of nomadic livestock breeders began to flow from over-populated Asia Minor into the Balkans, particularly to Bulgaria. Soon not only the officials and "*shipahi*" settled there but also soldiers from the Turkish garrison, merchants and craftsmen. In any case, it was probably the newcomers from Asia Minor who brought to the Balkans the cultivation of rice, cotton, silk and especially maize,

---

[60] N. Maghiar and S. Oltenau, *Din Istoria Mineritului in Romania*, Bucuresti, 1970, pp. 118–129.

[61] R. Samardzic, *Belgrade, centre économique de la Turquie du Nord au XVIe siècle*, "Studia Balcanica", Vol. III, pp. 34–36, 41f. The author emphasizes the enormous increase in importance of trade and manufacture of the town under the Turkish rule as compared with the earlier period. At that time the Danube became a great waterway for trade likewise. Cf. T. Stojanovic, *Model and mirror of the premodern Balkan city*, "Studia Balcanica", Vol. III, *passim*, and J. Tadič, *L'unité économique des Balkans et de la région méditerranéenne*, "Ier Congrès des Etudes Balkaniques et Sud-Est Européennes", Vol. III, Sofia, 1969, p. 633ff.

which became so important in feeding the population under the prevailing conditions of primitive agriculture.[62] J. Tadič has drawn attention to the fact that in the XVIth century there were no outbreaks of
famine in the peninsula due to the poor harvests whereas later exports
of corn to Italy became possible.[63] The Turkish scholars Ö. L. Barkan
and particularly H. Inalčik have grossly exaggerated the alleged beneficial effects of Ottoman rule in the Balkans in the XVth and XVIth
centuries, but it must be admitted that by the XVIth century at the
latest large increases in population and progress in urbanization had
been achieved.[64] What the conquered people felt about this is a different matter. The vast majority were relegated to the status of subjects
of the Sultan and his representatives. They were driven off the more
fertile lands and those nearer to the important routes of communications. They were forced to hand over to the Turks several thousand
children annually as tribute (devshirme).[65] The large-scale emigration
of Serbs to the bordering Hungarian province at the turn of the XVth
and XVIth centuries proves that life under Turkish rule was not easy
for the majority of Christian subjects of Mehmet II and his immediate
successors. Again this is a problem which has to be treated very carefully. The Turkish authorities, at least in the XVIth century and the
beginning of the XVIIth century, after strengthening their position in
the conquered territories, pursued a fairly flexible internal policy. In the
territory of Bosnia, they succeeded in gaining over the local population
for Islam without religious persecutions, thus making it possible later
to use Bosnians as a military force in Hungary. This success was relatively easy to achieve in Bosnia because of the earlier oppression there
of numerous Bogomils by the Catholic Church supported by Hungary.
In Serbia and Bosnia, at the beginning of the Turkish rule, there existed
large Christian groups, "shipahi", most likely consisting of former boiars
who received privileges similar to those of the Turkish military feudal

---

[62] J. Tadič, op. cit., p. 635; H. Inalčik, L'Empire Ottoman, "Ier Congrès des Etudes
Balcaniques", pp. 78, 81, 84, 87, 89f.
[63] J. Tadič, op. cit.
[64] H. Inalčik, op. cit., p. 90; Ö. L. Barkan, Essai sur les données statistiques des registres
du recensement dans l'Empire Ottoman au XVe et XVIe siècle, "Journal of the Economic
and Social History of the Orient", Vol. I, 1957, passim. Carefully presented statistical
material of primary importance.
[65] H. Inalčik, op. cit., p. 82f.

lords.[66] It has been known for a long time that the Turkish authorities treated the Orthodox clergy with toleration and that they, in turn, behaved loyally on the whole to their new masters. All this helped to pacify the peninsula. In Bulgaria and Serbia the Turks took advantage of and maintained some of the old divisions within the population, and in return for protecting roads or guarding the frontiers many were relieved from the payment of taxes. Miners were one of the privileged groups.[67] A proclamation of the orders of Mehmet II and Baiezid II concerning mines in Serbia indicates that the conqueror and his son were most anxious to get the mines working. Consequently, the ruler did not put particularly strong pressure on the miners and the merchants from Dubrovnik who were buyers of the ores and only required that the ores should be taken to the mints. From there the metal passed into possession of foreigners in the form of coins after a deduction of the ruler's share.[68] This did not differ in any way from the legal requirements in force in Christian Europe. Neither did the mining legislation of Soliman the Great depart from the principles generally accepted at that time. Thus the gradual decline in the production of metals in Serbia and Bosnia under Turkish rule cannot be considered as a consequence of the conquest but must rather be attributed to the exhaustion of the deposits. On the other hand, in contrast to the situation in Christian Europe at the turn of the XVth and XVIth centuries, in the Ottoman empire there were no substantial investments in mining, either by merchants' feudal lords or the state authorities. This is a problem which requires some explanation. It is understandable that German and Italian financiers, who were so closely linked with the Habsburgs, did not dare to invest capital in the domain of the Sultan who was not only a deadly enemy of the rulers of Austria and Spain but was also the leader of Islam. Dealings in properties in the countries engaged in combat would have been too dangerous, and the citizens of Dubrovnik did not have adequate resources at their disposal. So far as the Great Porte, the merchants and the great Turkish feudal lords were concerned, it would appear that they lacked both capital and the essential

---

[66] H. Inalčik, *op. cit.*, p. 85. This agrees with materials published by Yugoslav and Bulgarian scholars.

[67] I. Sakazov, *op. cit.*, pp. 178–185; V. Tapkova Zaimova, *Sur les débuts des colonies ragusines dans les territoires bulgares*, "Studia Balcanica", Vol. III, p. 127f.

[68] N. Baldicenau, *Les actes des premiers sultans conservés dans les manuscrits turcs de la Bibliothèque Nationale de Paris*, Paris/La Haye, 1960, Nos. 1–5ff.

specialists in mining technology.[69] Besides, for a time war and trade provided fairly quick returns, whereas profits from mining investments would have taken longer to accrue. It is known that the Turks attracted miners from Hungarian Slovakia to their territories by assuring them sufficiently favourable conditions, and gave far-reaching privileges to miners in Macedonia and Bulgaria.[70] I agree with Stojanovic, that the survival of the mining of metals, ores, lead and iron in the Chalkidike peninsula and its development in the region of Kratova and in Ciprovci should be attributed to the larger and more easily accessible natural wealth than that found in Serbia and Bosnia.[71] This problem requires further research, and the whole question has not yet been adequately studied from the point of view of the history of technology which, in this case, is of basic importance.

There is no doubt that the structure of trade in the Balkan countries after the Turkish conquest underwent gradual but far-reaching changes, particularly in so far as foreign trade was concerned. Silver, lead and other metals lost their leading role as exports. Livestock and later agriculture generally moved to the top as well as Levantine goods of all sorts. Consequently, the flow of silver underwent a gradual change of direction, compared with the earlier period. The Ottoman empire, in spite of the import of textiles, metal products etc. from Italy and from both Western and Eastern Europe had, in all probability, a favourable balance of trade with its trading partners, and it can be assumed that this was also true of the Balkan peninsula. We are, nevertheless, still a very long way from explaining the problems of the economic history of this part of Europe in the Middle Ages.

I believe that the material collected here allows us to draw some conclusions about which factors favoured and which restrained the economic growth of Central-Eastern Europe and to some extent of South-Eastern Europe in the late Middle Ages. We can also reach some conclusions on the nature of their economic relationship with the West and with Italy. The late economic development of the territories of Poland, Bohemia, Hungary and the Balkan countries in the early Middle

---

[69] H. Inalčik did not explain this in his article *Quelques remarques sur la formation du capital dans l'empire ottoman*, in "Mélanges en honneur de Fernand Braudel", Vol. I, Toulouse, 1973, pp. 235–244.
[70] Cf. note 68.
[71] T. Stojanovic, *Discussion*, "Studia Balcanica", Vol. III, p. 191f., J. Tadič, *L'unité*, p. 634; I. Sakazov, *op. cit.*, p. 245ff.

Ages was due to the fact that conditions for a "take-off" were inferior to those in the West, particularly due to the scarcity of population. Economic contacts between these two areas were fairly loose. Until the XIIth century such contacts were mainly confined to the export of slaves and small quantities of metal ores and furs from Eastern Europe. This permitted the import of a certain amount of luxury goods, weapons etc. A number of factors led the ruling classes to develop the economy intensively, such as the establishment of great estates in Central-Eastern Europe and of many forms of the feudal system in the XIIth and XIIIth centuries, the drop in revenue from wars of aggression, the increased need for defence, and the greater demands of the ruling classes. This explains the acceptance of institutions and legal forms from the West as well as the encouragement given to foreign and native colonization. All the factors mentioned acted as a stimulant to economic growth in many spheres of social life. The relative over-population which was becoming apparent in many countries in the West and also the great increase in demand for silver, gold and other metals, furs, hides, wax, food and timber products which Eastern Europe came to supply in increasing quantities favoured these developments. These trends were reflected in migration to Eastern Europe as well as in the considerable development of trade between the two parts of the continent, and the formation of strong commercial centres such as the Hanse, Vienna and Dubrovnik. The export of slaves at that time was maintained only in the most backward countries of Eastern Europe, mainly in Bosnia and in the Golden Horde, as increasingly labour came to be required on the spot. One aspect of this process was the "promotion" of slaves to the position of bondsmen. The slave trade by itself was of marginal importance in the economic life of Europe at that time.

The severe economic crisis in Western Europe in the XIVth century and the first half of the XVth century intensified these trends still further. Although the flow of settlers to the East stopped, the increase in the local population, the developing mining industry, agriculture and livestock rearing in Central-Eastern Europe not only encouraged the investment of merchant capital but also considerably increased the area's purchasing power and demand for luxury goods, together with many types of manufactures and other articles, which resulted in a trade deficit. This was of major importance to countries in the West as it occurred during a period of enormous economic difficulties. At that time, then, a division of labour on an international basis began to evolve, with Central-Eastern Europe becoming a major source of raw materials as well as a market for numerous articles manufactured in the West. The growth of both the rural and urban economies in Poland, Bohemia, and to some extent, in Hungary and the Balkans, enabled the local production of manufactured goods to continue expanding. However, certain aspects of the one-sided economic development of Eastern Europe, stretching from the Baltic to the Adriatic, were already evident.

It was this last phenomenon which assumed greater importance in the XVIth century and especially in the XVIIth century. As agricultural production and livestock rearing increased in Eastern Europe, and were accompanied by a huge increase in exports of both, there was a corresponding increase in imports from the West. These imports were encouraged by the gentry who were able to buy in large quantities and wished to prevent price increases in the goods they required. This phenomenon was accompanied by the expansion of serfdom and the gradual weakening of the economic links between the peasants and the towns. It was to lead Central-Eastern Europe to a situation dominated by a system of some sort of monoculture and to heavy economic dependence on markets and production of Western Europe. Thus the crisis of the XVIIth century, the reconstruction and modernization of English agriculture, the intensification of animal rearing in Denmark and the Netherlands, and the development of Western trade with countries overseas dealt a heavy blow to many countries of Eastern Europe and in particular to Poland. The effects were felt for a long time, and I have written about the historical process which made our region a kind of economic colony of some of the Western countries which were developing towards capitalism.[72] The origins of this phenomenon reach far back into the Middle Ages.

---

[72] M. Małowist, *Poland, Russia and the Western Trade in the 15th and 16th centuries*, "Past and Present", No. 13, 1958. Chapter 6 in this volume pp. 37–38.

CHAPTER NINE

EAST AND WEST EUROPE IN THE 13TH–16TH CENTURIES. CONFRONTATION OF SOCIAL AND ECONOMIC STRUCTURES*

I would like here to reconstruct elements of the model of economic relations between the two great European regions. I have no doubt that, despite many differences and even considerable asynchronism in their histories, the countries of eastern and east-central Europe showed many similarities with the West as regards economy and social organization.

The first problem I encountered was that of the relative backwardness of those areas in comparison with many western European countries, let alone with Italy, Europe's leader not only in economy but in every other aspect of medieval civilization. The areas of the former Roman Empire, from the 7th and 8th centuries at the latest, and of Germany from the next century, laid the foundations of the feudal system. They were able to do this, thanks to the size of their population and the possibility of taking advantage of certain older elements of culture and technique. What is often described as population pressure, i.e. the pressure of the urgent needs of growing numbers of population, required not merely an increase in arable land but also better methods of cultivation. In Western Europe, these better methods involved development of the three-field system and the use of heavier tools in agriculture. In the 11th century, the relatively densely populated Netherlands began reclaiming the coastal regions, leaving the ground dry enough for arable farming and cattle grazing. The two-field system lingered on along the shores of the Mediterranean. However, other sources of living existed there. All this took place in an atmosphere of fierce social struggles and constant conflicts among feudal lords representing different regions and positions. In the 9th century, the attacks of Normans and Hungarians

---

* Originally published as *Wschód a Zachód Europy w XIII–XVI wieku. Konfrontacja struktur społeczno-gospodarczych*, Warszawa: PWN, 1973, pp. 370–385. The following is a translation of the published text, as subsequently revised by the author. Translation from Polish by Maria Chmielewska-Szlajfer, revised by Robin Kimball.

and the continuing, albeit weakening, assaults of the Arabs rendered the life of the Carolingians a misery. The next century alleviated the situation somewhat, at least on the frontiers, and things in the West grew very much better. The Italian port cities, led by Bari and Amalfi, followed by Venice, Pisa, and Genoa, began to control the profitable Mediterranean trade, where they acquired a very strong position long before the Crusades. The Germans continued their attacks upon the Western Slavs. The French not only pursued the colonization of their own country, but actively participated in the extension of Christian possessions in the Iberian peninsula, and also supplied a growing quota of knights attempting to conquer Palestine and Syria.

By now it was no longer only at river mouths or on sea coasts but also further inland that a growing number of towns accommodating merchants and artisans were being founded. Developing agriculture provided them with food, the necessary raw materials, and buyers for their merchandise.

Clearly, medieval Western Europe cannot be treated as one unit. The differences in the level and rate of development of Flanders, Picardy, Ile de France, the Rhineland, and especially the northern and central parts of Italy on the one hand, and, say, Lower Saxony, Bavaria, or the northern and central regions of Spain on the other were enormous.

The development of feudalism was accompanied by increasingly wide contrasts in the living standards and resources of particular groups of population. Big and medium-sized landowners, both religious and secular, owned the largest estates. They laid a heavy burden on the peasants, thus reducing the overwhelming portion of the population to subsistence level. In the early stages of the growth of cities, first the itinerant merchants who had settled in town, then artisans, too, worked primarily to satisfy the needs of the ruling elite. The progress in agriculture led to an important rise in population in Western Europe in the 11th, 12th, and 13th centuries. Prices for agricultural produce were rising fast. In those circumstances, peasants, too, were drawn into the growing commodity trade.

Monarchs and great lords, interested in the growth of their property, supported the development of rural and urban settlements. New settlers were often granted better economic and legal status. This tendency was particularly marked in France, Spain, and eastern parts of Germany. Already in the 11th and 12th centuries, the cities of the West acquired or, more often, bought themselves urban privileges, indispensable to their further growth. The Netherlands, northern and central Italy, and the Rhineland developed metal and cloth industries. In some places they worked on the put-out system, attending to the needs of wealthy lords and merchants throughout Europe, including even the Mediterranean area and the more distant countries of Islam.

These leading countries, Italy in particular, amassed a relatively large merchant and banking capital, established marine and land insurance, and extended loans to borrowers in the whole of western and central Europe. So when, in the 12th and 13th centuries, the countries of east-central Europe began to develop rapidly, they were already backward compared with the West, even with its German periphery which, although relatively primitive, was nevertheless developing very intensively. It thus became clear to the Polish, Czech, and Hungarian lords who maintained contacts with the West, with Germany and France in particular, that they should make use of the means and methods which had proved effective elsewhere. Lords in eastern Europe took advantage of the relative surplus of population in the Netherlands, Germany, and France to improve the situation in their own domains. From these countries, too, they took over the legal patterns useful in the increase and territorial expansion of production.

Starting from the 12th century, the alluring prospects of the Baltic trade, of the supply of metals and ores and of land to colonize, led to the strengthening of contacts between Europe's East and West. Conquests by German liege lords definitely accelerated foreign settlement, even though this was limited to a certain area only. What is important is the fact that from the 12th century onwards Western manufactures, particularly the high-quality ones, occupied a significant position in east-central European markets. There, Western merchants found for themselves agricultural and forest products, important raw materials such as furs, hides, wax, etc., and also, which was of major consequence, considerable amounts of silver, gold, copper, and tin. Imports of the latter allowed the economically stronger West to strengthen its economy and to bring—at least temporarily—some order into its financial system. The rapid growth of Bohemia, Poland, and Hungary at that time, followed by the Balkan countries, is unquestionable. By the 13th century, both urban and rural economies were expanding enormously, being as yet favourably affected by trade and immigration.

The first half of the 14th century brought with it an intense crisis and depression in the West. Economic relations between East and West changed their former character. Epidemics decimated populations in the West, so rendering any major emigration impossible. For the following one hundred years the whole of Western Europe suffered from an acute labour shortage. The turbulent process of re-adaptation of the economy and political organizations to the changed demographic and social circumstances lasted until the last quarter of the 15th century. At the same time, the economies of Bohemia, Poland, and Hungary, followed by those of Lithuania and Russia, expanded substantially. I believe this was the reason why merchants and capital from Italy and Germany began to flow into the three leading countries of east-central Europe.

The developing eastern countries were very attractive to those western merchants whose old markets had declined and undergone serious organizational transformation. Sales of luxury as well as medium-quality goods increased because local artisans in Poland, Hungary, and Bohemia, let alone the Balkan countries, were unable to meet the demand. The rich food and mineral resources and their transfer to the West through Hanseatic traders and their numerous competitors—from the 14th century merchants from southern Germany and Nuremberg, Italians and Ragusans—encouraged growing imports from the West, sometimes from intermediary centres as well.

The long-term interests of Poland, Hungary, and Bohemia were not identical. Western imports would seem to have been of minor importance to the Polish economy. Polish handicrafts and trade were clearly on the rise in the 14th and 15th centuries, although imports probably hindered the establishment or development of certain lines of production in the country. This was to some extent made up for by the imports of merchant capital which, together with other factors, had a beneficial effect on such fundamental sectors of the economy as agriculture, forestry, and mining. I think that the growth of these three sectors, and this at a time when rent was becoming increasingly popular in the countryside, contributed to the improvement of relations between the rural population at large and the towns, to the further growth of towns, and to the development of trade in general. All in all, this marked considerable economic progress. It is no coincidence that, in the 14th and 15th centuries, the wool and linen industries in Great and Little Poland, and even in Mazovia, showed substantial dynamism; or that iron mills and many other non-agricultural areas were developing, despite large imports. In Bohemia and Hungary, however, exports of precious metals, copper, and tin were a much stronger incentive to imports of foreign manufactures and luxury items than the humbler Polish exports. In both Bohemia and Hungary, but especially in the latter, local producers found themselves in a difficult situation, facing fierce competitors lavishing all sorts of goods on their countries. The poverty of handicrafts, particularly in Hungary, the urban patriciate's interest in the import-export trade, and lack of state protection hindered the increase in urban production (again, particularly in Hungary). The Hussite revolution and the recession in Czech mining ultimately bettered the life of Czech craftsmen and lesser merchants. But in Hungary, things remained as they had been.

The situation in Serbia and Bosnia was far less advanced. Local handicraft emerged from the rural economy only at the beginning of the 13th century. At the same time, imports of luxury goods and those in common use, organized by Ragusans, Dalmatians, and Italians, grew as mining in these two Balkan countries developed. The example of these two shows that economically backward areas with resources of international importance can suffer serious and lasting damage if their relations with stronger partners are too close. This does not mean that trade of this kind did not contribute to the rise in living standards of the more affluent groups of the population. Still, such trade affected the pattern of the weaker countries, making their development one-sided and, more often than not, making them dependent on distant markets. It was all the more dangerous inasmuch as medieval mining technology was primitive, and serious crises in that industry proved unavoidable.

Thus in the late Middle Ages one can already observe the formation of a definite type of economic relationship between Europe's East and West. The latter supplied the former with finished artisanal and luxury products, capital, and, to some extent, labour. The countries of the East were first and foremost exporters of such important raw materials as bullion and other metals. Such division of labour favoured the diversification of the economy of the then "developed" countries of north- and south-western Europe, and the acceleration over those territories of the growth in artisanal and, in some measure, industrial production. It also increased the rate of accumulation of merchant capital. This was a factor creating elements of capitalist organization in the West, based on the production of increasingly mass-consumption goods. This, of course, was not a decisive but merely an additional incentive. In the East, which, due to unfavourable conditions at the start, was economically backward, trade with the West certainly exerted a civilizing influence, enriching local and foreign merchants and seigniors. At the same time it caused a certain one-sidedness in the economy, even if at times it helped increase the power of rich state organizations, as was manifest in Hungary under the Angevines, in Bohemia in the 13th and 14th centuries, and in Serbia under Stephen Dushan.

It would seem that the development of Poland at that time was more diversified, though less spectacular, than that of her two southern neighbours. In Russia, there obtained marked differences between Novgorod and the nascent Moscow state. Novgorod played a role similar to that of Ragusa in the Balkans or, somewhat later, of Gdańsk in the river-basin of the Vistula and Neman rivers, and greatly profited from this. At the same time it was developing as a strong base of production. In the 15th century, north-eastern Russia—persistently offsetting the ravages of Mongolian raids and oppression, yet at the same time remaining very distant from the West and therefore less exposed to its pressures—achieved an explosive economic growth which, at the turn of the century, allowed it to conquer Novgorod itself. All the same, the incipient centralized Russian state long felt acutely the effects of its former retrogression. Eager to make up for its economic shortcomings, it had to work hard to establish economic relations with the West.

In the second half of the 15th century, the countries of western and north-western Europe were busy extricating themselves from the long crisis. In the southern and northern Netherlands, in England, in Upper Germany, in Saxony, and in the Rhineland, the rate of economic development grew considerably faster, and the gap separating these countries from those of northern and central Italy shrank. It was at this time that economic differences between the dynamic north of Italy and the stagnating south became apparent. All experts on the late Middle Ages emphasize the partial filling of the population gaps caused by the epidemics of the 14th and early 15th centuries. Greater emphasis should however be placed on other economic transformations, such as the adaptation of industrial and handicraft production to the growing circles of consumers, the consolidation of the rural economy in England, and, following the Hundred Years War in France, a certain rise in productivity and an intensification of ties with towns, not only through trade but through drawing vast numbers of peasants into various important, albeit auxiliary, tasks of industrial production. The mass appearance of peasant-artisans was particularly typical of England, the Netherlands, Upper Germany, and also of central and northern Italy, where it had already emerged earlier. Despite the partial reconstruction of agriculture in the West, the unsatisfied demand for agricultural and forest products during the 15th century continued to rise.

Overseas expansion was of critical importance here. Ventured by the nobility from the less developed countries of Portugal and Castile, it opened up new vistas to the capital held not only by burghers of those two countries but to merchants and financiers from Italy, the Netherlands, and Upper Germany as well. In Africa, they gained access to cheap gold. They managed to establish new maritime connections with India which yet did not ruin, in the 16th century, the old Levantine trade, despite the momentary turbulence at the beginning of the century. Historically of the greatest importance was the Spanish and Portuguese conquest of Central and South America, where the Spaniards and Portuguese plundered the conquered peoples on an unprecedented scale and where, with time, they discovered extensive possibilities of mining precious metals and organizing sugar plantations, with the use of imported African slave labour, etc. The slave trade itself soon turned out to be for European merchants and numerous aristocrats a peculiar "gold vein" and a major source of vast fortunes.

Still, to take advantage of those new vistas required the mobilization of resources enormous for that time. In America, it was long possible to plunder but, with time, one needed to invest considerably as well. In Africa, and especially in Asia, it was possible to buy the desired goods, but from difficult partners. The latter showed great interest not only in certain sorts of European fabrics—linen and thin woollen cloth, made primarily in the Netherlands and in France, also in Silesia—but especially in silver, copper, and brass and their products. Changes in the equipment of European armies, with the increasing use of guns and other firearms, brought about a rise in the demand for copper and iron. To supply the strong Habsburg, French, and Turkish armies, plus the armed forces of other countries, constituted a major economic task in itself. It also provided incentives to the development of mining and the metallurgical industry. Just at this time, owing to the shortage of charcoal, the metallurgical works in Liège province and in England switched to a new fuel—hard coal. As emphasized long ago by J. U. Nef, this was particularly advantageous to the English coal industry, which had hitherto operated on a relatively small scale.

Thus, there is no exaggeration in the dictum that the 16th century was a period of extensive development for many countries of Western Europe, with northern and central Italy remaining the richest region. Yet, in the rate of their development, the advanced Italian cities had already fallen behind England, the Netherlands, and France. Upper Germany would seem to have gradually receded into the background, although its big financiers were still playing an important part, operating however in other countries, usually in the Habsburg possessions in Europe and America, also in Antwerp, Seville, and Lisbon, the main emporia of the emerging world trade. Antwerp, whose population soon totalled 100,000, became the leading centre of world trade, of money circulation, and also the one to impart dynamism to the industrial production of the southern Netherlands and, indirectly, to more distant territories also. When, in the 1560s, Antwerp was involved in grave social, religious, and economic troubles, its functions were gradually taken over by Amsterdam and Dutch cities, and later by London.

It has long been known that all these processes could hardly have taken place without the countries of east-central and eastern Europe. Portuguese historians maintain that their country's overseas expansion would have been impossible without the deliveries of timber, other forest products, and grain from the Baltic lands. Although there may be some exaggeration in what these scholars say, it is less than might seem at first glance.

From the 13th to the end of the 15th century, a certain model of trade relations between European West and East took shape. It involved exchange of handicraft and luxury products for raw materials. In the 16th century, this form of trade became even more popular. A general increase in population, still the main source of labour, took place in both parts of Europe, with the West remaining in the lead. Particularly important was the rapid process of urbanization in Western Europe, manifest not only in the economically most advanced countries, but also in their less developed peripheries such as Spain, Portugal, and southern Italy where, after all, towns abounded not just in workmen but in all conditions of poor people and beggars. True, no western European city could match Constantinople with respect to its size of population, but it was an exception in Europe at the time. It confronted the Sublime Porte with gigantic organizational and economic problems related to the feeding of 400,000 and ultimately 700,000 people.

In this new situation, the 15th century already witnessed a marked increase in the demand for grain, timber and its products from the Baltic region, for Czech, Hungarian, and Swedish metals, for Polish, Lithuanian, and Russian linen and hemp. Russian high-quality furs continued to play an important role in 15th- and 16th-century international trade. Of great importance also were a more or less fifty-year-long heyday of mining in Bohemia and Hungarian Slovakia, and presumably also in 16th-century Transylvania, and progress in lead ore mining in Little Poland and Silesia. In nearly all these areas, as in the Tyrol, Carinthia, Saxony, Spain, and to some extent America, the progressive development of mining was a result of the investment of merchant and mixed merchant-financier capital and partly that of feudal lords. Poland and, in some measure, Bohemia were the areas where feudal lords invested in mining. Whereas, however, in the initial periods capitalists' profits usually remained in the country because the merchants involved settled down in the vicinity of their businesses, in the 16th century the profits were collected by big financiers, usually from Upper Germany and Italy. They re-invested these profits elsewhere, particularly in the risky financing of the Spanish and Austrian Habsburgs, or their enemies—the kings of France. This capital considerably diminished as a result of the bankruptcies of the Spanish Crown and of other monarchs in the second half of the century. This notwithstanding, for many years to come this capital ensured the development of western industry and trade, and the exploitation of overseas territories. Nearly all important Upper German and Italian financiers were gradually made noblemen, which after all was characteristic of the rich European burghers in the final years of feudalism.

Mining organized according to capitalist rules, based on hired free labour lacking their own tools, was a new occurrence accompanying the large mining investments mentioned above. In this way, the primary accumulation of capital took place in mining, yet the resources thus earned were ultimately spent on non-productive purposes. This was because even the "advanced" countries of 16th-century Western Europe had not as yet demolished the core elements of the feudal system, particularly in the rural areas. They were only just setting off in that direction. The great merchant-financiers of the 16th century largely facilitated the formation in Western Europe of large centralized states which, although still feudal, in their own interest defended their burghers and peasants more or less effectively.

As early as the end of the 16th and on through the 17th century, such co-existence of feudalism and unfolding capitalism in the long term proved difficult, as shown by the examples of the Dutch and particularly the English revolution. In France, the social organization of feudalism, protected by royal absolutism, was so strong that the country's rich bourgeoisie dreamed of purchasing aristocratic titles rather than of strengthening their own economic and political position. At the same time, western absolutism, even if it heavily burdened the productive groups of society, in its own interest somehow protected them against excessive exploitation by the feudal lords, to whom it offered an outlet for their energies and a chance to enrich themselves in the bloated state apparatus. In such conditions, any factious freedom of the nobility was out of the question in the absolutist states of western and central Europe, and in England and Holland, which were heading towards capitalism. Instead, the legal norms in force made at least a sizable development of the economy possible.

The situation in the countries of east-central and eastern Europe was different and less auspicious. The great boom of the 16th century also found expression in the economy, but in a different form from that in the West. I mean here the growth of mining in the first half of the 16th century. This, however, was accompanied by other circumstances, much less advantageous.

A steady progression of seigniors' private estates based on serf or (as in Turkey) slave labour became a characteristic feature of the economies of Poland, Hungary, Bohemia, the Ottoman Empire, and Russia. Poland was the country where these traits occurred earliest. The Ottoman Empire was apparently the last one to adopt this mode of production (the matter is not sufficiently investigated as yet). I have tried to explain the genesis of this new system, assuming that it was primarily due to the low productivity of agriculture and to the limited incomes of the seigniors who (save in Royal Prussia and for a long time in Bohemia) could not usually afford the extensive use of hired labour.

It should be emphasized that the beginnings of the so-called "second serfdom" (in Prussia, based on the forced labour of the sons of liege subjects) coincided with a period of low agricultural prices both in Poland and in the West. The situation gradually changed to the advantage of the countryside in the second half of the 15th and during the 16th century, with prices for agricultural products rising rapidly from the 1550s onwards, thus affecting the agricultural market in Poland and in other countries of eastern and central Europe. Today, it is increasingly (and accurately) believed that the rise in food prices at the time resulted from the declining value of coin, caused by the influx of American bullion, as well as from the population increase, and especially from the urbanization and more rapid industrialization of many countries in Western Europe. The latter provided a great opportunity for the rural economy, not only of the Baltic zone, producing grain, industrial plants such as flax and hemp, hides, etc., but also for those parts of eastern Europe which could export cattle to the west and to Italy—for Hungary in particular, and, to a lesser degree, for southern Poland and Moldavia.

The latter however was forced to rid itself cheaply or free of charge of some of its livestock on behalf of Turkey and its capital.

We should not overlook the rise in the demand for all these goods in the producer countries themselves. After all, serf-based estates thrived in the larger part of Great Poland, where the main recipients of their products were the local towns, in western Little Poland, and in Hungary, where they grew grain primarily for the local market and for the imperial army defending the borders against the Turks. In the Balkans, from an early stage *cifliks* were taking part in the export of grain to Mediterranean countries, where at the turn of the 16th century agricultural productivity suddenly fell. In 16th- and 17th-century Russia, exports of grain were of no consequence. Neither could her exports of flax and hemp to England and Holland bring about any reorganization of Russia's rural economy. The growth of the serf economy in that country was a result of local demand. However, in the Russian context "local" also included the vast northern territories, initially including Western Siberia as well. (Somewhat later the Western Siberian region developed its own agriculture.) For a long period Poland was one of the leading grain exporters. In the case of the grain exporting countries, several aspects of the "second serfdom" should be taken into consideration. It is well known that massive exports of grain and forestry products contributed to a substantial surplus in sea trade between Poland and the West in the 16th century. The same can be said of Russia even in the early Middle Ages. It is an established fact that, in the 16th century, first Hungary and then the Balkan countries were receiving cash from the West. But very little of that cash was re-invested. Most of it was simply consumed. This was due to various causes. The fast-increasing burden of the serfs and their partial severance from urban markets caused a decline in the purchasing power of the overwhelming majority of the population, at the end of the 16th and at the beginning of the 17th century in particular. This in turn had an adverse effect on the condition of small and later medium-size towns linked mainly to local and regional markets. This was evident first in Poland and Hungary, much later in Bohemia and the Balkans. As regards Russia, it would seem that the continuous increase in the area under cultivation and the exploitation of natural resources in the north saved the situation for a long time to come. Thus there was no purpose in investing in growing production for a wider market.

This period also witnessed a piecemeal impoverishment of the petty and even the moderately rich nobility, which presumably stemmed from the sinking yield from the primitively cultivated land, the natural growth of this social group, and the parcelling of their property. Increasingly large areas became transferred to big landowners. Inevitably, this made the central European aristocracy and a similar, though socially not identical, group of Turkish dignitaries even stronger politically. The Austrian and Spanish Habsburgs, the tsars of Russia, and later particularly the Hohenzollerns of Prussia managed to enhance their political power *vis-à-vis* the nobility by ensuring the latter very profitable positions in the state apparatus and only seldom limiting their control over the peasants and the urban populace. These rulers could afford it as they had vast wealth at their disposal. Their revenues came not only from rural taxes but from other sources as well. By the 16th century, towns and industry in Bohemia and Austria, later also in Russia, were incomparably stronger than in Poland and Hungary and, with time, in the Ottoman Empire, too. Unlike Austria, Prussia, and Russia, in Poland and Turkey the spreading influence of oligarchies was accompanied by a rise in centrifugal and even distinctly separatist tendencies.

At the turn of the 16th century and in subsequent years, the great demand for agricultural products from east-central Europe diminished, prices for these commodities went down, and in the end it was difficult to sell them at all. The economic crises in 17th-century Western Europe were severe but transitory. Yet their effect on the east was much more perilous. The issue requires further study, but it is already clear that the excessively one-sided economies of Poland, Hungary, and later the Balkans were deficient in strong development incentives. These countries ultimately fell into a protracted state of stagnation, which led to a peculiar feudal reaction with regard to political and social organizations. Such a course of events was particularly dangerous to Poland at a time when strong absolutist states both to east and west became firmly established. In point of fact, it is only from the 17th century that one may speak of the so-called unfavourable "geopolitical" situation of Poland. This situation resulted however not so much from her particular position on the map as from the increasingly unfavourable correlation of economic and political forces between Poland and her neighbours. Turkey was able to hold on as an important power for a longer period, thanks to its own resources, which were still considerable, and to its relatively strong state apparatus. As for Russia, she achieved quick growth in the 18th century. At the same time, powerful elements of feudalism survived until the 20th century, exercising a decidedly noxious effect on the country.

To sum up, I believe that, in the early modern period, one can already discern the beginnings of the *sui generis* economic colonization of Eastern Europe by its western partners. This was a result not only of trade with the West but also of social relations in Europe's eastern part.

CHAPTER TEN

ECONOMIC AND POLITICAL DIVISIONS IN MEDIEVAL AND EARLY MODERN EUROPE[*][1]

As a result of Wallerstein's theses, with which I concur only in part, the problems of the economic and political division of Europe from the early Middle Ages through the so-called long 16th century are again the subject of widespread interest. It is an obvious fact, though one sometimes obscured by nationalistic bias, that in the early Middle Ages there were already marked differences in the level of social development in Europe. They resulted, I believe, from the respective population density, a factor of utmost importance in pre-industrial epochs, from the level of productive forces, and from the political and cultural infrastructure, including the legacy from Roman civilisation.

In examining these factors, I am inclined to indicate three main areas. The most developed area would embrace Byzantium, the territory along the western shores of the Mediterranean Sea, and more particularly Italy and Muslim Spain. A part of the Netherlands and Lorraine, northern France, the Rhineland, and the British Isles made up the second, less developed, area. The third, least developed, area comprised east-central Europe and Scandinavia. The particular areas differed precisely in population density, in the standard of agriculture, and in their social, political, and cultural development. I do not intend to dwell on the period discussed here; I only wish to emphasise that the period was decisive as marking the point of departure for the further development of each of those areas. It may be worthwhile paying attention to a certain factor usually overlooked. Until the end of the 10th century, or even somewhat later, the countries of eastern Europe had been second only

* Originally published as "Podziały gospodarcze i polityczne w Europie w średniowieczu i w dobie wczesnej nowożytności", in *Przegląd Historyczny*, Vol. 82, No. 2, 1991, pp. 233–244. Translation from Polish by Maria Chmielewska-Szlajfer, revised by Robin Kimball.

[1] From the posthumous manuscripts of Professor Marian Małowist, we print the text of the paper he presented at the conference of Polish and Hungarian historians in autumn 1986. In place of the footnotes the author had no time to prepare, we append the bibliography of works he used, compiled by Igor Kąkolewski and Andrzej Wyrobisz.

to Africa in supplying the more developed countries, particularly the world of Islam, with slaves. These slaves were by no means prisoners of war alone, but also included people sold by their destitute relatives. It has been established that in the 10th century, Prague was still a major export market for slaves. It is characteristic that in the 11th century, the export of slaves from eastern Europe (except Bosnia) tapered off, due, in my view, to the organisation of states and to the economic needs of both the rulers and the nascent feudal classes interested in the intensification of economic life. It is fair to assume that, from the mid-11th century at the latest, and perhaps even somewhat earlier, Western Europe, reaching as far as the eastern bank of the Elbe, began to develop intensively both economically and politically. I mean here the intensive development of agriculture, towns, crafts, and commerce and the establishment of the new political forms of the feudal state, including the Italian city-states. When all is said and done, the patriciate, with its feudal roots, played an enormous role, direct and indirect, in the development of Genoa and Venice. One should observe moreover that the development of crafts, commerce, and towns led not only to the development of their links with the countryside, but was also largely oriented towards the satisfaction of the needs of the affluent social groups. This is indicated, for instance, by the nature of the textile industry in its largest centres in Italy and the southern Netherlands. It was the time when Christian western Europe began to expand into other territories, sending military expeditions to Palestine and Syria, when the process of ousting Arabs from Spain and Portugal was speeded up and, last but not least, when the Germans began their economic and political expansion into almost all east-central and eastern Europe. All these were certainly the result of demographic and institutional growth. At that time, hubs of economic life in the West and South were moving elsewhere. As a result, the economic importance of southern Italy began to wane, whereas the northern and central parts of the peninsula were showing great dynamism in every sector. Manufacturing even began showing certain symptoms of the early capitalistic forms of production, although this production catered primarily for the needs of the international wealthy and feudal strata, i.e. the nobles, the hierarchy, and the nascent urban patriciate. This was particularly evident in the textile industry. The situation that evolved in the woollen and fustian industries of Flanders, of Brabant, and, to some extent, of Upper Germany was similar. Northern France, too, was undergoing extensive economic development, while the south of the country was diminishing in importance.

In the 12th and especially in the 13th centuries, the Levantine trade was assuming its final shape. It was not, as was earlier believed, trade in luxury products alone. Recent studies, particularly by Ashtor, prove that such Levantine imports as, first and foremost, cotton, alum, dyes, etc. were indispensable to European production. The Hanseatic League excelled in such trade as early as the 13th century. At that time, food products, including grain from the Baltic region, and great quantities of cheap furs from Novgorod, timber, etc. made up its main imports to the West; in its exports to the East, great importance was attached not only to woollen cloth and other handicraft products, but more specifically to salt, first from Lüneburg and later from Brittany. All this indicates an enormous growth in the commodity economy and, what is very important, an incipient international division of labour, which eventually proved very much to the advantage of western and southern Europe, save the Iberian Peninsula.

The 13th century marked the apogee of the medieval economic development of western Europe. One should, however, note the inherent causes of its future collapse. Thus, large-scale rural settlement went beyond the zones fit for farming, and degenerated into what the Germans call *Fehlsiedlung*. In many areas, the just proportions between cultivation and animal husbandry were infringed. Given the low levels of mining technology and of capital investments, the intensive exploitation of shallow lodes of precious and non-ferrous metals predictably led, first, to the depletion of accessible deposits, and subsequently to bottlenecks and problems of money circulation. E. A. Kosminsky and R. H. Hilton emphasise the principal fact that the whole of that growth was based on low wages paid both in town and country, on the steady deterioration in the living conditions of the peasants, and on the poverty of a part of the artisans. This resulted from the abundant supply of labour and from price rises. The populace lived in very hard circumstances. Morbidity was inevitably soaring. All this was the cause of the future crisis in many Western countries.

The situation in eastern Europe presented a different picture. I would at once point out that I shall not at this stage broach the problems of *Rus'*, for, as Russian scholars affirm, the Mongol invasions and Mongol rule hampered the economic development of those lands for a long time to come, and one cannot speak of any serious signs of regrowth until the 14th century. As regards Hungary, Poland, Bohemia, and to some extent also the Balkan countries, it would seem that they made rapid progress in the 13th century and, in the case of Bohemia, perhaps even in the 12th. These problems are relatively well known, so I will recall them only briefly. What was most important at the time was a marked, quantitative and qualitative, growth in agriculture. Not only was the acreage under cultivation increased, but also, owing to the spread of better tools, agriculture became more intensive. Productivity of farming and animal breeding was rising. Meanwhile money rent for farming land was spreading, albeit unevenly. This was possible due to the development of towns and crafts, and to the strengthening of their economic links with the countryside. Although not always appreciated by science, primary importance attaches to the development of mining in Bohemia, in Hungarian Slovakia, in Transylvania, in the Balkans, and also in Poland where, starting from the 13th century, first rock-salt and then lead mining developed vigorously. Mining contributed to the growth of settlements and towns in all areas mentioned here, even in backward Bosnia, starting from the 13th–14th century. Nor must we overlook the external factor of development. Economic dynamism was the reward for the initiative taken by the Church and lay lords, and by the state authorities. They exploited and encouraged Walloon, Flemish, and first and foremost German immigration to raise agricultural and urban potentials; they propagated German law, which gave stimulus to growth in agriculture and crafts. The same took place in the new mining sphere, where initially the German element clearly prevailed. One should nevertheless pay attention to certain specific attributes of this phenomenon. The serious economic growth of east-central Europe and the Balkans took place only in the 13th century, i.e. at a time when many western countries were already past their medieval economic prime. In this way our territories ushered in the stage of long-duration development, lagging, however, very much behind the West. That somehow made large-scale eastward migration possible. However, in the long run, certain factors worked definitely against the East. I mean here the inflow of western artisan products and exports of large quantities of raw materials. This created circumstances not particularly favourable to the development of crafts and thus to the development of towns in east-central Europe. This is the factor stressed by Czech scholars; nonetheless the same applies to Hungary and Poland. Maybe this was one of the reasons why in the entire region discussed here there were practically no large and populous towns save Prague, with its 30,000–40,000 population. Polish and Hungarian towns were far below 20,000 inhabitants, with Gdańsk being a cut above even Wrocław and Cracow. This does not mean that small towns, in all the countries mentioned here, were not fulfilling meaningful economic tasks. Yet the burghers there had always been weak, which was one of the factors which motivated Casimir the Great and also the rulers of Hungary to encourage the immigration of Germans and Jews from the West, and Armenians from the East. In this I see one of the major sources of religious toleration that typified Poland between the 13th and 16th centuries.

The whole development process was particularly conspicuous in Poland and Hungary in the 14th and 15th centuries; in Poland it even extended into the long 16th century, although in the end there appeared symptoms of stagnation and even recession. As regards Hungary, it seems to me that the Turkish invasion of 1526 led to the division of the country into three parts. Royal Hungary, i.e. the part of the country under Habsburg rule, and particularly Transylvania, continued to develop economically. Yet, in the second half of the 16th century, Habsburg Hungary was adversely affected by the decline of mining, whereas Transylvania continued to develop, coming within the sphere of the Ottoman economy. In the Habsburg kingdom, the burden of maintaining sizeable armies to defend the country against the Turks weighed heavily; on the other hand, as Hungarian scholars point out, the presence of the Habsburg armies stimulated the development of agriculture which supplied them. The part occupied by the Turks would seem to have stagnated. The manpower loss resulting from wars and emigration could not be made good by immigrants from the heart of the empire because there was no manpower surplus there. As a result, central Hungary became a pasture-land, which in the course of time acquired a greater international significance. From the political and military angles, the Porte treated the country as a kind of sally-port, and later as a fortified glacis to stave off attacks from the Austrian Habsburgs, whose might had been growing since the beginning of the 17th century.

The situation in Bohemia developed quite differently. Out of the Hussite wars the country emerged exhausted. Its agriculture, however, recovered quickly. Thanks to capital input from south Germans and from big landlords, for example from the Szlik family of Jáchymov, at the turn of the 15th century, silver, tin, and in some measure copper mining developed extensively. In towns, the guilds, for a long time free from foreign competition, managed to consolidate their position. The growth of towns and the strengthening of their links with agriculture were conducive to the continuance in Bohemian agriculture of the money rent system, in most cases until the beginning of the Thirty Years'

War. In this way, Bohemia, east-central Europe's economic leader, was becoming very similar to the western European countries at their early stage of economic development. Yet, at the turn of the 16th century, difficulties appeared, to which I will return later.

The 15th century also witnessed the rapid development of north-eastern Russia, both in agriculture and in urban economy, which was reflected in the steep increase in Muscovite power. The distinctive feature of the entire development of eastern Europe was its continuity, starting from the 13th century, particularly in east-central Europe. Even such events as the Mongol invasions, especially harmful to Hungary, did not halt economic progress. It should be added here that in this part of Europe, the grave epidemics of the 14th and 15th centuries were apparently less severe than in southern and western Europe. The flow of Italian and south German capital into Hungarian and Polish mining and trade was a significant occurrence. On the other hand, it must be stressed here that as these two countries' prosperity grew, so did their imports of western and Italian industrial products, of woollen cloth and metal-ware in particular. The undeveloped crafts of Poland and Hungary were hardly in a position to compete with foreign imports. Despite these two countries' unquestionable progress in the crafts, compared to the West they still remained backward. This is in clear contrast to the examples of the woollen industry of Great and Little Poland which, ever since the 14th century, had step by step been capturing the market, not only in Poland but also in neighbouring countries, and even in Switzerland in the West, as well as in Transylvania and Novgorod. Yet what they usually sold was unbleached and undyed, very cheap woollen cloth, i.e. a product that was none too refined. Rural settlement, farming and cattle breeding continued to develop, even though some fields remained abandoned. In urban economy, money rent was becoming increasingly popular, which shows that it was acquiring a commodity character, as best illustrated in Poland, Hungary, and especially in Bohemia. But even in those towns where rent was still paid partly in kind, as in Prussia, Sweden, or Novgorod, a considerable amount of the produce collected by landlords served not so much for direct consumption as for commercial purposes. During all that period, and particularly in the 14th and 15th centuries, Hanseatic League merchants were developing relations with their hinterland, and even with distant regions offering produce that was of interest to them. P. Johansen was right when he argued that, to the Hanseatic League, trade with its ports' vast hinterland was no less important than trade along the Brugge-Novgorod line. The

Hanseatic merchants widely used the system of payment on account for future deliveries, so binding the producers to themselves. This was evident in Norway, Prussia, and Livonia, as indicated by comprehensive records set down by V. Niitemaa, M. Biskup, and myself. I consider this occurrence as very important, since it gave Polish, Lithuanian, and Livonian agricultural and forestry products access to wider markets. I am by no means persuaded that such trade was accompanied by undue exploitation of the producers. We should realise that, had Norwegian fishermen and peasants from the Baltic hinterland not received their advances, they would have had no market for their goods, and thus the goods would not have been produced at all. I think that this system operated not only in the Baltic region, and that it was in its way analogous to the putting-out system throughout Europe.

I wish moreover to draw attention to one more phenomenon typical especially of the entire Baltic region from Denmark to Livonia, of Hungary in the 15th century, of Prussia from the first half of the century, and of other countries somewhat later. I mean here the great political and economic activation of the nobility. Their aim was to strengthen the dependence of the peasants and increase the services they rendered. The landlords wanted to engage in international trade directly by breaking the barriers erected by Hanseatic merchants, particularly in such harbour towns as Gdańsk, Revel, Riga, and others. How should we explain the phenomena manifest in so many regions at the turn of the 15th century? It was, I believe, a result of the decline in the landlords' incomes due to depreciation of the coin, the relatively high cost of labour, and the opening market prospects for forestry, agricultural, and animal breeding products in the West, which had just surmounted an immense crisis and entered a new stage of dynamic development. In this situation, liege lords in Poland and Livonia tried, initially on a small scale only, to increase the amount of the *corvée*. In the entire region discussed here the nobility were strong and numerous. They scored major political successes, even though they did not manage to subdue the larger Hanseatic towns. It is nevertheless worth noting that on the vast territory between Denmark and Livonia, and from the Baltic region to Hungary, there emerged a political system which in Poland led to the formation of the republic of the gentry.

The socio-economic situation in the West developed altogether differently. Earlier, I mentioned certain difficulties besetting western rural economy at the end of the 13th and in the first half of the 14th centuries. They were of the utmost importance. The Black Death and later epidemics killed more than a quarter of the population in western Europe, in Denmark, and especially in Norway, as well as in an economically highly developed country like Egypt. This came as a severe shock to those countries. In effect, they suffered from an acute shortage of labour, which became very dear, and from a concurrent decline in prices, food prices in particular. Those peasants who survived the calamity found themselves in a considerably more favourable situation as the number of candidates to man the abandoned holdings proved quite inadequate. The landlords' forcible attempts to keep their incomes at an unchanged level at the peasants' expense aroused active resistance from the latter, for example, in England, the Iberian Peninsula, and, to a certain extent, Scandinavia. The peasants' active and passive resistance defeated the landlords' attempt to continue or even increase oppression. The frequently published ordinances regarding maximum prices came to nought. It is fair to assume that in England, the Iberian Peninsula, and also in central and northern Italy, the situation of the peasants, especially the better-off among them, improved considerably. The transfer of a part of the landlords' property into the peasants' hands, the maintenance of rent payments at the old or even a lower level when the coin was losing value, indemnified them for the drop in prices for agricultural products and cattle. As regards the incomes of the landlords themselves, they unquestionably declined, a fact which they tried to make up for by downright robbery (*Raubrittertum*) and wars. It is worth remembering here that the Hundred Years' War was very popular in England, that in Spain and Portugal civil wars raged all the time, that the Danish Schleswig and Holstein nobility, under the aegis of the Danish crown, repeatedly invaded Sweden, and became *de facto* rulers of Norway. The struggles for power in France must also have played some part in the economic processes discussed above. Significant changes occurred in the structure of the largest industries, particularly in the textile but partly also in the metal industry. The high cost of labour and the decline of the market for expensive products gradually forced manufacturers to adjust to new circumstances. The old woollen industry of Flemish and Italian cities flagged or collapsed but at the same time, in the same Flanders, in England, Holland, and Languedoc, there arose the so-called new industry, and also *draperie légère*, destined for less affluent buyers: landlords poorer than in the past, burghers, and even peasants, particularly the wealthier ones. In this way the extent of the market economy widened, notwithstanding the decline in population and the long period of demographic stagnation that ensued. In some measure, the restructuring of production ensured western industry and trade additional profits. It facilitated the West's expansion in eastern Europe and in the Middle East. Thus, during the 14th and especially the 15th centuries, new woollen, fustian, and metallurgical products from the Netherlands, Germany, England, and Italy reached central and eastern Europe, where they found a wide market. As regards Hungary, suffice to mention the published registers of the custom-house of Pressburg (Bratislava). The great demand for western goods should be attributed, I believe, to the underdevelopment of crafts in the entire eastern region, as well as to the population's higher living standards. E. Ashtor recently observed that precisely in that period, exports of European medium-quality woollen cloth to Egypt underwent a very sharp rise. Egypt was a country particularly affected by the Black Death, and also by many symptoms of crisis already known from western Europe. Ashtor believes that it was as a result of western industrial competition that Egyptian trade, hitherto flourishing, subsequently collapsed. I have the impression that this scholar somewhat simplifies the whole problem, but here is not the place to discuss this.

Occurrences similar to those taking place between Italy and western countries on the one hand and eastern Europe on the other also took place in the former countries' relations with the Iberian Peninsula. In the 14th and 15th centuries, there was a marked rise in Iberian imports of Italian, Dutch, west German, and other products in exchange for Spanish wool, iron, and wine, Portuguese resin, etc. The active role of Italian merchants, especially those from Genoa, in the Kingdom of Castile and in Portugal, likewise since the 14th century, was favourable to such trade. The Iberian Peninsula was also where Flemish merchants, ousted from other areas of their former activities by Hanseatic competition, held their ground the longest. Besides, it is worth noting, ever since the 14th century, the growing Italian and upper German investments in Hungarian, Polish, Saxon, and Spanish mining, which, from the end of the 15th century, were of great importance to the European economy.

I would like to draw attention to one more occurrence related, I believe, to the serious crisis of the feudal structures. I have in mind the beginnings of the overseas expansion of Portugal in the first half of the 15th century, and of Castile somewhat later. Initially, the driving force of the expansion was the lower nobility, and especially the younger sons of the nobility, seeking fortune and fame. It was the lower nobility who most painfully experienced a decline in their incomes. Merchants joined the expansion only when Africa proved to constitute a risk smaller than initially thought, and actually began bringing in handsome profits.

We should moreover bear in mind the building of strong monarchies in England, France, and the Iberian Peninsula, particularly during the 15th century. This, too, was in my view related to the crisis of feudalism. M. Postan already called attention to the fact that the appearance of robber barons in Germany and sharp struggles for power in England were a result of a certain impoverishment of the nobility and landed aristocracy. After all, they were engaged in both robbery as well as the seizure of the major power centres which at the same time were centres with great resources at their command. Certain feudal groups, often represented by the monarchs themselves, tried, in their own interest, to restore order necessary to the normal functioning of the state and society. They had the support of broad circles of burghers interested in the same policy. This could be observed in nearly all of western Europe. It was the core of the policy of the powerful Burgundian dukes in the 14th and 15th centuries. The same policy was more successfully advanced by the Yorks and Tudors in England, by Louis XI in France, by the Catholic monarchs in Spain, and by the rulers of Portugal. In this way a new political system was constituted, which to some extent owed its existence to the intense social crisis. It is clear that the system was in some measure the opposite of what was taking place in east-central Europe, particularly in the 15th century. The despotic rule of the grand princes of Muscovy, already apparent at the turn of the 15th century, was established in quite different circumstances, but no doubt it was one of the principal factors of political and economic development. As regards western Europe, in my opinion, from more or less the mid-14th to the second half of the 15th century, it was the result of a serious crisis which, however, found its expression not just in a business slump, but also in such transformation of economic and social structures as facilitated further development in all areas of social life.

It is generally accepted that the serious crisis passed in the second half of the 15th century, and was followed by an era of new economic growth, lasting until the 1620s or 1650s. This precisely was the "long 16th century", as F. Braudel termed it. Before passing on to it, I must devote a few words to the theory of I. Wallerstein. He maintains that in that century the "world economic system," capitalist in nature, was already in operation. I do not agree with him. It would seem that in the period under discussion there were conditions conducive to the later development of capitalism in only two countries: the Netherlands and England. Meanwhile, in northern and central Italy, once highly developed, the capitalist forms that emerged in industry in the late Middle Ages disappeared. But in principle I accept his division of the world into economic spheres, although it does not seem to me flexible enough. I have the impression that Wallerstein underestimates the autonomous development of the "semi-peripheral countries" and "peripheral countries," whose development he treats as a function of the processes taking place in what he calls "core countries."

The problems of economic development in western Europe in the "long 16th century" are already relatively well known, particularly thanks to research by Braudel and his school. At this point, it is enough to remember that the main characteristics of the dynamics of that period were a new population rise, development of farming and animal husbandry, the emergence of such hubs of commerce as Antwerp, Lisbon, Seville, and Amsterdam, and the related rise in agricultural prices and somewhat smaller rises in other areas of the economy. This rise in prices became particularly rapid in the second half of the 16th century, when great volumes of American bullion reached Europe; that rise already started however at the turn of the previous century. A further factor was the substantial increase in silver and copper yields over a period of 100–150 years, starting from the second half of the 15th century, which made money circulation and equipment of increasingly numerous and strong armies so much easier. One should pay attention to two important factors. The first concerns the massive rise in the demand for timber, to build towns as well as powerful fleets, established in Portugal as early as the beginning of the 15th century, and somewhat later in Spain, Holland, and England. The other involves the rising demand for grain, which accompanied the population increase and intensive urbanisation. In several countries, such as Norway, Portugal, northern Spain, and the northern Netherlands, grain shortages became critical. England had been fringing upon self-sufficiency for quite a time, and it was only towards the close of the epoch we are interested in that the situation changed. It must therefore be assumed that several million Europeans had to rely on food imports, of grain and meat in particular. Frequent crop failures magnified the problem. That undoubtedly exerted a strong influence on production prices in the nascent international market and in the producer countries. Brisk trade in forestry products and grain between Europe's West and East appeared already in the 15th century. At the same time, the importance of cattle exports from Hungary, Moldavia, and Polish Ukraine to Bohemia, Germany, and even Italy was steadily growing. In the century that followed, these trends grew very much stronger.

At this point I must give some attention to Holland, whose march towards economic importance started in fact already in the 14th and 15th centuries. At that time Dutch fisheries and the Dutch fleet developed markedly, as did also the woollen industry, which offered mostly medium-quality goods, hence available to wider circles of consumers. The shortage, first of timber, then grain, prompted the Dutch, and especially the merchants of Amsterdam, to turn their attention to the Baltic countries. They focused their interest first and foremost on Gdańsk, but did not neglect Livonian and even Mecklenburg ports either. Initially, the Dutch bought large numbers of ships in Gdańsk, but from the close of the 15th century they developed their own shipbuilding industry, based on the timber they imported from Poland and Lithuania through the agency of Gdańsk merchants. The latter, as we have already seen, ensured themselves regular supplies from their hinterland through paying advances. The method of purchasing grain was similar, although initially not so popular. By the second half of the 15th century, the Dutch had already become the dominant power in the Baltic. Very quickly, they extended their sphere of influence to the West. To the Baltic countries, first of all to Gdańsk, they supplied their own and English woollen cloths, and salt from Brittany, and themselves purchased timber and grain in volumes exceeding domestic demand. Already in the 15th century, the Dutch embarked on the so-called *duurgaende vaertem*, involving voyages for goods from the Baltic coast, which they next imported into their own country, but also sold to Flanders, Spain, and Portugal. In this, they merely followed the example of the Gdańsk and Livonian merchants who had from the 15th century been regularly providing timber, and later also grain, to the southern Netherlands, to England, and especially to Portugal. The rulers of the latter country actively supported the imports necessary to their rapid overseas expansion. As regards the Kingdom of Castile, the relevant problems have not been sufficiently studied as yet. Throughout the 16th century, all this trade flourished, with the Dutch having the largest share in it and the Gdańsk shipping trade gradually declining, unable to compete with Dutch competition. Grain exports increased greatly in the 16th century, especially in the second half, when western demand was particularly great, with grain prices shooting up during the so-called price revolution. In the 16th and 17th centuries, the Dutch treated the Baltic trade as *moedernegotie*, the mother trade. The capital earned on the Baltic trade helped them bring about their great overseas expansion. This is the view held in Dutch historiography. Grain and forestry products of the Baltic region were a very important element of Holland's economy, as indicated by countless local and Hanseatic sources. In the 16th century, agents of the king of Portugal in Antwerp carefully watched the situation regarding deliveries of Baltic grain because these had a great impact on prices in the Netherlands and in Portugal. The Sound custom register shows clearly that great volumes of rye, wheat, and other grains were involved. In the Baltic region, Poland was the main grain producer, while Gdańsk was its leading seller. It was predominantly with the city of Gdańsk that the Dutch merchants were connected. In Gdańsk they provided themselves with grain from the Polish Commonwealth. I do not agree with those of my colleagues who maintain that at that time Poland exported a mere fraction of her grain output and that Polish agriculture was oriented towards the domestic market. The estimates of these scholars should be revised, precisely in view of the ample information available indicating the great significance of Polish grain in international trade. I also think that one should not overestimate the role of the Polish domestic market for food products. In the 16th century, the overwhelming majority of Polish small- and medium-size towns remained rural or semi-rural in character, which means that demand for countryside produce must have been limited. All this applies chiefly to the Vistula River basin; in Great Poland the situation may have developed somewhat differently.

I will not go here into the process of the establishment of the second serfdom and the *corvée* system, because these have already been sufficiently discussed. I can only say that I consider it, and always did consider it, to have been a result of the interaction of two factors: of the international market situation and of the social structure of the nations of east-central and eastern Europe. It concerned all the Baltic countries with the exception of Sweden. In some measure, it concerned the Hungarian economy, too, especially with regard to its animal husbandry. In this case, however, I prefer to rely on the opinion of my Hungarian colleagues.

At the close of the 16th century, the increase in the *corvée*, although gradual, seriously complicated the further development of Poland and, as I believe, of other countries of east-central Europe. I have in mind the impoverishment of a considerable number of peasants, which again had its adverse effect on medium- and small-size towns linked with the rural economy. At the end of the 16th century, one could place the decline in Poland of certain areas of urban trades working to satisfy the needs of the wider market. This presumably led to a certain polarisation of society. At a time when the majority of peasants and the poor strata of the burghers were getting poorer, the owners of medium-size estates and the aristocracy, engaged in the production of and trade in grain—so much valued in the foreign market—were getting richer. As a result, the latter could step up their demand for imported western and eastern industrial and luxury products. All in all, Poland landed herself in a dangerous predicament because the situation in the grain market, on which the Polish economy increasingly depended, was all-decisive. I would add here that many similar occurrences could be observed in eastern Germany. At the end of the 16th century, the *corvée* increased also in Hungary, in Russia, and somewhat later in Bohemia, too. This, however, seems to have been caused by factors different from those affecting the Baltic countries. At all events, in Eastern Europe at the turn of the 16th century, there appeared a wide sphere of inefficient *corvée* economy where, in the absence of a proper domestic market and because of foreign competition, industry could not develop. I regard this occurrence as regression, which assumed its most severe form in Poland, and not just in the economic sphere alone. The great progress in Dutch, English, and later also in Lombardian and Venetian agriculture, and the general economic stagnation of the 17th century, had been damaging the market for Polish grain from the first half of the century. The earlier dependence of Polish agriculture on the western market led to the *sui generis* colonisation of the Polish economy; at the same time, it ensured a considerable income to the Poles, thanks to the foreign trade surplus and the inflow of money from the West. Still, in the 1620s, and even more so in the middle of the 17th century, the relatively prosperous long 16th century in Poland came to an end.

Thus I do not agree with Wallerstein, who treats the estate based on forced labour but producing for the market as a capitalist enterprise. Neither do I agree with J. Topolski, who perceives in 17th- and especially in 18th-century Poland a new nobility, corresponding to the English gentry. On the contrary, I consider this period marked the perpetuation of feudal structures, and not in the area of economy alone.

I say nothing here of the extremely important problem of the advent of the second wide sphere of economic stagnation in Spanish and Portuguese America, where slave plantation and the so-called system of peonage played an enormous role. In Latin America, great importance also attached to its dependence on foreign and distant markets and production centres, in north-western Europe in particular. In the vanguard of economic, political, and even cultural progress came countries such as first Spain, then England, and finally France, and these were the countries to draw the greatest profit, not just from their own economy, but also from the backwardness of the others.

Bibliography

W. Abel, *Agrarkrisen und Agrarkonjunktur im Mitteleuropa vom 13. bis zum 19. Jahrhundert* (Berlin 1939).
—— *Die Wüstungen des ausgehenden Mittelalters* (Stuttgart 1955).
J. G. Alekseev, *Agrarnaya i social'naia istoria severo-vostocnoi Rusi XV–XVI vv.* (Moskva-Leningrad 1966).
E. Ashtor, *Levant Trade in the Late Middle Ages* (Princeton 1983).
Ö. L. Barkan, "Essai sur les données statistiques des registres de recensement dans l'Empire Ottoman au XVe et XVIe siècle", in *Journal of the Economic and Social History of the Orient*, Vol. I (1957).
I. Bieżuńska-Małowist, M. Małowist, *Niewolnictwo* (Warszawa 1987).
M. Biskup, *Zjednoczenie Pomorza Wschodniego z Polską w połowie XV wieku* (Warszawa 1959).
M. Bogucka, *Handel zagraniczny Gdańska w pierwszej połowie XVII wieku* (Wrocław 1970).
F. Braudel, *Civilisation matérielle, économie et capitalisme XVe–XVIIIe siècle*, Vols. I–III (Paris 1979).
—— *La dynamique du capitalisme* (Paris 1985).
M. A. Cook ed., *Studies in the Economic History of the Middle East* (London 1970).
F. Graus, *Cesky obchod se suknem ve 14 a pocatkem 15 stoleti* (Praha 1950).
R. H. Hilton, "Y-eut-il une crise générale de la féodalité?", in *Annales* (1951).
H. Inalčik, "L'Empire Ottoman", in *Actes du Ier Congrès International des Études Balcaniques* (Sofia 1969).
J. Janaček, "Der böhmische Aussenhandel in der Mitte des 15. Jahrhunderts", in *Historica*, Vol. IV (1962).
P. Johansen, M. Mollat, M. Postan, A. Sapori, C. Verlinden, "L'économie européenne aux deux derniers siècles du Moyen-Age", in *Relazioni del X Congresso Internazionale di Scienze Storiche, Vol. III: Storia del medioevo* (Firenze 1955).
A. Keckowa, *Żupy krakowskie w XVI–XVIII wieku (do 1772 roku)* (Wrocław 1969).
Z. Kirilly, L. Makkai, J. N. Kiss, V. Zimanyi, "Production et productivité agricoles en Hongrie à l'époque du féodalisme tardif (1550–1850)", in *Nouvelles Etudes Historiques*, Vol. I (1965).
E. A. Kosminsky, *Studies in the Agrarian History of England in the 13th Century* (Oxford 1956).
Y. Koreckii, *Zakreposcenie krest'ian i klassovaia bor'ba v Rossii vo vtoroi polovine XVI v.* (Moskva 1970).
W. Kula, *Teoria ekonomiczna ustroju feudalnego* (Warszawa 1962).
A. Mączak, *Sukiennictwo wielkopolskie XIV–XVII wieku* (Warszawa 1953).
A. Mączak, H. Samsonowicz, "La zone baltique; l'un des éléments du marché européen", in *Acta Poloniae Historica*, Vol. XI (1965).
A. Mączak, H. Samsonowicz, P. Burke, eds., *East-Central Europe in Transition. From the Fourteenth to the Seventeenth Century* (Cambridge 1985).

M. Małowist, "Le développement des rapports économiques entre la Flandre, la Pologne et les pays limitrophes du XIIIᵉ au XIVᵉ siècle", in *Revue Belge de Philologie et d'Histoire*, Vol. X (1931).

—— *Studia z dziejów rzemiosła w okresie kryzysu feudalizmu w Zachodniej Europie w XIV i XV wieku* (Warszawa 1954).

—— "The Economic and Social Development of the Baltic Countries from the Fifteenth to the Seventeenth Centuries", in *Economic History Review*, Vol. XII (1959).

—— "Certain Trade Techniques in the Baltic Countries in the 15th–17th Centuries", in *Poland at the XIth International Congress of Historical Sciences in Stockholm* (Warszawa 1960).

—— "Les produits des pays de la Baltique dans le commerce international au XVIᵉ siècle", in *Revue du Nord*, Vol. XLII (1960).

—— "The Problem of Inequality of Economic Development in Europe in the Later Middle Ages", in *Economic History Review*, Vol. XIX (1966).

—— *Europa a Afryka Zachodnia w dobie wczesnej ekspansji kolonialnej* (Warszawa 1969).

—— "Croissance et régression en Europe au XIVᵉ–XVIᵉ siècles", in *Cahiers des Annales*, Vol. XXXIV (1972).

—— "Górnictwo w średniowiecznej Europie Środkowej i Wschodniej jako element struktur społeczno-gospodarczych w XII–XV w.", in *Przegląd Historyczny*, Vol. LXIII (1972).

—— *Wschód a Zachód Europy w XIII–XVI w. Konfrontacja struktur społeczno-gospodarczych* (Warszawa 1973).

—— "Problems of the Growth of the National Economy of Central-Eastern Europe in the Late Middle Ages", in *Journal of European Economic History*, Vol. III (1974).

—— *Konkwistadorzy portugalscy* (Warszawa 1976).

—— "Constitutional Trends and Social Developments in Central Europe, the Baltic Countries and the Polish-Lithuanian Commonwealth", in J. Pelenski, ed., *State and Society in Europe from the Fifteenth to the Eighteenth Century* (Warszawa 1981).

D. Molenda, *Górnictwo kruszcowe na terenie złóż śląsko-krakowskich do połowy XVI wieku* (Wrocław 1963).

—— *Kopalnie rud ołowiu na terenie złóż śląsko-krakowskich w XVI–XVIII wieku* (Warszawa 1972).

V. Nitemaa, *Der Binnenhandel in der Politik der livländischen Städte im Mittelalter* (Helsinki 1952).

Z. P. Pach, "Die Abbiegung der ungarischen Agrarentwicklung von der Westeuropäischen", in *Agrartorteneti Szemle*, Vol. I (1961).

—— "Osteuropa und die Anfangsperiode der Entstehung des modernen internationalen Handels im 15. Jahrhundert", in *V Internationaler Kongress der Ökonomischen Geschichte* (Moskau 1970).

M. Postan, "The Fifteenth Century", in *Economic History Review*, Vol. IX (1939).

—— "Some Economic Evidence of Declining Population in the Later Middle Ages", in *Economic History Review*, Vol. II (1950).

W. Rusiński, "Die Agrarkrise des 17. Jahrhunderts in Ostmitteleuropa", in *Vierteljahresschrift für Sozial- und Wirtschaftsgeschichte*, Vol. LXXIV (1983).

R. Rybarski, *Handel i polityka handlowa Polski w XVI stuleciu* (Warszawa 1958).

J. Topolski, *Gospodarka polska a europejska w XVI–XVIII wieku* (Poznań 1977).

—— *Narodziny kapitalizmu w Europie XIV–XVII wieku* (Warszawa 1987).

I. Wallerstein, *The Modern World-System. Capitalist Agriculture and the Origin of the European World-Economy in the Sixteenth Century* (New York 1977).

—— *The Modern World System II: Mercantilism and the Consolidation of the European World-Economy, 1660–1750* (New York 1980).

A. Wyczański, "Próba oszacowania obrotu żytem w Polsce w XVI w.", in *Kwartalnik Historii Kultury Materialnej*, Vol. IX (1961).

—— *Polska w Europie XVI stulecia* (Warszawa 1973).

A. Wyrobisz, "Warunki rozwoju przemysłu w Polsce w XVI i pierwszej połowie XVII w.", in *Studia i materiały z historii kultury materialnej*, Vol. LI (1976).

B. Zientara, *Kryzys agrarny w Marchii Wkrzańskiej w XIV w.* (Warszawa 1961).

—— "Z zagadnień spornych tzw. 'wtórnego poddaństwa' w Europie Środkowej", in *Przegląd Historyczny*, Vol. XLVII (1956).

—— "Walonowie na Śląsku w XII i XIII wieku", in *Przegląd Historyczny*, Vol. LXVI (1975).

CHAPTER ELEVEN

EASTERN EUROPE AND THE COUNTRIES OF THE IBERIAN PENINSULA. PARALLELS AND CONTRASTS*

These modest observations are dedicated to the memory of a great scholar to whom I was bound by ties of friendship which were to prove, alas, all too short-lived.

Joachim Lelewel, the great pioneer of Polish historiography in the first half of the 19th century, was struck even in his time by certain analogies in the evolution of Poland on the one hand and Spain on the other.[1] The rapid growth of both countries in the course of the 15th and 16th centuries, followed in each case by a long and painful period of decline, captured the attention of this great scholar and man of action, anxious to discover the deeper causes of our national catastrophe. In the culture and civilization of the two peoples, he observed similarities in which he detected dangers for the lives of both nations.

Today, we know that the picture traced by Lelewel contained a number of inaccuracies. Notwithstanding his impressive erudition, he lacked both sufficient documentation of the period concerned and truly modem methods of research. However, recent studies in the field of economic and social history bring us once again face to face with matters of comparative history. It is an incontrovertible fact that, from the close of the 16th century, two large zones of "underdevelopment" made their appearance in Europe, one in the East and the other in the South-West, the latter extending far beyond the confines of Europe into the lands of Latin America and Africa. These latter also constituted economic zones *sui generis* complementary to the countries of North-Western Europe, more advanced and notably more dynamic in their industrial and commercial drive. But these periods of decline had in each case been preceded by totally contrasting phases. Spain and

---

* Originally published in French under the title "L'Europe de l'Est et les pays ibériques. Analogies et contrastes", in *Homenaje a Jaime Vicens Vives*, I, Barcelona, Universidad de Barcelona, Faculdad de Filosofia y Letras, 1965, pp. 85–93. Translation from French by Robin Kimball.

[1] J. Lelewel, *Parallèle historique entre l'Espagne et la Pologne au XVI, XVII, XVIII siècles*, Paris, 1835.

Portugal had founded vast colonial empires, the former even establishing preponderance in the Old and New Worlds. Meanwhile, Poland, on a far more modest scale, had succeeded in occupying vast areas in Eastern Europe, where for long years to come she would exercise a dominance limited only by the influence of the Ottoman lands in Europe. It is also an established fact that, at the dawn of their expansionist enterprises, Castile and Portugal, like Poland, represented the less advanced sector of the European economy, especially in comparison with the countries of the North-West, let alone with Italy or Southern Germany.

I would like here to advance certain observations concerning the social significance of these expansionist movements and the influence they exerted on the economic life of the peoples of the Iberian Peninsula on the one hand and those of Poland on the other.

The Kingdom of Poland, reunited at the end of the 13th century, entered a period of full economic and political development in the century which followed, marked by striking progress in the fields of agriculture and urban trade and industry. It would seem that none of the great epidemics rife at that time seriously affected any sector of national life. Given the lack of relevant sources, one can only surmise that they spared the Polish territories at least in part. Nevertheless, one can observe certain symptoms, even in Poland, of the grave economic crisis that affected the West. This was evident in the depreciation of coin, which the last two kings of the Piast dynasty did their best to counter, albeit without achieving tangible results. There was also a certain *malaise* in the ranks of the nobility who, held in check by Casimir the Great (1333–1370), were on the look-out for possibilities of expansion which, no longer on offer within the confines of the realm, could only be sought elsewhere. It is fair to assume that the monetary crisis exerted a nefast influence on the revenues of the nobles drawn in coin. The towns, in full growth, attracted large numbers of peasants. The shortage of manpower and its consequent dearness, reflected in the sources of the following period, perhaps stemmed from as far back as the 14th century. Even King Casimir, subsequently saddled by the nobility with the contemptuous sobriquet of "king of the peasants," felt constrained to publish an ordinance restricting in some measure the freedom of movement of the rural population, in order to ensure a sufficient workforce for the needs of agriculture. It was not only the commercial interests of the urban merchants but also the expansionist aspirations of the nobility that drove Casimir the Great towards the territories bordering the Ukraine, which he conquered after long years of intense struggle. There were also his principal allies—the nobles of Little Poland—to whom he granted considerable estates in those regions. We now know that the nobles from other provinces likewise profited from these conquests, and that the king probably regarded the occupied territories as the keystone of his realm, still subject to upheavals from factions of nobles in various regions of Poland.

These, however, were only the beginnings of the vast Polish drive towards the East. In the eyes of the *grands seigneurs* of Little Poland, who held the real power in the country, the dynastic Union with Lithuania (1386) was destined to open up new possibilities for expansion in Ruthenian territory, while simultaneously strengthening Poland's defences against the Teutonic Order. In the 15th century, the Polish nobility were still very active in the cause of territorial expansion. The powerful lords of Little Poland consolidated and extended their domains in the Ukraine, and it seems probable that the anti-Turkish policy preached by Zbigniew of Oleśnica, the powerful bishop of Cracow, echoed the expansionist designs of this same group. At the same time, the bitter struggles against the Teutonic Knights brought about the reunification of Central Pomerania (1466), thereby facilitating the export of agricultural produce towards the West. It is now known that the nobles of Central Poland likewise aimed at the acquisition of new estates and lucrative titles in those areas. The nobles of Mazovia province began their penetration into neighbouring Lithuania, while groups of peasants from the same region started settling in the woodland spaces of East Prussia, so forming the nucleus of the future "Masuria." One thus witnesses in several different fields a wave of expansion, in part warlike, in part peaceful, in which the nobility played a considerable, if not always dominant, role.

Now it seems to me that, from the turn of the 15th and during the 16th century, this warlike frame of mind grew progressively weaker. In their large majority, the Polish nobles lost their taste for adventure. The descendants of the former warriors turned their attention more and more to their own estates which, with the favourable turn in the marketing of cereals (in Poland, roughly from the last decades of the 15th century), promised safe profits with few risks attached. This transformation, remarked upon by contemporaries, showed itself clearly on several occasions during the 16th and 17th centuries, even in moments of crisis in the life of the state. The adaptation of agriculture to the needs of new markets, opening up mainly abroad but also exerting a great influence on the price of cereals in Poland, especially during the

price revolution, demanded great political and organizational efforts
on the part of the nobility. Given the shortage of manpower and the
weak financial status of the nobles, the latter were obliged to saddle the
peasants with the *corvée* which, in the absence of noteworthy resistance,
they progressively increased. This long process required the creation of
a whole coercive apparatus directed against any recalcitrants. Moreover,
the new economic situation also encouraged the nobles to limit the
rights of the burghers, with a view to obtaining direct access to foreign
buyers and sellers. In the course of the 16th century, the masses of the
middle nobility waged an unremitting struggle against the powerful
landlords on whom, towards the middle of the century, they inflicted a
victory that was as spectacular as it was ultimately to prove illusory. All
these struggles and conflicts so absorbed the majority of the nobles that
they turned their back on ideas of further foreign expansion. However,
in the second half of the century, and especially during the last three
decades, we again witness a change in the situation. This took the form
of a new, initially peaceful, eastward drive, directed at once against the
Russo-Lithuanian lands and the fertile plains of Livonia, an undertaking which aroused the antagonism of Russia and the opposition of the
Swedes. The wars of Sigismund Augustus and the victories of Stephen
Bátory over the Russia of Ivan the Terrible led to a wave of colonization by Polish nobles in the lands of Livonia. The strengthening of the
Union with Lithuania (1569) aided the colonization of vast areas of
the Grand Duchy and of the Ukraine. In both cases it was Mazovia,
sorely overpopulated as it was, that provided the hard core of the new
immigrants.

It is fair to assume that this new colonizing drive was due, not only
to the rise in native population, but also to the favourable turn in
the market for agriculture and stock-breeding. This might explain a
certain extension of colonization even in the Ukraine, despite its very
unfavourable geographical position in relation to the great markets of
North-West Europe. This new wave of settlement was largely rural in
character, consisting mainly of nobles and peasants anxious to move
to the eastern territories in order to avoid the *corvée*; the bourgeois
who joined this movement were few in number and represented no
significant political or economic forces. The turn of the 16th century is
marked by two factors of extreme importance. One was the formation
of new oligarchies—families of Polish or Russo-Lithuanian origin—who
settled mainly in the large estates situated in the east of the country.
The courts of these powerful magnates became the centres of a vast

clientele drawn from the ranks of the small and middle nobility who had fallen into a state of dependence on the *grand seigneurs*. This process—the "refeudalization" of the Polish nobility—has not so far been accorded the attention it deserves. Towards the beginning of the 17th century, the magnates took over the direction of eastward expansion into their own hands. It was they who created the immense *latifundia* in the Ukraine, they who organized and directed the Polish invasion of Russia in the Time of Troubles, prior to the accession of the Romanov dynasty there. With large numbers of poor nobles at their disposal, they impelled the Polish State into useless and unsuccessful campaigns against Russia and Turkey. The Ukrainian revolt of 1648, together with the attacks on Poland by foreign powers, put an end to this policy of eastward expansion, so restricting the margin of manoeuvre of the upper gentry to the confines of the country proper.

The "imperialism" of the Polish nobility at the turn of the 16th century contained other aspects of note. It developed against a background of favourable conditions on the agricultural and stock-breeding markets. Yet this was precisely the reason why the nobles tried to run their estates on the *corvée* system, being forced to do so on account of the shortage of manpower, and its consequent dearness, in their underpopulated territories. The spread of this system, accompanied by the impoverishment of the peasants and their (more or less effective) attachment to the soil, together with the intrusion of the nobles into the commercial domain—all this caused disruption in the life of the towns, cutting them off from both home and foreign markets. From the end of the 16th century onwards, the impoverishment of the peasants and of the majority of the bourgeois class led to the stagnation and eventually to the virtual demise of industry. Only a few branches of the luxury industry managed to keep going, and even to expand, by producing goods destined for the well-off sections of the population. As I have stated on a previous occasion, one may consider the Poland of this period as a country of cereal monoculture, at the mercy of conditions on the large foreign markets.[2]

One other important factor should be mentioned here: the fact that neither Poland's eastward expansion nor the formation of the "second serfdom" encountered any serious resistance inside the country. By

---

[2] M. Małowist, "Poland, Russia and Western Trade in the 15th and 16th Centuries," in *Past and Present*, XIII, 1958, pp. 26–41, p. 38. Chapter 6 in this volume.

the same token, the wars of the 16th and early 17th century, up to the time of the first Swedish invasions, were fought out mainly in lands far removed from the centre of the country, and did not materially affect the interests of the majority of nobles.

At the same time, the latter were careful to avoid any steps that might provoke the wrath of the fearsome Turk. In these conditions, the Polish nobility, and *a fortiori* the magnates, saw no reason to strengthen the central power of the state. Thanks to recent findings, we now know that in the 16th century this power was by no means so weak as was long thought.[3] Yet, notwithstanding the efforts of all the kings involved, the nobility, later under the leadership of the magnates, put up a stubborn resistance to the centralizing efforts of the monarchy and wrested from it a series of concessions. The evolution of the seigneurial economy in Poland was thus accompanied by the refeudalization of the state, effected by the leading gentry with the aid of their clientele. In this way, the economic and social stagnation and regression came to be reflected in the vital domain of the country's institutions.

In his studies on the Great Discoveries, Mr. Verlinden emphasized more than once the fact that, in the territories they occupied, both Spanish and Portuguese conquerors applied the norms and notions of feudal law. In my view, this fact not only reflected their aims, but also affords us some insight into the social aspect of the initial phase of the great wave of colonization. Some years ago, I advanced the suggestion that this whole vast movement was originally set in motion by the crisis in the seigneurial economy which probably affected the Iberian Peninsula at that time, as it did several other countries in the West. Unfortunately, the economic history of Spain and Portugal in this period has not so far been sufficiently studied. The works of J. Vicens Vives and the studies of P. Vilar and other scholars throw much light on the situation in Catalonia, but the economic and social history of Castile and Portugal, for all its intense interest, still requires much effort on the part of investigators. Here I would only mention the persistent wars between the peninsular states themselves and the brutal struggles between the aristocratic clans which disturbed life in Castile under the Trastamaras, together with the Portuguese revolu-

---

[3] K. Grzybowski, *The Theory of Parliamentary Representation in Renaissance Poland* (in Polish), Warszawa, 1959.

tion on the eve of the accession of the Aviz dynasty. If to this we add the effects of the crisis which played havoc with the monetary system and the shortage of manpower provoked by the epidemics of the 14th century, it seems fair to admit the existence of serious shortcomings in the seigneurial economy in various parts of the Peninsula. The widespread peasant revolts, so admirably analysed by J. Vicens Vives in the case of Catalonia, together with the resistance opposed by similar groups in the other Spanish states during the 15th century, all go to show that the increased pressure brought to bear on the peasantry by the nobles provoked problems with which the ruling class, and even the central authorities, were often unable to cope. Portuguese historians long ago, and more recently Mr. V. Magalhães Godinho, recognized the connection between the revolution of 1380–1381 and the beginnings of overseas expansion towards Morocco, the Atlantic islands, and West Africa. Mr. Godinho observed a direct relationship between the end of the civil wars and the conflict with Castile on the one hand and the expedition against Ceuta (1415) and the colonization of the Atlantic islands and the coast of West Africa on the other. He rightly pointed out that the Portuguese nobility were in absolute need of new fields of expansion, now that the former outlets no longer existed. In support of this contention, one may add the testimony of King Duarte on the eve of the expedition against Tangier. As one of the grounds for his decision to act, the King confessed his fear that, in the absence of other means of acquiring wealth, his noble vassals might seek their fortune abroad in the service of other monarchs.[4] From the chronicles of Zurara and other Portuguese writers of the period, it is clear that it was the leading Portuguese nobles who drew up and executed the plans for the Great Discoveries, with the aid of countless *fidalgos*. It was the circles of the nobles that provided the captains and a large part of those taking part in the overseas expeditions, taking with them numbers of the common folk as well. It was these same Portuguese nobles who acquired the glory and the wealth inherent in these exploits, which to us sometimes seem more like plain acts of brigandage than laudable crusades, though regarded by their contemporaries precisely as the latter. The Portuguese merchants joined in these expeditions

---

[4] V. Magalhães Godinho, *Documentos sobre a expansão portuguesa*, II, Lisboa, 1945, p. 96; likewise the extract by Zurara, *Crónica da Tomada de Ceuta*, ch. VI, pp. 35ff.

somewhat later than the *fidalgos*, and it was the nobles who pioneered these undertakings and whom Prince Henry, the regent Don Pedro, and succeeding monarchs presented with all the lucrative posts in the conquered lands and the territories opened up to the commercial penetration of the Portuguese. This state of affairs was patently evident in Africa, in the Indies, and even in Brazil from the time when King John III organized his captaincies there. It thus seems fair to assume that the overseas expansion of the Portuguese was largely the work of the nobility, in search of new sources of wealth and social advancement no longer on offer at home. It is worth noting that even Fernão Gomes, the great bourgeois entrepreneur who in 1469 was accorded a licence for the African trade, turned mainly to the nobles to assist him in his conquest of the African coast. All this also demonstrates that the Portuguese merchants in general showed scant interest in the enterprise of the discoveries, especially in the 15th century. The backward state of commercial and industrial development, together with the virtually insignificant accumulation of urban bourgeois capital, would seem to support this hypothesis.

The social aspect of the great Castilian overseas expeditions is less easy to define, though here, too, it is evident that the nobles played a preponderating part, even though they may not have provided a clear majority of the *conquistadores* and colonizers. But in the lands of the first Catholic Kings and the Habsburgs, the powerful lords and the great mass of the nobility still had other outlets for their expansionist aims, notably in the service of the various armies engaged in fighting in the four corners of Europe, or again in the constantly swelling bureaucracy at home. Obedience to the Crown henceforth became one of the classic virtues of the Castilian nobles. The dying phases of the revolt of the *Comuneros* prove that this once so turbulent faction was already regrouping round the throne. This bond of loyalty, so characteristic of the 16th and 17th centuries, provides a striking contrast with the preceding period. It is explained by the fact that, to a wide fraction of the nobility, and especially to its more powerful circles, Spanish absolutism ensured considerable profits. In summing up this somewhat cursory analysis, I would stress that the vast expansion of the Iberian countries during the 15th and 16th centuries contained typical feudal features, not only from the point of view of the legal norms imposed but also in that, as in Poland, it reflected the vital interests of the feudal classes, for whom all chance of economic and social advancement at home was severely restricted, sometimes even to the point of stagnation.

There has long been discussion of the effects exerted by colonial expansion on the economic life of Spain and Portugal. As far back as the 17th century, serious doubts were expressed concerning the allegedly favourable influence of the great overseas conquests on the lives of these two nations. It seems to me that these doubts had at least some justification in fact. The traffic in oriental merchandise and in gold and silver did not fundamentally alter the economic climate of the Peninsula. While a number of individuals undoubtedly profited from the situation, the grand colonial enterprise as a whole failed to bring about any progressive or lasting changes in the economic and social structures of the mother countries.

The influx of gold and silver into Spain only increased the cost of living and aggravated the shortage of the workforce, many of whom were attracted towards the fighting forces or the colonies; this was to have dire consequences for Castilian agriculture and industry. The rise in prices due to the same factors, which incidentally in the course of the 16th century preceded the general rise in other European countries, encouraged the import of industrial goods and agricultural produce from abroad. In this way Spain remained what she had been in the Middle Ages—a country mainly exporting its primary resources, with the addition of metals acquired in the colonies. Her industry, still underdeveloped, despite a temporary boom in the 16th century, had difficulty in facing the increasing competition of foreign merchandise, which not only penetrated into the metropolis but even found its way onto the overseas markets. This trade may be regarded as the forerunner of the colonial expansion of the Dutch, the British, and the French. Certainly, it is hard to imagine the huge empire of Charles V and Philip II without the influx of American coin. On the other hand, it is a well-known fact that this wealth was nowhere near sufficient to ensure the upkeep of the vast state apparatus of the Habsburg monarchy, but passed instead into the hands of foreigners having the necessary means for the maintenance of Spanish power. The drain on wealth due to the exorbitant level of taxation in the Castilian provinces reduced the purchasing power of the population, while simultaneously depriving agriculture and industry of the sources of investment essential to its development. The acquisition of wealth by certain leading merchants, bankers, and the more powerful members of the nobility does not materially alter this picture, given the weakness of those factors susceptible of stimulating productive investment. The negative effects of the great colonial enterprise made themselves felt even earlier in tiny Portugal, which found itself confronted with grave financial difficulties as early as the mid-16th century, and subsequently lacked both the economic means and the human resources to defend its vast overseas territories against the attacks of the Dutch. The Spaniards and the Portuguese opened up vast areas of the world to European influence, but it was not they who reaped the real harvest from this gigantic undertaking. On the contrary, they only succeeded in exhausting themselves in the effort, and found themselves obliged to make way for other nations whose economic systems were more advanced and hence more dynamic.

At this point I should like to call your attention to one more factor. In establishing the colonial economy in Spanish America and in Brazil, the invaders were obliged to introduce the system of forced labour for the Indians and especially the black slaves. This was the plain consequence of the shortage of manpower. But the system of slavery, while it might ensure the export of mineral resources, sugar, and other plantation produce, did little to encourage the development of a modern economy in the conquered countries. The restricted nature of the internal markets prevented the growth of a modern industrial system in the Iberian "New World," which with time became nothing more than an immense reservoir of the produce of a primitive economy based on agriculture and cattle-raising. The consequence was the advent of a new zone of "underdevelopment" which found itself at the mercy of certain European countries in full industrial evolution. Nor should one underestimate the disastrous effects of the black slave trade inflicted on the African continent.

Can one fairly speak of the negative results for the Spaniards and Portuguese of their great expansionist efforts? To me, these seem self-evident. Overseas expansion demanded an extraordinary deployment of forces on the part of the two peninsular powers. It drained off some of the most energetic and enterprising members of the population towards far-flung lands. True, the riches brought from the colonies contributed in decisive fashion to the rise of the great Spanish Empire but, for want of a solid basis of national production, these riches passed on to other countries. Indeed, the very Empire itself was an important factor in the progressive exhaustion of economic life in Spain and in the ossification of social structures too backward to ensure any dynamic development of the mother country. Many of these negative factors associated with overseas expansion appeared in Portugal even earlier than in Spain.

The immense territories conquered in America and exploited by means of black labour led to the emergence of a slave economy of plantations, little adapted to rapid progress and, from the start, dependent on countries disposing of a far more advanced economy.

The question arises: is it fair to speak of parallels between events in Eastern Europe (especially Poland) on the one hand and the nations of the Iberian Peninsula on the other? Conditions in the historical evolution of these three nations were very far removed from what Lelewel could imagine. He sought his analogies mainly in the customs, the civilization, and the political events of the countries concerned. Writing as he did in the first half of the past century, he could neither know nor grasp the importance of the economic factor in the life of human kind. Even so, I consider that there was some justice in his observations. The Spaniards and Portuguese on a worldwide scale, Poland within the far more modest framework of Eastern Europe, created huge states many times the area of their own countries. This gave rise to problems difficult and sometimes impossible to resolve, owing to the backward nature of their native economies. The policy of expansion, conducted by the nobles primarily in their own interests, exhausted the demographic potential of the home countries and, in the case of the Iberian peninsula, diverted the people, directly or indirectly, from productive labour. In Poland, it favoured the extensive development of agriculture but ruined the chances of industrial growth by mobilizing all available resources in the interests of the rural economy. In both cases, it contributed to the establishment over vast areas of an economy based on forced labour and the ruthless exploitation of original producers, so creating zones of age-long stagnation. One might add here that, despite all differences, the gulf between the "second serfdom" in Eastern Europe and the Iberian system of slavery overseas in fact narrowed with the course of time.

This process served the interests of those nations which, ever since the end of the Middle Ages, possessed the nucleus of industrial organization and of capital accumulated in the course of trade. The Dutch, the British, and the French very soon insinuated their way into the traffic between Spain, Portugal, and their colonies, and derived considerable profits from them. Their industrial and commercial organization enabled them to supply themselves with agricultural and forestry products from Eastern Europe, paying for these partly with coin and partly with colonial produce direct from the Iberian Peninsula. In this way they contributed, indirectly at least, to the consolidation and further spread of serfdom and of the *corvée* in the East, not only in Poland but also in the Eastern Germany and in Russia. The countries of North-West Europe absorbed a large part of the agricultural and stock-breeding market from the Spanish and Portuguese colonies, supplying them in return with industrial goods. This only reinforced the archaic socio-economic structures and condemned the respective peoples to a state of economic servitude, together with its inevitable consequences, poverty and stagnation.

The great expansionist adventure furnished both Spain and Portugal with the material wherewithal for the establishment of centralized states. Whatever one's view of the value of the Spanish bureaucracy of the 16th and 17th centuries, it undoubtedly contributed to the greater coherence of the state and succeeded in suppressing the anarchical tendencies rife among the nobility. By contrast, the eastward expansion of Poland produced exactly opposite effects. Not only did the eastern provinces, underpopulated and underpoliced, present a picture of chronic anarchy, but it was these same regions which gave rise to the huge fortunes of the aristocracy who, with the aid of their noble clientele, paralysed the central power of the state in the course of the 17th and 18th centuries. The national rebirth of the Age of Enlightenment came too late. The anachronistic character of the Polish régime, its backward economy, and its unfavourable geographical position—all these factors condemned the Republic of the Nobles to extinction.

CHAPTER TWELVE

THE SOCIAL AND ECONOMIC STABILITY OF THE WESTERN SUDAN IN THE MIDDLE AGES*

It is well known that African social and economic structures remained stable from an early date until the twentieth century. I propose to discuss here certain questions concerning the states of the western Sudan during the later Middle Ages; states which achieved a level of development in the fourteenth and fifteenth centuries, beyond which they were unable to advance before the Moroccan invasion of 1591, which began a decline that lasted several centuries. I shall draw on some analogies with eastern European countries, which during the eleventh and twelfth centuries were at more or less the same level of economic development as the western Sudan two centuries later. In so doing I am discounting the important differences of time and place. For what interests me is why Sudanese social and economic structures did not develop further, whereas those of eastern Europe underwent profound changes in the course of the thirteenth and fourteenth centuries. I intend, in fact, to attempt to pinpoint those elements of social and economic progress and more particularly of stagnation which were to be found in Mali and its successor state, Songhai; and in so doing I hope to contribute to the general discussion on economic incentives in primitive societies.

Agriculture was the basis of life for the vast majority of people in the two extensive regions in question, a primitive agriculture which had hardly yet adopted either the iron tools or two- and three-course rotation of crops which had been widespread in western Europe for some considerable time. In the western Sudan the soil of the savannah and the wide open spaces encouraged a relatively small population to retain the method of burning vegetation in order to fertilize the cultivated area. In many parts of eastern Europe this method was long out-of-date, yet agricultural productivity there seems to have remained very low. In both cases a subsistence economy predominated among

---

* Originally published in *Past and Present*, No. 33 (April, 1966), pp. 3–15. Translated from the French by Mr. Howard Clarke.

the peasantry, though a certain amount of exchange of products was necessary particularly because of differences in the natural environment. There seems to have been little social division of labour. Crafts and agriculture were still not separated in any clear-cut way. Until the thirteenth century and perhaps even the fourteenth, a considerable number of craftsmen in the Slav lands lived in villages and were also engaged in agriculture. Only in the thirteenth century did all crafts begin to be concentrated together, especially in the towns. Mention should be made here of "service villages," which probably existed up to the eleventh and maybe to the twelfth century and traces of which are preserved in the place-names of Slav countries. These were settlements whose inhabitants were tied to fixed services, often consisting of delivering to the prince or to his officials certain craft products, such as pots and weapons. The existence of this service system shows that many products were difficult to purchase, even for powerful men who wanted to be certain of obtaining them. It is further proof of low economic productivity in the Slav lands.

Archeological investigation has demonstrated the existence of towns in eastern Europe before the thirteenth century. But apart from a few exceptions like Prague—which, according to some sources, was an important slave market in the tenth and eleventh centuries—Kiev or Wolin, the evidence is that these towns were tiny groupings of people around princely residences and were inhabited only by a small number of craftsmen and possibly merchants, whose main task was to satisfy the needs of the prince, his officials and their courts. Relations between town and countryside must have been rather limited at first, although the towns naturally received their supplies from the surrounding district. The archaeological evidence also shows that these towns covered such a limited area that it was impossible for their inhabitants to engage in agriculture within them. In the economic life of a few more important towns, luxury products in particular played a considerable role, but these products, which were destined for a very limited section of the population, cannot have been very common.

It is often said that the great landed estate developed in Poland in the course of the eleventh and twelfth centuries and a little earlier in Bohemia. This is also the period when serfdom was becoming more and more prevalent. This process could have taken place only at the expense of the free indigenous population. There was, however, another source of slaves, or rather of serfs, although it seems to have been of less importance, namely, prisoners of war taken during the frequent invasions by Poles, Czechs and Russians of the lands of their temporarily weaker neighbours. It is known that these captives were often settled by the conquerors on their lands and obliged to cultivate them and pay taxes. No one seems to have asked whether, among the Slavs, prisoners taken in the course of invading enemy territory were useful in the slave trade. The lack of sources does not permit us to resolve this problem. But it should be remembered that slaves originating in the Slav lands were common everywhere in the Muslim world up to the eleventh century. And the sale of prisoners of war cannot be altogether excluded.

Our evidence for the economic life of the Mali Empire in the western Sudan is thin and very scattered but some conclusions can be drawn from it. This immense state was established by the Malinke tribe, who subjected a large number of different peoples dwelling between the upper courses of the Niger and Senegal rivers and the western limits of the Niger bend. The Mali Empire also exercised strong influence over the Berber tribes of southern and central Sahel. According to the evidence of two Sudanese chronicles of the sixteenth and seventeenth centuries, based on ancient traditions, the Mali or rather Malinke were warriors and traders.[1] Taking into consideration the structures of more recent and better known African states, it may be said that the Malinke were a kind of privileged group within the empire. From them were drawn not only the royal clan of Keita but also an aristocracy of powerful families, who surrounded the sultan and supplied the high officers of state. As for the native merchants active in Mali, they were called Wangara, which shows that they belonged to the great ethnic group of the Mandingoes.

We do not know for certain what the obligations of subjects were towards the sovereigns of Mali and its successor, Songhai. The Malinke were undoubtedly liable to military service. They were probably summoned frequently, for according to Sultan Mansa Musa in 1324–5, his empire used to wage incessant war against the infidels.[2] Written sources also mention the right to lodging which the sultan's subjects owed him in the Mali period. No doubt there were other dues to the sovereigns and their officials, paid probably by the free population, but their

[1] Mahmoud Kati ben el-Hadj el-Motaouakkel, *Tarikh el-Fettach [Chronique du Chercheur]*, French translation by O. Houdas and M. Delafosse (Paris, 1913), p. 65.
[2] Ibn Fadl Allah Al-Omari, *Masalik el Absar fi Mamalik el Amsar [L'Afrique moins l'Egypte]*, French translation by Gaudefroy-Demombynes (Paris, 1927), p. 81.

character is not known. As for territories conquered by the Mali, we know that they paid tribute to the sovereigns. Thus the sultan collected two thirds of the taxes paid (in gold) by the townsmen of Timbuktu.[3] The town and small but relatively rich principality of Jenne sent its tribute to the senior wife of the sultan. The peoples engaged in washing gold sifted from the river sand of Bambuk-Galam and Bure paid tribute in kind.[4] Privileges bought by merchants, who exported gold in exchange for salt and other foreign commodities, probably constituted a valuable source of revenue for the royal treasury.

Our knowledge of the dues rendered by the population to the monarch is therefore very limited. The authors of the two Sudanese chronicles reveal very clearly that during the period of the Mali Empire the institution known by scholars as the "castes" was already in existence. These were groups of sultan's slaves, who occupied a particular piece of land and were liable to uniform dues in kind. I have analysed this phenomenon in another place[5] and wish here merely to draw attention to the striking analogy between these "castes" and the inhabitants of "service villages" in the Slav world during the early Middle Ages. I believe that, in both cases, the emergence of these institutions was caused by the low productivity of the societies in question and that the sovereigns and dominant social groups needed to compel a section of their subjects to produce a surplus of essential articles, a sufficient supply of which could not be guaranteed in the markets. But I do not think that the nature of the renders was always determined by the occupation of the people in question. There is every likelihood that even those who appear in the sources as smiths or other craftsmen also cultivated their fields or lived off fishing; for it is improbable that there was any large number of professional craftsmen in a peasant society living at the stage of a subsistence economy.

Employing a term invented by E. Heckscher for a different purpose, however, one could speak in this case too of a barbaric prosperity. This is well shown in the narrative of Ibn battutah, the famous traveller of the mid-fourteenth century. He tells us that during his stay in Mali he

---

[3] Abderrahman ben Abdallah ben Imran ben Amir es-Sa'adi, *Tarikh es-Soudan, [Chronique du Soudan]*, French translation by O. Houdas (Paris, 1900), p. 40.

[4] *Ibid.*, p. 21; Al-Omari, p. 58.

[5] M. Małowist, *Wielke państwa Sudanu Zachodniego w późnym średniowieczu [The Great States of the Western Sudan in the Later Middle Ages]* (Warsaw, 1964), pp. 147–149, 380–382.

could easily obtain food supplies in each locality he passed through. Everywhere peasants offered travellers necessary provisions in exchange for small quantities of salt or luxury commodities like spices and jewels.[6] It is evident that the only essential commodity which the Mali peasants lacked was salt, which they had to import from the Sahara. From an examination of Al-Omari's writings, which come from the same period and are based on Sudanese accounts, it may be concluded that particularly agriculture and fruit-gathering, and also, in certain parts of the country, hunting and the rearing of livestock, assured the Mali peasants of a relatively prosperous and independent life, satisfying their needs without much contact with the outside world.[7]

This prosperity did not demand any great efforts on the part of the Mali peasants. Their needs in clothing and shelter were much less than those of the European peasantry. The wide expanses of savannah were well suited to a rudimentary agriculture, based on firing the countryside and using the wooden hoe as the principal tool. These open spaces also offered enough opportunities of food supply for a population which in any case increased relatively slowly. Collecting fruit yielded much necessary food, particularly in southern Mali, and it was often done by women and children. Thus the Mali peasants did not need to intensify their labour. Their small surplus production probably sufficed to procure them salt and a few luxury objects, if only modest ones at first. In the internal life of the Mali countryside, therefore, I can find no incentives which might have encouraged the peasants to improve and intensify their methods of work and consequently to change those old social structures which were so closely bound up with the agricultural system, such as the system of large families cultivating their land in common.

We must now ask whether these incentives could not have come from outside: that is, either from merchants or from the state. Arab travellers from the fourteenth to the sixteenth centuries all tell us that Mali towns—Timbuktu, Gao and lesser places—were in general well supplied with victuals, and there is no doubt that the towns obtained some of their provisions by trade with the peasantry. The rural areas had a surplus of agricultural and animal products which was dispatched

---

[6] Ibn Batoutah, *Voyages*, French translation by C. Defrémery and B. R. Sanguinetti, Vol. iv (Paris, 1858), pp. 392–4.

[7] Al-Omari, pp. 61f.

for sale in the towns. Ibn battutah and other sources indicate that the western Sudan even exported a certain amount of millet and rice to the Sahel regions, not only to Walata but also farther towards the districts where rock-salt and copper were exploited for import into the Sudan.[8] Yet the export trade of agricultural and animal products was not of sufficient quantity to cover the cost of importing salt, copper, silver and other commodities from the Sahara, North Africa, Egypt and Europe. The really valuable Sudanese commodities were gold and slaves. Both were at the disposal of sovereigns of Mali and later Songhai, and likewise of native and Arab-Berber merchants who visited or established themselves in the country.

Arab and Sudanese sources show that the Mali emperors collected tribute in gold from the regions of Bambuk-Galam and probably Bure. Cadamosto and certain Portuguese authors, relying no doubt on native accounts, have let us a description of the traffic in gold exchanged for salt between the Sahel, Timbuktu, Jenne, Gao, the Mali capital and the areas supplying gold.[9] We do not have any figures relating to this trade but the indirect evidence gives some indication of the scale of the trade in gold and in particular of its export northwards. It should be remembered here that during the fourteenth and fifteenth centuries there was an acute shortage of precious metals in Europe and in the Muslim lands and that the only really important source of gold was in the western Sudan and its hinterland. This metal had no place in local internal trade for its value was too high. Instead we see that salt, Mahgreb and Egyptian cloths, copper, weapons and horses from North Africa and even from Europe were paid for in gold. In this connection the accounts of Malfante, Cadamosto and Leo Africanus are quite explicit, and give a good deal of information on the subject. Valentim Fernandes and Malfante tell us that even in their own day—in the mid-fifteenth century—gold had the same value as silver in the Sudan.[10] We know that the Sudan did not possess any silver mines and that this metal was

[8] Ibn Batoutah, pp. 378, 391, 431f.; Leo Africanus, *Description de l'Afrique*, ed. A. Epaulard (Paris, 1956), ii, pp. 455, 463.

[9] *Delle navigazioni e viaggi di Messer Alvise da Ca'Da Mosto gentiluomo Veneziano*, ed. R. Caddeo (Milan, 1929), p. 196f.; P. Cenival and T. Monod, *Description de l'Afrique de Ceuta à Sénégal par Valentim Fernandes, 1506-7* (Paris, 1938), pp. 84ff.; Leo Africanus, Vol. ii, pp. 464, 468f., 471, etc.; C. de la Roncière, "La découverte d'une relation de voyage datée du Touat en décrivant en 1447 le bassin du Niger", *Bulletin de la Section de Géographie*, (Paris, 1918), pp. 28–31.

[10] Valentim Fernandes, pp. 60, 94; de la Roncière, *loc. cit.*, p. 32.

imported. In any case, even if Cadamosto and Malfante exaggerated, it must be noted that from the foreigners' point of view the price of gold in the Sudan was very low, probably because there was an abundance of it in comparison with local needs. The Maghreb, Egyptian and Sudanese sources give a good deal of information about the activities of the large number of North African and Egyptian merchants who visited the large towns of Mali and later Songhai in order to buy gold. It is well known, thanks especially to the narrative of Leo Africanus, that Jewish jewellers from the Maghreb often settled in southern Morocco, the Sahara and even the Sudan, evidently in order to intercept some of the gold transported northwards and to buy it at a low price.[11] Jaime Cortesão has drawn historians' attention to Portuguese sources of the early fifteenth century, according to which Portuguese gold currency was at that time based on importing from Morocco gold which must have come from the Sudan. The same author is of the opinion that it was above all in Sudanese gold that Morocco paid the import costs of European and Levantine goods brought by the Genoese and the Venetians[12]—a suggestion confirmed by several Italian documents. It should be added that Sudanese trade was not the only way in which Sudanese gold in large quantities reached Egypt and the Near East. Sudanese pilgrims, who each year visited Egypt and the holy places of Islam in Arabia, brought with them very considerable quantities of gold to spend on the journey and on arrival in Cairo, Mecca and Medina. The greatest expenses were incurred by the sultans of Mali and Songhai, members of their families and high officials.[13]

A substantial amount of gold was at the disposal above all of the sovereigns, who collected it as tribute and certainly also in the form of taxes from merchants. According to Al-Omari and later sources, the fourteenth-century sultans of Mali and the sovereigns of Songhai in the following century would give away a good deal of gold as presents or payments to Muslim scholars and civil and military officials.[14] It is obvious that gold was a very important source of revenue for the sultans of Mali and Songhai and similarly for their entourage and for

[11] *Ibid.*, pp. 28, 31; Leo Africanus, Vol. i, pp. 87–90, 93, Vol. ii, p. 422f.

[12] J. Cortesão, *Los Portugueses–Historia de America y de los pueblos americanos*, Vol. iii (Barcelona/Buenos Aires, 1947), p. 506.

[13] Al-Omari, pp. 77–9; *Tarikh el-Fettach*, pp. 25f., 58ff.; Ibn Khaldoûn, *Histoire des Berbères et des dynasties musulmanes de l'Afrique Septentrionale*, ed. Slane, Vol. ii (Paris, 1927), p. 112f.

[14] Al-Omari, p. 66.

all powerful men in the western Sudan. It is, however, impossible to determine just how much gold was at the disposal of the sultans and the ruling classes of Mali; similarly nothing can be said about the quantities exported.

The sources of gold supply were not, however, directly controlled by the sovereigns of Mali. They received the metal as tribute from animistic peoples inhabiting regions loosely attached to the empire or even situated outside its frontiers. The sultans were extremely careful in their relations with these peoples. They even gave up imposing the Islamic faith there for fear that any coercion might reduce the flow of gold.[15] We hear repeatedly that the gold suppliers were exceedingly suspicious of foreigners, with whom they conducted only dumb barter in order to procure the salt which they needed. These accounts are probably exaggerated but they do show that neither the sultans of Mali nor the merchants could completely subdue the suppliers of precious metal. It was feared that at any moment they might break off deliveries and so Mali wished to maintain as friendly relations as possible with them.

Nothing is known of the volume of gold production in powdered or lump form. But the sources suggest that from the thirteenth century onwards, the extraction of gold somewhat increased in the vast hinterland of Mali and Songhai, a development which may be attributed to growing demand. It is generally accepted that the setting up of Portuguese trading stations on the Atlantic coast and in particular at São Jorge da Mina considerably decreased the flow of gold towards the Niger region and the Mediterranean. I do not wish to discuss this view here but I do not believe it to be entirely justified. The description of the Sudan given by Leo Africanus and likewise in the Sudanese chronicles shows that in the early sixteenth century there was plenty of gold on the markets of the large towns of Mali and Songhai and that it was exported among other places to North Africa and Egypt.[16] At this period Mali was declining but it was replaced in the Niger bend by Songhai, another very powerful state which controlled most of the commercial routes leading from the tropical zone towards the Maghreb and Egypt. But it seems that the political influence of Songhai over the southern parts of this area was not so well consolidated as that of Mali. The sources of the Songhai period do not mention any tribute paid by

[15] *Ibid.*, p. 58.
[16] Cf. n. 11.

the miners to its sultans. So it is probable that their revenues in this field were limited to rights exercised over Wangara merchants, who secured relations with the Bambuk-Galam, Bure and High Volta districts, whence the metal came. It might also be asked whether American gold imported into Europe did not affect, in a negative way, this sector of the Sudanese economy. However that may be, the town of Jenne was still considered an important commercial centre for this precious metal during the first half of the seventeenth century.[17]

It is quite evident from all that I have said here that the gold trade was an extremely significant factor in the economic life of the Sudan and a most important source of revenue for its sovereigns and wealthiest social groups, notably officials, merchants and Muslim scholars. But there was yet another source of wealth, probably no less considerable. This was the traffic in black slaves with Muslim countries. It is commonly recognized from the accounts of El-Bekri and other Arab writers that slaves were already being exported in the time of ancient Ghana and that this trade developed particularly from the period of occupation of North Africa by the Arabs.[18] The trade was conducted during the Mali period, too. Ibn battutah frequently mentions the presence of slaves in the houses of well-to-do people and he also tells us something about the slave trade with North Africa. Its scale cannot be estimated but we do know that there were numerous black slaves in Egypt and the Maghreb and that they were also to be found in Muslim Spain.[19] In the two last instances they probably came in particular from the western Sudan. Thanks to the accounts of Valentim Fernandes' informants we have some idea of the trade between the Berbers and Senegal, where the nomads regularly exchanged horses for slaves destined for Morocco.[20] From the middle of the fifteenth century the Portuguese followed the example of the Tuareg in importing horses and other merchandise in order to buy slaves and gold.

---

[17] *Tarikh es-Soudan*, p. 22.
[18] R. Mauny, *Tableau géographique de l'Ouest africain au Moyen Age d'après les sources écrites, la tradition et l'archéologie* (Mémoires de l'Institut Français d'Afrique Noire, No. 61, Dakar, 1961), p. 336f.
[19] Ibn Iyâs, *Journal d'un bourgeois du Caire. Histoire des Mamelouks*, Vol. ii (Paris, 1960), pp. 60, 161; M. K. Radziwiłł, *Podróż do Ziemi Świętej, Syrii i Egiptu, 1582–4* [*Travels to the Holy Land, Syria and Egypt*] (Warszawa, 1962), pp. 141, 159f.; A. N. Poliak, *Les révoltes populaires en Egypte à l'époque des Mamelouks et leurs causes économiques* (Paris, 1936), p. 272f.; C. Verlinden, *L'esclavage dans l'Europe médiévale*, Vol. i (Brugge, 1955), pp. 210, 226, 388, 757f.
[20] Valentim Fernandes, p. 70.

Sources for the slave trade in Mali territory are not available, although the slave markets at Timbuktu and Gao, which were under Songhai rule in the early sixteenth century, are relatively well known. It is often claimed that there was one great difference between the two successive empires of Mali and Songhai. According to certain contemporary authors, Mali was a pacific state, whereas Songhai cruelly oppressed its subjects, ravaging neighbouring territories during frequent warlike expeditions and reducing to slavery the inhabitants of the lands upon which they had encroached. I am not convinced that this contrast is justified. For we know almost nothing of the political and military history of Mali, whereas the military expeditions organized by the sultans of Songhai are described in great detail in the two Sudanese chronicles. The provenance of black slaves in the Maghreb and Muslim Spain is attested by a variety of sources of the thirteenth and fourteenth centuries. According to Al-Omari, Mansa Musa, the famous sultan of Mali, said, during his stay in Cairo in 1324–5, that Mali was conducting unceasing warfare against the infidels.[21] In my view, the economic aim behind these wars was to capture slaves for export northwards. The great slave markets at Timbuktu and Gao, which figure in the early sixteenth-century description of Leo Africanus, do not seem to represent a situation which was in the least novel. Fifty years earlier, Cadamosto tells us that the Tuareg regularly bought slaves in the western Sudan and he states this while describing the trade of these nomads with Timbuktu.[22] There is no doubt, therefore, that the slave trade was being conducted on the banks of the Niger during the period of Mali supremacy.

But it cannot be denied that the Songhai conquest of the bend in the great river may have caused an increase in this traffic. Songhai possessed a relatively powerful military organization by comparison with its neighbours and derived considerable advantages from this in frequent invasions of adjacent territories. The Songhai often took a large number of prisoners. At the turn of the fifteenth and sixteenth centuries some of these captives were settled by Sultan El-Hadj Muhammad in special villages, whose inhabitants were treated as the sovereign's slaves.[23] This policy was probably pursued by the following members

---

[21] Al-Omari, p. 81.
[22] Ca'Da Mosto, p. 187f.
[23] *Tarikh el-Fettach*, pp. 141, 159f.

of the Askia dynasty, though there is nothing in the sources about this. Furthermore, we know that after each large-scale and successful expedition, there was a resurgence of the slave trade at Timbuktu and Gao. Slaves of both sexes and of all ages were sold, even children, the prices varying with the quality of the slaves and in relation to supply and demand.[24] And during the second half of the fifteenth and far into the following century, the slave trade in the Niger area seems to have been even more widespread than that organized by Europeans on the Atlantic coast and in the Gulf of Guinea. The Polish traveller, Duke Christopher Radziwiłł saw slave markets in Egypt in 1582, when Negro transports often holding 2,000 persons appeared each week from Algiers and other west African ports.[25] It must be concluded that a significant proportion of these people was bought in the western and central Sudan. The history of the Mamlukes also mentions people coming from this area, who sometimes rose to positions of importance,[26] although in general the condition of slaves recently introduced into Egypt was most lamentable, provoking them to revolt. It is thus clear that there was a great number of slaves from the western Sudan to be found in North Africa and Egypt in the fifteenth and sixteenth centuries.

Arab and Sudanese sources show that slave hunting presented no great difficulties in the Songhai period. The author of the *Tarikh el-Fettach* explicitly says so in citing a statement by the sons of Daud, Sultan of Songhai, in the second half of the sixteenth century.[27] Whether it was always restricted to the inhabitants of foreign territories is not clear. The two Sudanese chronicles mention several regulations of Songhai sultans forbidding third parties to sell "caste" individuals belonging to the sovereign. From these same sources we have proclamations of sultans banning in addition the sale of descendents of people freed from slavery or even of certain freemen.[28] The author of the *Tarikh el-Fettach* adds that these royal mandates were not always carried into effect.[29] From the early sixteenth century taxation list of royal slaves it can also be seen that some of these people were bound to give the

---

[24] Cf. n. 11.
[25] Radziwiłł, *op. cit.*, pp. 141, 159f.
[26] Ibn Iyâs, *op. cit.*, Vol. ii, pp. 60, 161.
[27] *Tarikh el-Fettach*, p. 195.
[28] *Ibid.*, p. 13ff.
[29] *Ibid.*

prince each year a small number of children, boys and girls, destined to be exchanged for horses.[30]

From all that I have said about the trade in gold and slaves, it is clear that these two branches of the west Sudanese economy were extremely valuable for Mali and for its successor, Songhai. It was for the most part owing to the export of gold and slaves that the western Sudan could supply itself with salt, horses, weapons and Maghreb, Egyptian and even European luxury products. These Sudanese export commodities were at the disposal above all of sultans and their families, officials and other rich men of the country and notably of merchants, both Arab-Berber and native, and Muslim scholars, who, as is well known, received gold from sovereigns and were often slave-owners. I believe, therefore, that throughout the period under consideration, neither sultans nor members of the dominant class were particularly interested in reorganizing the country's economy with a view to any marked expansion in production. They had no need to do this. The author of the *Tarikh el-Fettach* tells us that towards the middle of the sixteenth century the Songhai sultans possessed many goods for which the inhabitants—their slaves, or rather their serfs—were obliged to do agricultural work on behalf of the sovereign. The two Sudanese chronicles also relate that the sultans of Songhai sometimes granted to pious scholars or descendants of the Prophet groups of "castes" with all their chattels and obligations. The same conclusions can be drawn from a few references in Al-Omari's account of mid-fourteenth-century Mali.[31] These features, however, were not fully developed. In all likelihood, revenues derived from the gold and slave trades were of prime importance to the sultan and ruling classes of Mali and Songhai, whereas taxes paid by the agricultural population played a secondary role. Under the prevailing conditions, any incentive towards intensifying agriculture and other vital sectors of the country's economy could not have come from the state and the ruling classes.

I have already suggested that the peasants forming the great majority of the population were no longer interested in such changes, so that in the circumstances both Mali and Songhai were condemned to social and economic stagnation. No one needed to make any changes in this field. The abundance of gold and the slave trade held up social and economic

---

[30] *Ibid.*, p. 109.
[31] *Ibid.*, pp. 16, 52f.; Al-Omari, p. 66.

progress, and Songhai in the late fifteenth and sixteenth centuries was not much different from Mali two centuries earlier. This stagnation was not restricted to their economic life; the same phenomenon is noticeable in the structure of the state, in its military organization and even, despite a few appearances to the contrary, in the culture of the western Sudan on the eve of the Moroccan invasion.

At the beginning of this article I mentioned some analogies between the situation in eastern Europe during the early Middle Ages and in the western Sudan from the thirteenth to the sixteenth centuries. Yet the peoples of eastern Europe developed in a different direction. The natural wealth of eastern Europe, modest compared with that of the Sudan, demanded much effort in order to profit by it. A certain balance of power between the states which had been formed in the twelfth and thirteenth centuries meant that reciprocal invasions could bring significant gains to no one. And German pressure on Bohemia and Poland constituted a very serious threat. In these circumstances the princes, the lay and ecclesiastical aristocracy, were forced to take more interest in developing their own landed resources.

This was possible, however, only with the co-operation of the peasants. All the while peasant obligations were uncertain and peasants were afraid of being deprived of their surplus production, they had no interest in improving their working methods. Lords, on the other hand, were in no position to increase their demands on their serfs, for the latter could easily run away. Princes and lords who wished to develop their property economically were thus compelled to encourage their subjects to work more intensively and to introduce new methods, particularly in connection with agriculture. They achieved these aims by introducing the German or rather Western custom whereby peasant dues were not only regulated but also reduced. Commutation of services and renders in kind into money rents, begun in Bohemia in the early thirteenth century and carried into effect a little later in Poland, already reflected the development of agriculture and progress in the social division of labour. These methods were applied not only to agriculture but also to the economic life of the towns and in the mines of several eastern European countries. They accelerated the economic and social progress of the peoples in this area and marked the beginning in the thirteenth century of a long process of development.

CHAPTER THIRTEEN

THE WESTERN SUDAN IN THE MIDDLE AGES.
UNDERDEVELOPMENT IN THE EMPIRES
OF THE WESTERN SUDAN*

Hopkins-Małowist Debate

Professor Małowist has made a bold attempt to interpret the causes of economic backwardness in the empires of Mali and Songhai, drawing on comparisons with eastern Europe in order to contribute not only to our knowledge of west African economic history, but also to the wider problem of economic incentives in pre-industrial societies.[1] Because of its general interest, it is likely that his article will be quoted by scholars who are concerned with the problem of underdevelopment in its historical perspectives, but who do not possess any detailed knowledge of the period and area in question. It is for this reason that the present article has been written. It will be suggested here that Professor Małowist's main argument suffers from weaknesses, both of data and method, which together make his general thesis untenable.

I

Professor Małowist's analysis may be summarized in the following way. In the fourteenth and fifteenth centuries the states of the western Sudan attained a level of economic development which was broadly comparable to that achieved in eastern Europe in the early Middle Ages. However, the Moroccan invasion of the western Sudan in 1591 dealt a fatal blow to the Songhai empire, and initiated a period of decline which lasted for several centuries. In eastern Europe, on the other hand, the thirteenth century saw the beginning of a long process of rural change which eventually was to assist in transforming the structure of the economy. Thus the important problem is to explain why the two regions, once

---

* This debate between A. G. Hopkins and Marian Małowist was originally published in *Past and Present*, No. 37, 1967, pp. 157–162.

[1] M. Małowist, "The Social and Economic Stability of the Western Sudan in the Middle Ages", *Past and Present*, No. 33 (April, 1966), pp. 3–15. Chapter 12 in this volume.

similarly placed, should have taken such divergent paths. According to Professor Małowist, the answer lies in the varying strengths of the economic incentives operating in the western Sudan and in eastern Europe. In the western Sudan, he argues, conditions of life were such that the peasants, who formed the bulk of the population, were assured of a relatively prosperous existence without having to exert themselves unduly. Therefore they had no incentive to raise productivity and to change their traditional social structure. Moreover, neither the merchants nor the rulers of Mali and Songhai were stimulated to alter the existing situation because they received large incomes from the export trade in gold and slaves. But in eastern Europe, which was far poorer in natural resources, a much greater effort was required to win a living, and consequently there was a strong incentive to improve productivity. Furthermore, the lay and ecclesiastical aristocracy were forced to take a keen interest in developing their landed resources in order to maintain their incomes. So it was that eastern Europe progressed, while the western Sudan was condemned, ironically by its very "barbaric prosperity",[2] to a long period of backwardness.

II

The view that life was easy for the inhabitants of west Africa is one of the most ancient and widespread of the myths about the tropical world, though it is many years since scholars took it seriously.[3] To attack the legend at the present time seems almost to require an apology: no one today would seriously investigate Huntington's grand but simple notion that "civilization" could flourish only where the crucial "storm levels" created a climate which encouraged man to be energetic, and that the tropics were backward because their climate induced a state of lethargy among the population.[4] Similarly, few would set out now to test Toynbee's heroic thesis that the major "civilizations" were a "response" to a "challenge" arising out of adversity, and that tropical Africa was a case of arrested development, where the stimuli had been too weak to

---

[2] *Ibid.*, p. 6. See p. 262 in this volume.
[3] For a valuable study of early attitudes towards Africa see Philip D. Curtin, *The Image of Africa* (Madison, 1964).
[4] Ellsworth Huntington, *Civilization and Climate* (New Haven, 1915) and *Mainsprings of Civilization* (New York, 1945).

produce the "optimum response".[5] Consequently, it is alarming to find that Professor Małowist has adopted an interpretation of the African past which appears to draw its inspiration, however indirectly, from assumptions that are no longer considered valid. Of course, a scholar as distinguished as Professor Małowist would not construct such an argument without first carefully investigating the relevant sources. Perhaps, then, it may be true that the case of the western Sudan lends support to an old-fashioned view of the African past, and that Professor Małowist has succeeded in reviving a fading legend on the basis of new evidence.

The problem arises now as to how far it is true to say that life was indeed "relatively prosperous" for the peoples of Mali and Songhai. Any attempt to answer this question immediately runs into the basic difficulty that the source material at present available is far from satisfactory. Professor Małowist notes that the evidence is "thin and very scattered",[6] but he still feels that it is weighty enough to support his very broad conclusions. Most of these conclusions are based on certain well-known Arabic sources, and these suffer from a number of major defects from the economic historian's point of view. In the first place, they are few in number, and even these few are records of relatively short excursions to the western Sudan, some being written at second hand a long time after the date of the actual journey. Secondly, the writers visited only a small part of the huge region covered by the empires of Mali and Songhai, and their travels were confined for the most part to the relatively prosperous areas which were linked to the main trans-Saharan trade routes.[7] Thirdly, these Arabic sources are not concerned primarily with economic matters, but are principally records of religious and political interest. Finally, such economic information as they do contain is mainly of a descriptive nature, and not of the kind that can be quantified in the way that statements about "relative prosperity" would seem to require. At best, therefore, these sources provide interesting and sometimes useful glimpses into a small part of the history of a small section of the empires of Mali and Songhai, but they are scarcely sufficient to serve as a basis for Professor Małowist's main thesis.

---

[5] For a short version of this argument see the *Abridgement* by D. C. Somervell of Arnold J. Toynbee's *A Study of History* (Oxford, 1960).

[6] Małowist, *op. cit.*, p. 5. See p. 261 in this volume.

[7] Al-Omari, of course, never visited west Africa.

If these general criticisms hold, then it should be possible to find some gaps between Professor Małowist's evidence and his conclusions. One important example must suffice. Professor Małowist notes the existence of "slave castes," which he explains as arising out of the low productivity of the Mali economy, and which led the rulers to "compel a section of their subjects to produce a surplus of essential articles, a sufficient supply of which could not be guaranteed in the markets".[8] But in the very next paragraph Ibn battutah is quoted to show that everywhere he went "peasants offered travellers necessary provisions in exchange for small quantities of salt or luxury commodities...".[9] As they stand, those comments are obvious contradictions. Why should the rulers of Mali have such difficulty obtaining essential commodities, while foreign travellers had their needs catered for wherever they went? One likely explanation is that Ibn battutah's evidence is not representative of the economy as a whole, for he travelled through villages which were part of the trans-Saharan trade network. The point here is that these villages were part of an important, but nevertheless small, exchange sector which derived its prosperity not from wholly indigenous economic activities, but from the external commercial link with north Africa. Therefore it is not surprising that relatively wealthy travellers, such as Ibn battutah, should find it easy to purchase food and shelter on their journey, especially if they offered in return spices, jewels and, most precious of all, salt. However, the great majority of the population was occupied in local agricultural and pastoral activities, and did not have the good fortune of making windfall gains from passing foreign tourists. Clearly, this was a vast area in which levels of income differed both regionally and socially. General statements about the prosperity of the inhabitants of Mali and Songhai must be suspect because they rest on such slender and unrepresentative evidence.

If the nature of the evidence makes it hard to substantiate Professor Małowist's case, it also places obstacles in the way of alternative arguments. However, a few general comments should be made about the western Sudan in order to show that there is further reason to doubt Professor Małowist's optimistic view of life in Mali and Songhai. The western Sudan is the area of west Africa which occupies the savannah corridor between the forest in the south and the desert in the north.

---

[8] Małowist, *op. cit.*, p. 6. See p. 262 in this volume.
[9] *Ibid.*, pp. 6–7. See p. 263 in this volume.

Whatever pleasures are enjoyed by the inhabitants of this region, an easy life based on the leisurely exploitation of rich natural resources is not one of them. Indeed, some writers take a very pessimistic view of the development potential of the area.[10] The following points can be made without necessarily subscribing to this gloomy interpretation of the data. In the first place, many of the savannah soils are not particularly fertile, being low in organic content and deficient in calcium and phosphorous. Secondly, the brevity and variability of the rainfall, combined with the long, hot, dry season, has always been a severe test of survival. Shortage of water could lead to competition for the most fertile land, to poor yields, and to the appearance of the so-called "hungry-gap" between the consumption of the remnants of the old harvest and the gathering of the new crop. Thirdly, the western Sudan had no local supplies of salt, a biological necessity for which there were only imperfect substitutes, so salt had to be imported at great cost from mines in the Sahara, and even then shortages and inequalities in distribution occurred. Finally, added to these natural hazards was the constant threat of civil disturbances, especially raids for plunder and slaves.

It should now be apparent that there is another side to the economic history of the empires of Mali and Songhai, a side which Professor Małowist has discounted, though without saying why he has done so. Dietary deficiencies, disease, and, at worst, famine, were the conditions of life that helped to determine the organization of the farming community.[11] Such conditions can have inspired little confidence in man's ability to control his environment, and they help to explain why the economic system was geared primarily to achieving stability—in the circumstances an ambitious aim. Far from life being too easy for the fortunate inhabitants of the western Sudan, it would not be hard to show that the "response" was "poor" because the "challenge" was too severe rather than too weak.

---

[10] For example, Pierre Gourou, *The Tropical World*, 4th edn. (London, 1966).
[11] The first travellers to take an interest in the lives of the ordinary people were not the Arabs, but the Portuguese, who noted some evidence of poverty and dietary deficiencies in western Mali in the late fifteenth century. For a summary see D. T. Niane, "Recherches sur l'Empire du Mali au Moyen Age", *Recherches Africaines*, No. 2 (1911), p. 47. For case studies of present-day problems of this kind see two articles by J. M. Hunter, "River Blindness in Nangodi, Northern Ghana", *The Geog. Rev.*, lvi (1966) and "Seasonal Hunger in a Part of the West African Savanna: a Survey of Bodyweights in Nangodi, N. E. Ghana", *Trans. Inst. Brit. Geog.*, xli (1967).

III

Whether it is wise to attempt to explain a subject as complex as the process of economic growth on the basis of a simple "carrot and stick" theory of development is, of course, open to question. This point leads to the second major criticism of Professor Małowist's article, namely the limitations of his methodological approach to the problem of economic backwardness. His model of underdevelopment may be stated thus: easy conditions = lack of incentives = failure to develop. Let us assume for the moment that Professor Małowist is right, and that there was a state of "barbaric prosperity" in the empires of Mali and Songhai. Does it follow logically that there was no incentive to change the *status quo*? An affirmative answer must assume that adversity is the sole condition for creating the right incentives. But this is to ignore completely the behaviour most commonly associated with economic man, namely that he responds positively to the prospect of increasing returns to his activities. If higher profits and prosperity are indeed just as much incentives to development as are low returns and adversity, then Professor Małowist has to explain why the producers and traders of Mali and Songhai did not wish to improve their conditions of life still further. It could be argued, of course, that life in underdeveloped regions, where economic man is in an embryonic state, is governed by different rules of behaviour. This is certainly a point worth discussing, though it is now becoming increasingly clear that producers in "traditional" economies respond far more readily to price incentives than used to be thought.[12] However, Professor Małowist does not consider this line of enquiry.

Two examples will illustrate these objections to the way in which Professor Małowist deals with the relationship between incentives and economic backwardness. The first example shows that Professor Małowist's argument is not wholly satisfactory, even if his general thesis is accepted. He states that the Moroccan invasion of the western Sudan in 1591 began a decline which lasted for several centuries. Certainly, this is a common view, though it is doubtful whether the events of 1591 were as significant in economic terms as is often asserted. However, assuming that 1591 was a major turning point, then it is important to know why

---

[12] See, for example, William O. Jones, "Economic Man in Africa", *Food Research Inst. Stud.*, i (1960), pp. 107–134.

this reverse, by introducing a "healthy" element of adversity, did not create the incentives which would have led to the economic development of the area. This is a problem which simply cannot be handled within the narrow analytical framework established by Professor Małowist. The second example makes it clear that his assessment of the motivation of entrepreneurs in the western Sudan is inadequate. He suggests that the slave trade inhibited growth because it assured the rulers of a secure income, and so removed any incentive they might have had to alter the existing economic situation. But the important point about the slave trade in this context is that it was a successful response to monetary incentives of precisely the kind that Professor Małowist excludes from his explanatory model. The slave trade inhibited economic development because it led to the investment of much of the productive capacity of the state in an activity which was aimed at exporting one of the most important factors of production, namely labour, in return for goods which, for the most part, contributed little to the growth potential of the importing areas. Not only are incentives more varied than Professor Małowist has indicated, but they can also produce a response which is not conducive to economic development.

The second part of Professor Małowist's thesis appears to state that, given the right incentives, economic development will follow inevitably. Again, the argument is epistemologically faulty, for the *nature* of the response cannot be explained in terms of the *strength* of the incentives. A stimulus, either of adversity or of prosperity, may evoke a great variety of modes of adaptation. It may even lead to efforts being made to introduce innovations into the traditional pattern of economic activities. But between the desire to achieve development and its actual realization there stands the power to achieve, the means to the goal. A consideration of the ways in which incentives can be translated into economic growth interposes a whole new set of institutional variables, which may act either as barriers or as stepping-stones. These include the political system, the social structure, the distribution of economic power, the accumulation and disposition of capital, the level of techno-logy, the nature of inheritance and land rights, demographic patterns, and practically every other aspect of the society in question. Even assuming that the western Sudan and eastern Europe had precisely the same natural resources, and had achieved exactly the same level of prosperity, there is no reason to think that the stimulus arising out of this situation would have produced an identical response in both regions, unless all the other relevant features of the two societies were also identical, which clearly they were not. Thus Professor Małowist's model of economic change has no explanatory power at all, and his attempt to understand the "stability" of the western Sudan by contrasting it with the "progress" made by eastern Europe fails because it omits so much that is pertinent and important.

In so far as Professor Małowist does take note of institutional barriers to economic growth, his discussion is less than satisfactory. For example, he concludes that he can find "no incentives which might have encouraged the peasants to improve and intensify their methods of work and consequently to change those old social structures which were so closely bound up with the agricultural system...".[13] If the "traditional" social structure is being considered here as an obstacle to development, then the argument is at best obscure. If changing "old social structures" is a *consequence* of improvements in agriculture, then it is important to know why such changes are necessary, since the primary economic aim has been achieved already. If, on the other hand, Professor Małowist really means that the social structure has to be altered *before* economic development is possible, then this is a point which needs to be stated most carefully, especially since the stock notion of the incompatibility between "traditional" west African societies and economic growth has been challenged most persuasively in a recent study.[14] Moreover, it is a mistake to treat "old social structures" in aggregate without specifying the relationship between particular features of particular societies and the economic activities of the members of those societies. This is where historians have so much to learn from economic anthropologists.

IV

Briefly restated, the two principal criticisms of Professor Małowist's article are first, that it advances a view of life in the western Sudan which cannot be substantiated on the basis of the sources at present available, and second, that it seeks to establish an explanation of economic backwardness which is unacceptable because it is so incomplete. Far from life in Mali and Songhai being "easy," there is some evidence that it was "difficult," and that the contrast drawn with eastern Europe is mistaken. This does not imply that the nature of the constraints operating

---

[13] Małowist, *op. cit.*, p. 7. See p. 263 in this volume.
[14] Polly Hill, *Migrant Cocoa-Farmers of Southern Ghana* (Cambridge, 1963).

on the economies of the western Sudan cannot be ascertained. But it does mean that economic backwardness is not simply a function of incentives. It seems likely that expansion was restricted more by lack of opportunities than by easy conditions of life. The influences which have to be studied are primarily those which prevented a rise in returns to customary agricultural factors, and also limited the size of the market.[15] This approach involves a recognition of the great variety of ways in which a region can be underdeveloped, and consequently of the variety of the paths leading to economic growth. Otherwise, the comparative "method" can so easily become simply a mechanism for interpreting the world in terms of the European past. In the last analysis, the hardest task is not to explain why the western Sudan, and indeed the greater part of the world, remained underdeveloped, but to explain why a small part of Europe began to industrialize in the first place.

Rejoinder

I am grateful to Dr. Hopkins for his close reading of my article on the problems of the medieval Western Sudan, though I am not at all convinced by many of his arguments, which I must oppose. Dr. Hopkins basically argues that I try to revive old theories, according to which Africans, as peoples living in a tropical climate, are fundamentally incapable of social and economic development, whereas a prime factor in such a development is the rather difficult conditions of life in temperate zones which oblige their inhabitants to make the maximum possible effort. This was not at all my intention. The point of view I adopt, which is probably clear to every historian, is that geographical location is one of the important factors in shaping social life, and that this factor is especially strong in the circumstances of the primitive techniques, which are characteristic both of medieval Europe and of Africa. What I have in mind here is the influence of geographical location on the immediate and most essential needs of men and the means of satisfying them. There is no doubt that the peasants of the Western Sudan were not obliged to worry about clothing or warm and permanent dwellings like the population in the temperate and rather cold climate of Eastern Europe. With regard to the food supply, moreover, the inhabitants

---

[15] "Traditional" agriculture has to be analysed, not simply dismissed as "primitive." See T. W. Schultz, *Transforming Traditional Agriculture* (New Haven, 1964).

especially of the southern part of Mali could depend not only on agriculture, but also on the gathering economy to a far greater extent than the inhabitants of the European regions I have mentioned. These circumstances show that the compelling factors forcing the population to productive work were much weaker here than in medieval Poland or neighbouring countries. The shortage of salt and the low fertility of the soil in part of Western Sudan were not features which made life especially difficult by comparison with many areas of medieval Europe. Indeed, salt appears only in certain regions and for that reason at an early stage became an item of international trade. With regard to the low fertility of the soil and its relatively rapid exhaustion, this is also a phenomenon which we frequently meet in the Middle Ages. The early response of men to these difficulties both in Eastern Europe and in the Western Sudan was precisely the form of cultivation based upon clearance by burning, which assured good crops at least for a short period of time. It should, however, be added that the meagre population density in the Western Sudan made human habitation easy. Men had at their disposal vast tracts of land, which they could exploit gradually with their slash-and-burn economy. This factor is not met on so large a scale in medieval Europe, except in the almost deserted areas of northern Russia, which were relatively inaccessible until the thirteenth century and even later. I think that this important circumstance is one of the reasons why primitive agricultural techniques used in the savannah of the Sudan persisted for so long, though obviously other factors played an important part here. It seems abundantly clear to me that for precisely this reason the system of large families tilling the soil in common had an especially strong economic basis in the Western Sudan, which consequently strengthened the traditional method of acquiring food. We have no proof that epidemics and endemic diseases decimated the population of the Western Sudan between the thirteenth and sixteenth centuries to a greater extent than in medieval Europe. It is worth noting that both of the great Sudanese chronicles, written by writers on the spot, make considerably less mention of these disasters than European sources of the same period.[16]

---

[16] Mahmoud Kati ben el-Hadj el-Motaouakke and one of his grandsons Tarikh el-Fettach [*Chronique du chercheur pour servir à l'histoire des villes des armées et des principaux personnages du Tekrour*], French translation by O. Houdas and M. Delafosse (Paris, 1913), p. 175. Here we find the sole mention of a great pestilence in Songhai, dating from 1535.

In spite of all these circumstances, I do not at all suggest that the life of the Sudanese peasants in Mali and especially in Songhai was easy. I merely wrote, and I maintain this view, that in the areas of Mali proper in the middle of the fourteenth century, on the basis of the observations of Ibn battutah, the situation of the peasants was not presented as being difficult. His statements show that the peasants of Mali proper in the middle of the fourteenth century not only did not suffer from hunger, but, on the contrary, accumulated a surplus of agricultural produce and livestock which permitted them to obtain salt and a small number of luxury items.[17] Indirect evidence of this is provided by the statements of Leo Africanus, who fairly clearly contrasts the abundance of food in Timbuktu, Jenne, the town of Mali and Gao, together with the relative prosperity of their inhabitants, with the poverty and backwardness of the population of Dendi.[18] It is this abundance of food, even if we take into account that agriculture was practised in the towns as well, which shows the existence of a surplus in the rural economy of the western portion of Mali and, later, Songhai. Indeed, it is obvious that African markets not only served economic purposes, but that the large number of them observed by Cadamosto in the middle of the fifteenth century in the region of Senegambia and mentioned by Sudanese chroniclers of the sixteenth and seventeenth centuries likewise confirms the view that there was a surplus of production in the economy of the peasants of the Western Sudan.[19] Early Portuguese sources, it is true, emphasize the poverty of the African population, but this information relates mainly to desert coasts north of the River Senegal.[20]

For these reasons I described the position of the peasants of Mali and Songhai in terms of the "barbaric prosperity" used by E. F. Heckscher with regard to the population of Sweden in early modern times.[21] In Sweden the prevailing mode of existence was the natural economy,

[17] See my article on "The Social and Economic Stability of the Western Sudan in the Middle Ages", *Past and Present*, No. 33 (April, 1966), pp. 6, 7. Chapter 12 in this volume.

[18] Leo Africanus, *Description de l'Afrique*, translated by A. Épaulard, new ed. (Paris, 1956), vol. ii, pp. 464–472.

[19] *Delle navigazioni e viaggi di Messer Alvise Da Ca'Da Moste gentiluomo Veneziano*, ed. R. Caddeo (Viaggi e scoperte degli navigatori italiani, vol. i, Milan 1929), pp. 237–238. Abderrahman ben Abdallah ben Imran ben Amir es-Sa'adi, *Tarikh es-Soudan* [Chronique du Soudan], French translation by O. Houdas (Paris, 1900), p. 24.

[20] Gomes Eanes de Zurara, *Crónica dos feitos de Guiné* [*The Chronicle of Guinea*], Vol. ii (Lisbon, 1949), p. 338.

[21] P. de Cenival and Th. Monod, *Description de la Côte de l'Afrique de Ceuta au Sénégal par Valentim Fernandes (1506–1507)* (Paris, 1938), p. 50. E. F. Heckscher,

within which the peasant population was able to meet its most urgent needs and at the same time to use its small surpluses mainly for the purchase of salt and a very small number of other items.

In my analysis of these problems I have used Sudanese chronicles and Arab, and to some extent Portuguese, sources. I was indeed rather surprised by the strange view of Dr. Hopkins that the sources I used relate mainly to political and religious affairs. Al-Bekri, Al-Idrisi, Al-Omari, Ibn battutah, Ibn Khaldun and Leo Africanus have transmitted to the historian a vast number of observations precisely on the economy of the territories which interested them. They can be very favourably compared with European writers of the same period. It is just here that Arab sources are especially valuable. It was the utilization of these which brought about a real revolution in the study of the economic history of Europe in the Middle Ages, a fact which is well known to all historians. We cannot renounce the use of them on the ground that they do not contain quantitative details which are generally trustworthy. If we were to adopt the point of view of Dr. Hopkins in this matter, we should also have to reject almost all we have achieved in the study of the economic history of the ancient and medieval worlds and content ourselves with studies of economic activity which date from the eighteenth or even the nineteenth century. Dr. Hopkins is perhaps in danger of approaching the question of quantitative detail as if there were some kind of magic in it—an exaggeration which for all its absurdity is to be observed at present among certain historians.

Dr. Hopkins accuses me of an obvious inconsistency when I write that in the states of the Western Sudan there was a surplus of production and, at the same time, ascribe the appearance of "castes" of unfree persons to the attempts of the authorities to assure themselves of a supply of produce which was difficult to acquire in the country. Dr. Hopkins does not perceive that in speaking of surpluses I had in mind above all agricultural produce, fish and livestock, whereas the majority of these unfree "castes" were engaged mainly in providing the court and army with iron, for which reason there are so many "castes" of blacksmiths, furnishing arrows and similar objects, as well as performing certain special functions. The fact that certain "castes" were obliged to provide food, in my view, in no way invalidates my hypothesis. The civil and

Sveriges Ekonomiska Historia fran Gustav Vasa [*Economic History of Sweden from the Time of Gustav Vasa*], Vol. i (Stockholm, 1935), p. 99.

military establishment in Mali and Songhai was very extensive, so that meeting its demands for food required large stocks. In the conditions of a natural economy, in a large degree self-sufficient, and of primitive methods of cultivation and transport, the acquisition of essential supplies by the authorities could easily meet with difficulties at any moment. In comparable circumstances there arose in certain Slavonic countries in the early Middle Ages the so-called "service villages," the population of which had similar obligations to the authorities as had the members of the "castes" in Mali and Songhai.

Turning to what appears to be Dr. Hopkins's main criticism—that the lack of economic incentives resulting from conditions favourable to the natural economy leads to economic backwardness—I must again insist that natural conditions in the Western Sudan required of the population less economic effort than was the case in medieval eastern Europe. On the other hand, I have never asserted that the life of the peasant in Mali or Songhai was easy. With regard to social political or religious structures, which obviously play an enormous part in modifying the operation of economic incentives, these very structures themselves are subject to the pressure of economic change. In my view the slowness and weakness of economic change in the Western Sudan, in the period I am interested in, contributed to the petrification of social and political structures, which, taken together, constituted an element of stagnation. I have expressed this view in my short article in *Past and Present* and at greater length in a book on this subject in Polish.[22]

It is generally known that in the feudal Europe of the Middle Ages the pressure of the ruling classes was one of the important factors compelling the peasant population to increase its production. This fact is no doubt to be deplored from the point of view of our contemporary morality, but without doubt it existed. Economic necessity more than once compelled a ruling class to reorganize its estates, always for the purpose of maintaining or increasing its income. Frequently, especially in Central and Eastern Europe in the twelfth, thirteenth and fourteenth centuries, the feudal lords made temporary concessions to the peasants in order to increase their productivity and indirectly their own incomes. In all these cases there were consequential changes in the social and

---

[22] *Loc. cit.* and M. Małowist, *Wielkie państwa Sudanu Zachodniego w późnym średniowieczu* [*The Great States of the Western Sudan in the Later Middle Ages*] (Warsaw, 1964), pp. 342–5, 429–35.

political structure, about which I wrote in my article. To accuse me of ignoring so obvious a problem is without foundation.

Both in my article and in my book I tried to show that the state and the ruling classes in the Western Sudan, together with the well-to-do merchants and the lawyer-theologian scholars, had such important sources of income, both direct and indirect, from the trade in gold and slaves, that they were not especially interested in increasing the productivity of their subject population. Dr. Hopkins criticizes this hypothesis, but offers no arguments in its place. I therefore hold to my view. The texts of the Sudanese chroniclers quoted in my article show that in the state of Songhai in the sixteenth century it is possible, probably as a result of the declining trade in gold, to detect certain tendencies towards the creation of larger estates. In my book I dealt with this problem at greater length than was possible in a short article.[23] But this short and unfinished process, accompanied by a growth of aggressiveness towards its neighbours, increased internal tension in the state of Songhai and at the same time increased the hostility of its weaker neighbours.[24] It was precisely for that reason that the Moroccan invasion of 1591 led so quickly to the destruction of the state and caused chaos for a long time to come.

Finally, I should like to say that I see nothing unscholarly in comparing two very similar social and economic structures for the purpose of explaining them. On the contrary, the application of the methods of comparative history seems to me to be completely justified from the scholarly point of view. Research into the history of Africa in isolation from the history of the rest of the world, it is true, avoids the danger of seeing the problem from a European point of view, but it leads to a dangerous narrowing of our investigation of the historical problems presented by Africa. With regard to Dr. Hopkins's view that we must above all answer the question why only a few countries developed, while the majority of mankind remained in backwardness, I think that this is a question of our point of view. Dr. Hopkins lives in a highly developed country, while I in my country have experience of the difficult struggle with the remainders of backwardness. It is not surprising that I am intensely interested in understanding them. I think this is essential if we wish to overcome them.

---

[23] *Op. cit.*, pp. 382f., 399, 408f.
[24] *Op. cit.*, pp. 413f.

CHAPTER FOURTEEN

SOCIAL AND ECONOMIC LIFE IN TIMUR'S EMPIRE*

Studies on the internal history of Timur's empire are not as yet far advanced. This holds true in particular with regard to the core of his state, Mavrannakhar. This problem is of special significance because it was there that Timur embarked on his great career and where, mainly in the early stages, he amassed the strength to conquer the whole of Central Asia. One should add here that Mavrannakhar, with its capitals at Samarkand and Kesh (Shahrisebz), was the area about which Timur truly cared, and to the development of which he contributed significantly. The social and economic history of the other countries he annexed in one or other form has not been properly investigated. All this makes it very difficult to understand the process of the building of Timur's state and of its subsequent rapid fall—a phenomenon which lies beyond the scope of the present study.

One should first pay attention to certain better-known elements of the general situation. Thus, Timur became active at a time of serious social, and partly also political, crisis in Central Asia and the Near East. The decline of the Mongol state of the Il-Khanids in Iran and in the adjacent part of Central Asia led to far-reaching political fragmentation and to instability of social life. Things took a similar turn in the territories of the Golden and White Hordes. The state of the Egyptian Mamluks grew considerably weaker, reaching a stage of acute economic, social, and political crisis. In India, the sultanate of the Tughluq dynasty began to decline in power. Only Ottoman Turkey continued to show dynamic growth. It is a remarkable fact that, while Central Asia, the Mamluk Empire, the Golden Horde, and northern India easily fell prey to Timur's forays, and for a long time could not offset the effects of the defeats and ravages suffered, Turkey, despite the disaster of the battle of Ankara, returned to its former power and international significance only twenty years later. Turkey's body politic showed magnificent resistance

* Originally published as Chapter 5, pp. 83–119, 175–178 of *Tamerlan i jego czasy*, Państwowy Instytut Wydawniczy, Warszawa 1985. Translation from Polish by Maria Chmielewska-Szlajfer, revised by Robin Kimball.

to such great reverses of fortune as the Chagatai invasion. One can even surmise that the panicky flight of the Turkmen in the face of Timur's advance, first to Anatolia and then to the Ottoman provinces in Europe, considerably strengthened the Turkish element there, and with time enhanced the dynamism of the Ottoman state in south-eastern Europe in the 15th and 16th centuries. The centre of Turkish power moved from Anatolia to the Balkans.[1] By mid-15th century, the Turks were already a threat to both Hungary and Italy. Nothing similar occurred in the other territories conquered by Timur, as they were already in regress when he attacked them. Timur and his associates seem to have been aware of the situation in Central Asia and the Middle East. The well-informed chronicler Sharaf ad-Din writes that, at the time when Timur began to be politically active, Asia was ruled by usurpers who had grasped power owing to the extinction of old dynasties or by deceit. Widespread chaos prevailed and as a result the peoples suffered. Strong remedial measures were necessary. God made use of Timur, who secured such peace that an unescorted man could safely transport his silver and gold treasures from east to west of Asia.[2] I shall discuss the ideological aspect of this problem later. Here, I would only like to emphasize that Timur and his companions were aware of the weakness of the Central Asian states and resolved to exploit it, which they did. The same problem played a certain, albeit smaller, part in the struggles against Tokhtamysh and Egypt. On the other hand, it is worth noting Timur's long hesitation before he decided to attack Ottoman Turkey. Considering his excellent intelligence service, one may suspect that it was not religious reasons alone, i.e. disinclination to go to war against Bayazid, a warrior of Islam, that restrained him. Timur presumably feared a military defeat, which might destroy the general belief in his invincibility and lead to the fall of the empire. In the struggle against Bayazid, he capitalized on crucial elements of Turkey's weakness, particularly on the antipathy of the newly-conquered peoples of Anatolia towards the sultan, representing extreme despotism and centralist tendencies which were unpopular not only among the nomads of Asia Minor but also among the settled Turkish population who had already experienced feudalism. It may thus

[1] Alexandrescu-Dersca-Bulgaru M., *La Campagne de Timur en Anatolie (1402)* (London 1977) (reprint), pp. II, III.

[2] Sharaf ad-Din, *Histoire de Timur-Bec, connu sous le nom du grand Tamerlan, Empereur des Mongols et Tatares. Ecrite en Persan par Charefaddin Ali, natif d'Yezd, auteur contemporain* (Delft 1722–1723), Vol. IV, p. 197.

be said that there were many external circumstances favouring Timur when he was building his great state.

Let us now consider those favourable external circumstances. This question cannot be settled explicitly, as we know very little about the demographic, social, and economic structures of Central Asia at the turn of the 14th century. Indeed, no serious studies of this subject have been carried out as yet. Both ancient and modern historians were too much fascinated by Timur's personality and his military successes to undertake methodical studies on his socio-economic environment. The situation has begun to change somewhat, thanks to the work of Soviet oriental historians, but we are still very far from an accurate picture of the internal situation in Central Asia, and particularly of Mavrannakhar, shortly before Timur's appearance and during his reign. Here, we shall concentrate first and foremost on Mavrannakhar, which was the centre of the empire and formed the initial base from which to embark on further conquests.

We do not have the basic data, i.e. the demographic situation of the country. There are reasons to believe, however, that it was relatively densely populated. This is indicated by the considerable number of set-tlements and by the fertility of land where, thanks to the well-developed irrigation system, large quantities of wheat, cotton, vine, fruit and other usable plants were grown. The same can be said about the neighbouring region of Bukhara.[3] All these were nearly centuries-old areas of settled agricultural civilization which gave rise to the development of many towns, Samarkand and Bukhara foremost among them. Cattle breeding, and that of sheep in particular, formed a major element of these areas' prosperity. Cattle breeding was the occupation of the clans or rather tribes of Turkic and Mongol nomads who arrived in Mavrannakhar from the east in the 13th and 14th centuries. The immigrant Mongols very quickly adopted the Turkish way of life, forgetting even their own tongue. Their particular tribes were headed by *begs* or emirs, who were

---

[3] This is indicated by the descriptions from the 1430s by the great traveller Ibn bat-tutah, also the account by Clavijo of his embassy to Tamerlane around 1400. H. A. R. Gibb, *The Travels of Ibn battutah AD 1325–1354* (Cambridge, 1971), Vol. III, p. 550f.; Clavijo de Gonzales Ruy, *The Spanish Embassy to Samarkand 1403–1406* (London, 1971), pp. 218, 226f., a valuable eyewitness, found Mavrannakhar a densely-populated country.

leaders of great families.[4] They obtained definite areas of land as a sort of fief, and it was there that, together with their fellow-tribesmen, they led their nomadic life. (On the nature of the Mongol fiefdom, called *soyurgal*, we shall say more below.) The Barlas lived in the heart of Mavrannakhar, in the Kashkadarya Basin, the Dzhalairs near the city of Khodzhent, the Arlats in the Termez region, and the Kauchins, whose origin still remains unknown, on the upper Amu Darya, in the territory of present-day southern Tadzhikistan.[5]

Timur was a member of the family of the Barlas elders. While fighting for power, he destroyed the Dzhalairs and secured the leading position for his own tribe, particularly in the army. We know little about the nomads' affluence. There is no doubt however that under the reign of Timur they acquired considerable wealth, as it was they who made up the overwhelming majority of his army, composed mainly of horse. They took part in all his wars, which brought them much booty. As regards the Barlas, military service was their only duty to the ruler. In return, they were exempted from all taxes. They were allowed to camp wherever they wanted. Clavijo, the source of this information, writes that these nomads called themselves Chagatai. Elsewhere, he writes that the name was given by the aboriginal population of Mavrannakhar to the Tatars who arrived and stayed in the country.[6] But Clavijo's information on this matter is not very precise. He writes that at that time the Chagatai name was already current and was adopted not just by the nomads but also, as he himself maintains, by the numerous residents of Samarkand who were not Chagatai. Such was the prestige of the name of Chagatai in Timur's reign. Clavijo describes Timur as himself a member of the Chagatai people.[7] The matter is of some interest. To begin with, it is not known for certain how far the name of Chagatai, a son of Genghis Khan and the Mongol ruler of Central Asia in the 13th century, had sunk into the minds of the nomads of Mavrannakhar who adopted it. The name of Chagatai continued to enjoy great respect, which even Timur's unparalleled successes did not diminish. Timur, for his part, never aspired to the rank of khan. He was satisfied with the additional title of *kurgen* (in Mongolian, son-in-law) which he obtained on mar-

---

[4] A similar account is given by B. G. Gafurov and A. M. Belenickii in their *Istoriya tadzikskogo naroda* (Moscow 1963), Vol. I, p. 303f.

[5] *Ibid.*, p. 304.

[6] Clavijo, *Spanish Embassy*, pp. 219, 243.

[7] *Ibid.*, p. 243.

rying a princess from the family of the founder of Mongol power. As a ruler, Timur was content with the title of *beg*, the equivalent of the Arab *emir*.

As we already know from Clavijo, under the impact of Timur's successes and the political promotion of the nomads, other groups of the population, particularly the residents of the capital city of Samarkand, also adopted the name of Chagatai. This may be viewed as an incipient element of the formation of a national group, subsequent to the establishment of the state. However, the process did not have enough time to develop fully because the empire of Timur and his descendants collapsed too soon. Due to lack of source materials, it is difficult to say anything about the condition of the sedentary agricultural population. The situation of peasants in particular parts of such a vast country must have varied considerably, but in this regard, too, it is difficult to say anything specific. As regards Mavrannakhar itself, one may surmise that, compared with the last stage of the Mongol period, under Timur agriculture improved. Chroniclers stress the fact that Timur did, after all, safeguard the population from foreign invasions and civil wars and, moreover, impose perfect order in the country. What is more, some of the huge influx of captives were settled on the land. Around Samarkand, Timur ordered the building of settlements to be named after conquered capitals or towns, such as Dimishk (Damascus), Misr (Egypt-Cairo), Baghdad, Sultania, and Shiraz.[8] These were presumably settlements populated by farmers and artisans, perhaps deported from the towns or areas mentioned—but this is not certain. Most probably, the population of the new settlements were of mixed origins, while the settlements' names were to emphasize the original towns' submission to Samarkand, the capital of Timur's empire. The list suggests that Timur was perhaps making plans for the seizure of Cairo also. Clearly, Mavrannakhar's agriculture gained by the compulsory influx of population—a fact mentioned by all chroniclers of the time. Clavijo assesses this influx at about 150,000, which does not seem to be a gross exaggeration.[9] That number would of course have included essentially exiles from the territories that Timur had conquered and pillaged.

---

[8] Ibn-i-Arabšah, *Tamerlane or Timur the Great Emir* (London 1936), p. 309. It should be emphasized here that Timur never seized Cairo.

[9] Clavijo, *Spanish Embassy*, p. 227.

It is, however, worthwhile paying attention to other methods adopted by Timur to increase the population of the Samarkand region. Thus, for example, Clavijo writes that in Persia and Khorasan he saw people who, on Timur's instructions, abducted orphans and poor homeless men and women whom they then dispatched to Samarkand. Every emigrant led a cow, a ram, a sheep, or a goat. On the way, they were fed by the authorities.[10] I imagine that the poor were settled on the land, whereas the skilled artisans, who made up the majority of this forced immigration, were assigned primarily to Samarkand. Unfortunately, there are no source materials to prove the whole of my hypothesis. Clavijo, a careful observer of the country, noted that Timur was carrying out a deliberate settlement policy in Mavrannakhar which, by the end of his rule, was a densely-populated and wealthy country.[11] According to the same author, while enforcing immigration, Timur tried at the same time to prevent exodus from the country. Thus he posted guards on the Amu Darya crossings; the guards let everybody in, but people making for the opposite direction had to produce special certificates.[12] This is an interesting detail in the history of the great conqueror who set out to make Mavrannakhar, and the Samarkand region in particular, the centre of his global empire. The repair and construction of the irrigation system were designed to serve the same purpose. According to the chronicler Hafiz-i Abru, on Timur's initiative, in the Merv oasis, in the Murgab River valley, in the western part of the country, about twenty canals were dug, along which numerous villages were set up. This was done on the orders of the men to whom the ruler had given land in fief (*soyurgal*).[13] On a smaller scale, irrigation work was also carried out in the other provinces of the empire. For example, when, on his march on India in 1398, Timur stopped in Kabul, he ordered the digging of a 5-mile-long irrigation canal near the village of Baran. Sharaf ad-Din writes that as a result many large villages were set up there, and the valley, till then unproductive, turned into a beautiful garden. The conqueror distributed this area among his commanders and soldiers.[14] Another case of this kind was the thoroughgoing repair of the ancient canal drawing off some of the water of the Aras (Araks)

---

[10] *Ibid.*
[11] *Ibid.*, p. 226f.
[12] *Ibid.*, p. 227.
[13] *Istoriya tadzikskogo naroda*, Vol. I, p. 340.
[14] Sharaf ad-Din, *Histoire de Timur-Bec*, Vol. III, p. 29.

River on the border between later Soviet Azerbaijan and Iran. Around 1400, Timur gave orders for the canal to be dug anew. Reportedly, a month later, 10 miles of the canal were already navigable. The ruler called the canal the Barlas River, to commemorate his own tribe. Along its banks, he set up many villages, built mills and palaces, and planted vineyards. From Sharaf ad-Din's further account, one can assume that this initiative was undertaken in connection with the reconstruction of the ruined town of Bailakan. The army dug the canal, and from then on the town thrived.[15] It may well be that more canals were dug, but we lack information on this matter. Both Sharaf ad-Din and the ruler's apocryphal memoirs, put down in the 17th century, maintain that Timur took great care of land cultivation.[16] These memoirs abound in numerous data concerning the conditions alleged to have prevailed in Timur's state. Yet it is clearly impossible to use them with regard to the history of Central Asia in the 14th century, given that all these data were compiled nearly two hundred years later, and this at the court of the Great Mughuls in India.[17]

Above, we mentioned that Clavijo formed a favourable opinion of Mavrannakhar's agriculture around the year 1400. Before him, Ibn battutah, in the 1330s, had called attention to the numerous orchards around Bukhara and Samarkand.[18] Clavijo tells of numerous orchards, fields of wheat, and vineyards around Tirmid (Termez), Kesh, and Samarkand. Cotton was also grown there.[19] Agriculture was developing thanks to the network of irrigation canals, harvests were rich, but it is very difficult to say anything about the condition of the rural population. Under the Mongols, their condition was rather miserable. Under Timur, this may well have improved, particularly in the central provinces. After all, there were no more raids or civil wars, and peace and order prevailed over vast territories. This alone ensured a relatively safe existence to the farming population, although they suffered brutal exploitation, manifest even to a foreigner like Clavijo. Unfortunately, the history of the Central Asian countryside in Timur's time has been poorly studied so far.

---

[15] Ibid., p. 401.
[16] V. Bartold, "Ulug-Beg," Four Studies on the History of Central Asia (Leiden 1963), Vol. II, p. 40f.
[17] Political and Military Institutes of Tamerlane (Delhi 1972), pp. 85, 94, 125f, 131ff.
[18] Gibb, Travels of Ibn battutah, pp. 550 and 567.
[19] Clavijo, Spanish Embassy, pp. 228, 232, 325f.

According to modern-day researchers, the cultivated land was divided into several categories. A large part of it was state property, administered by the fiscal authorities of the day. This land was called *mamlaka-i diwani*. However, under Timur, the process of giving land in fief started. Such land, usually outside Mavrannakhar proper, was distributed among members of the dynasty, among outstanding military leaders, and later among civil servants, too. Down the years, among the liegemen there appeared clergy, merchants, and even wealthy artisans. Similarly to the European fiefs, *soyurgal*, which was initially allotted only for a certain period or for life, was later transformed into an hereditary fief, but only around the middle of the 15th century. Timur exercised full control over land distribution, and did not permit its appropriation by private persons. *Soyurgal* gave the suzerain complete immunity from any fiscal duty or administrative or court penalty. We shall return to this issue later.

Much of the land belonged to religious foundations, i.e. the *waqfs*. The profits derived from such lands were allocated to the maintenance of madrasahs, i.e. religious schools, mausoleums erected on the graves of pious men, mosques, etc. *Waqfs* often owned large acreages of land. True, as in other Islamic countries, a part of the revenue went to the donors, their families, or the donor-appointed attorneys. Many areas belonged to private persons. This category of land was called *muelk*. *Muelk* lands belonged to representatives of various social groups: to the military aristocracy, to merchants, to the clergy, and to other people, including a few peasants and the still existing peasant communities.[20] As for the peasant population, they were very much differentiated, both economically and socially. The few landowners among them paid lesser services to the ruler than the mere tenants did, but the tenants made up the overwhelming majority. About the latter we know the most, but still not enough to make a full assessment of their conditions. Soviet scholars conducted a long dispute on the peasants' legal situation and their relation to the land. Some supposed that, under Timur and his successors, Central Asian peasants were attached to the land. In the absence of any other evidence, they drew comparisons with Iran and the conditions there from the turn of the 13th century onwards. This was however not

---

[20] B. Gafurow, *Dzieje i kultura ludów Azji Centralnej. Prehistoria, starożytność, średniowiecze* (Warszawa 1978), pp. 488 and 490; Gafurov, in *Istoria tadzikskogo naroda*, Vol. I, p. 340; A. Y. Yakubovski, "Timur. Opyt kratkoi kharakteristiki," *Voprosy istorii*, 1946, No. 8–9.

a very convincing method. At present, the prevailing opinion seems to be that held by Vyiatkin and Gafurov, who found no evidence that the peasant population were attached to the land. It is assumed rather that they were free to move from place to place. This, of course, did not apply to the slaves.[21] In the Central Asian rural system, tenancy was most popular. The relevant law provided that peasants, usually small holders or people with no land of their own, leased a plot of land owned by the state or the local aristocracy for a period limited to two or three years.[22] When the labour supply was plentiful, this made them very much dependent on their superiors; on other occasions, their position was relatively strong. It is hard to say what the situation was like in Timur's time. Peasants who cultivated land belonging to religious foundations (*waqfs*) paid them, presumably in kind, one third of their crops.[23] Tenants of land owned by the state, or included in *soyurgals*, paid a land tax called *mal*, similar to the earlier *kharadzh*, which presumably corresponded more or less to the *waqf* burden. Besides this, they were probably obliged to pay a *kosh* tax on the area of land tilled by a pair of oxen, a hearth-tax, and several other taxes as well. Peasants were very heavily burdened by the *begar* tax, which involved the contribution of their own labour to road building, to the maintenance of city walls, fortresses, etc.[24] Particularly burdensome was the *ulag*, the obligation to provide horses and carts, and to maintain the postal service.[25] This is what Clavijo called attention to when, on his journey to Samarkand, he made use of the state post. One has the impression that the *ulag* duty was a heavy burden on all the peasants, irrespective of the category of land they cultivated.

The state post was organized on the following lines. Post stations were operated in both populated and unpopulated areas where inns (caravan-saries) were run. In both cases, peasants were obliged to deliver horses and food to the detachment in charge of the station and to travellers in the ruler's service. The travellers changed horses at these relay stations. If the horse died, they had the right to seize the horse of anyone they met on their way. Any objection was liable to end in death. Clavijo adds that, thanks to the post-station network, Timur disposed of a swift

---

[21] A. Y. Yakubovski, "Timur," p. 68. *Istoria tadzikskogo naroda*, Vol. I, p. 311f.
[22] *Istoriya tadzikskogo naroda*, Vol. I, p. 342. Gafurow, *Dzieje i kultura*, p. 489.
[23] Gafurow, *Dzieje i kultura*, p. 489.
[24] *Istoriya tadzikskogo naroda*, Vol. I, p. 343.
[25] *Ibid.*

inflow of information from the entire country. Clavijo notes that, as a deputy, at every post station he obtained everything he needed, but the system operated at the merciless expense of the local population. If supplies were late, the deputy's escort cruelly victimised the local elders. At the news of deputies' arrival, the people from the area would flee their village, thus saving themselves from gross exploitation.[26] It is well known that both the Mongol and the Timurid postal systems imposed a very heavy burden on the country's residents, ever since the time of the first descendants of Genghis Khan. It was not only the khan, but also his dignitaries and even merchants who availed themselves of the postal system. Meanwhile, the abuse of authority by the ruler's representatives and their escort led to the imposition of certain limits to their powers, and this as early as the 13th century. There is nothing to indicate that in Timur's time the postal system became any less onerous. It was efficient, in any event. As the reader will see below, it constituted a major element in the ruler's control over the entire territory of the state and also an effective tool for spying on territories remaining both within the state boundaries and beyond. It is worth remembering here that such a system had been used in Central Asia since remote ancient times, to be successively adopted by later rulers. From the Mongols, the system was then taken over by Moscow, who established similar postal stations known as *yamy*. The derivative word *yamshchik*, with a slightly changed meaning, obtained in Russian until only recently.

In the Mongol period, numerous extraordinary taxes were levied on peasants, usually for war purposes. However, chroniclers from Timur's time do not mention anything of this nature. It may be that, having captured sizable war booty, Timur waived such duties, usually very burdensome to the population. But undoubtedly, even under his rule, the peasants were still obliged to maintain the local administration, the supervisors of the irrigation system, etc.[27] Timur is alleged to have regulated the system of collecting taxes on state property. Thus, reportedly, he forbade the sending of tax collectors to pester taxpayers before harvest time. The tax collector might threaten the taxpayer in arrears with flogging, but himself had no right to flog anyone. But this information, coming as it does from apocryphal 17th-century sources, is by no means certain. The same applies to reports of a one-year grace period for those

[26] Clavijo, *Spanish Embassy*, pp. 198–201, 213.
[27] *Istoriya tadzikskogo naroda*, Vol. I, p. 343.

who had dug a canal or recultivated a plot of abandoned land, although this sounds quite plausible.[28] Generally speaking, it must be admitted that we do not have a clear picture of the rural economy in Timur's state. Certainly, the conditions of the countryside in particular parts of the empire differed widely, Mavrannakhar having been in a clearly privileged position. It never suffered any negative effects from wars, and even profited by them as it drew in the riches and the cheap slave labour seized from other countries. It must be borne in mind that the Chagatai infantry were recruited among the sedentary population, presumably in the first place among the peasants. Chronicles often mention infantrymen who, as a result of victorious campaigns, enriched themselves greatly. This must have affected the wealth of the countryside in general. Still, we have no basis to assess the tax burden imposed on peasants. Although we know that they were obliged to pay numerous taxes and perform all sorts of work on behalf of the state, we do not know how substantially it affected them economically. All researchers agree that, under Timur and his successors, the acreage under cultivation was increased in Mavrannakhar and certain other provinces. On the other hand, in areas more distant from the centre and repeatedly reconquered, in Iraq in particular, there was presumably marked regression as a result of population losses and destruction of the canal system or neglect of its supervision.[29] All these questions remain subjects for future studies, as and when source materials become obtainable.

Let us now review the condition of the towns and their population in Timur's state. One should start by emphasizing that medieval towns of the Near and Middle East differed considerably from the towns in Europe. Unlike European towns, those in Asia did not enjoy any autonomy. They were subordinated to the ruler directly, while their inhabitants were, theoretically, in the same legal situation as the rural population.[30] This was a major factor which precluded the development of that urban civilization, which was so important for the dynamics

---

[28] *Political and Military Institutes*, p. 132f. In certain years, following campaigns that had brought in much booty, Timur granted a tax holiday to the population.

[29] E. Ashtor, *A Social and Economic History of the Near East in the Middle Ages* (London 1976). The author emphasizes that in 1401 Timur destroyed Iraq particularly harshly; this had its adverse effect on the economy, which had anyway long been in depression.

[30] Very instructive on the history of oriental towns is the work by I. M. Lapidus, *The Moslem Cities in the Later Middle Ages* (Harvard University Press, 1967).

of western and central Europe in the Middle Ages. In large cities of
the East, there usually resided the lords or their deputies, and other
members of the feudal aristocracy, who had not only their abodes but
also large landed property there as well. The same could be said of
religious institutions such as mosques, *waqfs*, madrasahs, etc. In point
of fact, however, town residents had quite a lot to say, especially in
stormy times when superior authority fell short of expectations.[31] Of
great importance were rich merchants, particularly those among them
who could offer more or less voluntary loans to the rulers. Unlike in
the West, such merchants enjoyed great social prestige. In the East,
trade was not a despised occupation—even the rulers and the feudal
aristocracy openly indulged in business. The situation of artisans was
more complicated. It largely depended on their respective trade, their
personal wealth, and their number in a given town. Court chroniclers'
observations concerning artisans, particularly at the time when the latter were making political pronouncements of their own, for example
during the Serbedar movement in Samarkand, reveal the upper classes'
contempt for the urban poor.[32]

This was presumably the prevailing feeling among the aristocracy and
the rich merchants. The situation in Europe, where social divisions in
medieval towns went very deep, was similar. The rule of Timur and his
heirs is believed to have been a period very favourable to towns. This
holds true primarily with regard to Mavrannakhar and other central
provinces, but much less so to the conquered territories, which suffered
greatly from wars and accompanying devastations.

The capital of Timur's state was Samarkand, which under his rule
enjoyed dynamic growth. Yet we have no data concerning the number
of the city's residents. Ibn-i-Arabšah writes that the Samarkand region
extended over seven so-called *tumens*, able to provide 10,000 soldiers
each.[33] On the whole, it would seem, either that Ibn-i-Arabšah grossly
exaggerated, or else the *tumens* must have been considerably smaller
than in earlier epochs.

Archaeological studies give reason to suppose that at its peak period,
in the 10th century, Samarkand with its adjacent suburbs could have

---

[31] As illustrated by the example of the Serbedar movement in Samarkand.
[32] Sharaf ad-Din, *Histoire de Timur-Bec*, Vol. I, pp. 91–94.
[33] Ibn-i-Arabšah, *Tamerlane*, p. 17.

had between 100,000–110,000 residents.[34] Thus it was a big city. When Ibn battutah visited Samarkand in the 1330s, he observed that it was very beautiful, but that many palaces were falling in ruins, and that the same could be said about the greater part of the town. Samarkand had no walls, and gardens occupied a large part of the town, he added.[35] Soon after he seized Samarkand, Timur had surrounded it with walls, something he had not done in any other town, perhaps fearing a residents' revolt. The sentry from the imposing castle, where the grand emir kept his treasures, also took care of the city residents' security and loyalty. The emir built many palaces and laid out magnificent gardens inside and outside the city.

Samarkand became the place where, following victorious campaigns, booty was brought to be sold, and where most of the people deported from the conquered cities were driven. Thus, for example, after the conquest of Damascus and the pillage of Syria, Timur carried off to his own capital many captive artisans, dyers, silk weavers, and other specialists.[36] Tabriz suffered a similar fate in 1386, even though it had not put up any resistance to Timur.[37] During their campaign against India, the Chagatai took vast numbers of captives, including all Delhi's stone-masons, whom they needed in order to build in Samarkand a mosque as magnificent as the grand mosque in India's capital.[38] Waves of forced immigration reached Samarkand after every major campaign of Timur's. Some of the new arrivals were settled in the town, many more in large settlements on the neighbouring plain.[39]

We have already mentioned the campaign of planned settlements in Mavrannakhar. Clavijo writes that Timur brought back arch and glass makers and armourers from Damascus, also arch makers, stone-masons, and goldsmiths from Turkey. At Samarkand there were also makers of siege-trains and of the requisite ropes; the latter also introduced to the city's surroundings the cultivation of flax and hemp.[40] Among the forced immigrants were both men and women, Turks, Arabs, Armenians, Greek followers of the Eastern Church (presumably from Anatolia),

[34] A. M. Belenickii, I. B. Bentovich, O. G. Bol'shakov, *Srednevekovyi gorod Srednei Azii* (Leningrad 1973), p. 266.
[35] Gibb, *Travels of Ibn battutah*, Vol. III, p. 567.
[36] Ibn-i-Arabšah, *Tamerlane*, p. 165f.
[37] Sharaf ad-Din, *Histoire de Timur-Bec*, Vol. I, p. 410f.
[38] *Ibid.*, Vol. III, p. 112f. Ibn-i-Arabšah, *Tamerlane*, p. 222.
[39] Clavijo, *Spanish Embassy*, p. 325f.
[40] *Ibid.*, p. 327.

Nestorians and Jacobites, Parsees from India, etc. Clavijo writes that there were so many of them that they could not be accommodated within the city walls, that they lived and probably practised their respective trades even under trees, outside the town and in caves.[41]

Among the multitude of artisans driven to Samarkand, many were slaves. Timur took along many of them, particularly the highly-qualified ones. Besides, after he seized any major town, he distributed the local artisans among his emirs. This was Timur's regular practice. Unfortunately, we know nothing specific about these artisans' circumstances. It was apparently of no interest to the chroniclers of the time. Timur employed carpenters and stone-masons in the construction of monumental buildings;[42] others worked on the interior decorations of palaces, in gardens, etc. We lack information on these people's economic condition or how they were treated. It is rash to refer to the Mongols' cruel treatment of slaves, as described in the 13th century by Giovanni da Pian del Carpine. After all, we are discussing the situation that obtained some one hundred and fifty years later. We can only entertain hypotheses, without any source materials to support them. The slave artisans of the grand emir and his dignitaries were certainly first concerned with satisfying the needs and demands of their masters. They may have been allowed to sell their surpluses on the "free market," as was done in the 13th century. This presumably allowed some of them to buy themselves out of slavery. Others, less fortunate, slaved in the old-style big workshops, the so-called *kor-chone*, often under the close eye of cruel supervisors, solely for the benefit of their master and his court, and possibly manufactured goods for sale, given—as mentioned earlier—that aristocrats did not shun commercial transactions.

Gafurov emphasises that, well before Tamerlane, in the 14th century, slavery already pervaded Central Asian society, and that slaves worked in crafts, in agriculture and, of course, in households.[43] This is corroborated by the fact that the Chagatai, once they had seized the town that had put up resistance to them, often killed off the men, but took the women and children with them. The polygamy prevailing in Central Asia was certainly conducive to such customs. To return, however, to Samarkand's crafts, there is reason to suppose that a considerable

[41] *Ibid.*
[42] E.g. in the construction of the grand mosque. See Ibn-i-Arabšah, *Tamerlane*, p. 222f.
[43] Gafurov, in *Istoriya tadzikskogo naroda*, Vol. I, pp. 306–308.

majority of the artisans were, nevertheless, free men and that, even if brought there by force, they belonged to the free men's category; otherwise their condition would have been noted in the relevant source materials, particularly in those by an observer as acute as Clavijo.

One should not think that most of Samarkand's artisans were foreigners. On the contrary, a significant majority of them were local residents. They were engaged in the production of various textiles such as satin, taffeta, and others, cotton and silk fabrics in particular. Well developed were furriery, arms production, metal working, and goldsmithery.[44] To these should be added new trades introduced by forced emigrants. Samarkand under Timur should thus be recognized as a great centre of the crafts of the time.

The condition of free artisans in 14th-century Samarkand has not yet been investigated. We know that they often rented workshops, stalls, and buildings from the feudal lords who, besides the ruler, were the large urban real property owners, but we do not know how much rent the tenants paid them.[45] Although the majority of artisans were doubtless free, as before, there must also have been slaves and freedmen among them, and the latter must have had to give a part of their earnings to their current or previous master. This issue requires deeper research, provided source materials permit it. Besides, free artisans, whose legal position was no different from that of the peasants, were obliged to pay the ruler the hearth- and poll-taxes, and also the *tamga*, a heavy indirect tax.[46] They were moreover exposed to all sorts of extortions on the part of himself and his officers. Such things happened on various occasions, for example during the building of roads, though it would seem that in such cases the authorities generally used slave labour. Shortly before his campaign against China, Timur ordered all artisans to abandon their stalls and workshops and gather in the vicinity of the town, where the army was already encamped. They were supposed to sell goods to the warriors and make them merry. In the place where they set up their stalls, he ordered the erection of gallows, and himself began to dispense justice. He sent one excellent administrator to the gallows for embezzlement. A certain merchant sentenced to death offered a huge sum, of 400,000 silver bezants, in exchange for a pardon.

---

[44] Clavijo, *Spanish Embassy*, pp. 325–327.
[45] Gafurow, *Dzieje i kultura*, p. 522f.
[46] *Ibid.*, p. 522.

Timur took the money, tortured the man to pay even more, and then ordered not only his execution, but also that of the two people who had pleaded for him. Moreover, he meted out heavy fines on artisans and merchants charged with demanding excessive prices for their goods. Clavijo maintains that the residents of Samarkand were very much displeased, complaining that they were summoned, only to be robbed by the ruler.[47] Such incidents took place more than once, but Timur at least saw to it that his officers did not oppress his subjects excessively. When his dignitaries grew too rich, he made them pay large sums to himself.[48] This was, after all, a custom widespread in despotic monarchies of the East, practised, for example, in Mamluk Egypt in relation to the wealthiest dignitaries and merchants. On the other hand, it happened several times within a single year that Timur exempted the population from taxes.

Gafurov agrees with Belenickii's view that, under Timur and the Timurids, trade guilds developed greatly, in Samarkand in particular. The guilds, which acted together at ceremonies, must have been to some extent self-help organizations. It is unlikely however that, as in western and central Europe, they enjoyed a monopoly of production in their respective town. The guilds' elders were not elected, but appointed by the ruler's representatives. Members of some of the guilds were obliged to deliver all their products to the court of the grand emir, while certain groups of armourers worked under the strict control of the armoury's head.[49] The Samarkand guilds were thus at a lower stage of development than the guilds of medieval Europe. There is nothing strange in this. It does not necessarily imply any inferiority of Mavrannakhar's civilization in relation to that of western and central Europe at the time. Guild organizations were something quite common in the Middle Ages, both in Christian and, starting from the 14th century and maybe even earlier, in Islamic countries also. Nevertheless, the forms of their respective organization differed widely. The degree of the guilds' independence from their European monarch, or from the town authorities controlled by the merchants, hung on the "balance of power" obtaining between the artisans and the other parties to their "contract." That balance was by no means steady. Strong central authorities in particular did not

---

[47] Clavijo, *Spanish Embassy*, pp. 282–284.
[48] H. Moranville, *Mémoire sur Tamerlan et sa Cour par un Dominicain en* 1403 (Paris: Bibliothèque de l'Ecole des Chartres, 1894), Vol. LV, p. 459f.
[49] Gafurow, *Dzieje i kultura*, p. 521f.

tolerate what they considered as any excessive autonomy of the guilds. Such was the case, for example, in France under the Valois and the Bourbons, or the Duchy of Burgundy in the 15th century. The urban aristocracy or even the groups of the moderate-income *popolo grasso* in Venice and Florence represented the same line of reasoning. In the world of Islam, i.e. in Western and Central Asia, in Egypt and North Africa in general, the urban population lived in direct subordination to despotic rulers and in the shadow of their military might. Development of urban self-government or autonomous trade's organization were out of the question in such circumstances. Guilds were always subordinated to the ruler of the day, while their main task was to satisfy that ruler's demands. Such was the situation in Mamluk Egypt, in Ottoman Turkey as late as in the 17th and 18th centuries, in Samarkand—and doubtless in other towns of the Chagatai state—under Timur and his descendants. In Samarkand, the main task of the centrally-appointed guild elder was to collect levies and other payments due to Timur and to his offspring. When people wanted to defend their interests, whether against the ruler or against external enemies, the centre of their organization and resistance was not the guild but the mosque, where they gathered for prayers. That was the case in Samarkand, and probably in other towns of Mavrannakhar and of other dominions of Timur's empire. It must be said to his credit that, to some extent, he fostered the development of crafts, at least in Samarkand. He had a wide bazaar street built, to run across the whole of the town. Both sides of the street were lined with tents, with benches of white stones in front of each of them. He covered the entire street with a roof, with openings to let the light in. Along the street, water tanks were deployed.[50] It was a huge bazaar where the sellers were grouped according to their trade. This was not only convenient for the buyers, but also facilitated state control over the tradesmen. Later, Timur's son Shah Rokh built a similar but bigger bazaar in his capital Herat, described by the chronicler Hafiz-i Abru.[51]

There is no doubt that crafts developed considerably under Timur, primarily in Samarkand but probably in other centres, too. There was marked progress in trade specialization, which indicates a rise in the technical level and, to some extent, an increase in the number of artisans and even customers. Unfortunately, we have no precise information

---

[50] Clavijo, *Spanish Embassy*, p. 316. *Istoriya tadzikskogo naroda*, Vol. I, p. 345.
[51] *Istoriya tadzikskogo naroda*, Vol. I, p. 345f.

about the crafts' internal organization. Neither towns nor guilds in Central Asia have left behind any statutes or other documents, so precious to the student of their times.

Above we mentioned the bazaars of Samarkand. It is obvious that they traded not only in handicraft products, but also in food and other goods meant for town residents of varying affluence. Thus, at the bazaar one could easily buy wheat, wine, fowl, and other kinds of meat or fruit, among which local melons were particularly tasty. Clavijo writes that bread, barley, rice, and sheep were extremely cheap. There was much cotton on display. The same author maintains, mistakenly, that it was the wealth of goods that gave Samarkand its name—from the combination of the words *simes* (big), and *kint* (settlement). This etymology, however, is quite wrong.[52] Clavijo's account shows that, in Samarkand at the beginning of the 15th century, retail trade in food and food products was well developed, taking place in numerous squares. The low prices indicate that food was abundant. There is no doubt that the number of petty merchants was very large. I also consider that they fared relatively well. It must be kept in mind that the city was also rich thanks to the inflow of booty from each of Timur's and his commanders' myriad military campaigns. As a rule, in the Chagatai army camps there were many craftsmen who purchased part of the soldiers' booty and supplied them in return with the things they needed.

We may therefore assume that, under Timur, the populace of Samarkand, and probably of Kesh and other towns too, lived in relative wealth deriving from the growth of handicraft and retail trades. Trade with distant places was of no less significance, particularly in Samarkand. At this point, we must turn our attention to Central Asia's network of major trade routes. The establishment of the great Mongol empire in the 13th century went hand in hand with the emergence of crucial trade routes connecting Europe with the Near and Middle East and with China. Francesco Balducci Pegolotti of Florence described the most important of these roads at the beginning of the 14th century. The departure point was Tana, an Italian colony on the Don River, near the present-day town of Azov, which had an easy water connection with the Black Sea coast and with Constantinople, and a land connection with

---

[52] Clavijo, *Spanish Embassy*, p. 326f. In fact, Samarkand derives its name from antiquity, when the Sogdian called it Maracanda.

central and eastern Europe. From Tana, people travelled to Saray-Berke on the Volga river, the capital of the Golden Horde, and thence further east to Saraychik on the Ural River, whence, after a long journey, they reached Urgench in Khorezm, which, after the devastation wrought by Genghis Khan, became, in its new site, a large and flourishing trade centre. From there, they moved on to Otrar in northern Mavrannakhar, to Almalyk in the Ili River valley, across Chinese territory to Kan-chou and Hang-chou, and from there to Peking.[53] This route by-passed Samarkand in the north and was thus of little interest to its merchants. But the expedition undertaken by Ibn battutah in the 1330s shows that, at that time and certainly later also, there were other routes, much more convenient for the large cities of central Mavrannakhar, which, in their farther stretches, led to China or India. Ibn battutah travelled from Astrakhan on the Volga River to Urgench in Khorezm, and next via Kiat (the present Khiva) to Bukhara, and through Nasaf to Samarkand.[54] From there one could head, via Otrar and Almalyk, to China, or south, through Balkh, Termez, Kabul, and the Khyber Pass, to India, towards Delhi. Yet Timur destroyed Urgench, and later allowed only a small section of it to be rebuilt. Moreover, in 1395, his armies razed Saray and Astrakhan as a result of which the latter lost its significance as a trade centre for many years. Scholars have therefore questioned whether Timur deliberately destroyed Saray, Astrakhan, and Urgench in order to paralyse the old trade routes controlled by the Golden and White Hordes. According to this concept, Timur carried out a conscious trade policy aimed at fully restoring the importance of the roads leading from Iran, the Mediterranean and Black Sea coasts to the Middle and Far East, but running through his capital, Samarkand. The main such road ran from the Near East and Iran, i.e. from Tabriz and Sultania, via Herat in present-day Afghanistan, via Balkh, Termez, and Kesh (Shahrisebz) to Samarkand, and further, via Semirechye, to China.[55] There were also other roads in this part of Timur's empire. They all ran to the capital, and connected it with Kabul and India. Although Gafurov and certain other scholars are ready to give an affirmative answer to the question

[53] F. Balducci Pegolotti, *La Pratica della Mercatura*, edited by A. Evans (Cambridge, Mass., 1936), p. 21f. Of the places mentioned here, Almalyk, the last stop on the way to China, lost its importance in the 14th century. V. Bartold, *Sochineniya*, Vol. III (Moskva 1965), p. 470. For Urgench, see Gibb, *Travels of Ibn battutah*, Vol. III, p. 549.
[54] Gibb, *Travels of Ibn battutah*, Vol. III, pp. 539–580.
[55] Gafurow, *Dzieje i kultura*, p. 507.

posed above, I have some doubts. It seems questionable whether Timur
would have conducted a deliberate policy of sparing rich towns on the
routes he wanted to seize on behalf of his own merchants and his own
exchequer. Although he did not destroy Herat, Sultania, or Tabriz, he
laid them under heavy and painful tribute. He did not rebuild Balkh,
nor many other towns. Herat gained significance as a large economic,
political, and cultural centre only under Timur's successors. Timur
himself would seem to have failed to appreciate the town's development prospects, evidently excellent in the past. He did indeed promote
the development of domestic and external trade, yet, in the course of
war, I believe he was first and foremost concerned with strategic and
tactical purposes: in the towns he conquered, he was out to grab the
biggest booty for himself and for his warriors. Personally, I would not
credit him with plans to change the trade routes, although this cannot
be altogether ruled out.

It is worth turning our attention here to two other routes which
became important, particularly after the disappearance of the northern
route to China. One of them, from Trebizond to Samarkand, was taken
by Clavijo, an emissary of King Henry III of Castile. Clavijo sailed via
Constantinople to the Black Sea city of Trebizond, then the capital of
the tiny empire of the Comnenian family, Timur's vassals. Trebizond
was a major trade centre where Venice and Genoa kept their factories
(trading stations), intermediary between eastern Anatolia and Iran, and
Kaffa in the Crimea and Pera in Byzantium's capital, and hence south-
western and central Europe as well. From Trebizond, Clavijo travelled
further across Erzincan and Erzurum, which were already within
Timur's state, to Tabriz, where he joined the road leading to Samarkand
via Zendzhan, a large town of Sultania, Tehran, Bostam, Dzhadzherm,
Neyshabur, Meshed, Andhai, Balkh, Termez, and Kesh. He returned
home via Bukhara, Abivard, Kabushan, and Dzhadzherm, and thence
along the same route he had taken when travelling to Samarkand.[56]

It should be added that, besides the sea-and-land route from Europe
via Trebizond, there was another one, along the western coast of the
Caspian Sea, the Iron Gate Gorge near Derbent to Iranian Azerbaijan,
i.e. to Tabriz and Sultania. The Iron Gate and the Iron Gate Gorge, on
the road from Samarkand to India, were under Timur's control, a situ-

---

[56] Clavijo, *Spanish Embassy*, pp. 149–231.

ation which secured him considerable revenues from customs duties.[57] Unlike Clavijo, however, I think that Timur's continued attacks against Georgia and Armenia, as also his devastating campaign against India (1398/99), significantly weakened trade between Central Asia and the Caucasus area and India, and that in the early years of the 15th century reciprocal trade was considerably less than before.

It is thus clear that, under Timur, Samarkand became a vital crossroads for commerce. The city's growth at that time should not be seen as a result of geographical factors alone. After all, the geography was always the same and yet, following the growth of Mavrannakhar's capital in the 8th and 9th centuries, came centuries of much humbler existence. Samarkand enjoyed prosperity again only under Timur, and later under his grandson Ulugh Beg. It may be assumed that the enormous wealth of the capital's feudal lords and merchants attracted large quantities of goods whose transportation was relatively easy, thanks to a convenient network of trade routes. Trade was of primary importance. Clavijo writes that Samarkand imported hides and cloth from eastern Russia and "Tataria" (possibly the Crimea or central and south-eastern Russia), silk cloth, and particularly exquisite satin, rubies and diamonds, pearls, and numerous delicacies from China. From India, it bought various spices such as cloves, nutmeg, ginger, cinnamon, etc.[58] Thus, Samarkand's trade in Timur's time was very extensive, embracing both popular products such as cloth and hides as well as luxury goods from Southern Asia and its islands. Conditions were ideal for flourishing trade, as both the city and the whole of Timur's state were absolutely secure.[59] Moreover, Timur lowered or even abolished many of the internal customs duties that were so vexatious to merchants, not only in Central Asia but everywhere in the medieval world. He decreed that duties might be levied only in large cities.[60]

Unfortunately, we know practically nothing about the rich merchants of Samarkand at the turn of the 14th century. I have already quoted Clavijo's report on a certain merchant sentenced to death, who unsuccessfully tried to save himself by offering a huge sum of 400,000 bezants to the grand emir.[61] That is the only information we have. But

---

[57] *Ibid.*, p. 230.
[58] Clavijo, *Spanish Embassy*, p. 329f.
[59] *Ibid.*, p. 355f. Moranville, *Mémoire sur Tamerlan*, p. 459.
[60] Moranville, *Mémoire sur Tamerlan*, p. 459f.
[61] Clavijo, *Spanish Embassy*, p. 329.

even under Timur there must have existed and operated a merchant class, just as it existed and operated both earlier and later, or as was the case in Mamluk Egypt, where information on the subject is ample. Merchants made up a social group that was rich and widely respected, being among the leading strata of the Muslim world. Merchants were engaged not only in trade, but were also property and (in the later period) fief owners as well. And yet the only thing we know about them in Timur's time is that they were there. Among them were foreigners resorting to the empire's capital or staying there only for a while. Clavijo mentions the Chinese, who came to Samarkand with exquisite silks, rubies, musk, and other commodities.[62] Chinese merchants often accompanied their emperor's envoys to Timur, or else were on their way home, ushered by Timur's messengers.[63] The Chinese treated all their foreign partners with disdain, saying, reportedly, that Moors (Muslims) were blind, Franks (European Christians) had but one eye each, and that the only two-eyed people were themselves, the Chinese.[64] This was presumably a reference to their partners' ineptitude with regard to craft and trade, and to the easiness of cheating them. At any rate, it is an amusing symptom of the medieval Chinese' feeling of superiority over western "barbarians."

It is hard to say anything about the population of Samarkand at the turn of the 14th century. At the time of its greatest prosperity, in the 10th century, the population exceeded 100,000. We may assume that under Timur their number was much the same, but this is a mere supposition. Clavijo describes the city itself, without the communities surrounding it, as somewhat larger than Seville,[65] but this does not tell us much, although we know that at the time Seville was the largest town in Castile and maybe even in the whole Iberian Peninsula. According to the estimates and hypotheses of J. C. Russell, at the time of the Arab Umayyads (8th–10th centuries), Seville had a population of 90,000 and covered an area of 286 hectares.[66] But these estimates are not certain, and we still do not know the exact number of residents at the turn of the 14th century. We only know that Seville was a large

---

[62] Ibid., p. 329f.
[63] E. Brettschneider, Mediaeval Researches from Eastern Asiatic Sources (London 1910), Vol. II, pp. 231–234, 256–260.
[64] Clavijo, Spanish Embassy, p. 329.
[65] Ibid., p. 325f.
[66] J. C. Russell, Medieval Regions and Their Cities (Newton Abbot 1972), p. 178.

and very active city, with numerous foreigners, the busy Genoese in particular. Thus, Samarkand may well have reminded Clavijo of Seville in some respects.

Let us now turn our attention to other towns of Timur's state. His immediate homeland was Kesh-Shahrisebz (Green City). The city was given its second name in the 14th century. Clavijo describes Kesh as a large municipality situated on a fertile plain, between brooks and orchards. There were many large houses and mosques there, the big mosque where Timur initially wanted to be buried towering over them. Clavijo saw there the tomb of Dzhehangir, the ruler's eldest son. At Kesh, Timur erected many palaces faced with glazing. We know nothing specific about the economic life of the town, which was presumably a centre for trade in local wheat, cotton, melons, and other products.[67] During his campaigns, Timur often sent captives, particularly scholars, to Kesh. Sharaf ad-Din quotes several chroniclers as claiming (exaggeratedly) that Kesh used to be a place which attracted the most learned experts in Islamic law, including three thousand imams, founders of different theological schools. Sharaf ad-Din also claims that Kesh was called Green City (Sheher Sebz) because of the green freshness of its gardens. In 1376, enchanted with the city's beauty, Timur made it the place of his summer residence and the second capital, which is why he ordered the construction of the new city walls and the palace (Ak Saray). He then divided Kesh between his emirs and his guardsmen.[68] Among the larger towns that Timur preserved, one should mention Termez. Clavijo indicates that the Termez region was densely populated. That was where people crossed the Amu Darya when travelling between Khorasan and Mavrannakhar. Several hundred families were reported to live there.[69] Balkh, situated in Khorasan, was also a large town, consisting of three parts, in keeping with the local town-planning system. Of these three parts, however, one remained empty, while another was only scarcely populated. Unlike the majority of the towns of Timur's state, Balkh was surrounded by walls.[70] This notwithstanding, after

---

[67] Clavijo, *Spanish Embassy*, pp. 232–235. The so-called "Geography of the Ming Dynasty" in E. Brettschneider, *Mediaeval Researches*, Vol. II, p. 273, gives a similar account.

[68] Sharaf ad-Din, *Histoire de Timur-Bec*, Vol. I, p. 306f.

[69] Clavijo, *Spanish Embassy*, p. 226. Figures quoted after Chinese sources, the so-called "Geography of the Ming Dynasty" in E. Brettschneider, *Mediaeval Researches*, Vol. II, p. 275.

[70] Clavijo, *Spanish Embassy*, p. 223.

Timur defeated the emir Hussein, who had fallen into enemy hands and been murdered there, the town was destroyed and its population dispersed in punishment for siding with Hussein. Since that time, however, Balkh would seem to have regained a certain degree of prosperity, thanks, *inter alia*, to its position on the major routes from India and Iran to Samarkand.

If we now turn towards the northern confines of Mavrannakhar, those encompassing some of the steppe zone, we should, like V. Bartold, examine the towns located in the Syr-darya region. Chief of these was Sygnak, or Sagnak, which remained within the White Horde's power. The town grew up under Urus-khan, against whom, it should be remembered, Tokhtamysh rebelled. Sygnak even served as Tokhtamysh's base of operations, but the town seems unlikely to have played any major economic role in Timur's empire.

Likewise, the other urban centres of the area, such as Sairam, Sauran, and the more distant Tashkent (Shash), were probably of no economic importance to Mavrannakhar either. Otrar, on the Syr-darya, was situated on the route from Samarkand to China. It was there that Timur died, at the beginning of his campaign against that country. Otrar was moreover an important location on the road from Saray to Almalyk and China.[71] It presumably lost a great deal of its importance after the ruin of Saray and the decline in 1395 of the great northern route connecting the Volga Lands with the Far East. In place of the old town of Binket (or Benaket), ravaged by Genghis Khan, Timur in 1392 ordered the building of a new one, which he called Shahrukhia, in honour of his youngest son and later successor, Shah Rokh. The town gained in importance only in the 17th century; for the time being it played a major strategic role on the Syr-darya, close to the border with western Mongolia, where the rebellious Dzhalair tribes, whom Timur did not trust, were encamped. Unfortunately, we know nothing definite about the situation and internal life of Mavrannakhar at the turn of the 14th century.[72] It should be stressed nevertheless that northern Mavrannakhar, although a rather backward and distant part of the country, was quite urbanised at the time.

Let us return however to Samarkand. One of the roads leading from that city to Iran, and further to the west, passed through Bukhara. The

---

[71] V. Bartold, *Sochineniya*, Vol. III, pp. 221–227. Balducci Pegolotti, "La Pratica," p. 21.
[72] V. Bartold, *Sochineniya*, Vol. III, p. 221.

years when Ibn battutah was travelling there were relatively prosperous for the Bukhara oasis. According to this voyager, there were plenty of orchards and rivulets (perhaps canals), trees, and housing estates. Ibn battutah knew that Genghis Khan's Mongols had dealt the town a heavy blow. He found many bazaars, mosques, and madrasahs in ruins, and believed that, since the invasion, local culture had been on the decline.[73] The history of Bukhara in the 14th and early 15th centuries is not well known. The town and the oasis were under the rule of the Sadrs, the line of imams glorying in their descent from the Prophet. They recognized Timur's dominion, and under his rule the town stood somewhat aside from great events.[74] According to usually reliable Chinese sources, its population amounted to some ten thousand relatively prosperous families. According to the same sources, in the oasis five grain varieties, hemp, and mulberry were grown, and silk produced. Cotton was undoubtedly grown there also. If the Chinese data correspond with the facts, under Timur Bukhara was a large town with a population exceeding fifty thousand. Another source records that cotton weaving and many handicrafts known from Samarkand were well developed at Bukhara. However, on the precise conditions obtaining about the turn of the 14th century it is impossible to say anything specific. As regards other towns of Timur's empire, those situated in Iran, Iraq, and Afghanistan, contemporary sources provide only scant information (save in the case of Sultania). Clavijo, who on his way to Samarkand and back took notes which he later collected in his memorial to the king of Castile, remains the chief provider of details. I would like to turn the reader's attention to this memorial because this is, I believe, indispensable to an understanding of the nature both of Timur's empire and also, as we shall see, of the personality of this great conqueror. Thus, among large towns Clavijo includes Meshed and Buelo (possibly Abdul-Abad), as having the largest populations in the area reaching as far as Sultania. Further, he mentions Neyshabur as a very rich and large city, situated in the area abundant in orchards. In Ibn battutah's time, there was a thriving production of silk textiles, exported to India and Tabriz, and from there, presumably, also to Europe.[75] Yet Neyshabur

---

[73] Gibb, *Travels of Ibn battutah*, Vol. III, p. 550f.
[74] I. M. Mumynov, ed. *Istoriya Bukhary s drevneishikh vremen do nashikh dnei* (Tashkent 1963), contains abundant information concerning the epoch which interests us.
[75] Gibb, *Ibn battutah*, Vol. III, p. 584f. Clavijo, *Spanish Embassy*, p. 203f.

suffered considerable losses during Timur's campaigns against Iran, and this probably led to a decline in the city's prosperity.

In neighbouring Afghanistan, it was Herat which came into prominence. According to Johann Schiltberger, it numbered as many as three hundred thousand houses, but this is clearly a gross exaggeration. Bostam was another large town along Clavijo's Iranian route, but we know nothing more of this place. Clavijo stopped in Tehran, the city that was beautiful and rich, but with no walls, while Rayy, once the region's largest city, was entirely destroyed.[76] From the sources mentioned here, we know nothing of either Asterabad or Kazvin. Clavijo did not pay any attention to them, probably because they lost their significance as a result of the wars of Genghis Khan and Timur. Schiltberger mentions more towns in Iran and in the neighbouring countries, and among them precisely Asterabad, Malaga, and Shiraz (we know that Shiraz was destroyed by Timur), and even rich Hormuz, at the entrance to the Persian Gulf from the Indian Ocean, but he does not give any details, probably because he did not survey them.[77] Clavijo, for his part, dwells on the wealth of Sultania and Tabriz, both situated on the route from Iran or Syria to the South and the Far East. Tabriz was already well known as a very important medieval place where Iranian, and even Indian, merchants encountered Genoese and Venetians to trade in European and Asian goods. Clavijo describes Tabriz as a very beautiful and rich market town. There were many mosques, baths, and, reportedly, as many as two hundred thousand houses—which again seems a gross exaggeration. The city was not encircled by walls at that time. It had many canals. The numerous shops and booths offered both locally-produced and imported silk and cotton materials, also pearls from the Persian Gulf, sandalwood, and other luxury goods. At the same time, Clavijo learned that in earlier days Tabriz had been more densely populated. All the beautiful houses outside the city limits were destroyed by Mirza Miranshah, Timur's son and administrator of Iran.[78] In addition, Tabriz suffered badly from Tokhtamysh's raid in 1385, and the heavy

---

[76] J. Schiltberger, *The Bondage and Travels of Johann Schiltberger, Native of Bavaria, in Europe, Asia and Africa 1396–1427* (London: R. N. Hakluyt Society, 1879), Vol. LVIII, p. 44f. Clavijo, *Spanish Embassy*, p. 186f. It is strange that on p. 44, Schiltberger describes Rayy as a large city. It was first destroyed in the 13th century by the Mongols, and later Timur also laid the region waste.

[77] Schiltberger, *The Bondage and Travels*, p. 44.

[78] Clavijo, *Spanish Embassy*, pp. 167–171. The author stayed in Tabriz for nine days, and would thus have had ample time to observe the city.

contribution the townspeople had to pay Timur two years later, as the price of saving their life and property. This was perhaps the cause of the population decrease. Despite these setbacks, Tabriz would seem to have recovered from its sorry plight, and continued growing. In the 15th and even the 16th centuries, it still played a significant role in East-West trade. But it was Sultania that earned our Castilian's unstinted admiration. In his time it was a large town, though smaller than Tabriz, with no walls, very densely populated, and attracting more trade than Tabriz. Numerous canals wound through Sultania. There were many streets and squares where people could engage in trade. There were also many inns (caravansaries) where numerous foreign merchants put up. Every year merchants arrived at Sultania from Christian countries (usually from Genoa and Venice), from Kaffa in the Crimea, and from Trebizond. Merchants from Syria, Turkey, Baghdad, and India appeared regularly. Those from Hormuz and India brought silk materials embellished with pearls, imported from Ceylon and China, as well as the most beautiful rubies. The latter, together with some of the spices exported from India to Syria (and Alexandria), such as cloves, nutmeg, cinnamon, and others, also reached Sultania. From Khorasan, merchants brought high-quality cotton yarn and bright-coloured cotton materials. Silk was imported from Gilan province on the southern coast of the Caspian Sea, renowned both for its abundance of silk and cotton and for its hot climate. The same could be said about Sultania, where foreigners often died from sunstroke.[79] This however did not deter prosperous merchants from expeditions to faraway Sultania, which was overflowing with superior-quality Eastern and also Western goods, where one could find luxurious woollen cloth from Italy, the Netherlands, and even from England, and where all Occident-Orient bills were settled in cash. It has long been known that in those days Europeans usually had a deficit in their trade with the East. They carried with them much gold and silver in order to acquire luxury Asian products to which Europe's upper and even middle classes had long been accustomed.

At this point, it is worth adding a few words about our own country, Poland. In the 14th and 15th centuries, a certain, albeit modest, volume of oriental products on offer in Tabriz and Sultania, through the agency of Italian, Armenian, and even Turkish merchants, reached Kaffa, a renowned trading centre. A smaller volume was brought to Tana, on

---

[79] *Ibid.*, pp. 176–179.

the lower course of the Don River. In mid-14th century, Casimir the
Great in distant Poland was busy conquering Red Russia in order, as
he put it, to enable his subjects to participate in the remunerative trade
with the East. It was beyond the means of Polish merchants, usually
from Cracow, to travel as far as Iran. However, the king made it possible for them to trade with Tana and Kaffa. Sometimes they travelled
to Constantinople, and even to Alexandria, the two centres of the lively
Levantine trade. It cannot be ruled out that Armenians from Lwów,
who had from the 14th century maintained very wide trade contacts
with the East, also reached, via the Crimea and Trebizond, as far as
Tabriz and Sultania, where many of their fellow-countrymen were living, and that from those far-off countries they imported luxury goods
to Lwów and Cracow. This is admittedly only an hypothesis, which I
cannot prove, but which seems to me very plausible.

We lack any source materials concerning crafts in the two large cities
of Iran discussed here. Undoubtedly crafts were very much advanced
there, given the considerable supply of raw materials such as silk and
cotton. Besides weaving, both luxury and cheap rug manufacturing
flourished. In all the larger cities of the Near and Middle East, guilds
were very much alike. Thus the situation in the Iranian centres was probably no different from that which we already know from Samarkand.

The possession of many towns, including very wealthy ones, brought
Timur and his governors enormous profits in the form of taxes and
duties. Archbishop John of Sultania writes that in large towns, on behalf
of Timur, taxes were collected which the same ruler had abolished elsewhere.[80] This was a rational decision, facilitating the collection of taxes
and at the same time, to some extent, protecting merchants against the
extortions and thievery of the multitude of uncontrollable local clerks
who ignored the fact that their crimes were liable to death. Archbishop
John maintained that every year Timur collected the tithe plus a quarter of the respective income of all his countries and towns.[81] We lack
however any other source materials to confirm the archbishop's statement. Another author, Schiltberger—who was a slave of Timur's and,
after Timur's death, of his sons Shah Rokh and then Miranshah, the
latter for many years the ruler of Iran and Iraq—asserted that, thanks
to the number of merchants, Tabriz alone earned the "king of Persia,"

---

[80] Moranville, *Mémoire sur Tamerlan*, p. 459f.
[81] *Ibid.*, p. 460.

i.e. Miranshah, an income higher than any that the most powerful Christian rulers obtained.[82] That, again, must have been an exaggeration; nevertheless, it indicates that duties and other tariffs charged in Tabriz constituted a major source of revenue for the governors of Iran, and indirectly for Timur as well.

Summing up the arguments outlined above, one may say that at the turn of the 14th century many, although not all, towns of the Chagatai state and of the dependent territories enjoyed a relative prosperity. This was due to their favourable geographical location, to safety on the roads, as well as to Timur's policies. Along the lengthy route from Trebizond to Samarkand, Clavijo noticed few traces of the wars Timur had been fighting in Iran. Such traces were probably quickly smoothed over by an inflow of people from places having suffered destruction, or from rural to urban areas. Again however we lack the necessary sources to confirm our supposition. But we do know that some centres suffered severely. Thus, for example, as a result of Timur's two campaigns, Baghdad lay in ruins and was depopulated. The same applied to Sivas on the Turkish border, previously a very prosperous city, which for long was unable to recover from Timur's plunder.[83] We have elsewhere mentioned the slaughters of Khwarezm and Iraq, which affected Mosul and other towns in the region, the bestialities committed in India, and the cruel ravage of Georgia, Syria, Anatolia, and the territories of the Golden Horde. The greater part of these territories had not joined the Chagatai empire, and perhaps this was why Timur ravaged them so ruthlessly. Yet this was not the case with Khwarezm and Iran, which were not annexed either. Suffice to recall the fate of Urgench and Esfahan. As mentioned before, in 1391 Urgench was razed and ploughed out, while its residents were either butchered or sent to Mavrannakhar. Only after a lapse of some time did Timur permit the reconstruction of a small part of the city. It never recovered the old splendour that had once so fascinated Ibn battutah. The fate of the citizens of Esfahan, a large city in Iran, was much more tragic. Schiltberger gives a fairly detailed account of what fell to their lot. Thus, upon his return from the campaign against India, Timur marched off to the region, which frequently rose in rebellion while he was away. Esfahan surrendered without putting up any

---

[82] Schiltberger, *The Bondage and Travels*, p. 44.
[83] *Ibid.*, p. 46. The author states all this as an eye-witness. Regarding Sivas, see Ibn-i-Arabšah, *Tamerlane*, p. 116.

resistance and hence was initially spared. Yet when the grand emir left, the local population, indignant at the extortions of the Chagatai garrison, killed about six thousand soldiers—whereupon Timur returned to the town to settle accounts. On his orders, twelve thousand archers who had put up resistance were killed. Next, Timur ordered the execution of all townsmen over fourteen years of age. Towers were built of their skulls. He then enjoined that all children under seven should be trampled. When soldiers shrank from carrying out his command, he himself set off to give an example; the soldiers then did the rest. Reportedly about seven thousand children perished in this way. The soldiers' initial scruples should presumably be attributed to the Muslim military ethos which forbids the killing of children, as being unable to fight. On Timur's orders Esfahan was burnt down, and the remaining women and children were driven to Samarkand.[84] Ibn-i-Arabšah places these events earlier in time, but he, too, emphasizes the savage cruelty inflicted on the defiant population.[85] All these details are important if we are to ascertain Timur's personality.

Thus Timur combined a policy of supporting towns, their crafts and their trade, with one of striking the most savage terror into all those who dared resist his authority. The chronicler Sharaf ad-Din writes that Timur was a very pious and far-sighted ruler, who was also very liberal and kind to everyone except those who refused to obey him. He punished the latter with the utmost severity, leaving no offender alive. Not surprisingly, in the eyes of this particular chronicler, everyone who showed defiance was guilty. Archbishop John of Sultania spoke in the same spirit when he arrived at the court of Charles VI of France.[86] It should be mentioned here that Timur even made efforts to lure to his country merchants from such distant lands as France, England, and Castile, albeit to no avail. It was thus the Genoese and Venetians who continued to dominate Iran's foreign trade.

Timur seems to have supported the growth of towns in Mavrannakhar, particularly of the capital city of Samarkand and of Kesh, from where he himself came. In course of time, however, he began treating the subjugation and pillaging of towns as a crucial source of funds for himself and for his army. Those towns spared from plunder, which remained

---

[84] Schiltberger, *The Bondage and Travels*, p. 27.
[85] Ibn-i-Arabšah, *Tamerlane*, p. 44f.
[86] Sharaf ad-Din, *Histoire de Timur-Bec*, Vol. I, p. 1f. Moranville, *Mémoire sur Tamerlan*, p. 451.

within the Chagatai state or its fiefdom, paid heavy taxes to him but, thanks to security at home and on the major trade routes, they could still prosper. There are even scholars who consider the period under Timur and his descendants to have been the golden age in the history of Central Asian towns. However, considering the sacrifices that this prosperity entailed, I think these scholars must be grossly exaggerating. Moreover, the effects of Timur's policy did not always last. Some of the people forcefully brought to Samarkand, or Mavrannakhar in general, never grew acclimatized there, and were quick to take advantage of the civil wars that erupted following Timur's death (1405–09) and return to where they had come from, with or without the authorities' consent. This emigration achieved such proportions that in Samarkand there were labour shortages, and prices rocketed, probably due to the want of artisans. Prosperity returned to the town only after Shah Rokh gained control over most of the empire.[87]

The artless Schiltberger offers another version of the same events. In a way his is a fairy story. When Schiltberger was still a slave, shortly after Timur's death, the imams of the mosque where the ruler was buried were rumoured to have heard his wailing every night of the year that followed. Only after the captives that Timur had brought from other countries were freed did the whimpering cries stop.[88] Both the fact of the forced immigrants' flight from the capital to their native homes, as well as the report that Schiltberger propagates (in good faith), show that deportees forcibly brought to Samarkand and other towns of Mavrannakhar felt alien there and seized the first opportunity to return home. Apart from the natural ties that bound them to their native country, they presumably resented the exploitation of forced immigrants, especially of those turned into slaves and set to work for the ruler and his emirs.[89]

At this point we should consider the whole of Timur's position regarding the towns of his empire. Did he employ any specific policy in this respect? He undoubtedly aspired to the advancement of his capital Samarkand, of Kesh, and perhaps of Shahrukhia, which had been built on his orders, but which only developed much later. As regards towns situated in other parts of the Chagatai state, some of them did indeed

---

[87] Ibn-i-Arabšah, *Tamerlane*, p. 281f.
[88] Schiltberger, *The Bondage and Travels*, p. 30.
[89] Gafurow, *Dzieje i kultura*, p. 507.

achieve a degree of prosperity. In this connection we have already mentioned Tabriz and Sultania. The situation of Tehran, which quickly made up for its war losses, of Derbent, of Herat, and of a few other towns was presumably also favourable. Their wealth was no doubt a consequence of the complete safety of the trade routes, tariff reductions, etc. Besides, important changes took place in the trade routes in the last decade of Timur's rule, after the year 1395. I refer here to the northern route leading from the Black Sea towards the Far East. The route lost its significance after Timur destroyed the major centres along it, such as Tana, Saray, Astrakhan, and Urgench. Urgench was razed because in the second half of the 1380s it had favoured Tokhtamysh. Astrakhan, for its part, rebelled against the Chagatai at the end of the 1395 campaign, and for this it was punished. The annihilation of Saray was a revenge for the havoc that Tokhtamysh had wrought in Iran, on Mavrannakhar's border.

Leaving aside the motives advanced by Timur himself, the seizure and plunder of a town always ensured the Chagatai not only political success but also very substantial or even enormous spoils. I believe this was the main reason behind the havoc sown by Timur and his army. It is quite another matter that, as a result, the northern trade route between Europe and the Far East declined quickly. In this situation, the Crimean port of Kaffa became the main Black Sea centre for trade between Europe and Asia. Kaffa however took advantage primarily of other transportation routes. As a result, the steppes of the Golden and White Hordes lost their significance almost entirely. Those to gain were the towns along major transportation routes within the Chagatai empire. The main route led from Syria through Mesopotamia to Tabriz, from there via Tehran and Balkh to Samarkand, and then, across the steppes of western Mongolia and southern Mongolia, to China, in the direction of Peking. Under Timur's successors, the trade route leading from Iran to Samarkand via Herat, a city which was also situated along the road between Samarkand and northern India, would seem to have acquired particular importance. Still, the development of Herat in the 15th century should not be attributed to the road network alone. At that time, Herat was the Timurids' capital, the seat of their court and their treasures, and these factors undoubtedly affected the city's economic growth. The possible policy of Timur himself I have mentioned elsewhere. Taking all in all, it seems to me unlikely that he could have taken any purposeful action towards this end; otherwise he would not have destroyed Aleppo, Damascus, and Baghdad, significant trade centres along the route from the Mediterranean Sea to the Middle and Far East. In point of fact, his great campaigns made a major contribution to the weakening of the Mediterranean and Syrian areas in trade with the East. Instead, Alexandria became the leading trade centre, where Indian and Chinese goods arrived across the Red Sea, Africa, or the isthmus of Suez. It took a long time before Aleppo (the Arabic Halab), Damascus, and Beirut recovered their strong position in international trade, a position seriously impaired, first by Timur's campaigns and then by the fighting between his remote descendants.

Timur did however unquestionably contribute to a considerable advancement of crafts, particularly in Mavrannakhar, and this irrespective even of the emigration of artisans that followed his death. Contact between local artisans and arrivals from Iran, Iraq, Turkey, and India, to say nothing of regular contacts with the Chinese, had a positive impact on the development of production methods in Samarkand and probably also in other towns of Mavrannakhar where the majority of deportees were resettled. It must also have exerted a favourable influence on the development of culture in Central Asia.

Above we discussed the situation of town and village and their inhabitants under the rule of Timur. We have incomparably more source materials concerning towns than the rural areas, which is a result of the specific arrangement of the materials preserved and investigated. One should not imagine, however, that in the economy of the Chagatai empire towns predominated. The overwhelming majority of the population lived in the countryside as peasants or nomads. From the countryside also came the aristocracy on whom the ruler relied. Let us then take a closer look at rural conditions. The Muslim and Turko-Mongolian East did not know the noble estate as it existed in Europe, nor did it know division into estates. We saw that, in certain countries, even slaves or people of slave origin could attain to the highest positions in the state. At the same time, there did exist a peculiar class division, sometimes very marked. With the despotic system of government prevailing, individual promotion and demotion depended, at least theoretically, on the ruler's will alone. In point of fact, however, there were various coteries of magnates who exerted a very powerful, sometimes decisive, influence on society. Yet they did not show any manifest signs of affiliation to upper classes, such as a family coat of arms, privileges, etc. As regards the Mongol state, and then the Chagatai empire, its feudal aristocracy came from three origins: from the ruling family, from the nomadic chiefs (the so-called beys or emirs), or from the sedentary feudal elements who had accepted the Mongol conquest and remained loyal to the new rulers. It should be stressed here that in Timur's state the differences between these three groups levelled out to some extent, as, for example, in the case of the Barlas, who had meanwhile adopted a sedentary life. Gafurov and other historians very strongly emphasize the objective of Timur, of his successors and of the aristocracy to increase and irrigate the acreage under cultivation.[90] This implies a noticeable increase in the importance of farming against animal husbandry, the classic domain of the nomads. Under Timur, great military commanders, usually descended from the tribal aristocracy and loyal to the ruler, grew enormously rich. Among this group one might also include commanders of units of a thousand or a hundred men (the respective unit's numerical name did not always correspond with reality). Civilian dignitaries coming from the highest social classes, from the merchant class, or those owing their promotion to talent and knowledge were of lesser consequence.

The position of Muslim leaders, ostentatiously supported by Timur, especially if famed for their piety or scholarship, was relatively strong. It seems probable that Christian priests, as for instance Archbishop John of Sultania, mentioned earlier, also achieved high rank in Timur's court and diplomacy, though little is known about them. On the other hand, Timur's attitude towards the so-called pagans, i.e. Hindus, Parsees, and others, was decidedly hostile. He is reported to have particularly hated the Jews, though the work by the archbishop of Sultania is the only source mentioning this.[91]

In Timur's time, the military-feudal aristocracy of nomadic origin occupied the highest position in the state, next to the ruler's family. These two groups were very close to each other, all the more so since Timur readily appointed his numerous sons and grandsons to important military and administrative ranks, often under the guidance of experienced emirs. It was to them that a substantial part of the spoils fell, including skilled artisans. It should be stressed here that, save for a few plots at the time when he was still strengthening his authority, the emirs generally remained loyal to him. In their understanding, this loyalty was to last also in the afterlife. Sharaf ad-Din writes that, when Timur ordered the building of a mausoleum for the deceased princes

---

[90] Gafurov, in *Istoriia tadzikskogo naroda*, Vol. I, p. 340.
[91] Moranville, *Mémoire sur Tamerlan*, p. 462.

of his family, the emirs, eager to manifest their other-worldly devotion to him, erected tombs for themselves next to his mausoleum, arranging them according to the future "resident's" respective birth and rank in the state hierarchy. Sharaf ad-Din considered this a proof of their love and loyalty to Timur.[92] The aristocracy had every reason to revere their ruler so deeply. His successful campaigns earned them enormous riches in the form of spoils, a considerable part of which fell particularly to the emirs. This consideration alone encouraged them to show blind obedience to Timur, knowing as they did that the war expeditions he led brought them considerably more profit than the old tribal strifes. Timur lavished high rewards on his emirs for their courage and other virtues. Last but not least, Timur's annexations opened up to them the prospect of significantly enlarging their own landed property by gaining new fiefs.

The institution of fiefdom (*soyurgal*) had long been known to the Mongols. Iakubovskii maintains that the system was widespread in the Mongol states, and especially in the Golden Horde. The khan gave away large areas of land, together with the people settled there, in fief. *Yarlyks*, or bequest charters, were often accompanied by an immunity called *tarkhan*'s *yarlyk*, which exempted the serfs from paying a part or all of the taxes on behalf of the ruler; instead, the taxes were to be paid direct to the *tarkhan*, i.e. the local lord, himself. In course of time, *soyurgal* was given in hereditary possession; it could be sold or bought in whole or in part.[93] Elsewhere, the same scholar states that under Timur the *soyurgal* system likewise flourished. Drawing on a wide knowledge of the relevant sources, Iakubovskii shows that Timur often turned over vast regions, sometimes even entire countries he had conquered, as *soyurgal*. Occasionally *soyurgal* made up a completely new territorial unit that had not existed before the fiefdom was bestowed. In principle, fiefs were awarded first and foremost to the ruler's sons and grandsons, but emirs also received their share. As in the old Mongolian states, vassals were entitled to collect the whole or part of taxes. Under Timur's descendants, *soyurgal* was hereditary, although in reality Timur's vassals at times lost their lands, or received others. The once sovereign rulers who gained Timur's favour kept their property, but as a fief for which

---

[92] Sharaf ad-Din, *Histoire de Timur-Bec*, Vol. II, pp. 272–274.
[93] B. Grekov et A. Iakoubovski, *La Horde d'Or. La Domination Tatare au XIIIᵉ et au XIVᵉ siècle de la Mer Jaune à la Mer Noire* (Paris 1939), p. 130f.

they had to pay him tribute.[94] Apparently it was only rarely that Timur
granted the *tarkhan*'s immunity to anyone. Hence he did not forgo all
of the rent due to him from his subjects. Archbishop John of Sultania
wrote that Timur collected from all towns and communities tithes plus
a quarter of all their incomes.[95] This would indicate that taxes were
collected from *soyurgal* lands as well. However the whole issue raises
many doubts because as yet not one *soyurgal yarlyk* from the 13th or
14th century has been found; instead, the matter has been studied on
the basis of later grants and chroniclers' notes, often inaccurate or
totally misleading. It should be stressed that the enormous expansion
of the state contributed to the increase in the number of fiefs of various
acreage, which was very advantageous first and foremost to Timur's
family and to other emirs.[96] Under the rule of Timur's descendants,
smaller *soyurgals* were turned over to imams, lower-ranking officers,
clerks, merchants, and even to artisans.[97]

It is impossible to say whether *soyurgals* or their division confronted
the Chagatai state with some elements of feudal hierarchy. It would seem
that they did not. We should, however, consider one other aspect. Like
the European fief, *soyurgal* was also a form of a ruler's rewarding of
the upper social classes. The individual endowed with such fief thereby
obtained a source of income. At the same time he was performing
important functions in the administration, judiciary, and finance, and
above all in the army, as he was obliged to turn up in arms and with a
precise contingent of warriors whenever the ruler demanded. He thus
represented a very real source of political and military strength. The
vassals of Timur, who was a despot and had the means to enforce his
will, showed absolute obedience to him. After all, as we have already
shown above, they were interested in maintaining the unity of the
empire, whose existence and enrichment ensured them growing profits.
In order to keep a tight rein on his vassals, Timur established an extensive spy system and exercised tight control over the entire territory of
the state. The system however contained the germs of dangerous crises,
which became manifest as soon as Timur died; these intensified under
his descendants, who were much less talented than he.

---

[94] A. Y. Yakubovski, "Timur," p. 66f.
[95] Moranville, *Mémoire sur Tamerlan*, p. 459f.
[96] Yakubovski, "Timur," p. 66.
[97] *Istoriya tadzikskogo naroda*, Vol. I, p. 341.

We are dealing here with a phenomenon typical of nearly all feudal monarchies. Their founders as a rule had very strong personalities. They were to conquer vast areas and multitudes of people, and unite all of them not only by force but also by ties of loyalty motivated by mutual benefit. The difficulties in the administration of an immense state in the Middle Ages required providing the provincial governors with vast material resources, extensive prerogatives, and considerable autonomy of operations. This in turn was conducive to the emergence of decentralising tendencies. As long as the state was led by an able person embodying adequate military strength and (which is no less important) unimpaired authority, such tendencies did not manifest themselves. However, as soon as the all-powerful founder of the empire died, a struggle at once broke out among the great lords eager to take his place or to break away from the central authority. This explains why in feudal countries the ruler's personality was of such vital importance. Such a situation is totally different from that obtaining in democratic organizations, with their institutions operating as it were independently of the person of the head of state. Although what we describe as the decline of the feudal state resulted primarily from the absence of real ties between its particular parts, one should also bear in mind the significance of the disappearance of a strong and able ruler, an important factor consolidating the political organism into one whole. That was evident for example in the Frankish state after Charlemagne's death, when Louis the Pious took over power. Similar examples are legion.

Analogous, though less evident, cases took place in Timur's empire following the founder's death. Many areas hitherto treated as *soyurgals* in fact became almost or totally independent state units. This was already evident under Shah Rokh, Timur's son and not very successful successor. Shah Rokh lost his influence in western Iran and Iraq, which were governed by local feudal lords. Meanwhile his son Ulugh Beg, wielding authority at Samarkand, behaved as a sovereign ruler, although he did not break with his father and formally recognized him as his suzerain. Thus, the crucial role of the individual in the history of great feudal (and despotic) states is undeniable.

In this chapter I have endeavoured to present an outline of social life in the state that Timur founded. The feudal nature of that empire is unquestionable. It is indicated by the rural organization, comparable in point of fact with those existing in medieval Europe. Specific of the Chagatai society was its strong nomadic element, which in fact was undergoing feudalization processes, too. The towns of the empire, although in some ways similar to those in Europe, nevertheless differed from them considerably. The former were fully subordinated to the despotic central authority, hence their lack of autonomy and the underdevelopment of trade guilds. However, this did not hamper the economic development of towns which, in this respect, attained a level no worse than that in western Europe. But the populations of Timur's towns were under the heavy-handed control of their ruler, they had no chance to show any organizational initiative in public life. They could seize the initiative only sporadically, in particularly difficult situations which led to rebellions, because the superior authority had been falling short of expectations. Such was the case at the time of Genghis Khan's raids, or the invasion of the Mongol nomads from the North-East. These, however, were rather exceptional situations. In any case, the upper classes, led by the aristocracy, restored the *status quo ante* fairly rapidly. As a result, the population of the towns of the medieval East, including Mavrannakhar, were fairly passive, both socially and politically. This was one of the consequences of despotic rule.

CHAPTER FIFTEEN

NEW SARAY, CAPITAL OF THE GOLDEN HORDE*

The study of the history of the town of Saray-Berke, or New Saray, is not an easy one. Written sources are few in number and of limited value. The excavations by Tereščenko and by Balodis, together with the more recent explorations of Fedorov-Davydov and his team, have unearthed only a few sectors of this large town. Great prudence is accordingly called for when presenting the current state of research and the conclusions that may justly be drawn therefrom.

All traces of the urban civilization of the Khazar period have long since disappeared, from the time when the Mongols invaded the Caspian steppes in the first half of the 13th century. The inhabitants of those steppes, the Cumans (or Kipchaks), lived by stock-breeding and by war, their agricultural prowess being virtually negligible.

The Cumans were decimated by the Mongols but, despite the massacres perpetrated by the invaders and their own massive flight westwards, they would still seem to have retained a clear majority status among the nomadic peoples of the steppes.

The Mongols living in this ethnic milieu quickly became assimilated among the Turkic population, a state of affairs remarked upon by Al-Omari, an Arabian observer writing in the first half of the 14th century, i.e. only one hundred years or so after the final conquest of the steppe and the creation of the Empire of the Golden Horde.[1]

Batu Khan, the founder of this empire, the man who destroyed countless agglomerations in the Bulgaria of the Kama, in Russia, in Poland, and in Hungary, is still known in Mongol tradition as Sayin Khan, "the generous khan". Oriental sources credit him with the foundation of at least two further towns in the steppes of the Volga and

---

* Originally published in French under the title "Saraï la Nouvelle, capitale de la Horde d'Or" in J. Schneider (ed.), *Wirtschaftskräfte und Wirtschaftswege. Festschrift für H. Kellenbenz. I. Mittelmeer und Kontinent*, Bamberg: aku-fotodruck, Stuttgart: Klett-Cotta (in Kommission), 1978, pp. 15–29. Translation from French by Robin Kimball.

[1] V. Tizengauzen, *Sbornik materialov otnosiaščykhsia k istorii Zolotoi Ordy*, vol. 1, Sanktpeterburg, 1884, pp. 234–235.

the Ural river, namely Old Saray, also known as Saray Batu, situated on the Volga estuary, and Little Saray (Saradjuk), on the lower Ural,[2] It seems probable that Ukek (or Uvek), lying at the junction of a river of the same name and the Volga, was founded on the orders of the same khan, and originally served as a postal relay, the inhabitants being obliged to ensure the safe crossing of the main river for travellers visiting the camp of the sovereign. These inhabitants were Russians, in all probability prisoners of war installed there by the Mongols.[3] Ukek was later to become a town of medium size and, according to Ibn battutah, one that was well constructed and prosperous.[4] Batu Khan and his successors were nomads. In summer they lived on the shores of the lower Volga; in winter they moved up towards the middle course of the river, where it approaches the Don.[5] These were the two sites on which were constructed the two towns bearing the name of Saray: the Old and the New. New Saray was situated on the banks of the Akhtuba, a former tributary of the Volga, in the territory of the town of Tsariov (Carey) in the region of today's Volgograd.[6]

There were also some agglomerations in the steppes of the Caspian Sea but, with the one exception of Hadji Tarkhan (now Astrakhan'), these were of little importance.[7] Al-Omari, an Egyptian writer of the 14th century and a man of outstanding intelligence, records, on the basis of travellers' testimonies, that the vast steppes of the Golden Horde were relatively well populated, but that there were few towns or villages, far less than in Iran. The nomads neglected agriculture, their diet consisting mainly of meat and milk. The revenues of the khans were inferior to those of the sovereigns in Iran. They imposed heavy taxes on the nomad population who, owing to these exactions and to frequent famines, were often forced to sell their children or near relatives to foreign merchants.[8] At the same time, we also know that the khans

---

[2] *Ibid.*, pp. 20, 85; *Les textes d'El Djouveini et d'Al Wassaf; Aboul Ghazi Behadour Khan, Histoire des Mongols et des Tatares publiée par le Baron Desmaisons*, vol. II, S. Pétersbourg, 1874, p. 181.

[3] C. R. Beazley (ed.), *The Texts and Versions of John De Plano Carpini and William de Rubruquis*, Hakluyt Society, 1903, p. 171 (account of Rubrucq).

[4] L. Défrémery et B. Sanguinetti, *Voyage d'Ibn Batoutah*, Vol. II, Paris, 1854, p. 370.

[5] *Ibid.*, p. 410; according to Al-Omari, the khan used to spend the summer in the Urktag (?) mountains; Tizengauzen, *op. cit.*, I, p. 243.

[6] F. Balodis, "Neuere Forschungen über die Kultur der Goldenen Horde", in *Zeitschrift für Slavische Philologie*, IV, 1927, pp. 1–5.

[7] *Ibid.*, p. 5f.

[8] Tizengauzen, *op. cit.*, I, pp. 229–234.

of the Golden Horde disposed of considerable treasures in precious metals, as evidenced by the large quantities and high quality of their money up to the second half of the 14th century.[9] These fortunes were amassed at the expense of the subjugated peoples, mainly Russians. The tariffs levied on merchandise and the spoils of war largely contributed to the opulence of the khans and the Tatar aristocracy.

Al-Omari's account is of immense value. It confirms, once again, that the economy of the Golden Horde was primitive, fragile, and unbalanced. Above all, it lacked an agricultural basis, the prerequisite condition of prosperity and progress in medieval societies.

The available sources concerning Old Saray and Hadji Tarkhan being insufficient for forming any coherent picture of their distant past, I shall confine myself here to examining certain features of the history of New Saray.

I will begin by distinguishing certain factors whose coexistence was indispensable for the growth of large medieval towns:

1. A population prepared to settle in the town, or sufficiently docile to be implanted there by the ruler (a common occurrence in the East).
2. A favourable geographical position.
3. A political regime capable of controlling and ensuring the safety of the lines of communication.
4. The existence of a purchasing power sufficient to attract and ensure the prosperity of merchants and artisans.
5. The ability to supply the needs of the local inhabitants.
6. A scale of productivity on the part of the population sufficient to meet both everyday needs and the demands of foreign trade.

I will endeavour to present the history of New Saray in line with the above criteria.

The exact date of the foundation of the town is hard to establish. According to Ibn-i-Arabšah, who lived in the early 15th century at the court of Tamerlane's successors and subsequently in Egypt, New Saray existed for 63 years in all.[10] Since it was destroyed in 1395, this would mean that it was founded around 1332. However, this latter date

---

[9] G. A. Fedorov-Davydov, "Raskopki Novogo Saraya v 1959–1962", in *Sovetskaia Arkheologiia*, I, 1964, pp. 269–270.
[10] Tizengauzen, *op. cit.*, I, p. 462.

strikes me as unacceptable, inasmuch as Ibn battutah, who visited the town two years after its alleged foundation, described the capital of the Khan Uzbek as a large urban centre in full flower. The true date of its foundation must therefore presumably be placed some years further back. Ibn battutah, Al-Omari, and other Arabian writers all refer to the town as Saray-Berke,[11] inferring that the real founder was in fact Khan Berke, who reigned from 1255 to 1266. But this date also gives rise to doubts. The Egyptian legation that visited the residence of Berke in 1264 does not mention the existence of the town; its members met the Khan in his camp on the banks of the River Itil (Volga), where he lived in a magnificent tent. Supplies were brought by river from Russia.[12] It is possible that we are dealing here with the beginnings of an urban agglomeration, but the source provides no details of this. It cannot be altogether excluded that the reference is to Old Saray. Another source, slightly more detailed, dates from 1297–1298. This was when the Khan Tokhtai, at war with his rival Nogai, set up his camp on the banks of the Don, described as near Saray.[13] Now New Saray, as we know, was situated in the area where the Don comes close to the bend in the Volga. From this, one may surmise that Saray already existed towards the end of the 13th century. The basis from which it evolved was probably the former camp of Khan Berke, which gradually developed into a permanent town. The erroneous date given by Ibn-i-Arabšah possibly corresponds to the period between the reign of Khan Uzbek (1313–1342) and the destruction of the town by Tamerlane's forces in 1395; during this period, New Saray became the capital of the Golden Horde, being accorded this function by the powerful Khan Uzbek, perhaps around 1332.[14]

The geographical position of New Saray—like that of the other towns of the middle and lower Volga—was a particularly favourable one. From time immemorial, it had been the centre of a network of trading routes used in the time of the Khazars but abandoned during the domination of the region by nomadic tribes, the Pechenegs and the Curnans. Thanks to the security safeguarded by the khans, they

---

[11] Ibid., pp. 241, 460; Voyage d'Ibn Batoutah, Vol. I, p. 446.
[12] Tizengauzen, op. cit., I, pp. 60–63 (chronicle of Muhieddin Aboulfadl Abdallah).
[13] Ibid., p. 110 (chronicle of Ibn Wassil).
[14] Voyage d'Ibn Batoutah, vol. II, p. 446. Ibn battutah was the first of the authors mentioned here to refer to New Saray as the capital of Khan Uzbek; he visited the town during the reign of the latter.

were reactivated under the rule of the Mongols. Both Pegolotti and Ibn battutah mention the important lines of communication running between Tana, Astrakhan', New Saray, and Urgench in Khorezm, thence continuing towards Almalyk (Kulja) in eastern Turkestan and finally to Peking.[15] The route leaving Saray downstream from the Volga provided easy access to Astrakhan', with its outlet to the sea, or alternatively its land communications towards the great industrial and commercial centres of Azerbaijan and Iran, the principal sources of Persian silk.[16] It should be added that the trans-Caucasian routes running between the Volga steppes and Iran were frequently interrupted as a result of fighting between the Golden Horde and the Ilkhans.

As for the routes of communication between the towns of Iran, notably Tabriz, Yazd, etc., which entertained trade relations with the Golden Horde to the north and with India to the south-east, these are well known to us thanks to the accounts by Marco Polo, Ibn battutah, and other writers; there is thus no need for me to enter into details here.

Arab authors mention the presence of Russian shipping on the Volga, especially upstream.[17] These ships maintained links between the capital, the Bulgaria of the Kama, and the Russian territories of the upper Volga. After its destruction by Batu Khan in 1238, the town of Bulgar was never rebuilt, but the surrounding country, fertile and rich in high-quality furs, retained considerable commercial importance. The commercial links between the Bulgaria of the Kama, western Siberia, Russia, and the Great North existed from time immemorial.[18] Thanks to these connections, Bulgaria disposed not only of stocks of cereals but also of large quantities of local and imported furs, leather goods, and other merchandise highly valued in the Muslim East.

There was another route linking Saray with Tana. It is surprising to read that Pegolotti considered this section of the great route to the

[15] Fr. Balducci Pegolotti, *Pratica della Mercatura*—G. F. Pagnini del Ventura, *Della Decima*, Bologna, 1967 (reprint), Vol. II, p. 1. Ibn battutah travelled by this route in the course of his journey to Bukhara and Samarkand. Cf. also H. A. R. Gibb, *The Travels of Ibn battutah AD 1325–1354*, vol. III, Hakluyt Society, Cambridge, 1971, pp. 539–567.

[16] Afanasii Nikitin, *Khoženie za tri moria...*, *1466–1472*, Moskva-Leningrad, 1948, pp. 53–55. This description dates from the second half of the 15th century.

[17] Tizengauzen, *op. cit.*, pp. 58, 241 (texts of Muhieddin Aboulfadl Abdallah and Al-Omari).

[18] *Istoriia Sibiri*, Vol. I, pp. 353ff.

East to be less safe than its further stretches in the direction of Central Asia.[19] At this point it should be emphasized that the majority of routes converging on the towns of the Golden Horde traversed thinly populated regions, especially following the massacres perpetrated by the Mongols. The populations of these steppes, mostly poor and warlike nomads, constituted a serious threat to travelling merchants. In these conditions, a strong authority was required in order to maintain the security of the routes. This was precisely what the Mongol empires of the 13th and the first half of the 14th century put into practice, in their own best interests. The very fact that the powerful khans of the Golden Horde resided along the banks of the Volga or its environs and kept control of the road networks was of supreme importance for the widespread commerce of the towns of that region. As we shall see in due course, the removal of this factor later contributed to the decline of the urban centres of the Volga basin.

The fact that the khans of the Golden Horde established their winter quarters at New Saray was of immense importance for the town. The court attracted thither members of the Tatar aristocracy, who then set up residence there. While archaeologists place the date of this phenomenon around the middle of the 14th century,[20] Al-Omari's account suggests that in fact it took place somewhat earlier, probably during the first half of the century.[21] All experts share the view that the court of the khans and the Tatar nobles together represented a purchasing force of immense size, thanks to the great wealth they derived from the taxes and tributes levied on their subject peoples, as well as the spoils of successful wars. The large quantities of Tatar coinage recovered, especially that dating from the 14th century, provides convincing proof of this.[22] It thus seems certain that the presence of the khans and Tatar nobles in Saray, by creating a widespread demand for goods of all kinds manu-

---

[19] Pegolotti, *op. cit.*, p. 3.
[20] G. A. Fedorov-Davydov, *op. cit.*, p. 251; A. G. Mukhamadiev and G. A. Fedorov-Davydov, "Raskopki bogatoi usad'by v Novom Sarae", in *Sovetskaia Arkheologiia*, III, 1970, pp. 240–241.
[21] Tizengauzen, *op. cit.*, I, p. 241. According to Al-Omari, Saray contained houses for "emirs", including Tatar dignitaries. The chronicler died in 1348/1349.
[22] Balodis, *op. cit.*, p. 10; Fedorov-Davydov, *op. cit.*, 1964, pp. 8–10; S. A. Janina, "Monety Zolotoi Ordy iz raskopok i sborov Povolzskoi arkheologičeskoi ekspedicii na Carevskom gorodišče v 1959–1962", in *Povolže v srednie veka*, Moskva, 1970, pp. 194, 196.

factured by local artisans or introduced by merchants from abroad, did much to promote the economic growth of the town.

Let us now consider the two basic factors from the viewpoint of the history of a town and notably the distribution of its population. In their various accounts, Al-Omari, Ibn battutah, and Ibn-i-Arabšah all emphasize the huge dimensions of the town of New Saray. Balodis, the archaeologist whose excavations date from the early twenties, has even suggested that the town covered 50 km² or thereabouts.[23] Until the middle of the 14th century, Saray was not walled in, which affords some idea of the sense of security felt by authorities and inhabitants alike. Written sources indicate that the houses were built so close together that Ibn battutah, for instance, could detect no interspace for gardens. The central parts of the town housed a teeming population. Bazaars were without number. According to Ibn battutah and to Al-Omari, the town contained aqueducts, thirteen large mosques, several smaller places of prayer, other religious establishments (*medersas*), and baths.[24]

In the course of the 14th century, the influx of foreign scholars led to considerable enhancement of the spiritual life of the capital.[25] Al-Omari records that the grand palace was surrounded by ramparts, several towers, and houses belonging to emirs.[26] According to Fedorov-Davydov, who undertook excavations in Saray during the 1960s, the Tatar aristocrats settled in the town in the 14th century, probably in the southern quarters, where they lived surrounded by their slaves. In the view of Soviet archaeologists, the progressive improvement in the quality of the slaves' living quarters shows that at least some of them rose to the rank of serfs and probably mingled with the rest of the inhabitants of Saray.[27] According to Ibn battutah, the population of the capital was very mixed, comprising Mongols—the rulers of the country—Alans from the northern Caucasus, Kipchaks, Circassians, Russians, and "Rumis" (perhaps Greeks), etc. Each ethnic group lived in its own district, complete with bazaars. Ibn battutah records: "As for the foreign merchants from the two Iraks, Egypt, Syria,and elsewhere,

---

[23] *Voyage d'Ibn Batoutah*, II, p. 446; Tizengauzen, *op. cit.*, I, pp. 241, 462.

[24] *Voyage d'Ibn Batoutah, loc. cit.*; Balodis, *op. cit.*, p. 16. According to Balodis, the excavations show that there were both gardens and orchards in Saray Batu and in New Saray.

[25] *Ibid.*; Tizengauzen, *op. cit.*, I, pp. 461, 462, 507 (accounts by Ibn-i-Arabšah and by El-Aini, 1361–1451).

[26] Tizengauzen, *op. cit.*, I, p. 241.

[27] Cf. notes 20 and 21.

they and their possessions are in a special district surrounded by walls".[28] This list of nationalities is not complete. Saray was visited by Italians coming from Tana, there were emigrants from Khorezm,[29] and certainly Armenians, large numbers of whom lived in the vicinity of the Black and Caspian Seas. The capital of the Golden Horde attracted peoples from all sorts of places. Towards the middle of the 14th century, the population of the country was swollen by the arrival of a group of rich bourgeois from Tabriz and other towns in Azerbaijan, from Greater Armenia, and even from Ardebil in Mesopotamia, all fleeing the oppressive rule of their sovereigns.[30] It seems reasonable to conclude that numbers of them settled in the opulent capital. Nor should one forget that the enforced transfers of population to places favoured by the Mongols played an important role in the growth of the urban centres in the khans' empires. At the same time, it seems to me that cases of voluntary migration also played an appreciable part. New Saray, in its status of a highly important centre of commerce and industry, required strong reserves of manpower and abundant merchant capital. There was thus ample occasion to earn a living and even to amass a fortune. The people drawn to the capital came from relatively far-off regions, for the nearby steppes, peopled as they were by nomads ill adapted to urban life, were not a satisfactory source from which to recruit immigrants. This factor perhaps explains the diversity of peoples living in Saray. Local industry employed a huge number of artisans, some of them slaves and some probably freemen. The excavations undertaken by Tereščenko in the middle of last century, despite the unsatisfactory nature of the methods employed, produced impressive results. Tereščenko unearthed eight (large?) furnaces, one of which had 70 tuyeres. "The centre of the furnace contained an oven in ruins, surrounded by water inflow pipes at intervals along the tuyeres. Not far from the oven, we discovered a number of night-lamps, pitchers, cauldrons, iron and copper lingots, smelting pans, and moulds". Tereščenko, like Iakubovski after him, considered this to be the remains of an industrial works belonging to the court, known in the East as *karkhane*. Both iron and copper industries

[28] Cf. note 23.
[29] Fedorov-Davydov, *op. cit.*, I, 1964. In the light of Iakubovski's views, the author considers that a large part of the pottery unearthed at New Saray is Khorezmian in type, which suggests that the town contained an ethnic group of similar origins. Cf. B. Grekov et A. Jakoubovski, *La Horde d'Or*, Paris, 1939, p. 142; Balodis, *op. cit.*, p. 18.
[30] Tizengauzen, *op. cit.*, II, Moskva-Leningrad, 1941, p. 101 ("History of Sheik Uveiz").

were well developed in Saray, where there was large-scale manufacture of arms, agricultural implements, and other metal objects. The capital also included numerous workshops for wool and cotton weaving, and leather goods were likewise produced. The wool and the leather were furnished by nomad breeders, while the cotton was imported from Syria or Egypt. Large quantities of pottery were also found, some locally produced and some of foreign pattern.[31] One may thus assume that the Saray artisans worked not only to meet local needs, but in part also for the export market.

It is not easy to form a picture of Saray's trading practices. Both Ibn battutah and Al-Omari record that there was a lively exchange of goods *within* the town and that the numerous bazaars were well stocked with wares. Both authors call attention to the presence of countless oriental traders in the town, mentioning merchants from Egypt, Mesopotamia, and elsewhere.[32] They do not, however, mention Italians, and it is a fact that New Saray nowhere figures in the acts of Kaffa by the notary Lamberto di Sambuceto of 1289/1290.[33] This is probably explained by the fact that at the time in question Saray's commerce was still in its infancy, whereas Italian trade in Tana had already reached a considerable volume, even though no regular colonies existed there as yet. I would remind you that Saray became the capital of the Horde in the 1320s or 1330s, which coincides with the period of the Italian colony's establishment in Tana. Is there any connection between these two events? It may be that the growth of Saray exercised a beneficial influence on commerce in Tana, a town which can be regarded as a commercial outpost of the Tatar capital. This in turn might perhaps have attracted the Venetians to Tana. Pegolotti leaves us little information concerning Saray, though he does tell us that the route from Tana to Saray was not very safe.[34] It would appear that the direct routes from Tana to Astrakhan and beyond presented less dangers. We know next to nothing concerning Saray's trade relations with the West. As regards the North, I have already cited the presence of Russian ships in the port of the town on the Akhtuba; we may therefore assume that Russian

---

[31] Grekov et Jakoubovki, *op. cit.*, pp. 138–142.

[32] *Voyage d'Ibn Batoutah*, II, p. 446; Tizengauzen, *op. cit.*, I, p. 241.

[33] M. Balard, *Gênes et l'Outre-Mer*, I: *Les Actes de Caffa du notaire Lamberto di Sambuceto 1289–1290*, Paris-La Haye, 1973. Contracts between traders in Kaffa and Tana are numerous.

[34] Pegolotti, *op. cit.*, p. 3.

traders brought with them furs and other northern produce, as well as Russian and Bulgarian grain. Tatar merchants are frequently mentioned in 14th- and 15th-century Russia, but their exact origin is still virtually unknown. We have as yet no studies concerning Saray merchants' activities beyond the borders of the town. It seems possible that Saray was primarily an important centre for consumer goods and the transit of merchandise. This suggestion perforce remains an impression rather than a conviction, inasmuch as I am unable to provide any proof.

Archaeologists take the view that New Saray attained the heights of its prosperity around the middle of the 14th century, in the reign of Khan Janibek.[35] The coinage of the Golden Horde dating from this period is both abundant and of fine quality.[36] The anonymous author of "The History of Sheik Uveiz" concurs with this interpretation of the history of the Golden Horde and its capital.[37] Nevertheless, I personally have some doubts concerning this system of periodization. The descriptions of Saray by Ibn battutah and by Al-Omari give pictures of a flourishing town, but they refer to the 1330s and early 1340s. According to both Arab and Russian sources, the Great Plague of 1347/1348 caused widespread ravages over all the territories of the Golden Horde. Ibn al Wardi records that 85,000 persons perished in the Crimea alone, and this figure strikes me as reasonable.[38] According to Russian annals, the epidemic produced a catastrophic death rate in Urgench, Astrakhan', Saray, and other towns of the Golden Horde among Muslims, Tatars, Armenians, Abkhazians, Jews, Circassians, and other races living in those parts.[39] Russian sources likewise tell of a recrudescence of the Plague in 1362. Starting from the South, within two years it engulfed the principalities of the basin of the Upper Volga.[40]

It is hard to imagine that Saray's period of prosperity went hand in hand with such a lethal epidemic. In view of this, I suspect that the

---

[35] Balodis, *op. cit.*, p. 8; Fedorov-Davydov, *op. cit.*, I, 1964, p. 8. On the depreciation in the value of the khans' coinage from the beginning of the 15th century, cf. A. G. Mukhamadiev, "Dva klada tatarskikh monet XV veka", in *Sovetskaia Arkheologiia*, II, 1966, pp. 260–261.

[36] *Ibid.*

[37] Tizengauzen, *op. cit.*, II, p. 101.

[38] Tizengauzen, *op. cit.*, I, p. 529; El-Aini, *op. cit.*, p. 530, note 1. Ibn-al-Wardi's account of the Black Plague in the Crimea; he received his reports while the plague was still rife.

[39] "Letopis' po Voskresenskomu Spisku", in *Polnoe sobranie Russkikh Letopisei* (PSRL), Vol. VII, S. Peterburg, 1856, p. 210.

[40] *Ibid.*, Vol. VIII, p. 13.

real zenith of Saray's fortunes occurred somewhat earlier than Soviet researchers suppose, in all probability during the first half of the 14th century.

We also know that the period of the two great epidemics just mentioned was followed by political disorders which led to a sudden decline in the power of the Golden Horde. The violent struggles between different groups of the Tatar aristocracy and the numerous pretenders to the throne of the khans then reached a pitch of intensity hitherto unknown. It was in the course of the 1360s that New Saray was walled round, in order to strengthen its defence against any assailants.[41]

It seems reasonable to assume a direct connection between the effects of the Plague and the troubles which afflicted the society of the Golden Horde. The once powerful nobles thereby lost a considerable number of their subjects, with a corresponding loss of revenue derived from this source. Access to the throne of the khan opened up ways towards the wealth accumulated by the sovereigns, from the taxes levied on the population etc. The epidemics also weakened the military power of the Horde. In 1380, the mirza Mamay, "the khan-maker", suffered a crushing defeat at the hands of Dmitrii Donskoi, Grand Prince of Muscovy. By this time, the khans were no longer able to ensure the safety of the more important lines of communication. In 1361, traffic between Russia and the Golden Horde had already been affected by the interruption of navigation on the Volga. With this, famine afflicted the peoples of the Horde territories, who were probably starved of the supply of Russian and Bulgarian grain on which they relied for their existence.[42]

In the summer of 1366, bandits from Novgorod the Great (known as Ushkuniki) appeared on the middle Volga and massacred large numbers of Muslim and Armenian merchants. These attacks were repeated in 1374 and 1375, when they penetrated as far as the outskirts of Bulgar, Saray, and towards Astrakhan' on the Volga delta, slaying numbers of Muslim traders in the process.[43] Security on the other main lines of communication was probably little better. The frequent changes of sovereign in Saray undoubtedly undermined their control over the State territory. During this same period there is a noticeable lack of interest in the trade with Tana on the part of the Venetians, as shown by the

---

[41] Fedorov-Davydov, *op. cit.*, I, 1964, p. 250. The wailed enclosure is dated in line with the Tatar coinage found *in situ*.

[42] "Moskovskii Letopisnyi Svod konca XV veka", in PSRL, XXV, Moskva, 1949, p. 181.

[43] *Ibid.*, pp. 189, 191.

poor quality of the *incanti* on the occasion of the annual departure of two or three galleys towards that port.[44] I can only surmise that the combination of plague, famine, and civil wars among the Horde led to a drastic reduction in the population of the Tatar state. It is probable that all this adversely affected the slave trade and the commerce of Tana, New Saray, and other towns of the Golden Horde. I find myself in fairly close agreement with Fedorov Davydov and the members of his expedition in placing the beginnings of the economic decline of New Saray at the time of the widespread disorders of the 1370s and 1380s, in other words some twenty to thirty years before the destruction of the Tatar capital in 1395 by Tamerlane's armies.[45] This is nothing more than an hypothesis, given that we have no information concerning the internal situation of Saray during the last thirty years of the 14th century. One may surmise that the reign of Khan Tokhtamysh (1379–1395) brought about a temporary improvement, but this pertains mainly to the first six years of this period. Tokhtamysh was a *protégé* of Tamerlane's and it was thanks to him that he acceded to the throne of the Golden Horde. He was powerful enough to restrain the force of the Tatar aristocracy and to reestablish for a time the suzerainty of the Horde in Russia. In 1382 he even set fire to Moscow.

But these were only passing triumphs. Overconfident of his military power, in 1385–1386 Tokhtamysh risked a quarrel with Tamerlane, who in 1391 inflicted on him his first serious reverse on the banks of the river Syr-Darya.[46] Four years later, Tamerlane organized a vast expedition against the Golden Horde. After crossing the Caucasus, ravaging the country as they went, the armies of the Conqueror pushed on into the plains of the Volga, crushing Tokhtamysh at the battle of the river Terek. According to Ibn-i-Arabšah, a well-informed chronicler, the various detachments of the invaders laid waste almost all the steppes occupied by the Golden Horde, burning and pillaging the towns, notably

---

[44] The following sources describe the difficult situation in Tana from 1369 onwards: F. Thiriet, *Registres des délibérations du Sénat de Venise concernant la Romanie*, Vol. I, Paris, 1958, pp. 474, 476, 486, 489, 498, 508, 523, 524, 540, 579, 588, 589; F. Thiriet, *Délibérations des Assemblées Vénitiennes concernant la Romanie*, Vol. II (1364–1464), Paris-La Haye, 1971, pp. 783, 933.

[45] Fedorov-Davydov, *op. cit.*, I, 1964. The author places the beginnings of the decline of the town around the end of the 1380s, during the reign of Khan Tokhtamysh. My personal view is that the process already began some ten years earlier.

[46] Tizengauzen, *op. cit.*, I, p. 456; Ibn-i-Arabšah, *op. cit.*, II, pp. 110–115; Nizam Ad-Din Chani, official chronicler, contemporary of Tamerlane.

Azak (Tana), Saray, Saradjuk, Uvek, and Hadji Tarkhan (Astrakhan'), as well as Kaffa and other settlements in the Crimea. Chami and El-Yezdi, the latter chronicler of Sakh Rukh, the son and successor of Tamerlane, both record that at Azak (Tana) the Tatars decided to massacre the miscreants (meaning the Christians, and hence the Italians) and to spare the Muslims. The descriptions of this invasion by these two authors do not differ in essentials from the account of Ibn-i-Arabšah. All of these writers emphasize the intensity and extent of the ravages and destruction perpetrated by the invaders, who carried off with them vast amounts of booty, chiefly in the form of slaves, livestock, cereals, silver, and other precious objects. In the words of El-Yezdi, Saray was "laid waste from top to bottom".[47] Here one should add that, at the turn of the 14th and especially in the course of the 15th century, the spread of famines, epidemics, and internecine strife combined to bring about the final collapse of the Golden Horde.

This led to the establishment of separate khanates, one in the Crimea, under the rule of the Ghirei dynasty, and another in Kazan'. Far to the East, in the basin of the Syr-Darya, the states of the Uzbeks began to emerge. With this, urban life disappeared from the steppes. Astrakhan', rebuilt after the disaster of 1395, was still only a small town one hundred years later. The sole commercial resource of this agglomeration was a salt-mine frequented by merchants from Russia; they also purchased small quantities of silk imported from the Caucasus and from Azerbaijan.[48]

The history of Tana in the 15th century remains somewhat obscure, for lack of source material. We do know that the Venetians and the Genoese used to stock up there with sturgeons and caviare.[49] The slave trade continued, though it would seem to have diminished gradually, especially the export of slaves to Christian countries, due to the depopulation of the Tatar steppes and to a variety of political events.[50] Outbreaks of famine and other disasters may have led to momentary

---

[47] Tizengauzen, *op. cit.*, I, pp. 465–470; II, pp. 118–122, 173–185.

[48] Di Messer Josafa Barbaro Gentil huomo Venetiano, "Il Viaggio della Tana", in *Biblioteka inostrannykh pisatelei o Rossii*, Vol. I, S. Peterburg, 1836, p. 94; "Il Viaggio del Magnifico M. Ambrosio Contarim 1473", *ibid.*, pp. 166–168.

[49] E. C. Skrzinskaia, "Storia della Tana", in *Studi Veneziani*, X, 1968, pp. 22–23; M. Berindel et G. Veinstein, "La Tana—Azac, de la présence Italienne l'emprise Ottomane (fin XIIIᵉ-milieu XVIᵉ siècle)", in *Turcica*, VIII/2, 1976, pp. 129–149. Both authors seem to me to overestimate the importance of trade in Tana during the 15th century.

[50] On the slave traffic in Tana, cf. the numerous studies by Ch. Verlinden.

rises in the slave traffic (as for example in 1427/1428), but these were probably only passing phenomena. The slave traffic was concentrated in Kaffa, at first Genoese and later Ottoman; but the slaves were recruited less from the Tatars than among the Caucasians. During the period of Turkish dominance, other slave trade markets—subsidiary to that in Kaffa—operated also in Azak, Kerch, Copa, on the Kuban river,[51] and certainly in Akkerman as well.

From about 1470 onwards, the slaves exported from the Black Sea basin to Egypt and the countries of the Ottoman Empire were predominantly Ukrainians, Poles, Russians, and Caucasians.[52] After 1475, it was Azak that became the leading outpost of Turkish trade with Russia.[53]

With the end of the 15th century, New Saray disappears completely from the historical scene.[54] The remnants of its population who survived so many disasters probably dispersed and settled elsewhere. There was no longer any political power in the area either willing or able to ensure the safety of the trade routes or lines of communication. The huge town (or what remained of it) was shorn of the very basis of its existence. Nor did things change much with the capture of Astrakhan' in 1569 by the Russians. It was not until the 17th and 18th century that waves of urban and rural colonization saw the settlement in the steppes of a fresh population pursuing a far more lively economic activity than their predecessors.

---

[51] J. M. Ramos, *Andanças e Viajes de Pero Tafur por diversas partes del mundo avidos (1435–1439) par J. M. Ramos*, Biblioteca Classica, Vol. 265, Madrid, 1934, pp. 120–128, contains a description of Kaffa and Tana. Also *L 'Egypte au commencement du XVe siècle d'après le Traité d'Emmanuel Piloti de Crête (incipit 1420)*, Cairo, 1950, pp. 14–17, 62, 63, 64.; deals with the problems of the traffic of slaves from countries of the Black Sea basin, especially Kaffa; cf. A. N. Poliak, *Feudalism in Egypt, Syria, Palestine and the Lebanon 1250–1900*, London, 1939, p. 1ff.; the author emphasizes that in the 15th and 16th centuries the Circassians were far more numerous than the Tatars among the Mamelukes of Egypt, in contrast to the situation prevailing in the 13th and 14th centuries. Cf. A. Darrag, *L'Egypte sous le règne de Barsbay 825–841/1422–1438*, Damas, 1961, pp. 320–324; H. Inalčik, *The Ottoman Empire. The Classical Age 1300–1600*, London, 1973, pp. 130–131.

[52] M. Małowist, *Kaffa—kolonia genueńska na Krymie i problem wschodni w latach 1453–1475*, Warszawa, 1947, pp. 50–55, 80, 84, 103.

[53] V. E. Syroečkovskii, *Gosti-Surožanie*, Moskva-Leningrad, 1935, pp. 47ff.

[54] Afanasii Nikitin, *op. cit.*, p. 9. The author records that he passed through Saray (probably New Saray) in 1466, but gives no description of the town. Nor does Barbaro or Contarini, although they knew the region well. One must conclude that, by the 1480s, Saray was no longer considered of any importance.

CHAPTER SIXTEEN

THE FOUNDATIONS OF EUROPEAN EXPANSION IN AFRICA IN THE 16TH CENTURY. EUROPE, MAGHREB AND WESTERN SUDAN*

The great Arab conquests of the 8th and 9th centuries did not completely interrupt the economic exchanges between the northern and southern shores of the Mediterranean. Indeed, there can be little doubt but that, in subduing Spain and Sicily, the Arabs tended rather to promote the flow of goods between these territories and those of North Africa. Nor, despite religious antagonisms, were the contacts between the Maghreb and southern France and Italy broken off, although—at least until the second half of the 10th century—it was primarily the Arab merchants and Jews living in Arab countries who played the leading role in trade and navigation in the western sector of the Mediterranean basin. Towards the end of the 10th century, we find intense activity on the part of the citizens of southern Italian towns such as Bari, Amalfi, Salerno, and Gaeta, reinforced in the 11th century by those of Pisa and Genoa. Thenceforth, the process undergoes a continuous increase. During the 12th and 13th centuries, Italian and Catalan merchants, later followed by those from the south of France, assert their economic, political, and military supremacy over the adepts of Islam—a supremacy largely boosted by the development of the Christian states of the Mediterranean basin, notably Catalonia, the kingdoms of Naples and Sicily, and the Italian republics of Pisa, Genoa, and Venice. The collapse of the caliphate and the unremitting internecine feuds in the Arab world enabled the Christians to assume a dominant position in navigation and seaborne trade. Not even the successes of western Islam, associated with the conquests of the Almoravides in the 11th and those of the Almohades in the 12th century, succeeded in impeding this process for more than a brief while.

* Originally published as "Les fondements de l'expansion européenne en Afrique au XVᵉ siècle: Europe, Maghreb et Soudan occidental", in *Acta Poloniae Historica*, 18, 1968, pp. 155–179. Translation from French by Robin Kimball.

The series of great empires across the Maghreb collapsed very rapidly, and this was also true of the Moroccan state of the Merinides in the 13th and 14th centuries. It is worth recalling that it was precisely during the period between the 10th and 13th centuries that western and southwestern Europe underwent a relatively swift process of economic and political development, as a result of which the balance of force in the Mediterranean basin swung more and more in favour of the Christian powers—a trend evidenced by the state of commercial and navigational relations. It was now no longer the Moslems but the Italians and the Catalans who gained the upper hand, reducing the former to the role of customers and suppliers of merchandise. True, the acts of piracy practised by the Moslems dealt painful blows at the Christians, especially from the 13th century onwards; but the latter dealt scarcely less brutally with their adversaries. The supremacy of the Christians in the field of navigation was also demonstrated by the fact that the transport of many of the goods which the Maghreb exchanged for produce from the Moslem Near East was effected by ships belonging to the Europeans. The same applied to the transport of passengers from the western to the eastern parts of Islam, a situation which opened the door to all manner of abuses on the part of the captains of Christian ships. In fact, they often confiscated the possessions of their Moslem passengers, whom they then sold off as slaves—a policy which inevitably led to reprisals against European merchants who found themselves at the time in one or other of the Islamic states. For the Christians, this type of transport represented first and foremost a source of additional revenue.

In the virtual absence of quantitative data, it is impossible to state with any exactitude to what extent the trade between the Maghreb and Europe represented a rewarding proposition for the interested parties. Inasmuch as it invariably picked up each time, even after the fiercest of conflicts, it seems fair to assume that the traffic brought in considerable profits. During the 13th and 14th centuries, merchants from Italy, Castile, Sicily, and the French Midi, plus their agents, formed widespread and often numerous colonies in the ports of North Africa. In some cases, so-called *fonducs* were placed at their disposal. The European merchants also enjoyed wide fiscal and juridical privileges. Beginning with the 13th century, Tunis became the main centre of European commerce in North Africa. Up till the 14th century, the Genoese likewise played a leading role, together with merchants from Catalonia and especially Barcelona and Majorca, from Marseilles, and many other centres.[1] European merchants were also regular visitors to other ports in the Maghreb. Every year, Catalans and Italians made regular stays in the ports of the sultanate of Tlemçen, notably in Honein and Oran, but also in Algiers, Bougie (today Bejaia), and Bône. Tripoli was in close relations with Sicily, southern Italy, and Venice, as well as with Catalonia and Majorca. During the 14th century, both the Venetians and the Florentines strengthened their positions in the Maghreb. It is also important to stress the great importance of Ceuta in the 13th and early 14th century. European traders were engaged in lively commercial activity there, especially those from Barcelona, Perpignan, Montpellier, and other towns of what was then Catalonia, together with merchants from Seville, Jerez, Marseilles, and, outnumbering them all, the "omnipresent" Genoese who, until at least the early 14th century, had their own *fonduc* in Ceuta and continued to reside there until the town was captured by the Portuguese in 1415. Besides all this, some Europeans used to visit the Moroccan ports on the Atlantic coast: Anfa (Casablanca), Arzila, Salé, Larache, Azemmour, and Safi. Even in the 15th century, the Genoese were still highly active in Massa.

During the 13th and 14th centuries, Majorca was an especially important trading centre in commercial exchanges with the Maghreb, serving as a relay point for traffic in the western Mediterranean. Its population, of Catalan and Aragonese origin, together with numbers of wealthy Jewish merchants and even some Moroccans who had settled there, not only served as middlemen in the trade between the two shores of the Mediterranean but deployed considerable initiative of their own. Their points of contact comprised, at the very least, the area extending from Bougie to the ports on the Atlantic coast. In concert with the Catalans, they penetrated into the interior of Morocco and, at the dawn of the 14th century, agents of Majorcan and Catalan societies were installed in Fez, the capital of the Merinides.[2] In the period between April 1314

---

[1] A. E. Sayous, *Le commerce des Européens à Tunis. Depuis le XIIe siècle jusqu'à la fin du XVIe*, Paris, 1929, pp. 25–26.

[2] This description is based on the classic study by Heyd, *Histoire du commerce du au Moyen Age*, Vols. I and II, Leipzig, 1923; the ancient works of Mas-Lattrie; the work by Sayous cited above; that of Ch. E. Dufourcq, *L'Espagne Catalane et le Maghreb aux XIIIe et XIVe siècles*, Paris, 1966; the study by P. Vilar, *La Catalogne dans l'Espagne moderne*, Vol. I, Paris, 1962; the two works of R. S. Lopez, *Studi sull' economia genovese*, Torino, 1936, and *Settecento anni fa, il ritorno all'oro nell'occidente duecentesco*, Napoli, 1955; finally, *l'Histoire du commerce de Marseille*, Vols. I–III, Paris, 1949–1951.

and March 1315, some 10 Majorcan vessels put in at Ceuta, prior to continuing their voyage to the Atlantic ports, while other ships made the trip direct. In 1328, at least 20 Majorcan vessels set sail for the central Barbary coast.[3] At the same time, one should bear in mind that the Majorcan ships were of comparatively small tonnage and as such were unable to compete with those from Barcelona, and even less with those of the Genoese. In Majorca's trade with North Africa, Jewish merchants played a highly important role thanks to their close contacts with their numerous coreligionists in the Maghreb, some of whom were relatives—a not insignificant factor in the circumstances. According to one document dating from 1327—cited by Dufourcq—the Majorcan Jews, who were highly active in the territory of Tlemçen, entrusted their goods to Moslems from the most outlying regions of the Maghreb, who delivered these wares to the interior of the country, and paid for them in cash only on their return to Tlemçen. The French historian just cited lays particular stress on the economic ties which bound the Jews of Majorca to their coreligionists in Tlemçen. It is also worth noting that, according to Dufourcq, in 1247 King James I (the Conqueror), sovereign of the kingdom of Aragon, Catalonia, and Majorca, accorded his special protection in this island to two Jewish families from Sijilmassa, and gave permission to all Jews anxious to leave that region to settle in Majorca, Valencia, or Barcelona. Dufourcq assumes, no doubt rightly, that the king took this decision in the hope of increasing the supplies of gold from western Sudan which reached the Mediterranean and Atlantic coasts mainly via Sijilmassa, situated on the borders of southern Morocco and the Sahara.[4] Apart from the Majorcan Jews, those from Aragon, with the strong backing of their sovereigns, themselves anxious to develop trade links, displayed remarkable initiative in their contacts with North Africa during the 13th century.

The present state of research affords us little insight into the contacts that existed between the Arabs in Spain and the Maghreb during the 13th and 14th centuries, most of the relevant sources having been destroyed. We do know, however, that in the second half of the 14th century, and even earlier, the ports of the kingdom of Murcia such as

On the subject of Ceuta, cf. R. Ricard, *Études sur l'histoire des Portugais au Maroc*, Coimbra, 1955, pp. 10, 11.

[3] Ch. E. Dufourcq, *op. cit.*, pp. 68, 69, 139, 142, 144.

[4] *Ibid.*, p. 143; M. Małowist, *Wielkie państwa Sudanu zachodniego w późnym średniowieczu*, Warszawa, 1964, p. 238.

Alicante, together with Malaga and Almeria in Andalusia, were in relations with towns in the Maghreb. In the 15th and 16th centuries, textiles from Granada and Valencia were on sale in markets in the Maghreb, and even as far off as Timbuktu and Gao.[5] It is natural to assume that trade relations with Africa were far more intense during the period of Arab domination in Spain and Portugal than after its decline, at which point a large number of Moslems abandoned the Peninsula. This view of things, incidentally, is confirmed by El-Bekri and Indrisi.[6]

It is difficult to provide much concrete evidence concerning the presence of Portuguese merchants in Africa during the 13th and 14th centuries. During the 1230s, the Portuguese conquered the Algarve. At that time, this region, which to this day constitutes the most southerly province of the country, contained a particularly large Jewish and Moslem population. It is all the more regrettable that the archives of the principal ports of this region, such as Lagos, Tavira, and Faro, should have been destroyed before anyone became interested in the doubtless precious information that they contained.[7] The geographical position of the ports of the Algarve, and even Lisbon, added to any number of other reasons, together predestined this region to participate in the trade with the Maghreb, and especially with the territories lying to the southwest of the Straits of Gibraltar. Unfortunately, such details as are at our disposal on this score are at most fragmentary and often indirect.

The Portuguese conquest of the Algarve was not followed by a wave of emigration on the part of the Moslem or Jewish population. The latter, who enjoyed wide tolerance throughout Portugal, were to exercise a strong influence on the royal court during the 13th and 14th centuries. In fact, the Jewish communities installed in the country represented an important source of revenue for the Portuguese crown. There can be no doubt that both the Jews and the Moslems, as well as Jewish merchants, few in number in the early stages, all maintained economic relations with the Maghreb, as evidenced by the large amounts of North

---

[5] Ch. De La Roncière, *La découverte de l'Afrique au Moyen Age*, Vol. III, Le Caire, 1927, pp. VIff.; *ibid.*, Vol. I, 1925, p. 163; Léon l'Africain, *Description de l'Afrique*, Vol. II, Paris, 1956, pp. 414, 415.

[6] *Description de l'Afrique septentrionale par Abou-Obeid-El-Bekri*, transl. by Mac Guckin De Slane, Paris, 1965, pp. 46, 47, 67, 117–120, 136, 161, etc. On the trade between the Algarve and Africa in the 12th and early 13th centuries, cf. A. Iria, *Descobrimentos Portugueses. O Algarve e os Descobrimentos*, Vol. II, Lisboa, 1956, pp. 248–253, 254.

[7] A. Iria, *op. cit.*, p. 4ff.

African coinage found in Portugal, and especially in the Algarve, during the 13th and 14th centuries. During this same period, the kings of Portugal banned both Moslems and Jews who were their subjects from visiting the "countries of the Moors" without special permission.[8] The very promulgation of such a decree proves that such departures took place, and were presumably not so rare, given that the Portuguese authorities, probably on both fiscal and military grounds, felt obliged to intervene.

According to Zurara, the eminent Portuguese chronicler of the mid-15th century, every year the Moors from Morocco used to buy in the Algarve large quantities of fruit which they paid for in gold currency, mainly in doubloons minted in Tunis, as well as in Tlemçen, Sijilmassa, and Marrakesh.[9] There can thus be no doubt that the Portuguese had long since been in personal and commercial relations with the inhabitants of the Maghreb, and that the ports of that area were well known to them. Nor should we forget that one of the pillars of the Portuguese economy was coastal fishing along the whole of its shores. It was probably the fishermen from the Algarve, who dealt mainly in sardines and tunny-fish, who came closest to the shores of the Maghreb.[10]

The facts just presented demonstrate beyond all doubt that, during the 13th and 14th centuries, large numbers of traders and navigators from the Iberian Peninsula, the Balearic islands, the south of France, and Italy undertook frequent voyages to North Africa and were well versed in the trade of that region, whose shores they knew well. If I emphasize this factor, it is because it throws a revealing light on the beginnings of European expansion, first in the Maghreb and subsequently in West Africa. The situation outlined above would seem to indicate that the exchange of merchandise between the Europeans and the peoples of the Moslem countries was of tremendous importance to both parties. On the other band, if we were to judge solely from the goods most

[8] *Ibid.*, pp. 29, 41, 248, 295, 343, 356, 389, 390. Iria records that in the 14th century Portuguese merchants resided in Ceuta, but does not indicate the source of this affirmation; *ibid.*, p. 291f.

[9] *Ibid.*, p. 388. Fragment of the *Cronica do Conde Dom Pedro de Meneses*, written by Gomes Eanes da Zurara towards the middle of the 15th century, concerning events around 1418.

[10] P. De Cenival et Th. Monod, *Description de la côte d'Afrique de Ceuta au Sénégal par Valentin Fernandes (1506-1507)*, Paris, 1938, p. 26. The author writes that Portuguese fishermen penetrated as far as the mouth of the Mamora on the Atlantic coast, to the north of Morocco, where they had to beware of attacks by the Moors.

commonly involved, we should hardly arrive at the same conclusion. Thus, Genoa, which was probably the Maghreb's most important trading partner, used to buy cereals, and especially sheepskin and goatskin, alum, and wax, the only items of value from the Barbary states. On the Maugrabin side, Tunis disposed in the 14th century of the widest assortment of goods for export. Besides the merchandise just mentioned, exports included indigo, olives, horses, cotton, textiles, carpets, coral, arms, and black slaves. Much of this merchandise was dispatched to Egypt on board Italian and Catalan ships, but the greater part of it was finally destined for ports in Europe. The choice of products imported from Europe by the Maghreb was somewhat more varied. Sayous has reported that, in the 14th and early 15th centuries, Tunisian imports from Europe included cereals (in times of poor harvest), Asian spices, wine, woollen, linen, and silk textiles, decorative glass objects, paper, metals (especially copper), wooden and metal products (again mainly copper), jewels, and silver. In the 13th and 14th centuries, the situation was roughly similar in Tlemçen (albeit on a more modest scale than in Tunis), in Ceuta, in Algiers, and the other ports of the Maghreb on both Mediterranean and Atlantic coasts.[11]

It is not easy to assess the balance of trade between the towns of the Maghreb and those of southern Europe. All the evidence suggests that the balance between North Africa and Genoa and Venice differed from that between the Maghreb and the Catalans, and even more so with the people of Marseilles and the Portuguese, both of whose economies were still fragile.[12] The Genoese and the Florentines, who visited the Maghreb from the 14th century onward, like the Venetians somewhat later, all offered a wide range of very expensive wares, such as Asian spices, metals, silver, copper (in especially high demand in Africa), and superior quality textiles from western Europe and from Italy. By comparison, the position of the Catalans, Castilians, and Majorcans

---

[11] A. E. Sayous, *op. cit.*, pp. 86, 87, 88; J. Heers, *Gênes au XVᵉ siècle*, Paris, 1961, pp. 64, 67; R. S. Lopez, *Studi sull'economia genovese*, pp. 30, 31; Ch. E. Dufourcq, *op. cit.*, pp. 543–548; *Histoire du commerce de Marseille*, Vol. II, p. 110.

[12] R. S. Lopez, *op. cit.*, pp. 30–33. This scholar is of the opinion that in their trade with the Maghreb the Genoese purchased only small quantities of merchandise and did not invest large sums. He also believes that in the 14th and 15th centuries they lost their outposts there—a view which, in the light of the relevant sources, raises certain objections. At the same time, the economic crisis during this period had appreciably weakened the position of the Catalan and Provençal merchants.

was less favourable, let alone that of the merchants from Marseilles and from Portugal. It is, however, possible that certain important wares from the Maghreb did not interest certain traders. Castile, the kingdom of Aragon, and Portugal, and to a lesser extent Catalonia also, already had extensive sheep farms in the 13th century, but their textile industries were still backward. Consequently, they had no need of large quantities of Maghreb wool, even though we know that Catalonia and Majorca did in fact purchase certain qualities of the latter.[13] In the same way, both Castile and Portugal had their own supplies of wax in considerable quantities. Apart from this, the import and export capabilities of the Maghreb region varied from one country to another. Tunisia, the wealthiest country in the area from the 13th century onward, imported European and Asiatic merchandise in far larger quantities than, say, countries such as Morocco, Tripoli, or Algeria, which were much poorer. In fact, some of the goods imported were not even for local consumption but destined for re-export to other regions. Tunis itself, an important centre for the production of woollen textiles and leather goods, also furnished numerous wares for overseas export. The situation was subject to periodic modifications as a result of the poor harvests which occurred frequently on both shores of the Mediterranean. We know, for instance, that both Morocco and even Tunisia, despite its more favourable situation, sometimes found themselves forced to import cereals from Europe, whereas in years of abundant harvests they themselves exported large quantities of grain.

Dufourcq's fragmentary statistics concerning the exchange of goods between the Catalan lands—including Majorca—and the North African countries would not seem to be particularly reliable, and are in any case confined to only a brief period of years.[14] By contrast, Dufourcq inspires much more conviction when he asserts that the trade balance between Catalonia and the Maghreb in the 13th and early 14th century was often even.[15] From this it might seem fair to conclude that the same was true of traffic between the Provence and the North African countries, but this is no more than a conjecture. At this point one

---

[13] J. Klein, *The Mesta. A Study on Spains' Economic History*, Cambridge, Mass., 1920, p. 32ff., p. 299ff.

[14] Ch. E. Dufourcq, *op. cit.*, pp. 68, 545.

[15] *Ibid., op. cit.*, pp. 552–555. The author estimates that the annual value of the goods imported from the Maghreb by the Catalan countries was often equal to that of the merchandise they exported there.

should add that, during the 14th century, Marseilles ceased trading with Morocco (or, to be more exact, was eliminated from this trade), while yet maintaining contact with Tunis, Bougie, Collo, and neighbouring ports. From about mid-century, both Catalonia and Majorca found themselves on the decline, whereas Barcelona continued to display a lively interest in North Africa. The Genoese engaged increasingly in trade with Castile and Portugal, but displayed rather less activity in the Maghreb, though their presence in both Tunisia and Morocco at this time is established beyond doubt. In Tunisia, it is henceforth the Florentines who assume the leading role. During the first half of the century, the agents of the banking and commercial institutions of the Bardi, Peruzzi, and Acciaiuoli families take up residence in the capital of the Sultanate, and it is the latter who maintain their presence the longest.[16] The economic crisis, which grew particularly severe from the middle of the 14th century onwards, and whose consequences dealt a painful blow to the Catalans and the Provençaux, did not spare the Florentines either, their commercial institutes, to which we have just referred, going bankrupt around the middle of the century. For a long time to come, the Venetians showed very little interest in the Maghreb, and it was only around 1440 that, following the example of the Florentines, they too established a line of regular communication, provided by the *galee di Barbaria*, which indicates an increase in trade on the routes connecting Maghreb-Florence and Maghreb-Venice.[17]

Available sources do not enable us to assess the state of the trade balance between North Africa and Europe. We can only assume that it was an unstable one, depending largely on the state of the harvests on either shore of the Mediterranean. At the same time, it seems highly probable that the balance of trade tended to be in favour of Genoa and other Italian towns, and perhaps also of Portugal, Andalusia, and Sicily, especially in those years in which they exported grain to the

---

[16] *Histoire du commerce de Marseille*, Vol. 1, p. 365, Vol. II, pp. 98–110; A. E. Sayous, *op. cit.*, pp. 60, 63, 69, 74; P. Vilar, *La Catalogne...*, Vol. 1, p. 461ff., 480, 538ff.; R. S. Lopez, *Studi sull'economia genovese*, p. 19; J. Heers, *op. cit.*, p. 65. The author stresses the fact that in the 15th century the gold imported to Genoa from the Maghreb was still vital to the former. Valentin Fernandes (*Description de la côte d'Afrique de Ceuta au Sénégal*, p. 38, cf. note 10 supra) recalls the sojourns of the Genoese in Massa, which, even at the turn of the 15th/16th centuries, was still an important Moroccan port on the Atlantic coast.

[17] A. E. Sayous, *op. cit.*, pp. 69, 82.

Maghreb.[18] Apart from this, both the Italians and the Catalans secured additional revenues by taking charge of part of the transport along the North African coasts and also part of the transport of goods and passengers between the Maghreb and Alexandria. Each year, merchants and scholars from the Maghreb arrived in this vast port on board Christian vessels. True, some of them made the voyage by Maghreb ships but, when the time came to leave, they usually embarked on Italian or Catalan vessels.[19] It thus seems likely that they sold their own boats to the Egyptians who suffered from an acute shortage of shipping and were unable to remedy this situation for lack of the necessary timber.

I purposely avoid any detailed description of the continuous acts of piracy perpetrated by Christians and Moslems alike. Prisoners on both shores of the Mediterranean were numerous. Some of them, however, were subsequently bought back in return for a ransom, a fact which contributed to the circulation of coinage and precious metals between the Christian countries and the Barbary states, but it is impossible to say who derived the greater advantage from these transactions. The situation doubtless fluctuated widely, depending on the measures deployed by the privateers of the interested parties and on the means of defence at the disposal of the vessels attacked.

The picture just painted gives only a summary account of the main aspect of the traffic between North Africa and the European shores of the Mediterranean, namely the Sudanese gold which found its way into southern Europe. Many years have elapsed since Marc Bloch first turned his attention to this problem. Estimating that this gold began arriving in North African ports not later than the beginning of the 12th century, he expressed the view that in the 14th century—along with Hungary and probably Asian sources—(western) Sudan was the main supplier of gold to Europe. F. Braudel and R. Lopez likewise attach considerable weight to the importation of Sudanese gold into the Mediterranean basin.[20] It should at once be noted that Sudanese gold arrived in this region even before the 12th century, though its

---

[18] Cf. note 9.

[19] Subhi Y. Labib, *Handelsgeschichte Ägyptens im Spätmittelalter (1171–1517)*, Wiesbaden, 1965, pp. 100, 101.

[20] M. Bloch, "Le problème de l'or au Moyen Age", in *Annales d'Histoire Économique et Sociale*, 1933, 19, *passim*; F. Braudel, "Monnaies et civilisation, de l'or du Soudan à l'argent d'Amérique", in *Annales E.S.C.*, 1946, fasc. 1, *passim; idem, La Méditerranée et le monde méditerranéen à l'époque de Philippe II*, IIe éd., Paris, 1966, Vol. I, p. 166, Vol. II, pp. 431, 432.

export increased appreciably later, at a time when the political situation in western Sudan grew more stable under the Mali empire, whose economy was closely tied to that of the Maghreb and of Egypt.[21] At the same time, Marc Bloch and other western historians failed to observe that in the 13th and 14th centuries both Bohemia and Hungary also played a role of considerable importance in the production not only of silver but of gold as well. In spite of all this, medieval Europe evidently lacked sufficient supplies of its own gold, a shortcoming that made itself especially keenly felt during the period of its rapid development which culminated in the 13th century.

Towards the middle of that century, the ever-increasing scale of commercial exchanges compelled northern Italy to adopt gold coinage: first the Venetian and Genoese ducat and subsequently the florin. These coins were also introduced in other European countries and soon became indispensable for all important transactions. This demonstrates that, towards the mid-l3th century and ensuing decades, the gold reserves, first in northern and central Italy and then in other regions, were sufficiently large to encourage such an experiment and justify putting it into practice.

Ever since the time of Henri Pirenne, historians have devoted serious attention to the problem posed by the exchange of precious metals between Christian Europe and the Moslem East in medieval times, and the extreme importance which this factor exercised on the economies of the regions involved. At the same time, our ideas on the subject have undergone great changes in the course of the past few decades. The hypotheses advanced by the great Belgian scholar have not been confirmed in the event, and the problems raised by such matters as gold and silver reserves and coinage circulation have since formed the object of exhaustive studies and numerous debates. The merit of having introduced the subject of Sudanese gold into these discussions belongs primarily to Marc Bloch, F. Braudel, S. Bolin, and R. Lopez. In recent years, the problem has captured the attention of more and more historians. The interdependence of Europe, the Moslem countries of the Mediterranean basin, and western Sudan in respect of their monetary situation and precious metal reserves is by now established beyond all doubt, even though numerous elements in the puzzle are still missing

---

[21] M. Małowist, *op. cit.*, pp. 239ff.

and prevent us from gaining an exact idea of the overall situation and the periodic changes to which it was liable.

In an article recently published, Watson has attempted to provide a synthesis of all these factors.[22] He bases his conclusions mainly on the ratio of the value of gold to that of silver, and in so doing distinguishes several phases. He points out that in the 10th century the silver mines in Afghanistan were in full flood, yet in the 11th century the Moslem countries gradually ceased minting silver coinage, or at least considerably reduced its value. This process ultimately encompassed the entire Moslem world, from the borders of India to those of Spain. In this period, the coinage minted was mainly gold, together with small change made of copper, lead, and iron, whose value was negligible. Watson is probably right in suggesting that this phenomenon was brought about not only by the loss of the mines in Transoxiana and the reflux of silver towards India, but also by the export of this metal to Europe, demonstrated *inter alia* by the numerous treasures of silver dirhems unearthed by archaeologists in southern and eastern Europe during the 19th and 20th centuries. The value of gold in relation to that of silver varied from one country to another, and in Europe the rate of the latter was more favourable than in the Moslem world. Beginning with the 1170s, the situation began undergoing certain changes, though these did not become really evident until the 13th century. At this time, the Moslems again began minting large quantities of silver coinage, probably as a result of imports of this metal from China and from Europe. Watson surmises that the Crusaders brought large quantities of silver to the Near East to meet their own needs in Syria and Palestine, and that they perhaps exported certain quantities of gold of African origin. It should be added that the Levantine trade, which had begun developing in the 11th century, in particular the import of spices and of silk into southern and western Europe, greatly contributed to the flow of silver eastwards on into the 12th century. Watson also cites sources according to which the silver exported to the Maghreb was there exchanged for gold imported from the Sudan. Towards the beginning of the century, numbers of mints in southern France began striking silver coins, known as *millarès*, modelled on the dinars of the Almohade dynasty. These coins, which were exported to Bougie, Ceuta, Oran, and Tlemçen,

---

[22] A. M. Watson, "Back to Gold—and Silver", in *Economic History Review*, Vol. XX, 1967, No. 1, pp. 1–34.

bore an Arab inscription dating from the time of the Almohades which read "There is no God save Allah, Mahomet is his prophet, and Mahdi is our leader". The bishops of Languedoc and of Provence, as well as the counts of Toulouse and the kings of Aragon, granted their minters special concessions for striking these coins.[23] The *millarès*, exported in large quantities to the Maghreb, circulated as legal currency there and—according to Watson—greatly boosted the flow of Sudanese gold towards Europe whence, in the 13th century, a sizeable quantity of it found its way back to Egypt and Asia.

This reflux of silver is also characteristic of Genoa, where we witness the same process in the second half of the 14th and throughout the 15th century. In many European countries, silver coinage rapidly depreciated in value during the 14th century. I would not ascribe this process solely to the reflux of silver towards the East. One other important factor was the decline of the mining industry in Europe, the more so since this went hand in hand with a rise in the trade of goods destined for the less well-off sections of the population, namely cheaper wares requiring payment in coinage better corresponding to their worth. There can be no doubt that in many European countries the standard of living of the broad masses of the population attained a higher level from the mid-14th century onward, and that it subsequently underwent little change for some one hundred years to come.

To return to Watson's article, one may question whether the import of Sudanese gold into Europe in the 12th and 13th centuries, by virtue of the exchange of currency and merchandise, was really as extensive as the author supposes. The scale of trade between the Maghreb and Europe such as we have just outlined does not support such a supposition. That silver coinage was exported from Europe to North Africa is beyond dispute. On the other hand, neither the notarial acts of Marseilles nor other sources of similar origin contain any mention of the import of gold from overseas, whereas in the 13th century Marseilles merchants themselves exported gold to the Maghreb on more than one occasion. In Barcelona, the situation was similar, despite the fact that, in the 13th and 14th centuries, the Catalonian capital occupied a stronger position

---

[23] *Ibid.*, pp. 7–9, 11–14; Ch. E. Dufourcq, *op. cit.*, p. 31. An extremely interesting contribution which highlights the mentality of the leading feudal ecclesiastics and laymen at the time of the Crusades, viz. in the period of increased religious zeal.

in traffic with the Maghreb than did Marseilles.[24] In the 13th and early 14th centuries, Europe suffered from a shortage of precious metals, and it seems fair to assume that such Sudanese gold as it received from the exchange of goods and currencies arrived in only limited quantities, which were seized on and exploited primarily by those countries and towns which, directly or indirectly, exported to the Maghreb such goods as were most in demand there. First and foremost among these was Genoa, together in all probability with Florence and Venice, Majorca and Andalusia, and Portugal, the latter often exporting large quantities of fruit and cereals destined for North African shores. At the same time, Lopez, and more recently Dufourcq, have called attention to one other means by which Sudanese gold found its way into Europe, pointing out that, beginning in the 12th century, the sovereigns of Catalonia, Majorca, and Sicily often compelled the Maghreb sultanates to pay their tribute in gold currency. The latter were prepared to pay vast sums, not only to guarantee their security against attacks from their increasingly powerful adversaries, but also in return for permission to recruit in their countries, especially in Catalonia, the mercenaries whom they constantly needed to fight their own internecine feuds.[25]

It was thus by these means, and also through the intermediary of the mercenaries themselves, that significant quantities of gold found their way to the Iberian Peninsula, Majorca, and Sicily. Commercial exchanges subsequently promoted the diffusion of this gold, not only to other countries of the Mediterranean basin, but also to lands in

---

[24] *Histoire du commerce de Marseille*, Vol. I, p. 175; Vol. III, p. 110. The export of gold and gold currency in the 13th century is mentioned, together with the export of silver coinage. On the other hand, there is no trace of gold imports, not even towards the end of the 14th century. Cf. also Ch. E. Dufourcq, *op. cit.*, p. 170.

[25] R. S. Lopez, *Settecento anni fa. Il Ritorno all'oro nell'Occidente duecentesco*, Napoli, 1955, p. 19ff.; Ch. E. Dufourcq, *op. cit.*, pp. 181, 277, 317, 321, 322, 326, 374, 558ff. In 1304, the Merinide sultan of Morocco, Abu-Jakub, paid 10,000 gold dinars to James II ("the Just"), king of Aragon and Catalonia, who in return concluded an alliance with the sultan and authorized him to recruit mercenaries. This represented an immense success for the king of Aragon. The Hohenstaufens, the Angevins, and the Aragonese dynasty which reigned in Sicily from 1282 onwards frequently forced the sultans of Tunis to pay them tribute. The kings of Aragon also obtained from the sultans the right to collect a part of the customs dues which Catalan merchants paid in Maugrabin ports. While the Arab sovereigns showed considerable delay in paying these tributes, they were still a source of very important revenue for the contracting parties. According to Ch. E. Dufourcq (*op. cit.*, p. 562), in the course of the years 1276 to 1331, these tributes represented up to 10%, and possibly even more, of the total revenues of the Aragonese court. For their part, the sultans also derived handsome profits from their trade with the states belonging to this dynasty.

western and northern Europe. There is no doubt that it was primarily
the gold previously imported by the Maghreb from western Sudan that
represented at that time almost the only source of the metal in North
Africa. It should also be remembered that, probably from as early as the
9th, 10th, and 11th centuries, the Moslem countries already received
Sudanese gold—extracted from auriferous sand, and known to the Arabs
as *al-tibr*—from Ghana, while from the 13th and 14th centuries gold
also found its way to Fez and the ports of Morocco and Tlemçen, having
passed via Mali, Djenné, Timbuktu, Ualate, Teghase, and Sijilmassa. The
other caravan routes, which traversed the Sahara further east, linked
Algeria and Tunisia with Gao, an important centre of the gold trade
in the eastern part of the bend of the Niger. From Tripoli, other routes
passed through Gadames towards the towns of Hausa and the region of
lake Chad. All these routes were concerned in the flow of gold towards
the North. In many cases, craftsmen established in the Saharan oases
and near its northern borders used gold in the manufacture of jewels,
which they probably sold for considerable profits. In the 14th century,
following the fall of Sijilmassa, the oases of Tuat and that of Uargla
situated further east played an important part in the traffic of Sudanese
gold destined for the Maghreb, Egypt, and the European countries of
the Mediterranean basin.[26]

The export of gold was a vital factor in the social and economic life
of the upper Niger regions, enabling them as it did to acquire extensive
stocks of Saharan salt essential to their existence. According to certain
mid-15th century sources, gold and silver were at that time of equal
value in western Sudan. This strikes us as quite probable, inasmuch as
the lands of the northern savannah were completely devoid of white-
metal reserves, which had to be imported from the North, whereas
they disposed of large quantities of gold, which served little purpose
in their weak economy and was mainly destined for export. The ratio
in the price of gold to silver and its relatively low value rendered it
an export item of predilection, and this export trade was organized
mainly by the Moslems.[27] It is impossible to say whether the value of
gold and silver in the upper Niger region remained constant in the 13th
and 14th centuries and up till the middle of the 15th, but this is by no

---

[26] M. Małowist, *op. cit.*, pp. 238–245, 297–300; R. Mauny, *Tableau géographique de
l'Ouest Africain au Moyen Age,* Dakar, 1961, pp. 426–435.

[27] M. Małowist, *op. cit.*, p. 276.

means impossible. However, I consider that, from the viewpoint of the Maghreb merchants, gold from the Sudan was not dear by comparison with the price it fetched in the Mediterranean basin, and that its transport in that direction, notwithstanding all the difficulties it encountered, brought in immense revenues to the Maugrabins and the Egyptians. As already emphasized, this export trade represented a vital necessity for the people of western Sudan, ensuring them sufficient supplies of salt and so helping to consolidate in large measure the empire of the Mali, including the whole state apparatus and the ruling classes.[28] At the same time, the development of the Mali empire, which helped to pacify relations throughout its territory, so convincingly described in 1352 and 1353 by Ibn battutah,[29] boosted the export of gold in its trade with the Maghreb and with Egypt.

In the light of researches carried out by historians in recent decades, it is clear that the minting of gold currency in Genoa, Venice, and Florence from the mid-13th century onward, and subsequently in Castile, Catalonia, and some other European countries, led to an appreciable rise in the demand for gold, not only from Transylvania and Bohemia but also from far-off Sudan.[30] Conversely, this situation stimulated the export of silver from Europe to the Maghreb. Watson records that large quantities of silver were exported from Montpellier in the 13th and early 14th century and also, over a much longer period, from Genoa, Florence, and Venice.[31] This export trade, which was primarily a key element of trade with the Near and Middle East, also extended to Tunis and probably to other towns in North Africa, whence certain quantities of silver found their way to Senegal and the upper Niger region. On the basis of somewhat fragmentary source material, Watson takes the view that the introduction of gold coinage in the 13th century led, first in Italy and subsequently in France, to a rapid rise in the value of gold compared with that of silver. At the turn of the 13th/14th centuries, the ratio between the respective metals was 1:13 and 1:14 in Venice, and 1:14, 1:15, 1:16, and even 1:19 in France at the time of Philip IV ("le Bel"). We witness the same phenomenon a little later in Italy and in Hungary, the gold-silver ratio in the latter country in 1339 reaching

---

[28] *Ibid.*, pp. 250, 251, 290, 291, 431.
[29] *Voyage d'Ibn Batoutah.* Arabic text accompanied by a French translation by C. Defrémery and Dr. B. R. Sanguinetti, IV, Paris, 1853, pp. 393, 394.
[30] R. S. Lopez, *Settecento anni fa...*, p. 22ff., 35, 44ff., 59, 61.
[31] A. M. Watson, *op. cit.*, pp. 16–19.

the exceptionally high figure of 1:21.6.[32] The data amassed by Watson concerning the Islamic countries are less extensive, but they are sufficient to show that in 1278, for instance, the price of gold in Tunis was roughly the same as in the European countries of the Mediterranean basin, though it was appreciably higher than it had been before the middle of the 13th century, when the rate in Tunis varied between 1:9.3 and 1:11.6. We have no details concerning the ensuing period. In Watson's view, data concerning Egypt and Syria prove that, from the mid-13th century onward, the price of gold likewise increased by comparison with the period 1175–1250, albeit to a lesser degree than in Europe, but the rate of exchange underwent severe fluctuations during the years in question.[33]

However, the situation in Tunis, Alexandria, and the Syrian ports was influenced not only by the influx of cheap Sudanese gold, but also by the appreciable rise in the value of this metal from the 13th century onwards, primarily in Italy but also in other Mediterranean countries in Europe who were in regular trade relations with the Moslem world. The Sultan of Tunis and his subjects realized important profits by exploiting the margin between, on the one hand, the market price of gold in the Sudan and the transport costs involved and, on the other, the high price at which they were able to dispose of it in Europe. Among their customers engaged in traffic with the Maghreb, the most handsome profits accrued to the Genoese merchants and—on a lesser scale—to those from Florence, Venice, southern France, and the Iberian peninsula. It seems likely that, in the 13th and 14th centuries, Tunisia owed at least a part of its economic and political development to the situation just described, and that merchants from many Maugrabin towns, engaged in trade with the Sudan and with European traders, also amassed considerable profits. This was, incidentally, the conclusion reached by the Genoese Malfante in 1447, following his sojourn at the oasis of Tuat. Nor is it surprising that, in the view of Leo Africanus, the Arab geographer who observed the situation in the Maghreb much later, at the turn of the 15th/16th centuries, trade with the Sudan was virtually a prerequisite condition of the welfare of the peoples of the southern Maghreb living on the Saharan borders and of those settled

---

[32] *Ibid.*, p. 26.
[33] *Ibid.*, p. 27, Table 2.

in the oases of that desert.[34] Given this situation, the tributes in gold which the Maugrabins paid to European princes were perhaps not so burdensome after all.

There can be no doubt that the states of the Mali and the Songhai reaped large revenues from the export of gold, but in the 13th and early 14th centuries they probably lacked a sufficient number of merchants to exploit the favourable situation to the full. In the Mali empire, this trade developed rather in the course of the 14th century. Merchants were recruited largely among the Moslems already established some considerable time in the region around the bend of the Niger, as well as among natives who had adopted the Islamic way of life. We also know that these were wealthy and influential persons, who included scholars in their midst.[35]

It is likewise quite possible that, in the face of the increasing demand for gold, its extraction was stepped up—though we lack the necessary data to confirm this. On the basis of the study by Mrs Meyerowitz, I have already called attention to the fact that the middle of the 14th century (or a little later) probably saw the beginnings of gold exports from the state of Bono-Mansu, situated in the bend of the Volta river.[36] I. Wilks has drawn attention to another region from which gold was exported (also mentioned by Mrs Meyerowitz), in the region of Beco (or Begho), situated at the point where the Black Volta veers southward, not far from the forests which later formed part of the land of the Ashantis. The merchants involved had penetrated that far. This was the location which also saw the foundation of an extensive agglomeration which, according to tradition, contained a special residential quarter for the Moslem merchants sent from the borders of the Niger and from Djenné (known as the "Uangara" merchants). The date of the foundation of this agglomeration remains uncertain. Mrs Meyerowitz suggests the 11th century, but Ivor Wilks, an outstanding specialist in the history of this region, maintains that it cannot possibly have been before the early 15th century, linking the foundation with the demand for Sudanese

---

[34] Léon l'Africain, *op. cit.*, I, pp. 74, 80, 87, 91, 93, 117, 135; II, pp. 334, 335, 422, 424, 428, 429, 432, etc.; Ch. De La Roncière, "Découverte d'une relation de voyage datée du Tuat en décrivant en 1447 le bassin du Niger", in *Bulletin de la Section de Géographie*, 1918, pp. 10, 13ff., 28, 29.

[35] M. Małowist, *op. cit.*, pp. 214, 215, 222, 226, 227ff.

[36] *Ibid.*, pp. 248, 249; E. L. R. Meyerowitz, *Akan Traditions of Origin*, London, 1960, p. 34. The works of this author have raised numerous objections on the part of her English and French colleagues.

gold which, even earlier, was widely sought after in Europe.[37] This latter surmise seems plausible. The gold exported from western Sudan, at the time of Ghana and in the 13th and possibly even in the 14th century, stemmed mainly from the regions of Bambuk and Galam, situated between the sources of the Senegal and the Niger, as well as from Bouré, somewhat further to the south-east. It thus seems fair to suppose that in the 13th and 14th centuries the demand for gold in Mediterranean Europe, and hence also in North Africa and in the towns lying on the bend of the Niger, promoted the exploitation of gold in other regions as well, namely in the confines of the savannah and the dense forests of the Volta basin. One can therefore assume that the economic development of Europe, so characteristic of the 13th century, also exercised an influence—albeit with a certain time lag—on territories so distant that not even the Genoese were aware of their existence.

Towards the middle of the 14th century, the price of gold in Europe lost its stability, thereafter undergoing wild fluctuations. According to Watson, the gold-silver ratio ranged at this time from 1:6.6 to 1:12. Towards 1360, the rate steadied somewhat, varying between 1:10.5 and 1:12. This remained the position until around 1500, i.e. until the arrival in Europe of gold and silver of American origin.[38] It is also worth recalling that, in the course of the 14th century, one European state after another began minting gold coinage, amongst which the old English "noble" stood out by virtue of its high content of gold.

The rise in the value of silver in Europe was due to several factors: above all, to the export of this metal to the Moslem countries and especially to the Near East; to the diminishing extraction of silver towards the end of the 14th century; and to the widening of the commercial and monetary economy to include the poorer members of the population during the crisis of feudalism.[39] However, if the price of gold during the period 1360–1500 settled at a much lower rate than previously, this might have been the result of the ever-increasing supplies of Sudanese

---

[37] E. L. R. Meyerowitz, *op. cit.*, pp. 45–48; I. Wilks, *The Northern Factor in Ashanti History*, Institute of African Studies—University College of Ghana, 1961, pp. 1–7; *idem*, "The Growth of Islamic Learning in Ghana", in *Journal of the Historical Society of Nigeria*, Vol. II, No. 4, pp. 410–413.

[38] A. M. Watson, *op. cit.*, p. 26.

[39] M. Małowist, "Zagadnienie kryzysu feudalizmu w XIV i XV wieku w świetle najnowszych badań", in *Kwartalnik Historyczny*, LX, 1953, No. 1, pp. 86–106, *passim*; *idem*, "Z hospodárské problematiky krise feudalismu ve XIV a XV stoleti", in *Ceskoslovensky Casopis Historicky*, Vol. IV, 1956, 1, pp. 85–101, *passim*.

gold already mentioned. In this connection, the records of the Genoese customs for 1376–1377, published by J. Day, provide extremely interesting information.[40] A comparison of these data with other documents of the last quarter of the 14th century affords us a more or less exact picture of the situation in Genoa as regards the import of gold from the Maghreb and from the Iberian peninsula. Part of the gold imported not later than the 13th century was known in Genoa and in Sicily by the name of *oro di Pagliola*, a fact that provides indisputable testimony of its western Sudanese origins. This same name was also in use subsequently in the south-west of France.[41]

In the 14th century, this metal was used in Genoa in the production of gold thread, large quantities of which were exported to Alexandria and other towns of the Near East. From Genoa, some gold found its way into north-western Europe, but there is no doubt that some of it was hoarded locally, and the Genoese mint began striking the so-called *genovini*, viz. coins whose value corresponded to that of ducats and florins.

The records of the Genoese customs throw a clear light on the problem of Genoese supplies of gold in 1376–1377. The gold reached the Ligurian port on numerous vessels hailing from a region known as "Yspania" or "Hispania". In Day's view, this official terminology indicated the territories of Spain lying to the west of the Straits of Gibraltar, together probably with the Atlantic shores of Morocco.[42] It should be noted that, for the Portuguese chroniclers of the 14th and 15th centuries, the term "Hispania" embraced the entire Iberian peninsula, as it did in the days of the Romans, who tended to use the word in its plural form, in view of the division of the country into several

---

[40] J. Day, *Les douanes de Gênes 1376–1377*, Vols. I–II, Paris, 1963.

[41] R. S. Lopez, *Settecento anni fa...*, pp. 19–21. In 1254, the English King Henry III received from Gascony a certain quantity of gold, some of which consisted of *oro di Pagliola*. In 1265, this gold was on sale on the markets of Champagne. "Pallola" (or "Paliola") was the name given to a non-existent island, allegedly situated to the east of Ghana, whence—according to Massoudi and Idrisi—this gold was imported. Cf. L. E. Kubbel and V. V. Matveev, *Arabskie Istočniki VII–X vekov po etnografii i istorii Afriki juznee Sakhary*, Moskva-Leningrad, 1960, pp. 257, 261; V. V. Matveev and L. E. Kubbel, *Arabskie Istočniki X–XII vekov*, Moskva-Leningrad, 1965, p. 287. In reality, the region in question was that of Bambuk-Galam, situated on the Falémé, a tributary of the Senegal river, and lying between the sources of the Senegal and the upper Niger. This probably explains why the informants of Massoudi and Idrisi believed it to be an island. The term *oro di Pagliola* was widely used in Genoa.

[42] J. Day, *op. cit.*, Vol. II, index of geographical names, p. 969, cf. "Yspania".

provinces. At all events, the term "Hispania" understood in this sense certainly included the territories of Portugal. It therefore seems fair to assume that in 1376–1377 the Genoese vessels, mentioned in Day's study, which transported gold from "Yspania" to their home port or to Alexandria, in fact put in to numbers of other ports as well, notably Seville and Cadiz, Majorca, towns in southern Portugal (Algarve), and Lisbon, as well, in all probability, as ports on the Atlantic coast of the Maghreb such as Salé, Massa, or Safi. The Genoese had long since been in close relations with these regions and, ever since the middle of the 14th century, represented a powerful economic force in Castile and in Portugal.[43] Besides this, smaller numbers of vessels used to bring gold from Majorca, from Valencia, which was subject to the Catalan-Aragonese dynasty, and above all from Malaga, at that time within the frontiers of Granada and hence closely linked to the Maghreb and to Tlemçen in particular. The import of gold from Barcelona and the Provençal ports was at this time minimal—in fact, it seems more likely that Genoa actually supplied them with gold. We have no clear-cut evidence of gold being imported from Tunis, even though we know that in the years 1376–1377 a number of Genoese vessels put in there before subsequently returning to their home port.

The gold was transported in sacks (*sacchi*) and small sacks (*sacchetti*) of clearly defined dimensions, as well as in Mauritian coinage (*dobras*) and in gold cords (*gordena auri*). Genoa used to import certain quantities of gold from Palermo and elsewhere in Sicily, either in coinage or in other forms. According to Heers, who examined the relevant sources prior to their publication by Day, gold imports by Genoa during this period took the following form:[44]

---

[43] Da Silva Marques, *Descobrimentos*, I, pp. 114, 116. Cf. the plenary powers of the Genoese envoys, appointed on 25 June 1370 to the court of the Portuguese king Dom Fernando, and the agreement of 25 October 1370 reached with him. The king undertook to return the vessels confiscated by the Portuguese and to pay extensive damages. We know that one of the three ships in question was on passage from Seville to the Maghreb, and that the captain was himself from Seville. The other two vessels had been captured by Portuguese privateers at the mouth of the river Guadalquivir. These events took place during the war between Castile and Portugal.

[44] J. Heers, *op. cit.*, pp. 69, 70.

Vessel sailing from	Value in Genoese lire
Palermo	1,000
Valencia	6,000
Malaga	6,000
Seville	9,500
Spain (sum total)	45,000
Origin unknown	1,100
TOTAL	68,600

Certain quantities of gold were also shipped direct to Alexandria, i.e. without transiting through Genoa.[45]

However, several questions arise. In his study, Day never once mentions Seville in connection with gold imports to Genoa; on the other hand, he several times refers to Majorca, which is not cited by Heers. One must conclude, either that one of the historians is guilty of error, or that Heers consulted different sources—which seems unlikely in the light of the explanations he gives.[46]

On the basis of Heers' findings, Dufourcq attempted to calculate the amount of gold imported into Genoa in 1377; he arrived at a figure in the region of 200 kg, which must be regarded as a considerable sum.[47] On the assumption that the technique of "fluvial" gold extraction in Africa has undergone no change since time immemorial, and that in our day Bambuk-Galam and Bouré together produce some 8,000 kg of gold, R. Mauny has calculated that in the early Middle Ages the annual extraction of gold in western Sudan amounted to roughly 9,000 kg, of which 5,000 to 6,000 kg were probably exported.[48] These quantitative assessments can at best be regarded as problematical. Among the towns deeply engaged, both directly and indirectly, in traffic with the

---

[45] J. Day, op. cit., Vol. I, pp. 254, 281, 307, 326, etc.

[46] J. Heers, op. cit., p. 69. The author claims to have studied the files which Day had prepared at the printers'. Concerning the gold which the Genoese exported from Seville, cf. R. Doehaerd and Ch. Kerremans, Les Relations commerciales entre Gênes, la Belgique et l'Outremont d'après les archives génoises (1400–1440), Bruxelles-Rome, 1952, p. 153. Data of 1412. Numerous documents published in this volume bear testimony to the lively activity deployed by the Genoese in Seville.

[47] Ch. E. Dufourcq, op. cit., p. 563. The author estimates that towards the middle of the 13th century the treasury of the Kingdom of Aragon received 70 kg of African gold annually; ibid., pp. 180, 561, 562.

[48] R. Mauny, Tableau géographique..., pp. 296, 376, 377.

Maghreb and the Iberian peninsula, Genoa represented the highest economic potential, and it is presumably by dint of this that it received the largest supplies of gold, which was indispensable to its commerce and to its unusually highly qualified craftsmen. On the other hand, it is extremely doubtful whether the above-mentioned 200 kg of gold supplied to Genoa in 1377 forms a sound basis on which to estimate the importance of African gold imports into Mediterranean Europe. For one thing, we have no idea whether the situation was not very different in other years. We must not forget that the Genoese imported their gold from Spain, Portugal, and all the Maugrabin countries, not only from the Moroccan ports on the Atlantic coast. We dispose of no data indicating how much Sudanese gold reached North Africa. From there, the gold was transported, in quantities unknown to us, to the kingdoms of Granada, Valencia, Andalusia, Catalonia, and Portugal. While part of this gold undoubtedly remained there, it is not impossible that from time to time the Genoese and the Florentines, as well as other Italian merchants from Milan and Piacenza who were then highly active in the Iberian peninsula, may have syphoned off the gold reserves that had long since been amassed there.

One thing, however, seems established beyond doubt: the fact that the gold which the Genoese purchased in Spain, Portugal, Morocco, and Sicily stemmed almost exclusively from the western Sudan, and that no other source was of any consequence in this connection.[49] In traversing the Iberian peninsula, especially its harbour towns, the gold found its way into western France, whose economy was closely linked to the Iberian one, into England,[50] and even further, towards the north-east. It was precisely at the end of the 14th century that Castile and Portugal captured the attention of the Hanseatic traders, and merchants from southern Germany began deploying an increasingly lively activity in the kingdoms of Valencia, Catalonia, and Aragon. Through their intermediary, part of the African gold may have found its way to central

---

[49] It should be added here that the Belgian scholar A. Grunzweig established that the Florentine galleys sailing from Spain to Italy in the 15th century transported quantities of *auro tiberi*, i.e. the same as the *al-tibr* already mentioned as being Sudanese gold obtained from fluvial sand. My source here is the work by J. Heers, *op. cit.*, pp. 66, 67. It may be presumed that in the early 14th century the agents of the Florentine banking firms of the Bardi, Peruzzi, and Acciaiuoli families were interested above all in obtaining gold; cf. A. E. Sayous, *op. cit.*, pp. 74, 75; Ch. A. Jullien, *Histoire de l'Afrique du Nord*, Vol. II, p. 151.

[50] Cf. note 41.

and even to eastern Europe, although at that time the latter territories relied primarily on Czech and especially Hungarian production. Large quantities of gold from the Transylvanian mines reached Venice, a fact which probably explains why this city evinced so little interest in the Maghreb during the 13th and 14th centuries. This interest only grew with the crisis in the Czech and Hungarian mining industry in the 15th century.

The details of gold circulation described above clearly demonstrate the extremely close economic ties binding Europe, North Africa, and western Sudan, and the notable influence exerted by the economic situation of the European Mediterranean basin on far-off regions in Africa.

Three items of merchandise stemming from black Africa played a lesser role in medieval Europe, namely: the pepper known as "malagueta" (*Aframomum melegueta*), ivory, and black slaves. The pepper, from the forests of present-day Liberia and further eastwards, was exported to the countries situated in the bend of the Niger, whence some of it was then dispatched to the Maghreb and to Egypt. In their turn, European vessels transported certain quantities to southern Europe, as evidenced by the data concerning the goods imported into numerous towns of the Mediterranean basin.[51]

Insignificant quantities of ivory from western Africa likewise found their way to Europe via the Maghreb.

The presence of black slaves in medieval Europe presents a very complex problem. At that time, serfs and freedmen exercised the basic functions of agricultural production, while the urban handicraft industry was largely dominated by free citizens. Nevertheless, the Mediterranean countries at times counted a very considerable number of slaves, mainly employed as servants. The studies of Ch. Verlinden have brought much new material to light, but they have not in principle done anything to alter our assessment of the significance of slavery in early medieval Europe. It has long been known that these slaves were mainly recruited from men bought up by the Italians in the regions of the Black Sea and the Caucasus, as well as from numerous others taken prisoner by the peoples of the Iberian peninsula in the course of their land and

---

[51] R. Mauny, *op. cit.*, pp. 249–362; J. Day, *op. cit.*, pp. 253, 489ff. In the case in point, this merchandise had been transported to Genoa from Provence, probably from Marseilles (*Histoire du commerce de Marseille*, Vol. II, p. 110).

sea battles with the Arabs. These slaves were far better adapted to the conditions of life in the European countries of the Mediterranean basin than their black counterparts, accustomed to very different climatic conditions. Even so, there were also a number of negro slaves in Europe, especially in the Arab states of the Iberian peninsula.

In the 11th and 12th centuries there were large numbers of negro slaves in Cordova and in Algeciras, where they were employed as oarsmen. At that time there were many of them in the southern part of Moorish Spain, but after this we have no further information.[52] It is difficult to admit Verlinden's hypothesis that the conversion to Islam of Senegal and western Sudan prevented the Arabo-Berbers, in their capacity of Moslems, from making slaves of their coreligionists.[53] In any case, the process of islamization in these two regions was purely superficial and embraced only small sections of the population. The vast majority of the people remained true to their ancient beliefs, and continued to be the victims of both local and Moslem oppressors, as well as of merchants engaged in the slave trade.[54] Meanwhile, the export of black slaves to the Maghreb and to Egypt continued. Researches have shown that in the 13th century the number of slaves increased considerably in Catalonia, Valencia, and Majorca. Moors formed the larger part of these slaves. This was partly the consequence of the conquest of Majorca and Minorca, as a result of which large numbers of the native population were captured and sold as slaves on the markets.

In the second half of the 13th and the early 14th century, the Catalans strove to attain the same objective by dint of a widespread policy of piracy. During this period negro slaves, albeit in relatively small numbers, made their appearance in the territories mentioned, as well as in Marseilles and Montpellier. These slaves had either been captured in the Barbary states or else removed from Moslem vessels, themselves engaged (supreme irony!) in transporting large numbers of slaves from the Maghreb to Egypt.[55] It is not impossible that the Europeans, at this time busily engaged in trade with North Africa, also purchased a certain number of negroes there. In Italy, towards the turn of the 14th

---

[52] Ch. Verlinden, *L'esclavage dans l'Europe médiévale*, Brugge, 1955, pp. 210, 226.
[53] *Ibid.*, pp. 226, 227.
[54] M. Małowist, *Wielkie państwa Sudanu...*, pp. 104, 109, 318, 319.
[55] Ch. Verlinden, *op. cit.*, pp. 251–275; *idem*, "Note sur l'esclavage à Montpellier au bas Moyen Age (XIIIᵉ–XVᵉ siècle)", in *Etudes d'histoire dédiées à H. Pirenne*, Bruxelles, 1937, pp. 452ff.; Ch. E. Dufourcq, *op. cit.*, p. 71; Subhi Y. Labib, *op. cit.*, p. 101; *Histoire du commerce de Marseille*, Vol. II, p. 412.

century, we find a growing awareness of the shortage of slaves and of the ever-increasing price of such labour,[56] It is conceivable that this price rise was part and parcel of the general rise in the cost of labour, characteristic of this period plagued by frequent epidemics. Nor is it impossible that the slave markets in the Black Sea region were at this time disorganized as a result of the troubles linked to the incursions of Tamerlane. It may well have been these difficulties that awakened a growing interest along the Mediterranean shores for black slave labour. Thus, in Sicily and Naples, where slaves were numerous at the latest by the 13th century, negroes did not constitute a significant proportion until the first half of the 15th century. The notarial acts of the period testify that the majority of them came from Barca in Tripolitania.[57] João Fernandes, the informant of the chronicler Zurara, who spent several months in Mauritania around the 1440s, reported that the Tuareg used to deliver in Mondebarque (viz. Barca in Tripolitania) negroes whom they captured from time to time in the Sudan. Ca'Da Mosto, well versed in matters of African trade, also wrote around the mid-15th century that, in the locality of Uadan in Mauritania, the Moslems used to separate the slaves they brought from western Sudan into three groups. One group was destined for Cyrenaica and Sicily, the second group for Tunis, while the third group was taken to Arguin, where a Portuguese trading station (*factorerie*) had been operating since 1448.[58] This information accords with Verlinden's findings concerning Sicily, and may hence be considered reliable. At the same time, 1 find it very strange that the merchants whose main activities were centred in the region of Senegal and the upper Niger should have chosen to follow the long and arduous route to Tripolitania, rather than the shortest and more important one used for the transport of gold and slaves leading to Uadan.[59] It should be added here that commercial routes also led

---

[56] R. S. Lopez, "Quattrocento Genovese", in *Rivista Storica Italiana*, LXXV, 1963, p. 713, note 5. In the correspondence of the eminent firm of Datini de Prato, complaints on this score were raised in 1393.

[57] Ch. Verlinden, "Schiavitu ed economia nel Mezzogiorno agli inizi dell'età mo--derna", in *Annali del Mezzogiorno*, Vol. III, 1963, p. 19; *idem*, "Esclavage noir en France Méridionale etcourants de traite en Afrique", in *Annales du Midi*, LXXVIII, 1966, pp. 338–340.

[58] Gomes Eanes de Zurara, *Cronica dos Feitos de Guiné*, II, Lisboa, 1949, pp. 342, 343; *Le Navigazioni Atlantiche di Alvise da Ca'Da Mosto*, ed. R. Caddeo, Milano, 1929 (2nd ed.) "Viaggi e scoperte", I, p. 198.

[59] Cf. M. Małowist, *Wielkie państwa Sudanu...*, p. 319. At the time the present study was passed to the printers, I was not yet acquainted with the article by Ch. Verlinden

from Libyan ports towards Lake Chad and the state of Bornu, whose sovereigns, as we know, organized frequent expeditions against their neighbours with the aim of capturing prisoners and selling them off to Maugrabin merchants.[60]

The data assembled by Verlinden and the information we owe to João Fernandes and to Ca'Da Mosto date from the period when the Portuguese were in the act of making their first purchases of slaves along the West African coast. It thus seems probable that the details of this procedure outlined above correspond in some measure to the situation in this field, at least towards the end of the 14th century.

All this goes to prove that in the early Middle Ages the negro slave was not an altogether unknown phenomenon in the European portion of the Mediterranean basin. It is also worth noting that in the 13th and 14th centuries the Catalans frequently hired out their slaves to local craftsmen, or set them to execute their own handicraft work where they lived, or again, employed them in petty commerce and so derived profits from their labour. In 15th-century Sicily, black slaves were employed on the land.[61] It would thus seem that, before actually participating in the slave trade, the Europeans already had some experience in the matter and realized how black slave labour could be turned to their advantage.

At this point I should like to draw attention to one other aspect of the store of knowledge which the Europeans had concerning the Maghreb and hence, indirectly, West Africa. I first recall what I stated earlier regarding the close ties uniting Majorca, and its Jewish population in particular, with the peoples of Morocco and its neighbouring countries. We know further that the Catalans not only reached the shores of the Maghreb, but penetrated as far as Fez, and that large numbers of them resided there at different periods. According to some reports, which I was unable to confirm in the relevant sources, it sometimes happened

---

(cited in note 61) concerning slavery in southern Italy, and I considered the account of Ca'Da Mosto as completely erroneous. While it still raises certain doubts in my mind, I can no longer dismiss it out of hand.

[60] Léon l'Africain, *op. cit.*, II, pp. 481, 497. The information relates to the turn of the 15th/16th centuries. From the shores of Lake Chad, slaves were also transported northwards during preceding periods. The slaves from this region, apparently distinguished by their striking beauty, were particularly appreciated in the Moslem world.

[61] Ch. Verlinden, *L'esclavage dans l'Europe médiévale...*, pp. 280ff. In the 13th century, slaves in Catalonia were not employed on the land. In Sicily, the situation was different, especially during the 14th and 15th centuries; cf. the same author's "Schiavitu ed economia...", pp. 15, 16, 27–30.

that the Genoese ventured into the most remote regions of the Barbary states, an undertaking not without its dangers for Christians.[62] It would even appear that a Genoese citizen settled in Sijilmassa in 1291, though this must have been a quite exceptional case, inasmuch as the Moors, on political, commercial, and religious grounds, did not normally allow Christians to penetrate into the interior of their country.

Those Christian prisoners who returned to Europe after being bought back out of slavery represented an important source of information on conditions in the Maghreb and its hinterland. In the 13th and 14th centuries, a huge number of Christians were captured by Moslem privateers, but some of them succeeded in regaining their freedom and returned home. There can be little doubt that, on their return, they recounted their experiences and through their intermediary a great deal of information about Africa reached the European shores of the Mediterranean.

The geographical maps of these territories drawn up in the 13th, 14th, and early 15th centuries testify to what was known in those times of the Maghreb and perhaps its hinterland also. As mentioned on a previous occasion, I would like to point out here that, on the 1367 planisphere (albeit very inaccurate) of the Pizzigani brothers, there appears an island situated in the middle of a lake and bearing the legend "*Insula Palola hic colligitur aurum*". It is no mere chance that the finest work of medieval cartography, the *Atlas catalan* of Abraham Cresques of Majorca, which King John of Aragon offered to Charles V of France, contains the most complete information then available concerning the Maghreb, the oases of the Sahara, and the empire of the Mali. It was preceded by various maps, planispheres, and portulans covering not only the Maghreb but also the territories situated further to the south. The "Ganuya" frequently encountered on these maps corresponds to Guinea, viz. the territories inhabited by negroes. It should be observed that these maps placed this region much nearer to the Maghreb than was in fact the case. All historians are unanimous in certifying that the Jews of Majorca who were in contact with those of the Maghreb, and perhaps the Sudan also, were in a position to obtain information

---

[62] J. Heers, *op. cit.*, p. 479.

concerning the interior of the black continent from their coreligionists established in the Saharan oases or in western Sudan.[63]

At the same time, I do not personally believe that these maps contributed much to the diffusion of knowledge concerning North Africa and its hinterland, if only because their access was confined to a restricted circle of persons, while their reproduction encountered immense difficulties at a time when the art of printing was still virtually unknown, let alone perfected. In my view, these cartographic works testify rather to what was known of Africa at that time to the best informed circles, but they did not constitute a source of information for the broad masses of the population.

It seems to me that the facts presented above enable us to draw a certain number of conclusions. There can be no doubt that the relations existing between Mediterranean Europe, North Africa, and western Sudan represented an important element in the economic life of all the countries concerned. In the Middle Ages, the role of the Maghreb in the exchange of merchandise was apparently a more modest one than that of the Near East. It was indeed poorer in all respects. But Sudanese gold flowed into the Maghreb, and part of this gold subsequently strengthened the European reserves of this metal, and so exerted an appreciable influence on the exchange of goods on both shores of the Mediterranean. This in turn was the key factor which determined the great importance of the Sudan and of North Africa for the economy of

---

[63] M. Małowist, *Wielkie państwa Sudanu...*, pp. 21–23, R. Mauny, *op. cit.*, pp. 42, 43, 44; Le Vicomte de Santarem, *Recherches sur la découverte des pays situés sur la côte occidentale d'Afrique au delà du Cap Bojador*, Paris, 1842, p. 237; A. Ballesteros Beretta, "Génesis del Descubrimento", in *Historia de America y de los Pueblos Americanos*, Barcelona-Buenos Aires, 1947, vol. III, pp. 476ff. The school of cartography in Majorca ceased its activities in the early 15th century—doubtless the consequence of the economic decline of the island and the resultant loosening of its commercial ties with the outside world. Bailesteros Baretta reminds us that, in the *Libro del Conoscimiento...* dating from the mid-14th century (the work of a Castilian Franciscan of whom we know no exact details), there is mention of a Rio de Oro, i.e. a river of gold, which was considered to be a western branch of the Nile reaching the ocean near Cabo Buyder (Cape Bojador). *Ibid.*, p. 375. In the face of Ballesteros' account, experts are convinced that the author in question in fact never undertook a voyage, and was no more than a naïve and simple compiler of information. What strikes us as important is the fact that information concerning African gold found its way into the cells of Spanish provincial monasteries: what Ballesteros writes of a western branch of the Nile is no more than the echo of the accounts of the Niger which the medieval Arabs likewise invariably described as a branch of the Nile.

the medieval world. As mentioned above, certain findings would seem to confirm the hypothesis that the demand for gold in the Maghreb and in Europe—together, no doubt, with the demand for black slaves—in turn affected the situation in western Sudan, not only as regards its economy, but also in the political and cultural domain.[64]

We know that merchants from almost all the countries bordering the northern shores of the Mediterranean, including the Balearic islands and Sicily, made frequent voyages to North Africa, and this throughout several centuries. It would seem that the leading role accrued to the Genoese, the Catalans, and the Majorcans, but North Africa was also well known to the Portuguese, the Castilians, and the peoples of other European countries. We know, too, that merchants from Majorca, Catalonia, and Genoa penetrated into the interior of the country, that some of them made lengthy sojourns in Fez, and that in exceptional cases they even reached Sijilmassa. The Maghreb also held numbers of prisoners of European origin, some of whom eventually managed to return to their home country.

As a result, the peoples inhabiting the European shores of the Mediterranean were probably well informed concerning the economic life of North Africa and, while aware of its shortcomings, they must also have known that gold reached those territories from the Sudan. It should also be noted that the sovereigns of Catalonia and Sicily themselves participated actively in traffic with the Maghreb,[65] and that they were presumably as well informed concerning its economy as simple merchants. They were also aware that the riches of the Maghreb, and its gold in particular, could be obtained not only in return for merchandise but also—as Dufourcq established—by means of diplomatic and military pressure, at times accompanied by certain political concessions.

The Europeans had only a vague idea of the origins of the gold which reached them from the Maghreb, although in Genoa, Majorca, and Catalonia many persons must have heard not only of the great importance of Sijilmassa as the point of transit for the supplies of gold destined for the Maghreb, but also of the existence of the Mali empire, with its vast reserves of gold. However, neither the Europeans nor the Maugrabins knew exactly which territories this gold came from.

---

[64] In the study referred to, I have given a more detailed account of the economic, political, and cultural influence which the Maghreb exercised on western Sudan.

[65] Ch. E. Dufourcq, *op. cit.*, pp. 129, 415, 556–562.

Contacts with this region were the monopoly of the black merchants from Uangara who, conscious of their own interests, jealously guarded their secret and never disclosed it to the Moslems.[66] In the 13th and 14th centuries, the peoples of south-western Europe already had some experience—albeit a very limited one—in the exploitation of black slave labour. The feudal system which then prevailed in Europe allotted the main productive tasks to the peasants and burghers, and allowed little scope for the exploitation of slaves in the principal sectors of economic life. Nor did natural conditions favour the establishment of negro slaves in Europe. It seems possible that the engagement of black slaves began in the 14th century, when manual labour in Mediterranean Europe became very expensive and was often in short supply.

The Portuguese likewise participated in the traffic between southern Europe and the Maghreb, though their role here was no more than a secondary one. At the same time, it is hard to imagine that the Jewish, Moslem, and Christian merchants of Portugal, as well as their political leaders, were any less well informed concerning conditions in the Maghreb than the Italians or the Catalans, given that they were such close neighbours of the Moslems.

Bearing in mind all that has been said on this subject, there is in my view a high degree of probability in the hypothesis that in the 15th century the Portuguese, followed by the Catalans, attacked the Maghreb for the sole reason that they were in search of Sudanese gold and, to a lesser extent, of African slaves.

---

[66] M. Małowist, *Wielkie państwa Sudanu...*, pp. 247–250, 326–328.

CHAPTER SEVENTEEN

PORTUGUESE EXPANSION IN AFRICA AND EUROPEAN ECONOMY AT THE TURN OF THE 15TH CENTURY*

In this article I would like to tackle the problem of the impact of Portuguese expansion in Africa upon the economy of other European countries towards the close of the 15th and the beginning of the 16th centuries, when the Portuguese assumed control over the eastern and western coasts of Africa, reached India, and established contact with the immense areas of the Far East. At that time Portugal was ruled by King Emanuel the Fortunate (1469–1521), whom Francis I reportedly named "the king of pepper" (*le roi-épicier*).

One may agree with the view of Portuguese historians that the great successes of Emanuel—both in foreign as well as internal policy—were all the result of the achievements of his predecessor John II. John II (1481–95) not only developed and fortified Portuguese colonies and missions on the West African off-shore islands and coast, but provided the conditions for further growth and, above all, prepared very carefully and pressed ahead with a plan for an expedition to India. Thanks to his considerable financial revenues derived from the rising imports of gold and slaves from Africa, he succeeded in enfeebling the great nobles and established absolutism in Portugal. The new ruler adopted a different position towards the nobles, no doubt because he was related to the Braganzas. He restored their confiscated estates and also allowed the banished participants in the conspiracy against John II to return to their country. I do not think, however, that he was motivated by family considerations alone. In the first half of his rule, the Crown had such vast resources that it could afford, at the cost of some concessions, to soothe its conflicts with the nobles, and Emanuel did just that. It used to be said that this king committed two fundamental errors, which were to tell on Portugal's economic life and on the Crown's finances.

* Originally published as "Ekspansja portugalska w Afryce a ekonomika Europy na przełomie XV I XVI w.", in *Przegląd Historyczny*, Vol. 59, 1968, pp. 227–244. Translated from Polish by Maria Chmielewska-Szlajfer, revised by Robin Kimball.

The first was the restoration of a huge fortune to the Braganzas. The second was the expulsion in 1498 of Jews who played an important role in trade and urban crafts and who made up a considerable source of the Treasury's revenues.[1] True, it was under the pressure of Castile, who had carried through a similar operation several years earlier, that a large number of Jews were expelled. The anti-Jewish campaign in Portugal was accompanied by much cruelty and pillage of Jewish property—with profit both to the Crown and individuals. Emanuel behaved ambiguously at the time. While persecuting the Jewish population, he made it difficult for them to leave Portugal, and it is presumed that in point of fact he wanted to keep as many of them as possible in the country, while forcing their conversion.[2] As a result, many affluent Jews became baptized and remained in Portugal, worshipping the God of their forefathers in secret. In this way the numbers of so-called new Christians (*cristiãos novos*) went up, but they were habitually suspected of renegation from the Christian faith. The new Christians were numerous, particularly among the well-to-do. In this situation the Portuguese Inquisition seized the opportunity to show its might. Yet this sinister institution became truly active only after Emanuel's death, under the rule of his fanatical and bigoted successors, John III and Sebastian.[3]

The main event in the history of Portugal at the time was the discovery by Vasco da Gama in 1498 of the sea route to the East Indies. Initially, dominance of the Malabar Coast was very advantageous to Portugal. For the time being, the rising share in the spice trade and the pillage of Muslim ships in the Indian Ocean and in the Red Sea ensured huge profits to the Crown and its agents in the Middle and Far East. Nevertheless, before long governor Affonso de Albuquerque, the conqueror of Goa and Malacca, needed more soldiers. Thanks to works by Braudel and many other scholars, we now know that the Portuguese did not obtain the exclusive control of trade between the East Indies and Europe, and that the new sea route from Lisbon, around the

---

[1] A. Braamcamp Freire, "O Livro das tenças del Rei," in Archivo Histórico Português, Vol. 2, No. 6, 1904, p. 207. See A. da Silva Costa Lobo, *História da Sociedade em Portugal no século XV* (Lisboa, 1904). According to this author, King Emanuel made it difficult for Jews to emigrate. See also Damião de Goes, *Crónica de El-Rei Dom Manuel*, ch. I, Biblioteca dos Classicos Portugueses, Vol. LIX (Lisboa, 1909), pp. 34f., 51–58.

[2] Damião de Goes, *Crónica*.

[3] Damião de Goes, an outstanding Portuguese humanist and historian, himself became one of the Inquisition's victims. He died four years after he was released from prison.

Cape of Good Hope to South-East Asia, in no way supplanted the old routes connecting India with Persia and Turkey, and even with Egypt and Italy.[4] All the same, the revenues of the Portuguese Crown, which under John II amounted to 60,000,000 reals a year, under Emanuel reached as many as 200,000,000 reals.[5] It is generally believed that a large income from trade with Africa, especially from imports of gold from São Jorge da Mina, and presumably even more so the profits from the colonies in the East Indies, contributed to this rise. It should be added here that by this time the Spaniards had begun to administer Central America and Mexico, and therefore demand for black labour already had its effect, albeit small as yet, on the increase in the export of slaves from the Portuguese missions in Africa and on their proceeds. On the other hand, the discovery of Brazil in 1500 did not initially produce any important economic repercussions.

Taking advantage of the complete political chaos obtaining in Morocco, King Emanuel managed to seize many footholds on that country's Atlantic coast. The most important events in this regard concerned the occupation of the city of Safi (1508), the instalment of a Portuguese corps in the fort of Santa Cruz do Cabo de Guer (Agadir)—built in 1505 and considerably strengthened later—and in Mazagan, on the borders of the fertile regions of Doukkala and Sous. On the strength of the 1509 treaty between Portugal and Castile, the two powers delineated their spheres of conquest in the Maghreb. The Spaniards already held Oran, Honein, and Melilla, but stopped their military expansion in Morocco proper. Thereafter, the residents of Andalusia, who did not give up their trade with Morocco, supported the Portuguese *presidios* (garrisons) in that country by extending not only food but even military assistance to them.[6] In this way the two countries captured the main ports of the western Maghreb, thus extending their control of the extreme points of the gold and slave routes, which had their origins as far afield as the Sudan.

If we agree with the hypothesis that this had been the gist of the old political concepts of Henry the Navigator, the Infante, we must admit

---

[4] The issue of Portuguese activities in India and Morocco has been comprehensively discussed by my students J. Kieniewicz, *Faktoria i forteca* (Warszawa, 1970), and A. Dziubiński, *Maroko w XVI wieku* (Wrocław, 1972).

[5] *História de Portugal*, Vol. III (Barcelos, 1931), p. 646.

[6] R. Ricard, "Etudes sur l'histoire des Portugais au Maroc," in *Acta Universitatis Coimbrigensis*, 1955, pp. 145–170. The Goes chronicle quoted here contains numerous accounts of Portuguese raids on Moorish settlements.

that at the beginning of the 16th century his concepts were brought to fruition, albeit with Spanish participation. However, the future was to show that these conquests were difficult to retain, and proved short-lived. But for the time being, as we shall see, they greatly facilitated Portuguese trade with Black Africa and the seizure of gold and slaves delivered from the Sudan to Morocco. Moreover, the outposts in Morocco made it easier to supply grain and animal products not only to the local garrisons but to the metropolis itself.

Other circumstances, too often overlooked by historians, also require strong emphasis. Thus, the development of overseas trade and the intensive development of apparatus for the exploitation of the colonies, especially of the missions in Black Africa, Morocco, and India, allowed the Portuguese aristocracy, nobility, and merchants to display their talents. As regards Morocco, the continuous attacks against areas inhabited by the Moors gave first and foremost the two upper social strata an outlet for their "knightly" energy and an opportunity to gain rich spoils. Such prospects in overseas posts in the 16th century also lured many people from poorer social strata who were looking for ways of getting rich quickly. As a result, great nobles opposed royal absolutism no longer. The parties to the old conflict came to terms with each other at the expense of the "infidels." In this respect, the situation in Portugal resembled that in Spain and even in Sweden when these countries were in the prime of their power in the 16th and 17th centuries.

Against these successes of the Portuguese monarchy must be set the negative side of the conquests, which with time entailed expenses incommensurate with the exchequer's revenues from the colonies. Although in the 15th and 16th centuries immigration into the colonies was not as yet massive, nevertheless the 1527 census revealed many abandoned farms at home. With time, the problem of desolate areas became much more acute. It should be added here that the colonies attracted the young and most entreprising elements, only a few of whom were later to return to the metropolis.[7] One of the indirect consequences of colonial expansion was the rapid and presumably excessive development of Lisbon as a hub of commerce and the seat of the royal court and aristocracy in the 15th and 16th centuries. At the end of that period, the population of the capital stood at 100,000. This however was achieved

---

[7] *História de Portugal*, Vol. III, pp. 286, 652.

largely at the expense of a flight from the countryside and from many other towns, which aggravated the already acute shortage of labour. And all this at a time of low birth rate,[8] and with the price and wage revolution just starting in the Iberian peninsula (the first half of the 16th century). True, not all the negative effects of Portuguese seaborne expansion were immediately visible. Nonetheless, the royal treasury had already run into serious debt to foreign merchants towards the close of Emanuel's reign.[9]

The problems of Black Africa occupied a much more modest place in this ruler's policy than in his predecessor's. The main task, especially on the West African coast and on the adjacent islands, involved, first of all, consolidation of the position already attained and the appropriate administration of those territories. Emanuel gave considerable attention to these issues, but his policy in this respect was wavering. He either imposed an extreme trade monopoly or licensed merchants to do business with particular stretches of the coast. As a rule, the fortresses of São Jorge da Mina and along the entire Gold Coast remained in the hold of the Crown. The old Portuguese missions there were developed and new ones established. Thus the castle of St. Anthony was built in the Axim settlement (1502?), where large quantities of gold were purchased.[10] Above all Mina, then Axim, and later also very distant Accra were of essential importance to the Portuguese gold trade in West Africa. In Emanuel's time, gold was also purchased in South-East

---

[8] *Ibid.* The size of the Lisbon population is quoted after the 1551 census. The whole of Portugal had at that time 1,326,000 inhabitants. Subsequently, such Portuguese publicists as Luis Mendes de Vasconcelos, who wrote in 1608, and particularly the outstanding theoretician of mercantilism Severim de Faria (1583–1654) believed emigration to the colonies to be the root cause of depopulation and of the acute manpower shortage, especially in agriculture, and of the weakness of the army and navy. De Vasconcelos gave attention to the excessive development of Lisbon, at the expense of the countryside. De Faria was right to observe that Portuguese colonies in South-East Asia caused greater population losses to the metropolis than their Atlantic possessions did. A. Sérgio, *Antológia dos economistas portugueses. Século XVII* (Lisboa, 1924), pp. 80, 86, 186–188, 194–196, 201.

[9] *História de Portugal*, Vol. III, p. 646.

[10] Duarte Pacheco Pereira, *Esmeraldo de Situ Orbis*, transl. G. H. T. Kimble (London, 1937), The Hakluyt Society (1936), series II, p. 117; G. R. Crone, ed., *The Asia of João de Barros*, I Decade, Book 2 (London, 1937), The Hakluyt Society (1936), No. 80, ch. 1, 2, p. 108, footnote 4. Kimble's publisher writes that, after some years, the population of Axim destroyed the Portuguese port, but in 1515 it was rebuilt. The local gold was obtained from the sand of the Ankobra river.

Africa, primarily in Sofala, where the Portuguese ousted the old Arab gold buyers.[11]

Manuel enthusiastically supported the penetration and evangelization of the state of Congo, undertaken in the 1480s. At the beginning of the 16th century, there were already many Portuguese residents there. In the Congo capital, Mbanza, renamed São Salvador after the king's conversion, the Portuguese possessed the privilege of extraterritoriality. They exercised a powerful influence on the country's ruler. Emanuel admitted the latter to his own coat of arms, sent him priests, craftsmen, and even chasubles and other necessary church utensils. The Congolese king sent his own brother Henry, later bishop of Congo, and other youths to Portugal to receive an education there.[12] The Congolese king behaved in a friendly manner because he hoped to receive Portuguese military assistance in the fight against his menacing neighbours and those local chiefs who had initially rebelled against him, proposed another candidate for the throne, and at the same time stood up for their old beliefs.[13] The outwardly very promising action of the evangelization of Congo turned out to be extremely superficial, having no effect on the mass of the native population.[14] We may assume that the fierce quarrels among the Portuguese and the crimes they committed, as described by Damião de Goes and mentioned by witnesses to the events, did not make the Portuguese particularly popular, and only undermined the prestige of the new religion. As for the religion's chief spokesmen, the Portuguese priests, they behaved no better than the rest

---

[11] Damião de Goes, *Crónica*, Vol. III, pp. 99–102. The Portuguese began to build new fortresses in Sofala, Kilwa, and elsewhere along the eastern coast, but not all these projects were brought to fruition.

[12] *Ibid.*, Vol. V, p. 127, Vol. VII, pp. 44–56. Prior to this, Hieronim Münzer, who visited Portugal in 1494, wrote that there were sons of many African rulers at the court of John II, where they were brought up in the Christian faith and manners. B. de Vasconcelos, *"Itinerario" do Dr Jeronimo Münzer (Excertos)* (Coimbra, 1932), p. 54. Emanuel adopted this policy of influencing Africans on a much larger scale.

[13] Damião de Goes, *Crónica*, Vol. VII, pp. 50–52. In the letter from King Dom Alfonso I of Congo to Emanuel, quoted by the chronicle's author, one can trace the legend of the dream of Constantine the Great on the eve of the Battle of the Milvian Bridge. The Congolese ruler, too, had a vision of the cross auguring a victory over the pagans. St. James (the patron saint of Portugal) and other apostles were to take part in the African battle. A much more exhaustive although very similar description of events is to be found in the work by Filippo Pigafetta, *Relazione del Reame di Congo e delle circonvicine contrade* (Roma, 1593), pp. 46–57.

[14] Filippo Pigafetta, *Relazione*, p. 57f.

of their fellow-countrymen.[15] In the 1520s and 1530s, the Portuguese were already strongly committed to the slave trade and to the export of slaves from Congo and neighbouring Angola. It would seem that the slaves were from outside Congo's borders, as the country's rulers did not oppose these exports. The Congolese kings merely insisted that exports should be concentrated at the mouth of the Congo River and be subject to duty.[16] Nonetheless, the wholesale export of slaves from this part of Africa, from Angola in particular, had as yet barely begun, reaching its apogee, due to the great demand in Brazil, as late as in the 17th and 18th centuries.

Although Emanuel was clearly the senior partner, he never raised the issue of Congo's formal dependence on Portugal. Even so, both Don Alfonso as well as his successors addressed and treated the Portuguese monarchs as their suzerains. This situation was very convenient for Emanuel, because it was not necessary to deploy Portuguese troops in Congo. This would have been very costly and, in point of fact, to no purpose, considering that profits from the Congo trade were very meagre, while the tropical climate and diseases caused a high death rate among Europeans. Portuguese efforts to exploit Congo's famous natural resources bore no fruit for a long time to come.

Thus, the reign of Emanuel saw the establishment of a strong framework for Portuguese rule in West and Central Africa. At the same time, a definitive system for the exploitation of trans-Saharan Africa took shape. All this required a huge economic and organizational effort.

On another occasion I pointed out that medieval Portugal did not belong to the leading countries in Europe. Not only did it lag far behind such developed countries as Flanders and Italy, but it could not even compare economically with France and England; Portugal was much weaker even than neighbouring Castile. Portugal's great overseas expansion, especially in the 15th century, served primarily the needs of the nobility, who represented its driving force. It was they who paved the way for merchants, who joined the campaign only later, when it was evidently worthwhile. Expansion, first in Africa and then in South Asia, assumed such vast proportions that it required not only a steady leadership of state, but also the allocation of vast financial resources,

---

[15] L. Cordeiro, *Questoes Historico-Coloniais*, I, Biblioteca Colonial Portuguesa, Vol. VII (Lisboa, 1953), pp. 346, 350.

[16] *Ibid.*, pp. 355–367.

which again only the Crown could provide. It is only natural that in
such a situation the monarchs sought to ensure revenue to the throne
through the establishment of a monopoly on the most precious African
goods. After all, such a monopoly was necessary to them, as even their
financial resources remained very meagre. All this was taking place at a
time when money circulation was still very slow, and the risks attach-
ing to long-distance sea trade very serious. In these circumstances, it
was of essential importance to the Portuguese Crown to be able to buy
goods as cheaply as possible and sell them at a high profit. This explains
why the whole trade with West Africa, formed in the 15th century
and ultimately developed in the reigns of John II and of Emanuel,
was monopolistic in character and subordinate to the interests of the
Crown. The Crown however had to share its revenues with the nobility,
as well as those working in the colonial machinery and in the national
state administration. Additionally, the monarchs tried to determine the
merchants' share in overseas trade in such a way as to ensure the best
revenue for the Treasury.

Yet, in the period of great discoveries, Portugal's economic backwardness brought it face to face with extremely difficult tasks. To
complete them was a prerequisite of the success of the whole colonial
enterprise. Portugal lacked a properly developed production base and
sufficient capital. As regards grain production, the country had already
been dependent on imports since the 14th century. As time went by,
so Portuguese grain imports went up. It was necessary to import wood
(despite the discovery of Madeira) and high-grade iron. Although in
the 16th century the copper output rose somewhat, this metal, very
much in demand overseas, was also imported in large amounts.[17]
Portugal produced hardly any brass, which proved so valuable in trade
with Africa. The textile industry was too weak to organize large-scale
production adjusted to the needs of tropical countries. Moreover, it is
worth remembering here that the demand of the affluent Portuguese had
for long been satisfied with imports of Netherlands and Italian cloth.
With a few exceptions, Portuguese merchants were unable, particularly

---

[17] F. Mauro, *Le Portugal et l'Atlantique au XVIIe siècle. 1570–1670* (Paris, 1960),
pp. 295–297. Referring to the works by R. da Silva and O. Ribeiro, Mauro writes that in
medieval and 16th-century Portugal grain acreage was approximately 550,000 hectares.
The average yield per hectare was a mere 8 hectolitres. This was a totally inadequate
amount, making large imports necessary. Regarding iron, copper, and timber, see
ibid., pp. 399–401.

in the 15th century, to make substantial long-term investments in a costly maritime venture. With time, however, the situation improved markedly. Even so, merchants did not engage themselves in increase of production. Sugar production was an exceptional case, but in Madeira Italian, and particularly Genoese, capitalists early managed to establish control over the distribution of the finished product. The situation in the same industry on the island of São Tomé was more promising.

Portugal's manpower shortage not only made it difficult to build up the country's industrial base, but also checked the development of the navy and armed forces vital to the preservation and exploitation of the colonies. This explains why, almost from the beginning of the great discoveries of the 15th century, the economic problems of Portuguese seaborne expansion were, in a way, of an all-European character. In fact, the Portuguese had to confine themselves to mediation in trade between West Africa (and later also India) and many countries of Europe and the Maghreb. The Portuguese aim was to derive maximum profit from their mediation, and to prevent other countries establishing direct relations with the overseas territories. The task had been difficult enough from the start; in the longer run, it proved impossible.

The hubs of international commerce in medieval and early modern Europe were the northern and central Italian cities and, north of the Alps, Brugge in Flanders and, from the end of the 15th century, Antwerp in Brabant. From the 12th and especially the 13th century, the Portuguese were very active in Brugge, to which they exported wine, southern fruits, resin, cork, and salt, and where they purchased, first and foremost, Netherlands cloth, but also metals and many other goods. And yet they only played second fiddle there. Starting from the 14th century, Portuguese traders became active at Middelburg in neighbouring Zeeland. In the next century, the kings of Portugal were represented in Brugge by a *feitor* (permanent agent). In 1499, when Brugge lost its importance, the *feitor* moved to more flourishing Antwerp. Despite many attractive offers from Brugge, Portuguese merchants likewise abandoned that city for Antwerp. In 1511, they were not yet numerous in Antwerp, but in that year they already secured a seat for their consul there. Starting from 1526, the number of Portuguese visitors to the large port on the Scheldt River began growing rapidly.[18] Brugge, and

---

[18] R. Häpke, *Brügges Entwicklung zum mittelalterlichen Weltmarkt* (Berlin, 1908), pp. 142–147. Such African merchandise as dates, alum, and Moroccan leather goods

then Antwerp, became the places where the Portuguese acquired, not just Flemish and Brabantine cloth, but also metals, particularly copper from Germany, Austria, and Hungary, brasses from Nuremberg, etc. Last but not least, in Brugge, the Portuguese came in touch with the Hanseatic League, the suppliers of wood and other forestry products, grain, furs, iron, and copper from Sweden, Hungary, and Poland.

Although the accumulation by Portugal of reserves of gold, of *malagueta* pepper, of ivory, and of other merchandise accompanying the flourishing trade with West Africa, increased the purchasing power of the Portuguese, and especially of the Portuguese Crown, her overseas expansion only amplified the country's need of foreign products. The issue became particularly sensitive once the sea route to India was discovered. Starting from 1503, Portugal flooded Antwerp with spices, thus forcing Venice to yield the palm. At the same time, however, Portugal's demand for copper and silver, for wood to build ships, and above all for credit from big Italian and southern German financiers increased rapidly.

Brugge, and later Antwerp, were not the only meeting points between Portuguese and international merchants. The position of Genoese and other Italian merchants in Lisbon was already strong in the 14th century. They became very active even in the interior—in spite of opposition from the Portuguese burghers. The enormous territorial expansion and the attendant needs became in the 15th century an irresistible lure to the Hanseatic League and merchants from southern Germany. As early as the 14th century, Portuguese grain supplies were increasingly dependent on transport from, first of all, Brittany and Normandy, and with time also from the northern Netherlands and the Baltic countries. Portugal's contacts with Brittany and Normandy are known well enough, so we will not dwell upon them here.[19] Portugal's relations with the Hanseatic League were of considerable importance to the economic history of

---

arrived in Flanders in the 13th century through the mediation of the Iberian peninsula. A. Braamcamp Freire, "A feitoria de Flandres," in *Archivo Histórico Português*, 6, 1908, pp. 337–350; J. A. Goris, *Etude sur les colonies marchandes méridionales (Portugais, Espagnols, Italiens) à Anvers de 1488 à 1567* (Louvain, 1925), p. 37ff., 53, 55. The author points to the minor role of the Portuguese among foreign merchants in Brugge. W. S. Unger, *Middelburg als Handelsstad (XIIIe tot XVI eeuw)* (Middelburg, 1935), pp. 52, 99f., 104.

[19] *Cf.* Ch. Verlinden, "Deux aspects de l'expansion commerciale du Portugal au Moyen Age (Harfleur au XIVe siècle. Middelbourg au XIVe et XVe s.)", in *Revista Portuguesa de História*, 4, 1949, pp. 177–207; A. da Gama Barros, *História da Administração Publica em Portugal nos séculos XIII a XV*, pp. 281–287.

Poland. It is regrettable that so far no one in Poland has paid due attention to Poland's very significant, even if outwardly passive, share in European overseas expansion. Particularistic leanings, still present in Polish historiography, have done much damage in this area also. For lack of space I cannot dwell on these problems here, but I shall try at least to state them. Thus, the Portuguese historian A. H. de Oliveira Marques observed that from the end of the 14th until the end of the following century, among the Hanseatic merchants visiting Lisbon, Oporto, and other Portuguese localities, those from Gdańsk apparently predominated. More than fifty Gdańsk merchants and skippers were at the time involved in the shipping trade with Portugal.[20] It should be added here that Oliveira Marques's data are incomplete. By a strange coincidence, he makes use only of the published Hanse documents but overlooks certain references to Gdańsk traders made in other sources.[21] Diligent archival studies in Gdańsk, Belgium, Holland, and Portugal will no doubt provide much more information. The Gdańsk books of the pile duty from the second half of the 15th century mention only one ship as having arrived from Lisbon in 1476. No Portuguese arrival was recorded in the years that followed. So far, we have not found any concrete figures concerning navigation from Gdańsk to Portugal.[22] This in no way detracts from the evidence provided by Oliveira Marques; it only shows how cautiously we should treat medieval statistics. On the basis of very fragmentary records, he writes that in the years 1400–11 there arrived in Portuguese ports an average of one to two Prussian, i.e. undoubtedly Gdańsk, vessels per annum. As in later years, the Hanseatic Portugal-bound ships were, as a rule, part of the fleet sailing to Brittany for salt, wine, and other French and Spanish products. They usually made the return voyage together also, after they had concluded their transactions at Baie de Bourgneuf and neighbouring harbours. Though few records are available with regard to the following years, it would seem that this policy continued. From 1430 onwards,

---

[20] A. H. de Oliveira Marques, *Hansa e Portugal na idade média* (Lisboa, 1959), pp. 55, 160–186.

[21] B. de Vasconcelos, *"Itinerario" do Dr Jeronimo Münzer*, p. 22. For example, in 1494 Hieronim Münzer visited, in Santa Maria de Luz near Lisbon, one Bernard Fechter from Gdańsk, on board his large ship. No other source material mentions Fechter. Presumably, the stay of many other Gdańsk skippers in Portugal left no trace in the documents.

[22] H. Samsonowicz, "Handel zagraniczny Gdańska w drugiej połowie XV w.," in *Przegląd Historyczny*, Vol. 47, fascicle 2, 1956, p. 290.

the trade along this route increased from one to three (exceptionally even six) ships a year. By 1452–54 at the latest, the concentration of Hanseatic merchants in Lisbon was sizable enough to obtain special privileges from the king. In 1456 alone, upwards of twenty Hanseatic ships arrived in Lisbon.

While information from the second half of the 16th century is very scant, there is no doubt that trade between Portugal and the Hanse expanded markedly. Thus, in 1462, forty-four Prussian vessels sailed across the Sound on their return route from Lisbon, carrying a large consignment of goods. In 1490, John II granted the Gdańsk merchants a three-year licence to leave their goods in Portugal without the need to pay any special storage charges.[23] The question arises: what could have prompted Hanseatic traders, and those from Gdańsk in particular, to sail as far as Lisbon, Oporto, or even Algarve? Such Portuguese products as wine, olives, raisins, figs, oranges, cork, etc. were readily available in Flanders and France. Oliveira Marques clearly exaggerates when he suggests that the Hanseatic merchants attached great importance to salt from Setúbal and Aveiro, for it is a well-established fact that the Baltic countries relied on salt imported from Brittany.[24] Hirsch emphasized long ago that in the 15th century Gdańsk traders carried wood, flour, beer, and herring to Portugal, and that they were encouraged to bring timber for the shipbuilding industry.[25] They probably used the cheap and low-grade Portuguese salt primarily as ballast necessary to ships when homeward bound. Otherwise, it was along the western coast of France that they used to supply themselves with salt throughout the 15th century. One can presume that it was her growing demand for shipbuilding timber and, to a lesser extent, grain from the Baltic region that stirred up Prussian traders' serious interest in Portugal. Oliveira Marques admits that the scanty records of Hanseatic cargo destined for Portugal mention wood in the first place. In 1460, a certain German resident of Lisbon complained, on his own and other Hanseatic merchants' behalf, about the unlawful seizure of wood they had customarily delivered to Lisbon.[26] In 1494, John II lifted for ten years

---

[23] A. H. de Oliveira Marques, *Hansa*, pp. 57–62, 143. But in all this time, only one Portuguese merchant, Jorge Gonçalves of Lisbon, visited Gdańsk, round about 1457.

[24] *Ibid.*, pp. 113–117.

[25] Th. Hirsch, *Danzigs Handels- und Gewerbsgeschichte* (Leipzig, 1858), p. 84f.

[26] Baltic countries exported primarily rye, while Portugal needed the wheat supplied by Brittany, Castile, etc. Nevertheless, Prussia already exported grain to Lisbon in the 15th century.

the import duty on masts. The Latin copy of this decree indicates that it concerned specifically Hanseatic imports. The royal licence granted to Hanseatic traders in 1502 stated that they would pay duty only on a *dizima*, i.e. one tenth, of the value of the masts they imported.[27] It should be emphasized here that wood for masts and masts themselves made up a major part of Gdańsk exports in the 15th and partly in the 16th century. At that time, agents of the Portuguese kings purchased them in Flanders.[28] The problem of shipbuilding timber was evidently piling up in Portugal. In 1517, Emanuel exempted Hanseatic suppliers from the duty on shipbuilding beams. In 1528, the regency performing the duties of the juvenile John III confirmed that privilege, whereupon it became one of the permanent rights that Hanseatic dealers enjoyed in Portugal.[29] The privilege concerned the so-called *borten*, exported from Gdańsk on a mass scale beginning from the 14th century. Along with wood, the city supplied Portugal with wood by-products such as tar and pitch. All these commodities constituted a major element of exports from the Baltic region, from Prussia in the first place and Livonia next. No wonder then that merchants from Gdańsk and Revel showed such a keen interest in relations with Portugal and reacted so swiftly to its growing demand for raw materials indispensable to ship-building. In the 15th century, Hanseatic dealers also provided Portugal with certain quantities of copper (presumably from Sweden), iron, and other goods. The ever-increasing privileges ceded to the Hanse at the turn of the 15th century[30] show how much importance the Portuguese government attached to supplies from north-eastern Europe. With time, this dependence on the Baltic region even increased. From the beginning of the 16th century Portuguese imports of grain, primarily from Prussia and Livonia, also rose.[31] To say anything more specific about the balance of trade between Portugal on the one hand and Prussia and

---

[27] A. H. de Oliveira Marques, *Hansa*, p. 111f.
[28] A. Braamcamp Freire, *A feitoria de Flandres*, pp. 413–415.
[29] J. Denucé, "Privilèges commerciaux accordés par les rois du Portugal aux Flamands et Allemands", in *Archivo Histórico Português*, Vol. 8–9, 1910–12, pp. 318, 388, 389–392.
[30] *Ibid.*, pp. 384–392.
[31] A. Braamcamp Freire, *A feitoria de Flandres*, Vol. VI, Nos. 19, 23, 50, 59. The letters of the royal agents stationed in Antwerp in the first half of the 15th century show that Portugal was acquiring grain there, and that the situation in the grain market depended heavily on Baltic deliveries. Data from the trade manual by Hans Paumgartner of Augsburg indicate the same. See A. K. Müller, *Welthandelsbräuche (1480–1540)*, 2nd edition (Wiesbaden, 1962), pp. 77, 261, 302f.

other Baltic countries on the other is impossible. The Prussians usually exported mass and relatively cheap products; however, the share of Hanseatic traders from the Baltic region in deliveries of Netherlands woollen cloth, copper, and even furs might have had an advantageous effect on the balance of payments. Portugal, for its part, exported wine, fruits, and salt, but the first two of these items belong to the category of more expensive products, and were not very popular in the Baltic area. We may assume that, during the 16th century, significant changes occurred in the structure of Portuguese exports to the Baltic region, as at that time they included Indian spices and almost certainly sugar from Madeira and São Tomé as well. It would seem, however, that initially Hanseatic merchants bought these products primarily in Antwerp, which became the leading centre for trade in these goods. It is thus difficult to say whether or when German traders were able to gain access to Portugal's African gold. Some of the Portuguese royal records indicate that the Hanse dealers, at least on occasion, brought silver coins with them and that, if they did not spend their silver in Portugal, they were free to take it abroad.[32] This offered them a certain opportunity to export gold from Portugal, which was strictly forbidden by the Portuguese authorities. Of course we have virtually no information on this subject since such transactions were naturally kept secret. We only have the testimony of a commanding officer of a large group of Dutch boats who in 1552 returned from Lisbon to Arnemuiden. The officer attested that the merchants had hidden large amounts of gold on board. He himself had hidden 7,000 ducats, and one Antonio del Rio (i.e. a Spaniard) more than 10,000 ducats. Had royal officials searched the ships, matters would have taken a tragic turn.[33] One can surmise that the case described here was not unique, and that passengers not only of Dutch but also of Hanseatic boats secretly shipped Portuguese gold overseas.

As already mentioned, Baltic forestry and agricultural products reached Portugal not through the offices of the Hanseatic merchants alone. The products were available, first in Brugge, later in Antwerp and Amsterdam. The Portuguese took a very active part in their transport, but first and foremost the Dutch. There are certain suppositions that

[32] J. Denucé, "Privilèges commerciaux," pp. 378, 381, etc.
[33] R. Häpke, *Niederländische Akten und Urkunden zur deutschen Seegeschichte*, Vol. I, No. 629, München u. Leipzig, 1913.

the English, too, showed great interest in the dispatch of Baltic products to Lisbon. During the 16th century, Dutch mediation in the shipping trade between the Baltic ports and the Iberian peninsula assumed large proportions, whereas the share of the Gdańsk fleet dropped. It rose again at the time of the Netherlands Revolution, when boats from the "rebel provinces" were often refused entry into the ports of Spain and Portugal, united from 1580 until 1640 under Philip II and his successors.

The question of Polish lands' indirect participation in European overseas expansion in the 15th–17th centuries thus deserves thorough examination. At that time Gdańsk was a large exporter of forestry and agricultural products from the Polish-Lithuanian state, whose reserves of these commodities were enormous. We may assume that, without East European deliveries, the development of the Portuguese (and also Spanish) fleet would have been impossible. It should be added here that for many years Portugal had to build ships capable of sailing not only to Africa, but also to Brazil and even to India. In view of the very short life of the ships of that time, especially of those sailing in tropical waters,[34] demand for wood rose together with colonial expansion. Thanks to grain deliveries primarily from the Polish territories, the chronically insecure food supply of the Iberian Peninsula eased off. On the other hand, the peninsular countries' overseas expansion strengthened Polish and Lithuanian forestry and agriculture. However, at the present stage of research, the precise effect of Iberian imports is not known and requires further study.

As soon as the Portuguese established trade relations with West Africa, they found that copper products and brasses were in relatively great demand there. However, in order to export them, the Portuguese had themselves first to import them—primarily from central and southern Germany. In the 14th and 15th centuries, the leading centre manufacturing such goods was Nuremberg. This was the period of the city's greatest prosperity as a trade centre. Town residents did not confine themselves to the distribution of products by their own craftsmen. They were active as merchants in general. Residents of other south German and Swiss towns, where linen and fustian production was prominent, acted in similar fashion. Although, in his monumental work on the

---

[34] According to information acquired by H. Münzer in Lisbon in 1494, a ship built of European wood could withstand no more than four voyages to Africa. After this, the wood rotted away. B. de Vasconcelos, *"Itinerario" do Dr Jeronimo Münzer*, p. 50.

great Ravensburg Trading Company of Bavaria, A. Schulte provides
extensive information concerning the activities of south German
merchants in Catalonia, Aragon, Valencia, and Majorca, he does not
mention their operations in Portugal.[35] We know however that in the
15th century copper products and brasses already played a considerable
role in the trade of Portuguese missions to Black Africa. In his account
of his trip to Portugal, Hieronim Münzer of Nuremberg wrote that
John II sent to Africa various products of Nuremberg crafts, such as
copper cauldrons, brass basins, gilded items, amber rosaries, woollen
cloth, etc.[36] In that period there already existed in Lisbon a colony of
south German merchants who enjoyed a certain degree of autonomy
and tax relief. The merchants from southern Germany would seem to
have attained the status of a privileged group sooner than the Hanseatic
salesmen. A Moravian or Saxon, one Valentim Fernandes, known as a
Portuguese writer and an outstanding printer from Lisbon, came from
that community. The settlement of German merchants in Lisbon or the
placing of their agents there, even before the discoveries of Vasco da
Gama, was no doubt related to the expanding West African trade. On
the one hand, the Portuguese were increasingly in need of the products
of southern German crafts, in order to export them to Africa. On the
other hand, the inflow of gold from that continent was rising at the
time, and must have attracted south German merchants. It should be
borne in mind here that the revival of European mining in the second
half of the 15th century did not include gold mining, but helped very
substantially to increase the manufacture of copper products and brasses
and augment European silver reserves.

In the present state of research, we cannot determine the effect of
Portuguese expansion in Africa as early as the 15th century on European
mining and crafts. It is obvious, however, that this expansion was one
of the factors of their growth. Further discoveries and the accompanying trade expansion magnified the importance of this factor. The rising silver, copper, and tin outputs and the development of European
metallurgy enabled not only the Portuguese but also the Venetians
and the merchant-financiers from southern Germany to develop their

---

[35] G. Reicke, *Geschichte der Reichstadt Nürnberg* (Nürnberg, 1896), pp. 112, 237–240,
646–648; G. Schrötter, *Geschichte der Stadt Nürnberg* (Nürnberg, 1909), pp. 22–25,
100; A. Schulte, *Geschichte der Grossen Ravensburger Handelsgesellschaft 1380–1530*
(Stuttgart/ Berlin, 1923), pp. 448–450.
[36] B. de Vasconcelos, *"Itinerario" do Dr Jeronimo Münzer*, pp. 13, 52.

overseas trade. I mean here the Fuggers, the Welsers, the Höchstetters, the Paumgartners and several other big German and Italian establishments. The quick rise of Antwerp at the turn of the 15th century to become the most important commercial centre was a direct effect of such development.

Portugal here played the role of intermediary between Europe and the overseas countries. Hans Paumgartner's merchant guidebook, from the first quarter of the 16th century, shows that at this time Portugal imported goods from Africa, India, and Brazil, as well as silver, copper, and all sorts of silk, woollen and linen cloths, grain, and wood from Western, Central, and Eastern Europe.[37]

However, this outwardly fascinating picture of the situation leaves no doubt about the weakness of the local production basis. At the same time, such a situation was favourable to the growth of the Portuguese merchants. Their chief representative was the king himself, who had the largest volume of the most desirable colonial goods and who, through the special system of checks and duties, effectively controlled the entire trade.

We lack sufficient source material to conduct a thorough analysis of the Lisbon market with regard to African trade. We can, however, state that foreign merchants operating in Lisbon offered only a part of the goods indispensable to trade with Black Africa. As regards the Netherlands, the situation is slightly clearer, thanks to the survival (and part publication) of the correspondence of the agents of the Portuguese Crown, together with certain details concerning the activities of other Portuguese there. But information about Portuguese trade in Brugge in the 15th century is very scanty. We know that Portuguese merchants appeared there in large numbers, particularly from the middle of the century. For more than fifty years they had been enjoying many privileges, had their own jurisdiction, their own superior with the title of consul, and, from 1445, their own trading-post in the town.[38]

From the text of the privileges, it emerges that already at that time the Portuguese in Brugge were buying such items as masts and grain, but first and foremost Flemish and Dutch cloth and canvas. In 1441 they purchased arms as well. It is worth stressing here that, in the 15th century, some of the vessels the Portuguese sailed to Flanders

---

[37] A. K. Müller, *Welthandelsbräuche*, pp. 288–301.
[38] A. Braamcamp Freire, *A feitoria de Flandres*, VI, pp. 337–339.

were owned by the Portuguese aristocracy.[39] To the Netherlands, the Portuguese supplied mostly wine, olive oil, southern fruits, wax, leather, honey, and cork. The Italians, who, under Alfonso V, held a monopoly of the procurement of Portuguese cork and resin, exported these wares to Brugge.[40] From 1441 at the latest, successive *feitores*, i.e. Crown agents, operated in Brugge, and they, of course, had the greatest trade opportunities. Initially, their transactions did not indicate any direct consequences of the growing trade with Africa. Perhaps this was due to the fact that trade in African goods was in the hands of Prince Henry, whose archives were lost at an early stage. There is little information available concerning the rule of King John II. At that time, exports of Madeira sugar to Flanders were increasing. Meanwhile, Alfonso Martins, royal *feitor* from 1495, delivered African goods to Brugge: the first pepper, presumably from Benin, sold in Flanders and England for 600,000 reals, and also a certain amount of ivory.[41] Manuel Fernandes, King Emanuel's first permanent agent, who was still in Brugge, offered a wider assortment of African products: cotton (perhaps from the Cape Verde Islands), over and above 274 Portuguese quintals of gum arabic from Arguin, a small amount of ivory, pepper (from Benin), and *malagueta*.[42] During the entire period preceding the discovery of the passage to India and the transfer of the *feitor* and other Portuguese merchants from Brugge to Antwerp, the list of goods they purchased in the Netherlands did not change much, though the transactions of the royal *feitoria* increased. In Brugge, the Portuguese continued to buy mainly cloth and canvas from Flanders and Brabant, copper, arms (including fire-arms), gunpowder, masts, hemp cordage, grain, flour, and many luxury products, primarily for the court.[43]

In the 15th century, the Netherlands merchants in Lisbon formed a group enjoying special privileges of the Crown. Their transactions were probably very similar to those of their Portuguese colleagues. In my opinion, the very flood of foreigners observed in Lisbon in the 15th century is indicative of the bright business prospects that trade with Africa offered.

---

[39] *Ibid.*, p. 351.
[40] *Ibid.*, pp. 327, 337, 359.
[41] *Ibid.*, p. 368.
[42] *Ibid.*, p. 371.
[43] *Ibid.*, pp. 347–371.

The question thus arises as to where in the 15th century did the Portuguese procure some of the chief items of their exports to Africa, i.e. *manilhas* or bangles, necklaces, cauldrons, basins and other wares made of copper, brass, and iron, and chains to fetter slaves. These were the products of Nuremberg which Hieronim Münzer mentioned. We find masses of them when examining details of the sales of the Portuguese missions in Africa. The first bills of the royal *feitores* in the Netherlands seldom mentioned these items, but it is hard to imagine that they did not buy such commodities in Brugge, the more so since, in a somewhat later period, in the years 1495–1498, the *feitores* used to buy them in very large quantities. For example, the agent Manuel Fernandes purchased 447,484 brass *manilhas*, weighing 258,173 Portuguese pounds, several thousand shaving bowls, 3,254 wash-basins, etc.[44] These were very important acquisitions, considering that, in his statutes concerning Casa da Mina, the central institution managing trade with Africa, King Emanuel stated that the lack of bangles often made transactions at Mina difficult, and that there should therefore always be 100,000 items in reserve, so that dispatching them to Africa should be always feasible.[45] The mass-scale sale of such merchandise by the Portuguese in Africa doubtless provided a potent incentive to European crafts, particularly in southern Germany, the Rhineland, and a part of the Netherlands.

The transfer of Portuguese agents and merchants from Brugge to Antwerp coincided and was no doubt connected with the discovery of the sea passage to India. True, the position of the Portuguese as the controllers of the spice-trade became very strong. At the same time, however, their demand for tin, silver, bronze, and especially for copper developed beyond measure. That is why the Portuguese Crown was quick to establish close relations with big south German houses in control of the exploitation and distribution of these metals in Europe. These houses were very active in Antwerp; their managers showed keen interest in the Lisbon market. Large-scale entrepreneurs had an enormous financial advantage not only over the Portuguese merchants but over the Crown as well. They wanted to exploit this to the full, but encountered sharp resistance. In 1504, Emanuel agreed that the Fuggers, the Welsers, the Höchstetters, the Imhoffs, and several other south German and Italian houses might send their agents and goods to India.

---

[44] *Ibid.*, p. 372.
[45] D. Peres, *Regimento das Casas das Indias e Mina* (Coimbra, 1947), chap. 5, p. 8.

This, however, was to prove a short-lived victory. In the following year, Emanuel decreed that Indian spices should be sold only by the Casa da India in Lisbon or the royal agent in Antwerp.[46] All this was bound to exert an impact on trade with Africa. In the absence of sufficient source materials, however, it is difficult to elucidate this question. At any rate, we know that at the beginning of the 16th century the Portuguese used to acquire in Antwerp large quantities of brass and copper bangles,[47] the lion's share of which must have been meant for African customers. The acquisition of copper became a very difficult problem for Emanuel. Copper formed a vital part of Portuguese exports to South Asia. It was also of significant importance in trade with West Africa, which lacked this metal. Even so, compared with the huge volumes of copper exported to India, exports to Africa were quite insignificant. Information on this subject is very meagre. Some idea of the circumstances at that time can be gauged, for example, from the fact that in 1517 a mere 210 quintals and 86 pounds of red copper were dispatched from Antwerp to the Casa da Mina in Lisbon, whereas contracts which the *feitoria* signed with the Fuggers, the Frescobaldis, and the Affaitadis amounted to the supply of 12,000 quintals of copper a year (with Portugal's own demand for that metal hardly exceeding a quarter of this volume).[48] German and Italian financiers, who captured the lion's share of European copper mining, the Fuggers in particular, frequently imposed high prices for that metal. They used to collect their Portuguese dues in Indian spices. This was most inconvenient to the Portuguese Crown, which in this way lost its freedom to sell its precious merchandise to the highest bidder. It is worth stressing here that from 1506 onwards, in order to keep prices for Indian pepper high, Emanuel restricted deliveries of African pepper to Antwerp, which might otherwise have had an adverse effect on the volume of imports of that commodity from Africa.[49]

---

[46] A. Braamcamp Freire, *A Feitoria de Flandres*, p. 377.

[47] *Ibid.*, pp. 382, 413 and *passim*. Shortly before 1510, the royal agent procured 550 barrels of bangles to exchange them for slaves. In the years 1494–1498 he had purchased brass and copper bangles weighing 937,586 pounds. We do not know the figures concerning acquisitions by private merchants.

[48] *Ibid.*, p. 410.

[49] *Ibid.*, VII: *Documentos*, Nos. 21, 23, 25, 37, 41, 42, 50, 58, etc. Letters from the *feitores* to King Emanuel from the years 1509–1522. Many of them give an interesting picture of the situation in Europe. For example, letter No. 41 of 9 December 1519 tells of the Fuggers' and other German firms' siding with Christian II who fought against Sweden. The Fuggers wanted to gain control over Swedish copper. In a letter dated 27 November 1520, *feitor* Rui Fernandes reports on the tragic situation in Hungary. He

Sugar was a major item of Portuguese exports to Antwerp and to the rest of Europe. At the turn of the 15th century, Portuguese sugar came mostly from Madeira. Within the next few decades, supplies from São Tomé became increasingly important. Then came deliveries from Brazil. African sugar was of relatively inferior quality. It was purified only in Antwerp, where many sugar refineries were established. One of the great Antwerp firms, the Schetzs, acquired large sugar plantations in Brazil as early as *c.* 1540. Previously they had shown keen interest in São Tomé sugar. From other sources we know that in mid-century the Schetzs were exporting sugar from Antwerp to Amsterdam.[50] It cannot be ascertained whether other Antwerp firms invested in sugar production. Inasmuch as the Portuguese Crown had a practical monopoly of the supplies of Indian spices to Antwerp and Italy, there were numerous Portuguese, Genoese, Castilian, and other merchants in the sugar exporting business, whence their understandable inclination to control production.

Summing up, it must be said that trade between Portugal and African countries had from the very beginning undoubtedly had a stimulating effect on western European crafts, first and foremost on metal-work in Germany and the Netherlands, and also on mining. In addition, Portuguese expansion in Africa offered great opportunities to the big capital represented at that time by Italian and German houses. To be sure, foreign capital made colonial conquest possible for the Portuguese, but at the same time made them increasingly dependent on foreign factors, and also caused the outflow of currency from Portugal to other countries. Seeking the help of the more developed European countries did not solve all the problems related to Portuguese overseas expansion. As early as under Prince Henry, it became essential

---

describes Sigismund I very favourably, writing that he reclaims the royal estates on pawn, and that he is alleged to have raised the Crown's revenues from 80,000–100,000 to 200,000 florins a year. He also mentions that Sigismund I is very popular in Poland.

[50] J. Denucé, *L'Afrique au XVIe siècle et le commerce anversois* (Anvers, 1937), pp. 37–40. The Portuguese were among the Schetzs' customers for large quantities of copper, and brass and lead products. The Schetzs came from Aix-la-Chapelle, a major centre of brass production. Also, the Schetzs held calamine mines in Limbourg on lease, as calamine was indispensable to the production of brass. For the relations between Antwerp's big merchants and São Tomé and for the distribution of São Tomé sugar in Europe, see *ibid.*, p. 42; F. Mauro, *Le Portugal*, p. 189; C. Laga, "O engenho dos Erasmos em São Vincente," in *Estudos Historicos*, Vol. 1, 1963, pp. 24, 26; M. Małowist, "Les produits des pays de la Baltique dans le commerce international au XVIe siècle," in *Revue du Nord*, No. 166, 1960, p. 192, footnote 73.

for Portugal to establish closer links with the Maghreb, in order to supply Black African markets with the goods in demand there, i.e. primarily light textiles which the Maghrebi in turn supplied to Sudan. Hieronim Münzer wrote that John II imported *tapetes*, i.e. carpets, from Fez and Tunis, and that he enjoined that they should be made in a certain town in Portugal, but Münzer forgot where. This could have been Redondo, east of Evora.[51] The Portuguese exported these carpets to Africa. Not later than the mid-15th century, their exports to Africa contained many more Maghrebi textiles—as indicated by the account given by Ca'Da Mosto with regard to Arguin.[52] The problem has been investigated by R. Ricard. Ricard mentions the so-called *hambels* or *alambees* and blankets produced in Oran, Tunis, Tenès, and Safi as the most important Maghrebi textiles that the Portuguese delivered to Arguin, Mina, and other trading points at the turn of the 15th century and later. Contemporary accounts also mention other kinds of Moroccan blankets, burnouses, and cheap, bright cloth, preferably red or blue, particularly popular with the black population, and many other textile products.[53] King Emanuel, probably preceded by John II, established contact with some of the Safi Jews who were able to supply him with *hambels*, which he could then export south of the Sahara. The Portuguese acquired horses and certain amounts of grain in Morocco, which they then supplied to Arguin and Senegambia.[54] Unlike textiles, grain was not exported to the Gold Coast, where the people had sufficient sorghum, and hence had no need for European or Maghrebi food products.

The occupation of the Atlantic ports of Morocco made it easier for the Portuguese to exploit the West African coast, to say nothing of their intercepting some of the gold and slaves that Sudan was exporting to Morocco. Although the Portuguese were in competition with Andalusian and Genoese merchants as early as the beginning of the 16th century, their control over a number of ports still strengthened their position vis-a-vis the Moroccans. Before long, however, it trans-

---

[51] B. de Vasconcelos, *"Itinerario" do Dr Jeronimo Münzer*, p. 54; R. Ricard, "Etudes," p. 85, footnote 1.
[52] Ca'Da Mosto, *Delle navigazioni e viaggi di Messer Alvise da Ca'Da Mosto gentiluomo Veneziano*, ed. by R. Caddeo (Milano, 1929), p. 187.
[53] R. Ricard, "Etudes," pp. 89, 93, 96, 107–111.
[54] V. Magalhães Godinho, *História económica e social da expansão portuguesa* (Lisboa, 1947), pp. 77–97. Valentim Fernandes maintains that the Portuguese also acquired textiles for export to West Africa at Azemniar and other Moroccan coastal towns.

pired that the Portuguese were unable to maintain that position when the Sà'di family established an independent state in Morocco, and when English, French, and Dutch merchants began to show a keener interest in that country's natural resources. But even at the time of Portugal's greatest influence in Morocco, its territory played a much lesser role than Europe as a base of Portuguese trade in West Africa. All this taken together supports the thesis that Portugal's production basis was very narrow, and that the great seaborne expansion did little to strengthen that basis in the 15th and 16th centuries. The result was that a high percentage of the profit made on trade with Africa and India immediately passed into the hands of foreign financiers and, to a lesser degree, producers. Portugal itself played the role of the relay station, which was of course an untenable position in the long run. Colonial trade and revenues from missions in Africa and India were not factors that could contribute in any great measure to the economic development of the metropolis.

CHAPTER EIGHTEEN

GULF OF GUINEA COUNTRIES IN THE 15TH AND EARLY 16TH CENTURY*

Let us now examine the situation of the inhabitants of the Gulf of Guinea coast at the time when the Portuguese appeared there, and the changes that occurred in the area in the early period of European expansion. To study these issues, particularly the first one, is not easy. The only available source concerning the epoch preceding the arrival of the whites is the oral tradition, which is at present being written down and analysed by English and African scholars. Although they have already met with considerable success, sources of this kind do not usually contain any indication of the chronology of the events described and are thus extremely difficult to interpret. What is more, they do not provide information on the economic and social problems that interest us.

The fact remains that it was precisely the areas situated round the Gulf of Guinea and the nearby islands that were of vital importance at the time of early European expansion. It was there, and especially on the Gold Coast, that the Portuguese finally achieved what had been their main ambition ever since the 15th century, namely the organization of the gold trade on a relatively large scale. In the territories further to the east, they discovered a rich source of slaves. Against their will, they paved the way for the English and the Dutch, who would later extensively develop the existing opportunities.

On the coast of the Gulf of Guinea, chiefly on São Tomé island, the Portuguese organized the first sugar plantations based on the black slave labour imported from the mainland. The system, much more highly developed than in Madeira, the Canary Islands, and even the Cape Verde Islands, became a model, not only for the Portuguese colonizers in Brazil, but also for other European colonizers in Central

* Originally published as Chapter V of *Europa a Afryka Zachodnia w dobie wczesnej ekspansji kolonialnej*, PWN, Warszawa, 1969, pp. 397–429. Translated from Polish by Maria Chmielewska-Szlajfer, revised by Robin Kimball.

and South America and in the British possessions in North America. It is worth adding here that São Tomé island became a leading centre for the transshipment of black slaves to the New World.

The São Tomé, Annobón, and Principe islands were probably discovered by members of the expeditions sent by Fernão Gomes, a well-known licensee in trade with Africa in the years 1469–74. It is generally believed that the discovery took place after 1471. It was then or soon after that Fernão Do Pó discovered the island subsequently named after him (Fernando Po).[1] All these islands were uninhabited. Their considerable distance from the metropolis and their severe tropical climate for several years prevented any serious attempt to colonize them. After some time, however, the Portuguese realized that, thanks to its volcanic, very fertile soil and numerous potable springs, São Tomé island was fit for cultivation. The climate of the areas slightly above sea level proved less lethal to European settlers, although even there a white man could not expect to live long.[2] Hence São Tomé island very early became a place of exile, not just for criminals alone. No doubt the Portuguese crown's chief motive for colonization of the island was the sound decision to introduce sugar there. On 24th September 1485, John II gave João de Paiva the rank of *capitão* of the island of São Tomé. In the deed of 16th December, the king made a reservation that settlers should pay him partly in kind, i.e. in sugar. In anticipation of the need to import manpower from the neighbouring continent, John II licensed future settlers to conduct trade "on five slave rivers" east of the castle of São Jorge da Mina.[3]

---

[1] J. de Barros, "Asia," in G. R. Crone, ed., *Voyages of Cadamosto and Other Documents on Western Africa in the Second Half of the 15th Century* (London, 1937), pp. 109–111; P. de Cenival et Th. Monod, *Description de la côte d'Afrique de Ceuta au Sénégal par Valentim Fernandes (1506–1507)* (Paris, 1951), p. 182f., footnote 239 (hereafter quoted as *Valentim Fernandes*); Damião Peres, *A History of the Portuguese Discoveries* (Lisboa, 1960), pp. 46–48.

[2] "Navigazione da Lisbona all'Isola di San Tomé scritta per un pilotto portaghese e mandata al magnifico Conte Raimondo della Torre di Verona (1551)," in R. Caddeo, *Viaggi e scoperte*, Vol. I, pp. 324–327 (hereafter quoted as "Navigazione"). An anonymous pilot, knowing the island well, described the diseases striking the whites, the often fatal "fever" in particular. Only a handful of whites passed the age of 50. The author emphasized the wide spread of *mal francese* and other venereal diseases.

[3] J. M. da Silva Marques, *Descobrimentos Portugueses. Documentos para a sua história*, Vol. II (Lisboa, 1944), pp. 299, 500; A. Brásio, "Monumenta Missionaria Africana," in *Africa Ocidental*, Vol. I, p. 50; V. Rau e J. de Macedo, *O Açúcar da Madeira nos finos do século XV* (Funchal, 1962), p. 9; *Valentim Fernandes*, p. 182f.; A. F. C. Ryder, "An Early Portuguese Trading Voyage to the Forcados River," in *Journal of the Historical*

For several more years the settlement campaign produced no results, though it is possible that the first convicts had already appeared on the island of São Tomé. It is not known either when John II began to apply the method, taken over by his successor Emanuel, which consisted of assigning a black female slave to every convict in the hope that their offspring would remain on the island for good. Children from such unions were later granted the status of free people (with some limitations).[4] With time, the island became the territory where some of the mulattoes and a small number of negroes enjoyed a certain degree of well-being and a relatively good social position. But this was not so much the result of alleged Portuguese tolerance towards "coloured" people as the effect of the heavy fighting on the island in the 16th and 17th centuries, as well as the geographical and climatic conditions, which, at the time, ruled out any large-scale or permanent European settlement.

In 1493, the knight Alvaro de Caminha was appointed the island's *capitão*. At the same time, John II took advantage of the fact that the Jews expelled from Castile in 1492, who had earlier paid him considerable sums of money for the privilege of staying on in Portugal for a short time, had not yet had time to leave the country. By the king's order, their children were taken away from them, forcefully baptized, and, with *capitão* de Caminha, sent to the island of São Tomé, where, as Garcia de Resende puts it, "separated from their parents, they were to become good Christians."[5] Valentim Fernandes maintains that there were 2,000 children under eight years of age. Compared with other sources, the age of the children seems unlikely. When all is said and done, children that young would not have survived the island's lethal climate. At the time de Resende was writing (about 1511), there reportedly lived a mere 600 of the deported children, as many of them had

---

Society of Nigeria, Vol. 1, No. 4, 1959, p. 294. Ryder believes the five rivers to have been Mahin, Benin, Escravos, Forcados, and Ramos.

[4] A. Brásio, "Mon. Miss. Afr.," Vol. I, No. 107. Emanuel's emancipation acts of January 1517. All these indicate only a small number of European women on the island. The above-mentioned pilot wrote that negroes and mulattoes on the island procreated very quickly, whereas white women remained barren. See "Navigazione," p. 327. The matter throws some light on the alleged lack of any feeling of racial superiority among the Portuguese, so emphasized by their historians and questioned, justifiably, by C. R. Boxer, "The Colour Question in the Portuguese Empire, 1415–1825," in *Proceedings of the British Academy*, Vol. 47, 1961, and in other works by this scholar.

[5] Garcia de Resende, *Chronica de El-Rei Dom João II*, Bibliotheca de Classicos Portugueses Vol. 3 (Lisboa, 1902), p. 37.

died on arrival. When they grew up, by the captain's order, they married, but they had very few children. In this respect, interracial black and white marriages produced much better results. A group of people, two carpenters among them, were also reported to have left for the island voluntarily, together with de Caminha. They all died there.[6]

It is possible that this influx of colonizers speeded up the development of the island somewhat. Nevertheless, the shortage of settlers remained acute. At the end of 1499 Emanuel made the knight Fernão de Mello the captain. Several months later, the king considerably extended the privileges of the island residents, arguing that the Portuguese did not want to settle there because of the great distance from the metropolis.[7] No doubt they were scared of the climate. In virtue of the royal act, they acquired the title to conduct trade along the coast of the Gulf of Guinea from the Rio Real and the island of Fernando Po to the Congo, without the need to seek royal licence. From the mainland trade, they were to pay a *quarto* to the Exchequer. It was taken for granted that the payment would be made in black slaves and in various goods. Upon their return from the African continent to the island and after paying duty, they were free to export their goods wherever they wanted, or to sell them on the spot. Foreigners who agreed to buy goods on the island, and then transport them to the metropolis or to other crown possessions, were excused from many customs tariffs. The island residents were exempted from depositing 10 per cent of the value of the goods they brought to the Portuguese possessions. The settlers moreover were accorded tax relief when buying or selling goods on the Cape Verde Islands, the Canaries, Madeira, and the Azores. In all the cases mentioned, they were merely obliged to produce a certificate of their residence on the island of São Tomé. They were also allowed to deliver food from their own island to São Jorge da Mina. There they might exchange food for gold—through the mediation of a royal official and in keeping with binding regulations. Last but not least, should the king lease the revenues drawn from the island to anyone, the colonizers' privileges were to remain in force. These privileges, greater than those granted to settlers on the Cape Verde Islands, are proof that the colonization of the island of São Tomé encountered considerable

---

[6] *Valentim Fernandes*, p. 118.
[7] J. W. Blake, *Europeans in West Africa 1450–1560*, Vol. I (London, 1942), p. 89.

difficulties. The new royal privilege, moreover, provided that the island residents might freely import slaves for the emerging sugar plantations, and export negroes, sugar, cotton, and other commodities, not only to the metropolis and its Atlantic territories, but to foreign countries as well. The licence, and even encouragement, to deliver food to São Jorge da Mina gave them some access to trade in gold, of which they took advantage to an extent that caused the crown's displeasure.[8]

It is not easy to assess the island's population at the turn of the 15th century. Valentim Fernandes, who based his description on the account of one obscure Gonçalo Pires, writes that, at the time of Captain Alvaro de Caminha, a settlement was established in the south-eastern part of the island. The captain erected for himself and his family a fortified tower and two churches of stone and lime shipped by John II. The settlement was inhabited by two hundred people, mostly convicts whose death sentence had been commuted to deportation to the island. In the margin there is a note: "sixty arrived of their own free will." The same author says that Fernão de Mello moved the settlement to a healthier area—presumably the other port settlement described, situated on the Bay of Ana Chaves, where ships were repaired. There were about 250 wooden, two-storey houses, more or less as many as covered the remaining territory of the island, primarily on the rivers. Valentim Fernandes estimates the number of field slaves at 2,000. Another 5,000–6,000 *espravos de resgate*, i.e. newly-acquired slaves due to be transshipped, often stayed on the island temporarily. According to another source, the first settlement mentioned was situated in the north of the island; the other, called first Povoação and later Cidade de São Tomé, on the north-eastern coast.

So, according to Valentim Fernandes, at the turn of the 15th century there were on the island some five hundred wooden houses inhabited by whites, by free or recently freed negroes and mulattoes, and their slave servants. This would represent a substantial number of 2,000–3,000 heads altogether. It is hard to say whether the above-mentioned two thousand field slaves should be included in this figure—probably not, as field slaves usually lived separately from their masters. It is more likely the house slaves that Fernandes must have had in mind. The number of whites is hard to estimate. Presumably some 50–100 of them were

---

[8] *Ibid.*

Portuguese family heads, with this reservation however that, as early as about 1500, these families were already very much racially mixed. If, as Valentim Fernandes writes, six hundred of the Jewish children deported in 1439 did survive—which seems unlikely—the number of whites would be correspondingly bigger. The freed mulattoes, negroes, and house slaves would make up the rest.[9]

The de Mello family exercised captaincy of the island, that is administration and jurisdiction, until 1522, when the last representative of the family, accused of many crimes, fled São Tomé. The crown deprived him of his fief and office, and took power into its own hands. By that time, sugar production had already increased. Already in 1499 there were on the island *engenho* mills to grind sugar-cane and press juice out of it. They were either water- or slave-operated. In 1517, regulations concerning the sale of sugar and the related charges were issued. On the island of São Tomé, primarily molasses were produced. These made a brown, poorly refined sugar, but one cheaper than that produced in Madeira.[10]

The first precise figures regarding sugar production on São Tomé date from 1529. At that time the island yielded about 5,000 arrobas, i.e. more or less 60 tons, of sugar a year. It was also in 1529 that the construction of twelve new *engenhos* was started. This was merely a modest beginning of the huge increase in production which, by the middle of the century, amounted to 150,000 arrobas (about 1,800 tons) of sugar from local plantations, processed by sixty mills. Meanwhile the number of houses occupied by free people and their servants only went up from 500 to a mere 600 or 700.[11] The explosive growth in production thus depended

---

[9] *Valentim Fernandes*, pp. 120, 128, 184, footnotes 241–243. In a letter to the king, dated 30th July 1499, a son of Alvaro da Caminha gives the number of fifty *moradores*, i.e. permanent free residents of the island. There were 60–62 signatures of *moradores e vezinhos degradados* (i.e. convicted, permanent residents and citizens of the island) under the petition to the king, dated 27th July 1499. It is impossible to say whether this number concerns only convicts or voluntary white settlers as well. At that time, freedmen were not yet included among the *moradores*, let alone the higher caste of *vezinhos*, the free property owners. A reference, in a letter of 30th July 1499, to young boys and girls being conscientiously instructed in the Christian faith, but lacking clothes and food, might refer to the Jewish children brought from Portugal in 1493. See A. Brásio, "Mon. Miss. Afr.," Vol, I, No. 137.

[10] V. Rau e J. de Macedo, *O Açúcar*, p. 10; F. Mauro, *Le Portugal et l'Atlantique au XVIIᵉ siècle 1570–1670* (Paris, 1960), p. 189f.

[11] V. Magalhães Godinho, "Crises et changements géographiques et structuraux au XVIᵉ siècle," in *Studi in onore di A. Sapori*, Vol. II (Milano, 1957), p. 983; "Navigazione," p. 316.

on the large influx of slave labour from the African continent, on the growth in the sales market, and on such organization of production and distribution as would enable São Tomé residents to import food and other necessities from Europe and the Atlantic islands.

We have already seen how the royal deeds from the final years of the 15th and the early years of the 16th century attempted to tackle the situation. The aim of the royal ordinance of 1524 was the same. It encouraged imports of food, iron, copper, tin, and other products the island needed, with the exception of those whose export to the African mainland was forbidden. The ordinance observed the principle of the free export of goods from São Tomé island to the metropolis, to the Atlantic islands, and to foreign countries. Moreover, it allowed foreigners to export sugar. The ordinance betrays some concern about the fact that sugar plantations were growing at the expense of grain production. The government had been trying to halt this process, but to no avail. Moreover, from the ordinance it transpires that island residents made expeditions for gold to the neighbouring continent without bothering to acquire the royal licence, supplying negroes in the process with banned commodities, maybe arms. This was strictly forbidden.[12]

The import of slaves to São Tomé began soon after the discovery of the island. Judging from the above-quoted royal deeds, slaves came from the Yoruba, the Igbo, and smaller ethnic groups of the population living in the Niger Delta, from Benin and, first and foremost, from Congo, with which the residents of the island had strong economic ties. This was confirmed by the anonymous Portuguese pilot who described the situation on São Tomé in the first half of the 16th century. He provided extremely valuable information on the system of plantation slavery on the island. Every prosperous settler willing to start a plantation received land from the island authorities. Then he procured slaves who dug up and burnt the trees, thus greatly raising the fertility of the soil. Sugar mills and plantations were set up along the rivers flowing from the mountains in order to exploit water power in the mill and irrigate the fields. Mills on the less advantageously situated plantations were operated by slave power alone. Planters at one time tried using horses, but they could not stand the climate and quickly perished. At the turn

---

[12] *As Gavetas da Torre do Tombo*, Vol. II (Gav. III–XII) (Lisboa, 1962), No. 1222. Officials from São Jorge da Mina advised King Emanuel in a letter dated 5th October 1509 that inhabitants of São Tomé island travelled to Mina, where they bartered banned goods for gold from negroes. J. W. Blake, *Europeans*, Vol. I, no. 20.

of the 15th century, ownership of fourteen field slaves was enough to be recognized as a prosperous person.[13] At the beginning of the 1550s, rich planters owned from 150 to 300 negroes.[14] This represented a great quantitative leap accompanying the growth of sugar plantations.

The maintenance of plantation slaves was not costly. They were allocated plots of land which they tilled on Saturdays, working for their master all the other days of the week. They ate yams, including *coco*, i.e. taro, sweet potatoes imported from America, and bananas, which abounded on the island. From 1502, the islanders began to grow sorghum, hitherto imported from mainland Africa. Valentim Fernandes also specifies other edibles, but only in passing does he mention meat as consumed by the slaves. They probably received very little. It is curious that the anonymous writer does not cite maize, which had been cultivated on the island from the end of the 15th century, though he did observe it in the Cape Verde Islands. From their masters, slaves received small quantities of cotton or palm bark, from which they made loincloths—they did not wear anything else. Cotton, too, was grown on the island.

The condition of the enslaved black population can only be deduced from a few scattered remarks by the author of this account. He wrote that in the rainy season slaves suffered from cold and wind, all the more so as they were as thin "as a tree and ha[d] no flesh." Every cold spell caused diseases and many deaths. This probably applied to the mountainous area. The slaves' diet described above indicates a deficiency of animal protein. The anonymous observer writes that pigs kept in the mills, where they were fed with production waste, were a source of meat for the whites only. The health of the entire population was bad, and not just because of the climate. Syphilis and other venereal diseases were common on the island. Negro women applied some remedies against them. Reportedly, until the 1540s no major epidemic had spread.[15]

Thanks to numerous works devoted to the history of plantations in South and Central America, we now know that the worst was the predicament of the slaves working in mills (*engenhos*). The average slave working on a plantation in Brazil did not live longer than seven to ten

---

[13] This last piece of information was provided by *Valentim Fernandes*, p. 120.

[14] "Navigazione," p. 315f.

[15] "Navigazione," *passim*. The introduction of pig, donkey, sheep, goat, and ox breeding and the cultivation of orange trees, etc. are also mentioned in *Valentim Fernandes*, pp. 122, 126, 128, 135, 137.

years. The situation in São Tomé was probably similar. If colonial Brazil was, as the saying went, black men's hell, the island of São Tomé had been the model for this hell. There were, of course, exceptions to this rule. These concerned primarily the mulattoes born from marriages between European men and negro women. A large number of their offspring were granted freedom. The author of the account referred to here writes that Portuguese, Castilian, Genoese, and French merchants residing on the island, on becoming widowers, would marry black women. The latter, however, were already daughters of free negroes, well-to-do people, *di grande intelletto*, brought up in the Portuguese manner and dressed according to European fashion.

The author we are quoting claims to have visited the island five times from 1520 onwards. He knew there one João Menino, a very old negro brought from mainland Africa at the initial stage of São Tomé colonization. The man had acquired freedom and even a considerable property, and established a family—with time a very big one.[16] As early as 1526, the royal government allowed the black freedmen to organize a rosary confraternity with privileges greater than the analogous one in Lisbon.[17] This shows that there was on the island a group of free or freed negroes, mainly mulattoes, whose social status was quite high. It is well known that such phenomena occurred in every slave society, even at times of the most extreme exploitation. More likely than not, the free mulattoes and negroes were mostly descendants of white colonizers and their black wives and slave-women, people freed on account of special services rendered to their masters, and those who managed to buy themselves out of slavery, their sons and daughters. Free and affluent negroes and mulattoes in São Tomé adopted the Portuguese way of living. It is unlikely that they treated their own slaves any better than the Portuguese did. "Racial" solidarity did not exist at that time. On the other hand, the white Portuguese did not treat them as their equals.

Due to the insignificant scale of European immigration and to the immigrants' high mortality and low birth rate,[18] the numbers of negroes and mulattoes presumably swelled much faster than the number of

---

[16] F. Mauro, *Le Portugal*, p. 179; C. R. Boxer, "The Colour Question," p. 131. For the condition of slaves in Brazil, cf. G. Freyre, *Maîtres et esclaves* (Paris, 1952); "Navigazione," pp. 314, 326.

[17] C. R. Boxer, "The Colour Question," p. 117.

[18] Comp. *Valentim Fernandes*, p. 118.

whites. This disproportion was further widened by the continuing import of slaves from the coast of Africa, destined not only for export to America and partly to Europe, but also for work on São Tomé plantations. At the time our anonymous pilot wrote his account, i.e. around 1540, the slave population on the island plantations was presumably much higher than 5,000–6,000. The author quoted here mentions 600–700 houses probably occupied by some 2,500–3,500 free whites, mulattoes and negroes, and their slave servants. At that time, some two-thirds of the island's surface were still covered by tropical rain forests. Thus, before the settlers there loomed dazzling prospects for the extension of plantations and, by the same token, for an increase in the number of slaves.[19] The situation changed markedly only at the end of the 16th century.

We do not know precisely when the first symptoms of organized resistance to the island's slave owners appeared. In either 1530 or 1531, a rebellion broke out which was still on in 1536.[20] It seems clear that the exploitation of slaves was not the only cause. It is a well-known fact that exploitation often reduced the oppressed slaves to extreme apathy. The realization that negroes were in a majority must have played a significant role. It cannot be ruled out that mulattoes, discriminated against by white colonizers, acted as the rebellion's leaders. I think, however, that the key factor was the continuous influx of negroes from Africa, of people who used to be free and who were unable to reconcile themselves with their new and helpless situation. The thick forests and

---

[19] "Navigazione," pp. 314, 318. Precise figures concerning the number of slaves on the island of São Tomé are not available. In the 17th-century, the average-size Sergipe (Brazil) sugar mill and plantation employed at least eighty slaves. F. Mauro, *Le Portugal*, p. 215. Our anonymous reporter writes that, in his time, on São Tomé island there operated sixty *engenhos* rendering 150,000 *arrobas* (about 1,800 tons), and that the São Tomé plantations were much larger than those in Madeira. On the other hand, we know that the São Tomé sugar mills and plantations did not usually compare in size and output with those in 17th-century Brazil. O. Dapper, *Description de l'Afrique* (Amsterdam, 1686), p. 490. Owners of 150–300 field slaves, mentioned by the anonymous pilot, could have, and often did have, more than one plantation. Calculating an average of eighty slaves for each of sixty plantations, we obtain 4,800 people, which number we may increase slightly. To this, we should add children and old men, the numerous servants in well-to-do households, etc. The total number of 10,000 seems to me somewhat too small.

[20] A. Brásio, "Mon. Miss. Afr.," Vol. I, No. 158 and Vol. II, No. 17. Data from 12th December 1531. Plantation slaves rebelled, killing many white settlers and their black assistants. See J. W. Blake, *Europeans*. Letters of John III, dated 22nd and 25th October 1536, mention the negroes' rebellion still continuing.

mountainous terrain of the island helped runaway slaves find shelter and, at the same time, defend themselves against their owners or even attack them. F. Mauro is probably right in suspecting that in the São Tomé mountains in the 16th and 17th centuries there existed permanent and continuous new centres of resistance of runaway slaves,[21] as was the case in Brazil and the West Indies.[22]

In the first half of the 16th century, the white colonizers of the island were first and foremost deportees and their descendants. The number of voluntary settlers was, as we have seen, insignificant, particularly at the beginning of the century, but with time it probably increased in view of the increasing production of sugar and the prospects of large and rapid profits. I have already mentioned that, alongside the Portuguese, the Castilians, the Genoese, and the French also settled on the island.[23] Despite the arguments advanced by Denucé, it is not certain whether Antwerp merchants also set up plantations there, although undoubtedly direct and indirect economic relations between the island and that city were close, and the imports of sugar from São Tomé had an effect on the growth of Antwerp's trade and sugar-refining industry.[24]

Besides wealthy planters and various-ranking officials, led by the captain and the clergy, the Portuguese residents of the island included poor whites as well. Little is known about these people's life. A certain royal deed of 1554 mentions two exiles, natives of Villa Viçosa in Portugal, who were appointed to guard one Luis de Roma, a resident

---

[21] In the second half of the 16th and at the beginning of the 17th centuries, rebellions were frequent and usually long-lasting. F. Mauro, *Le Portugal*, p. 191.

[22] C. R. Boxer, "The Colour Question," pp. 122–138; idem, "Negro Slavery in Brazil," in *Race*, Vol. 5, 1964, pp. 38–47.

[23] As indicated by the description of this group by the Portuguese pilot; "Navigazione," pp. 314, 317.

[24] J. Denucé, *L'Afrique au XVIᵉ siècle et le commerce anversois* (Anvers, 1937), pp. 42f, 95. According to Denucé, between February 1546 and February 1556 as many as eighty-two ships sailed to the island of São Tomé. The Schetz business of Antwerp had from 1540 had a sugar plantation and a mill in the captaincy of São Vincente in Brazil. See C. Laga, "O engenho dos Erasmos em São Vincente," in *Estudios Históricos*, Vol. I, No. 4, 1963, p. 26. In the years 1542–44, Erasme Schetz and other merchants staying in Antwerp frequently dispatched sugar to Amsterdam and other ports but the origin of that sugar is unknown. See Brussels, Archives du Royaume. Chambre des Comptes 23367, 30th July 1543; 23368, f. 81; 23369, f. 13, etc. The first notices concerning the transport of sugar produced on São Tomé from Antwerp to Amsterdam date from 1543. *Ibid.*, 23367, 23368, data from August and September 1543; Vazquez de Prada, *Lettres marchandes d'Anvers*, Vol. I (Paris, n.d.), pp. 93, 105, 184, and Vol. II, p. 337. When Spanish mercenaries were plundering Antwerp in 1576, fires burnt down three streets occupied by sugar refiners and spice merchants (*açucareiros y espeçieiros*).

of São Tomé imprisoned for his participation in the anti-Portuguese
rebellion. The reference is to the riots of 1550–54. In fact these arose
from conflicts between colonizers, but they were accompanied by a
slave rising which threatened the town. Luis de Roma was a white
participant in the rebellion against the town and royal authorities.
Owing to his guards' negligence, he managed to escape, as a result of
which his two guards first spent a long time in prison, and were then
sentenced to a two-year exile in Africa, for which they were shortly due
to be deported. But the king pardoned them in view of the fact that
they were from very poor peasant families and that they were earning
their living on the island as husbandmen (*piães*), and moreover were
exhausted by disease. Luis de Roma was also pardoned.[25] There must
have been very few white small farmers if membership of that group
was an argument for pardoning the two offenders. By contrast, the more
affluent Portuguese, the larger plantation owners in particular, were
the actual aristocracy of the island. They lived at Povoação or on their
own estates. The richest of them, aided by their armed slaves, could
effectively oppose officials trying to enforce sentences against them.
Family ties and the resulting bonds of solidarity among planters made
the situation of the more zealous officials really dangerous.[26]

The information supplied by the anonymous pilot concerning the
diet of the white people most probably refers only to the group of the
very well-off. They are said to have consumed food imported from
Europe and excellent pork from their own estates. The pilot observed
that they drank too much.[27] He evidently meant wine. He showed no
sympathy for the rich Portuguese, but no compassion for the oppressed
negroes either. Presumably, the white population of the island lived
in great fear of the slaves—especially when the latter revolted—and
were prone to victimize the rebels indiscriminately. There is a relevant
royal document, unfortunately from as late as 1566, from neighbouring
Principe, where the situation was very similar. The document throws
some light on the issue discussed here. The royal *ouvidor* (magistrate),

---

[25] P. d'Azevedo, "Os Escravos," No. XIII; A. Brásio, "Mon. Miss. Afr.," Vol. II, No. 106.
[26] P. d'Azevedo, "Os Escravos," No. XII. The royal deed of 30th January 1554. The
king allowed a certain clerk to carry arms permanently and arm his slaves. This in
view of the danger of attack by relatives of a certain powerful planter who had, with
the help of his armed slaves, for a long time been resisting the colonial authorities. The
latter had sentenced the planter to death. The clerk mentioned in the royal deed had
managed to imprison the planter, but had been in fear for his life ever since.
[27] "Navigazione," pp. 315–317, 325.

a nobleman named Manuel Teles, was sentenced to a three-year exile to the African mainland for having murdered rebellious mulattoes without the court inquiry required by law. Seeking pardon, he invoked the pressure emanating from other white residents of the island. The king granted his plea. From the text it emerges that Teles had served his monarch well by suppressing rebellions and taking great care of the royal treasury. Had he chosen to abide by the law with regard to the rebels, the crown would have lost the island, and many white people would have perished. Teles argued moreover that he himself had killed no one, he had merely tried to be absent when others had perpetrated the murders. After all, Teles observed, such behaviour was normal on the island.[28] King Sebastian would seem to have agreed with him.

I think this document to some extent reflects the tense situation on the islands of the Gulf of Guinea from the time when negroes and mulattoes seriously outnumbered the whites, viz. not later than in the second or third decade of the 16th century. Many scholars dealing with the problems of slavery emphasize the fact that slave societies were in constant terror of revolts and attacks, and that this fear drove slave owners and their environment to cruelty.[29] This reflects the situation obtaining in São Tomé, Principe, and other Atlantic islands before similar developments took place in Brazil and the West Indies.

In São Tomé, the ruling group was led by the island's administrators. This group included the white clergy. At the turn of the 15th century, the island was an hereditary fief of the Crown administered by the de Mello family. The captain's authority was not confined to the island alone; theoretically (but not in practice), it extended to all Portuguese residing in the territory between the Niger Delta and the Congo. The captain held the administrative, judicial, and military power. This being so, he collected some of the charges but received no pay from the treasury. Representatives of the crown or leaseholders of its revenues collected 1/4th and 1/20th of the duty on goods sold or bought by island residents and merchants doing business on the African continent. Even so, the situation of the captains was a promising one.

In the tenth year of his "rule" (i.e. in about 1509), Fernão de Mello, who lived on the island together with his family, had at least five estates

---

[28] P. d'Azevedo, "Os Escravos," No. XVIII.
[29] In the 1630s, when the number of black slaves in Portugal and Andalusia became relatively large, the laws against them were made considerably tougher.

(*fazendas*), conveniently located on the island's rivers. These were probably sugar plantations, but this is not certain. He also bred pigs, grew grain, etc.[30] De Mello engaged in trade with the continent, where he sent two locally-built vessels, of one trunk each. Reportedly, they were no smaller than an average caravel. Each of them could carry 400 quintals (over and above 1.8 tons). According to Valentim Fernandes' informant, had Fernão de Mello committed himself more seriously to trade with the coast, he could have gained 10,000 cruzados a year, which represented a very considerable sum.[31] We know that Fernão de Mello was very much involved in trade with the African continent and with Portugal. Presumably somewhere around 1509, he signed a contract with the Casa da Mina to exchange 16,000 bronze and copper bracelets for slaves and pepper from *nos rios da dita ilha*—doubtless an allusion to the five rivers of the Slave Coast. Both from the reference to pepper (not to malaguette) and from the text following, it is clear that it embraced trade with Benin as well. De Mello delivered a certain number of chains to "put negroes in."[32] The captain's accounts do not indicate how he paid his dues to the Casa da Mina; he probably paid them in kind, i.e. in slaves and pepper. That was a major transaction. It is another matter, though, whether he signed such transactions often. His interest in the export of slaves from Congo was so great that he allegedly urged the Portuguese clergy and merchants there to concentrate first and foremost on the slave trade, and pay less attention to the conversion and enlightenment of the populace. He was not ready to assist the ruler of Congo militarily against the "pagans," a fact which prompted Alfonso I to intercede with Emanuel.[33]

We are dealing here with an interesting type of rich Portuguese nobleman, a landowner (no doubt also of sugar plantations), a high state official, and holder of an hereditary overseas fief, who was also

---

[30] A. Brásio, "Mon. Miss. Afr.," Vol. I, Nos. 46, 47, 108; *Valentim Fernandes*, pp. 128, 130. These documents indicate that Fernão de Mello embezzled big funds of the Crown, oppressed the free populace of the island, and sold freedmen.

[31] *Valentim Fernandes*, pp. 132, 136.

[32] A. Braamcamp Freire, "Cartas de quitação del Rei D. Emanuel," in *Archivo Histórico Portuguez*, Vol. I, No. 8, 1903.

[33] The letter from Alfonso I, king of Congo, of 5 October 1514, with a complaint about Fernão de Mello. See A. Brásio, "Mon. Miss. Afr.," Vol. I, Nos. 83, 99, etc. Many documents imply exports of slaves from Congo at the beginning of the 16th century. The king of Congo himself took part in this; at the beginning of 1517, he appealed to Emanuel for a ship, or exemption from duty on the slaves he sent on Portuguese ships. *Ibid.*, No. 111.

committed to large-scale trade. Fernão de Mello did not disdain even illegal revenues obtained at the expense of the treasury, the free residents of the island and, of course, the slaves. He was rather typical of the great Portuguese feudal lords involved in the early colonial expansion. Thanks to their high social position and standing in the state hierarchy, they had a much freer hand than the merchants of bourgeois origin. Inevitably, such situations tempted high colonial officials into corruption, and one should thus not be surprised by the vast number of court sentences passed upon them once they had accomplished their respective missions. Duarte Pacheco did not escape this fate. He died in poverty, but he did not belong to the aristocracy.

Around 1522, authority over São Tomé was transferred to representatives of the Crown. The *corregedor*, the administrator and chief justice, was the highest official, followed by the *ouvidor*, i.e. the magistrate, then the junior executives, and finally the royal agent, who engaged in trade on behalf of the treasury and who was subordinated to the Casa da Mina. It is a well-known fact that officials were often in conflict with one another. In 1526, the settlement of Povoação was given Portuguese municipal rights as Cidade de São Tomé, which placed its citizens in a markedly better social position.

Since 1534, the island of São Tomé had been the main seat of the bishop, whose diocese extended to the neighbouring islands and coasts, including the Congo territory. But the bishops did not always reside in their diocese, out of fear of its lethal climate. By the end of the 15th century, there were two churches on the island; one was monastic, but there were no monks there at that time. It is not known when blacks first appeared among the island's clergy. In the case of the Cape Verde Islands, their existence is confirmed by source material from as late as the 17th century. But the first negro priests might already have been ordained under the rule of Emanuel (1495–1521), as the cadre to organize the church in Congo. There, the European clergy mostly died soon after their arrival. At any rate, mulatto priests existed in São Tomé no later than the middle of the 16th century.[34]

The above attempt at depicting the characteristics of São Tomé society seems to me important inasmuch as its findings throw some light on

---

[34] A. Brásio, "Mon. Miss. Afr.," Vol. II, No. 108; *Valentim Fernandes*, p. 120. In 1528, the affluent mulattoes were admitted to the Cidade de S. Tomé city council, despite the *corregedor's* objection. C. R. Boxer, "The Colour Question," pp. 117, 121.

the formation of new societies on other islands of the South Atlantic and also in Brazil in the 16th and 17th centuries. Unfortunately, owing to the inaccessibility of the Portuguese archives, I am unable to study these very interesting problems more thoroughly.

I have already emphasized the dependence of São Tomé settlers on the sugar plantations and on trade with the African continent. The latter provided manpower not just for the needs of the island but also for export to Portugal and, with time, primarily to the West Indies and Brazil. We have also seen that the island's merchants dealt with São Jorge da Mina, where they delivered food for which they bought gold. However, the successful development of the trading-post at Mina castle required a supply of slaves for the black merchants who brought the metal from the interior, and probably for the local black chiefs, too. We already know that at the beginning of the 16th century the Portuguese brought to Mina slaves they had bought in Benin, and that these slaves sometimes came from as far away as Arguin Island. In view of numerous deaths among ships's crews, due to the bad climate, in 1506 King Emanuel began signing special contracts with people engaged in trade between São Tomé and the African continent. In exchange for certain goods from the Casa da Mina and for tax reliefs, they undertook to supply São Jorge da Mina with slaves. Presumably the contract between Fernão de Mello and the central colonial authorities was of a similar nature. As the Crown's partners were making huge profits, in 1519 Emanuel scrapped the system once again. On condition that only local sailors be hired, he entrusted transactions with the Slave Coast to the Crown's resident agent in São Tomé. The local sailors were either mulattoes or negroes, who easily endured the climate that was lethal to the Portuguese. Moreover, the residents of the island engaged in trade on their own account. Thus, in 1516 they imported 4,072 "heads" of slaves on fifteen ships, in addition to 235 slaves brought there on Captain Fernão de Mello's personal account. Inasmuch as this was reportedly a very good year for the slave trade, we may assume that the average yearly number of imported negroes must have been smaller.[35]

Ryder has published the log-book kept on board a small caravel named "São Maria da Comçeiçam," which left the island on 12th

---

[35] A. Brásio, "Mon. Miss. Afr.," Vol. I, No. 108; A. F. C. Ryder, "An Early Portuguese," p. 294.

March 1522. Her destination was the rivers Forcados and Benin. The ship was dispatched by a royal agent. The caravel arrived at Forcados on 1st April 1522, and left on 25th April. On her way back, in Gwato (the port of the city of Benin), the crew had to transship their cargo to another vessel from São Tomé, as their own was seriously wrecked. The agent furnished them with 15 quintals (about 675 kg) of cowrie shells, brought as ballast by Portuguese ships on the return route from India, 4,010 copper *manilhas* [bracelets], 4,000 glass beads (from Venice), canvas from Brittany, and twelve hats. On the Forcados River and in the state of Benin, the crew managed to acquire 136 slaves (adults of both sexes, also boys and girls), 18 tusks weighing about 3 quintals (about 150 kg), palm oil, beads (very much in demand on the Gold Coast), cotton cloths, and various odds and ends. Two crew members and five slaves died, and another two ran away. In Benin, the price for an adult slave, male or female, reached 6,370 cowrie shells, and for a ten-year-old child—3,720 shells. On the Forcados, a standard-value male or female slave sold at 50 copper *manilhas*. Ships' crews were paid in slaves, usually one per individual.[36] Unfortunately, it is impossible to convert these prices, even into the Portuguese currency of the time. It seems, nevertheless, that the exchange of 50 copper bracelets for a healthy male or female slave was a good deal for the residents of São Tomé. If we recall the argument on Portugal's growing dependence in the 15th and 16th centuries on other European countries' manufactures, the log-book discussed here corroborates such a thesis. After all, among the commodities exchanged, none were of Portuguese make. What is more, there is absolutely no reason to believe that the transactions described here were in any way exceptional.

At the beginning of the 16th century, São Tomé residents and Portuguese notables there were strongly committed to trade with Congo. They must have engaged in such trade earlier, and the relevant royal privilege of 1499 merely legalized an already existing situation. It was a period of intensive Portuguese penetration of Congo, of christianization of the country's ruling groups, and of close relations between Alfonso I of Congo and his successor and John III on the one hand,

---

[36] A. F. C. Ryder, "An Early Portuguese," pp. 294–321. In his 1499 letter to the king, Pero Alvares de Caminha maintained that, in new trading-posts, a new slave cost no more than six bracelets of good-quality copper. A. Brásio, "Mon. Miss. Afr.," Vol. I, No. 44, p. 177. This presumably applied also to the Niger Delta. It is therefore clear that there, too, prices for slaves rose markedly.

and the Papal State on the other.[37] The Congolese ruler used Portuguese
assistance to fight neighbouring tribes. He was, however, afraid of their
growing influence in his own state.[38] São Tomé was the base from where
Portuguese influence permeated Congo the most powerfully. We have
already seen that in 1516 nearly 4,700 slaves, mostly from Congo, were
brought to São Tomé alone. The Congolese king, Alfonso I, also wanted
a share in this trade. He sought a special ship from Emanuel to transport slaves or an exemption from duty on the slaves exported on his
account.[39] After a time, Alfonso came to observe some of the adverse
consequences of the slave trade. In 1526 he announced he would no
longer tolerate the slave trade or the export of slaves because this caused
anarchy and led to the depopulation of his country. Various "rascals," as
he put it, kidnapped his subjects, even children of the nobility, in order
to sell them to foreign slavers. He therefore insisted that John III (or
rather the regency) forbid royal agents to send merchants with goods
to Congo, or at least that the slave trade in Congo should be subject
to local authority. Alfonso complained that the Portuguese were flooding his country with banned imports and that, as a result, numbers of
his subjects and "vassals" were growing richer than the king himself.[40]
Perhaps Alfonso I had in mind the import of weapons which he feared
his subjects might use against him.

The Portuguese did not wish to stop slave imports from Congo. In
the 1530s they (São Tomé residents included) reportedly exported more
than 5,000 "specimens" a year, which roughly translates into more or
less 7,000 heads.[41] Slaves were gathered in the port of Mpinda, south of
the estuary of the Congo River. Many of them died while waiting for
ships. Portuguese with a royal licence to carry on trade in São Tomé
and the succeeding resident agents were very much engaged in that

---

[37] Many sources indicate this. See A. Brásio, "Mon. Miss. Afr.," Vol. I, Nos. 55, 97,
99, 105, etc.; F. Pigafetta, *Relazione del Reame di Congo e delle circonvicine contrade*
(Roma, 1593), p. 55; Damião de Goes, *Chronica d'El Rei D. Emanuel*, Vol. II, Bibliotheca
de Classicos Portugueses Vol. 59 (Lisboa, 1909), p. 119f.

[38] L. Cordeiro, *Questoes histórico-coloniais*, Vol. I (Agencia Geral das Colonias, 1935),
pp. 106–108. Letter from Manuel Pacheco da Lima to John III of 20th May 1536.

[39] A. Brásio, "Mon. Miss. Afr.," Vol. I, No. 111. A document dated 26th May 1517.
Alfonso reminds Emanuel that he had already asked for a ship before, but received no
reply. But later, he had at his disposal a ship to conduct trade.

[40] *Ibid.*, Nos. 142, 147.

[41] L. Cordeiro, *Questoes*, p. 108.

trade.[42] As early as the second decade of the 16th century, the Portuguese were seeking trade with Angola. Once again, the residents of São Tomé played a considerable role therein. This aroused misgivings among the Congo rulers and led to conflicts with Europeans.[43]

A note sent by Simão da Mota to John III in 1548, on behalf of the king of Congo, contributes some very interesting information on this subject. Alfonso I reminded John III that his grandfather had already forbidden São Tomé residents to organize slave expeditions to Angola, and that he himself had repeated that order. Alfonso had already written on this matter to Emanuel. The Congolese king knew that the resident agent and officials in São Tomé wanted to resume sending ships to Angola and Congo, by-passing the port of Mpinda. The island's slave traders maintained that such a move would be most expedient, as the ships sent from São Tomé trading-post to the mouth of the Congo River delivered no more than 40–50 "specimens" of slaves a year, and often returned empty. In his note, the Congolese king sharply disagreed with such reasoning. He argued that in the port of Mpinda there was always a plentiful supply of male and female slaves ready for loading onto ships but such ships were lacking and as a result many "specimens" died. In recent years, Alfonso I continued, no ship arriving from São Tomé had taken on board less than 400 slaves.

Enclosed with the letter was a written statement by the Portuguese residing in the Congo capital. They presented their case in the same manner as the king. They complained moreover about heavy losses, because in Mpinda many slaves had died for whom there had been no room on board ships from São Tomé.[44] From Alfonso I's note it is clear that he still treated Angola as a dependent state, even though by the end of the 15th century the Angolan rulers had practically thrown

---

[42] *Ibid.*, p. 108f.

[43] A. Brásio, "Mon. Miss. Afr.," Vol. II, No. 7, 1953. On 2nd August 1532, John III forbade his intermediary to conduct trade with Angola. The king justified his decision, arguing that such trade annoyed the king of Congo. If the Portuguese gave up this trade, the Congolese ruler would certainly make the purchase of slaves, copper, and ivory in his country easier.

[44] L. Cordeiro, *Questoes*, pp. 356–362. The enclosed statements by the Portuguese in Congo were evidently specially selected and prepared. Their reports betray their fear that the main entrepôts for the export of slaves might switch from Congo to Angola. The approximate number of 400 slaves carried on one ship frequently recurs in the documents.

off Congo control and only seldom paid tribute.[45] At this point, however, we are primarily interested in the argument between the king of
Congo and the São Tomé authorities. From later information it emerges
that Congo did not regularly supply large numbers of export slaves,
although on occasion it did, particularly after victorious wars against
its neighbours. The kings of Congo wanted to control these exports in
order to profit by them. This explains why they tried to concentrate
all exports, not only from Congo but also from Angola, in the port of
Mpinda. By the same token, this was inconvenient to the São Tomé
residents, anxious to reduce their operating costs. Hence the argument
which, as the document from 1548 indicates, had been going on for
many years.

It shows at the same time the great involvement of the island's
Portuguese officials and local merchants in the trade in Congo-exported
slaves, and the beginning of their interest in relations with Angola.
The whole affair only goes to prove that African rulers not only did
not oppose the trade in black slaves, but actually fostered it, eager to
skim off the maximum profit therefrom. This particular case concerned
slaves from countries neighbouring upon Congo, to be delivered to the
Portuguese by their resident agents.

The development of the Portuguese island of São Tomé had from the
very beginning depended on the source of manpower from the African
continent, primarily from the Niger Delta, Congo, and later Angola. It
was predominantly to this supply of manpower that São Tomé planters, merchants, and sailors, of both Portuguese and African extraction,
owed their incomes.

The incomes of the island's priests and Church institutions included
not only a slice of customs duties, but also a certain number of imported
slaves.[46] Moreover, numerous documents show, not only that the bishop
and other priests owned slaves, but that many of them were very much
engaged in the slave traffic in Congo.

In this way the society of the small island of São Tomé emerges as the
earliest example of the full development of the modern slave economy,
characteristic also of Latin America, in particular of Brazil, the islands
of Central America, and even of the later colonized territories of the

---

[45] F. Pigafetta, *Relazione*, p. 19.
[46] A. Brásio, "Mon. Miss. Afr.," Vol. II, No. 97.

Mississippi basin. In all these instances, the slave economy was always tightly bound up with monoculture, its purpose being to supply sugar, coffee, and other products to the markets of more advanced countries. Predominant in the main line of production slave labour was based on the import of negroes from the African continent and "breeding" them on the spot. In the case of São Tomé, slavery pervaded all aspects of its life. We have already seen that the island's mode of production was quite primitive. At the same time, the numerous sugar-cane plantations on the island were closely linked with international trade in which the great companies of Antwerp and later those of Amsterdam took part. In those great centres of economic life, numerous sugar refineries were established in the 16th century thanks to increasing supplies of molasses from São Tomé. It should be noted that, despite the very active role of Portuguese merchants in the export of sugar from the island, the process of refining was not undertaken by Portugal, whose economy was weak, but by countries then thriving economically which had important capital resources and skilled labour, i.e. countries already on the road of capitalist development. This is not to say that Portugal did not derive large profits from São Tomé's slave labour. Nonetheless, a considerable portion of the profits from the sugar plantations went to the more advanced countries, thanks to their role in the distribution of sugar as well as in its refining and adjustment to the needs of the population in Europe.

It should be added here that São Tomé's economy rested on very weak foundations. The prevailing mode of production caused quick impoverishment of the island's fertile soil. Moreover, the island's total dependence on external trade exposed the producers to the turmoil accompanying the incipient rivalry among European states competing for access to overseas markets. In addition, in the course of time São Tomé residents came up against keen competition with new and stronger sugar-production centres, first and foremost Brazil. All these factors would decide the colony's fate only in the 17th century.

The other Equator islands, viz. Annobón, Principe (first called São Antão), and Fernando Po, played a far smaller economic role than São Tomé in the 16th century. They were very thinly populated, although there, too, sugar plantations were set up.[47] Neither in sugar production

---

[47] Duarte Pacheco Pereira, *Esmeraldo de Situ Orbis* (London, 1937), p. 107.

nor in the re-export of slaves imported from the continent were they any match for São Tomé. Nonetheless, Fernando Po undoubtedly played a major role in Portuguese trade with the Niger Delta and the state of Benin, from where in the first half of the 16th century not only slaves were imported but also cotton cloths (from Benin, very useful in Portuguese trade with other parts of the African continent), Guinea pepper, and other goods.

SELECTED BIBLIOGRAPHY

Articles on Marian Małowist

1966:   *Times Literary Supplement*, 8 Sept., p. 812.

Books

1935:   *Handel zagraniczny Sztokholmu i polityka zewnętrzna Szwecji w latach 1470–1503*, Rozprawy Historyczne Towarzystwa Naukowego Warszawskiego, T.15, Warszawa.

1947:   *Kaffa—kolonia genueńska na Krymie i problem wschodni w latach 1453–1475*, IH UW, Warszawa.

1954:   *Studia z dziejów rzemiosła w okresie kryzysu feudalizmu w Europie Zachodniej w XIV i XV wieku*, PWN, Warszawa.

1964:   *Wielkie państwa Sudanu Zachodniego w późnym średniowieczu*, PWN, Warszawa.

1969:   *Europa a Afryka Zachodnia w dobie wczesnej ekspansji kolonialnej*, PWN, Warszawa.

1972:   *Croissance et régression en Europe, XIVᵉ–XVIIᵉ siècles. Recueil d'articles*, Cahiers des Annales 34, Armand Colin, Paris.

1973:   *Wschód a Zachód Europy w XIII–XVI wieku. Konfrontacja struktur społeczno-gospodarczych*, PWN, Warszawa.

1976:   *Konkwistadorzy portugalscy*, PIW, Warszawa.

1985:   *Tamerlan i jego czasy*, PIW, Warszawa.

1987:   with Iza Bieżuńska-Małowist, *Niewolnictwo*, Czytelnik, Warszawa.

Articles

1931:   "Le développement des rapports économiques entre la Flandre, la Pologne et les pays limitrophes du XIIIᵉ au XIVᵉ siècle", *Revue belge de philologie et d'histoire*, T. 10, pp. 1013–1065.

1948:   "Polityka gospodacza Zakonu Krzyżackiego w XV w.", *Pamiętnik VII Powszechnego Zjazdu Historyków Polskich*, T.1, Warszawa.

1953:   "Zagadnienie kryzysu feudalizmu w XIV i XV wieku w świetle najnowszych badań (próba krytyki)", *Kwartalnik Historyczny*, 60(1), pp. 68–106.

1954:   "Podstawy gospodarcze przywrócenia jedności państwowej Pomorza Gdańskiego z Polską w XV wieku", *Przegląd Historyczny*, 15, pp. 141–187.

1955:   "Le commerce de la Baltique et le problème des luttes sociales en Pologne aux XVᵉ–XVIᵉ siècles", *La Pologne au Xᵉ Congrès International des Sciences Historiques à Rome*, Varsovie.

1956:   "Z hospodarske problematiky krise feudalismu ve XIV a XV stoleti", *Československy Časopis Historicky*, 4(1).

1957a: "L'évolution industrielle en Pologne du XIVᵉ au XVIIᵉ siècle", *Studi in onore di Armando Sapori*, Instituto Editoriale Cisalpino, Milano/Varese, pp. 573–604.

1957b: "Über die Frage der Handelspolitik des Adels in den Ostseeländern im 15. und 16. Jahrhundert", *Hansische Geschichtsblätter*, 75. Jahrgang, Graz, pp. 29–47.

1958:   "Poland, Russia and Western Trade in the 15th and 16th Centuries", *Past and Present*, No. 13, pp. 26–41.

1959a: "The Economic and Social Development of the Baltic Countries from the Fifteenth to the Seventeenth Centuries", *The Economic History Review*, 12(2), pp. 177–189.
1959b: "Z zagadnień popytu na produkty krajów nadbałtyckich w Europie Zachodniej w XVI w.", *Przegląd Historyczny*, 50.
1960a: "L'approvisionnement des ports de la Baltique en produits forestiers pour les constructions navales aux XVe et XVIe siècles", in: *Le navire et l'économie maritime du Nord de l'Europe, du Moyen Age au XVIIIe siècle* (Travaux du Troisième Colloque International), Paris, pp. 25–43.
1960b: "A Certain Trade Techniques in the Baltic Countries in the 15th to the 17th Century", in: *Poland at the 11th Congress of Historical Sciences*, Warsaw, pp. 103–116.
1960c: "Les produits des pays de la Baltique dans le commerce international au XVIe siècle", *Revue du Nord*, 42(166), pp. 175–206.
1962:   "Les mouvements d'expansion en Europe aux XVe et XVIe siècles", *Annales E.S.C.*, 5.
1963:   "Les problèmes de la Pologne avant et après les Grandes Découvertes", *Comptes rendus de l'Academie des Inscriptions et Belles Lettres*, Séance du 14 juin 1963, pp. 196–206.
1963:   "O społecznych aspektach wczesnej ekspansji kolonialnej", *Przegląd Historyczny*, 54.
1964:   "Les aspects sociaux de la première phase de l'expansion coloniale", *Africana Bulletin*, 1, pp. 11–40.
1965a: "L'Europe de l'Est et les pays ibériques. Analogies et contrastes", in: *Homenaje a Jaime Vicens Vives*, Vol. l, Universidad de Barcelona, Barcelona, pp. 85–93.
1965b: "Uwagi o roli kapitału kupieckiego w Europie wschodniej w późnym średniowieczu", *Przegląd Historyczny*, 56, pp. 220–231.
1966a: "Le commerce d'or et d'esclaves au Soudan Occidental", *Africana Bulletin*, 3, pp. 43–72.
1966b: "The Problem of the Inequality of Economic Development in Europe in the Later Middle Ages", *The Economic History Review*, 19(1), pp. 15–28.
1966c: "The Social and Economic Stability of the Western Sudan in the Middle Ages", *Past and Present*, 33, pp. 3–15.
1967:   "The Western Sudan in the Middle Ages. Rejoinder", *Past and Present*, 37, pp. 157–162.
1968a: "Ekspansja portugalska w Afryce a ekonomika Europy na przełomie XV i XVI w.", *Przegląd Historyczny*, 59, pp. 227–244.
1968b: "Les fondements de l'expansion européenne en Afrique au XVe siècle: Europe, Maghreb et Soudan Occidental", *Acta Poloniae Historica*, 18, pp. 155–179.
1969:   "Les débuts du système de plantations dans la période des grandes découvertes", *Africana Bulletin*, 10, pp. 9–30.
1970a: "Die Ostseeländer und die frühe europäische Übersee-Expansion", in Fritze, K., Müller-Martens, E. et al. (eds.), *Neue Hansische Studien. Forschungen zur Mittelalterlichen Geschichte*, Berlin, pp. 301–310.
1970b: "Quelques observations sur le commerce de l'or dans le Soudan Occidental au Moyen Age", *Annales E.S.C.*, 25, pp. 1630–1636.
1970c: "Les routes du commerce et les marchandises du Levant dans la vie de la Pologne au bas Moyen Age et au début de l'époque moderne", in: *Méditerranée et Ocean Indien* (Travaux du Sixième Colloque International d'Histoire Maritime, Venise, 20–24 septembre 1962), Paris, S.É.V.P.E.N., pp. 157–175.
1972a: "Les bases économiques du retour de la Poméranie de Danzig à la Pologne au XVe siècle", in: *Croissance et régression en Europe, XIVe–XVIIe siècles. Recueil d'articles*, Cahiers des Annales 34, Paris, Armand Colin, pp. 63–90.

1972b: "L'évolution industrielle en Pologne du XIVᵉ au XVIIᵉ siècle", in: *Croissance et régression en Europe, XIVᵉ–XVIIᵉ siècles. Recueil d'articles*, Cahiers des Annales 34, Paris, Armand Colin, pp. 191–215.

1972c: "L'expansion économique des Hollandais dans le bassin de la Baltique aux XIVᵉ et XVᵉ siècles", in: *Croissance et régression en Europe, XIVᵉ–XVIIᵉ siècles. Recueil d'articles*, Cahiers des Annales 34, Armand Colin, Paris pp. 91–138.

1972d: "L'inégalité du développement économique en Europe au bas Moyen Age", in: *Croissance et régression en Europe, XIVᵉ–XVIIᵉ siècles. Recueil d'articles*, Cahiers des Annales 34, Paris, Armand Colin, pp. 39–52.

1972e: "Les mouvements d'expansion en Europe aux XVᵉ et XVIᵉ siècles", in: *Croissance et régression en Europe, XIVᵉ–XVIIᵉ siècles. Recueil d'articles*, Cahiers des Annales 34, Paris, Armand Colin, pp. 217–223.

1972f: "La politique commerciale de la noblesse des pays de la Baltique aux XVᵉ et XVIᵉ siècles", in: *Croissance et régression en Europe, XIVᵉ–XVIIᵉ siècles. Recueil d'articles*, Cahiers des Annales 34, Armand Colin, Paris, pp. 175–190.

1972g: "Les produits des pays de la Baltique dans le commerce international au XVIᵉ siècle", in: *Croissance et régression en Europe, XIVᵉ–XVIIᵉ siècles. Recueil d'articles*, Cahiers des Annales 34, Paris, Armand Colin, pp. 139–173.

1972h: "Quelques problemes économiques de la zone baltique dans le haut Moyen Age", in: *Croissance et régression en Europe, XIVᵉ–XVIIᵉ siècles. Recueil d'articles*, Cahiers des Annales 34, Armand Colin, Paris, pp. 13–38.

1973a: "Le commerce du Levant avec l'Europe de l'Est au XVIᵉ siècle. Quelques problèmes", in: *Histoire économique du monde méditerranéen 1450–1650. Mélanges en l'honneur de Fernand Braudel*, Toulouse, Privat, pp. 349–357.

1973b: "Z problematyki wzrostu gospodarczego Europy Środkowo-Wschodniej w późnym średniowieczu i na początku XVI wieku", *Przegląd Historyczny*, 64, pp. 655–680.

1976: "Some Aspects of the Early Colonial Expansion as Presented by Zurara in the Chronicle of Guinea", *Africana Bulletin*, 25, pp. 75–93.

1974: "Problems of the Growth of the National Economy of Central-Eastern Europe in the Late Middle Ages", *Journal of European Economic History*, Vol. III.

1978a: "Capitalismo commerciale e agricoltura", in *Storia d'Italia. Annali I: Dal feudalismo al capitalismo*, Torino, pp. 451–507.

1978b: "Saray la Nouvelle, capitale de la Horde d'Or", in J. Schneider (ed.) *Wirtschaftskräfte und Wirtschaftswege. Festschrift für Hermann Kellenbenz, Vol I: Mittelmeer und Kontinent*, Bamberg, Klett-Cotta, pp. 15–29.

1981a: "Constitutional Trends and Social Developments in Central Europe, the Baltic Countries and the Polish-Lithuanian Commonwealth", in J. Pelenski (ed.), *State and Society in Europe from the Fifteenth to the Eighteenth Century*, Warszawa.

1981b: "Merchant Credit and the Putting-Out System: Rural Production during the Middle Ages", *Review*, IV(4), pp. 667–681.

1986: with Adelheid Simsch, "Polen 1450–1650", in: H. Kellenbenz (ed.), *Handbuch der Europäischen Wirtschafts- und Sozialgeschichte*, Vol. 3: *Vom ausgehenden Mittelalter bis zur Mitte des 17. Jahrhundert*, Stuttgart, pp. 1074–1096.

1989a: "Marian Małowist on the Origins of a Periphery. Evolution of the Economic Division of Europe, 13th–16th Centuries", *Estudios Latinoamericanos*, 12, pp. 40–55.

1989b: "Sobre la historia y los historiadores habla Marian Małowist. Bibliografía selecta," *Estudios Latinoamericanos*, 12, pp. 11–39.

1991: "Podziały gospodarcze i polityczne w Europie w średniowieczu i w dobie wezesnej nowożytności", *Przegląd Historyczny*, 82, pp. 233–244.

INDEX OF NAMES[1]

---

[1] Footnotes and bibliographies excluded.